Politics and Economics of the Middle East

Fragile Mideast Countries: Afghanistan and Yemen

POLITICS AND ECONOMICS OF THE MIDDLE EAST

Additional books in this series can be found on Nova's website
under the Series tab.

Additional E-books in this series can be found on Nova's website
under the E-books tab.

POLITICS AND ECONOMICS OF THE MIDDLE EAST

FRAGILE MIDEAST COUNTRIES: AFGHANISTAN AND YEMEN

ROBERT P. DEEN
AND
ALLISON D. BURKEN
EDITORS

Nova Science Publishers, Inc.
New York

Copyright © 2011 by Nova Science Publishers, Inc.

All rights reserved. No part of this book may be reproduced, stored in a retrieval system or transmitted in any form or by any means: electronic, electrostatic, magnetic, tape, mechanical photocopying, recording or otherwise without the written permission of the Publisher.

For permission to use material from this book please contact us:
Telephone 631-231-7269; Fax 631-231-8175
Web Site: http://www.novapublishers.com

NOTICE TO THE READER

The Publisher has taken reasonable care in the preparation of this book, but makes no expressed or implied warranty of any kind and assumes no responsibility for any errors or omissions. No liability is assumed for incidental or consequential damages in connection with or arising out of information contained in this book. The Publisher shall not be liable for any special, consequential, or exemplary damages resulting, in whole or in part, from the readers' use of, or reliance upon, this material. Any parts of this book based on government reports are so indicated and copyright is claimed for those parts to the extent applicable to compilations of such works.

Independent verification should be sought for any data, advice or recommendations contained in this book. In addition, no responsibility is assumed by the publisher for any injury and/or damage to persons or property arising from any methods, products, instructions, ideas or otherwise contained in this publication.

This publication is designed to provide accurate and authoritative information with regard to the subject matter covered herein. It is sold with the clear understanding that the Publisher is not engaged in rendering legal or any other professional services. If legal or any other expert assistance is required, the services of a competent person should be sought. FROM A DECLARATION OF PARTICIPANTS JOINTLY ADOPTED BY A COMMITTEE OF THE AMERICAN BAR ASSOCIATION AND A COMMITTEE OF PUBLISHERS.

Additional color graphics may be available in the e-book version of this book.

LIBRARY OF CONGRESS CATALOGING-IN-PUBLICATION DATA

Fragile Mideast countries : Afghanistan and Yemen / editors, Robert P. Deen and Allison D. Burken.
p. cm.
Includes bibliographical references and index.
ISBN 978-1-61209-709-1 (hardcover)
 1. Afghanistan--Politics and government--2001- 2. National
security--Afghanistan. 3. Drug control--Afghanistan. 4.
Afghanistan--Foreign relations--21st century. 5. Afghanistan--Foreign
relations--United States. 6. United States--Foreign relations--Afghanistan.
7. Yemen--Politics and government--21st century. 8. Yemen--Foreign
relations--21st century. 9. Yemen--Foreign relations--United States. 10.
United States--Foreign relations--Yemen. I. Deen, Robert P. II. Burken,
Allison D.
 DS371.4.F73 2011
 958.104'7--dc22
2011001547

Published by Nova Science Publishers, Inc. † *New York*

CONTENTS

Preface		**vii**
Chapter 1	Afghanistan: Post-Taliban Governance, Security, and U.S. Policy *Kenneth Katzman*	**1**
Chapter 2	Afghanistan: Politics, Elections, and Government Performance *Kenneth Katzman*	**89**
Chapter 3	Afghanistan: Narcotics and U.S. Policy *Christopher M. Blanchard*	**137**
Chapter 4	Yemen: Background and U.S. Relations *Jeremy M. Sharp*	**161**
Chapter Sources		**199**
Index		**201**

PREFACE

With limited natural resources, a crippling illiteracy rate and high population growth, Yemen faces an array of daunting development challenges that some observers believe make it at risk for becoming a failed state. As the country's population rapidly rises, resources dwindle, terrorist groups take root in the outlying provinces, and a southern secessionist movement grows, the Obama Administration and the 111th Congress are left to grapple with the consequences of Yemeni instability. Additionally, limited capacity and widespread corruption at all levels of Afghan governance are growing factors in the debate over the effectiveness of U.S. strategy in Afghanistan. This new book provides an overview of the fragile mideast countries of Afghanistan and Yemen.

Chapter 1- Following two high-level policy reviews on Afghanistan in 2009, the Obama Administration asserts that it is pursuing a well resourced and integrated military-civilian strategy intended to pave the way for a gradual transition to Afghan security leadership beginning in July 2011. The pace of that transition is to be determined by conditions on the ground, as determined by a formal DOD and a White House review of the Afghanistan situation in December 2010. The policy is intended to ensure that Afghanistan will not again become a base for terrorist attacks against the United States. At the same time, the Administration is attempting to counter the perception in the region, particularly among Pakistan, India, the Afghan insurgency, and within the Afghan political establishment that U.S. involvement will be sharply reduced after July 2011. That perception may, among other consequences, be inflaming the traditional rivalry between Pakistan and India, in this case to deny each other influence in Afghanistan. As of November 2010, the Administration is stressing that a transition to Afghan leadership would not likely be completed until 2014, with only gradual handover to the Afghans prior to then. The November 19-20, 2010, NATO summit meeting in Lisbon is to map out the transition to Afghan lead and presumably convince partner countries to remain deployed until at least that time.

Chapter 2- The limited capacity and widespread corruption of all levels of Afghan governance are growing factors in debate over the effectiveness of U.S. strategy in Afghanistan, although Afghan governing capacity has increased significantly since the Taliban regime fell in late 2001. In a December 1, 2009, policy statement on Afghanistan, which followed the second major Afghanistan strategy review in 2009, President Obama stated that "the days of providing a blank check [to the Afghan government] are over." During 2010, the Administration has been pressing President Hamid Karzai to move more decisively to address corruption within his government, with mixed success. Karzai has agreed to cooperate with U.S.-led efforts to build the capacity of several emerging anti-corruption institutions, but these same institutions have sometimes caused a Karzai backlash when they have targeted his allies or relatives. Purportedly suspicious that U.S. and other donors are trying to undermine his leadership, Karzai has strengthened his bonds to ethnic and political faction leaders who are often involved in illicit economic activity and who undermine rule of law. Some of the effects of corruption burst into public view in August 2010 when major losses were announced by the large Kabul Bank, in part due to large loans to major shareholders, many of whom are close to Karzai. Addressing U.S. public complaints that U.S. lives are being lost in part to defend a corrupt government, some in Congress have sought to link further U.S. aid to clearer progress on the corruption issue.

Chapter 3- Opium poppy cultivation and drug trafficking have eroded Afghanistan's fragile political and economic order over the last 30 years. In spite of ongoing counternarcotics efforts by the Afghan government, the United States, and their partners, Afghanistan remains the source of over 90% of the world's illicit opium. Since 2001, efforts to provide viable economic alternatives to poppy cultivation and to disrupt drug trafficking and related corruption have succeeded in some areas. However, insecurity, particularly in the southern province of Helmand, and widespread corruption fueled a surge in cultivation in 2006 and 2007, pushing opium output to all-time highs.

Chapter 4- With limited natural resources, a crippling illiteracy rate, and high population growth, Yemen faces an array of daunting development challenges that some observers believe make it at risk for becoming a failed state. In 2009, Yemen ranked 140 out of 182 countries on the United Nations Development Program's Human Development Index, a score comparable to the poorest sub- Saharan African countries. Over 43% of the population of nearly 24 million people lives below the poverty line, and per capita GDP is estimated to be between $650 and $800. Yemen is largely dependent on external aid from Persian Gulf countries, Western donors, and international financial institutions, though its per capita share of assistance is below the global average.

In: Fragile Mideast Countries: Afghanistan and Yemen
Editors: Robert P. Deen and Allison D. Burken

ISBN: 978-1-61209-709-1
© 2011 Nova Science Publishers, Inc.

Chapter 1

AFGHANISTAN: POST-TALIBAN GOVERNANCE, SECURITY, AND U.S. POLICY

Kenneth Katzman

SUMMARY

Following two high-level policy reviews on Afghanistan in 2009, the Obama Administration asserts that it is pursuing a well resourced and integrated military-civilian strategy intended to pave the way for a gradual transition to Afghan security leadership beginning in July 2011. The pace of that transition is to be determined by conditions on the ground, as determined by a formal DOD and a White House review of the Afghanistan situation in December 2010. The policy is intended to ensure that Afghanistan will not again become a base for terrorist attacks against the United States. At the same time, the Administration is attempting to counter the perception in the region, particularly among Pakistan, India, the Afghan insurgency, and within the Afghan political establishment that U.S. involvement will be sharply reduced after July 2011. That perception may, among other consequences, be inflaming the traditional rivalry between Pakistan and India, in this case to deny each other influence in Afghanistan. As of November 2010, the Administration is stressing that a transition to Afghan leadership would not likely be completed until 2014, with only gradual handover to the Afghans prior to then. The November 19-20, 2010, NATO summit meeting in Lisbon is to map out the transition to Afghan lead and presumably convince partner countries to remain deployed until at least that time.

The December 2010 reviews will take into account the effect of the addition of U.S. combat troops to Afghanistan in 2009 and 2010, intended to create security conditions to expand Afghan governance and economic development. A total of 51,000 additional U.S. forces were authorized by the two reviews, which has brought U.S. troop levels to about 104,000 as of September 4, 2010, with partner forces holding at about 41,000. Until October 2010, there had not been clear indications that U.S. strategy has shown clear success, to date. However, in October 2010, the top U.S./NATO commander in Afghanistan, Gen. David Petraeus, as well as other U.S. and partner military officials say that signs are multiplying that insurgent momentum has been broadly blunted. One particular sign is that insurgent commanders are exploring possible surrender terms under which they might reintegrate into society. Still, some experts remain pessimistic, asserting that the insurgents have expanded their presence in northern Afghanistan, and that President Hamid Karzai's refusal to forcefully confront governmental corruption has caused a loss of Afghan support for his government. U.S. officials are reinforcing the U.S. insistence that Karzai move more decisively against governmental corruption, but reportedly will focus on lower level corruption such as police and governmental demands for bribes.

In order to try to achieve a strategic breakthrough that might force key insurgent leaders to negotiate a political settlement, Gen. Petraeus is attempting to accelerate local security solutions and experiments similar to those he pursued earlier in Iraq, and to step up the use of air strikes and Special Forces operations against Taliban commanders. In order to take advantage of an apparent new willingness by some insurgent commanders to negotiate, Karzai has named a broad- based 68-member High Peace Council to oversee negotiations. However, there are major concerns among Afghanistan's minorities and among its women that reconciliation could lead to compromises that erode the freedoms Afghans have enjoyed since 2001.

Through the end of FY2010, the United States has provided over $54.5 billion in assistance to Afghanistan since the fall of the Taliban, of which about $30 billion has been to equip and train Afghan forces. (See CRS Report RS2 1922, *Afghanistan: Politics, Elections, and Government Performance*, by Kenneth Katzman.)

BACKGROUND

Afghanistan has a history of a high degree of decentralization, and resistance to foreign invasion and occupation. Some have termed it the "graveyard of empires."

From Early History to the 19th Century

Alexander the Great conquered what is now Afghanistan in three years (330 B.C.E. to 327 B.C.E), although at significant cost and with significant difficulty, and requiring marriage to a resident of the conquered territory. From the third to the eighth century, A.D., Buddhism was the dominant religion in Afghanistan. At the end of the seventh century, Islam spread in Afghanistan when Arab invaders from the Umayyad Dynasty defeated the Persian empire of the Sassanians. In the 10th century, Muslim rulers called Samanids, from Bukhara (in what is now Uzbekistan), extended their influence into Afghanistan, and the complete conversion of Afghanistan to Islam occurred during the rule of the Gaznavids in the 11th century. They ruled over the first vast Islamic empire based in what is now Ghazni province of Afghanistan.

In 1504, Babur, a descendent of the conquerors Tamarlane and Genghis Khan, took control of Kabul and then moved onto India, establishing the Mughal Empire. (Babur is buried in the Babur Gardens complex in Kabul, which has been refurbished with the help of the Agha Khan Foundation.) Throughout the 16th and 17th centuries, Afghanistan was fought over by the Mughal Empire and the Safavid Dynasty of Persia (now Iran), with the Safavids mostly controlling Herat and western Afghanistan, and the Mughals controlling Kabul and the east. A monarchy ruled by ethnic Pashtuns was founded in 1747 by Ahmad Shah Durrani, who was a senior officer in the army of Nadir Shah, ruler of Persia, when Nadir Shah was assassinated and Persian control over Afghanistan weakened.

A strong ruler, Dost Muhammad Khan, emerged in Kabul in 1826 and created concerns among Britain that the Afghans were threatening Britain's control of India; that fear led to a British decision in 1838 to intervene in Afghanistan, setting off the first Anglo-Afghan War (1838-1842). Nearly all of the 4,500-person British force was killed in that war, which ended with a final British stand at Gandamack. The second Anglo-Afghan War took place during 1878-1880.

Early 20th Century and Cold War Era

King Amanullah Khan (1919-1929) launched attacks on British forces in Afghanistan (Third Anglo-Afghan War) shortly after taking power and won complete independence from Britain as recognized in the Treaty of Rawalpindi (August 8, 1919). He was considered a secular modernizer presiding over a government in which all ethnic minorities participated. He was succeeded by King Mohammad Nadir Shah (1929-1933), and then by King Mohammad Zahir Shah. Zahir Shah's reign (1933-1973) is remembered fondly by many older Afghans for promulgating a constitution in 1964 that established a national legislature and promoting freedoms for women, including dropping a requirement that they cover their face and hair. However, possibly believing that he could limit Soviet support for Communist factions in Afghanistan, Zahir Shah also entered into a significant political and arms purchase relationship with the Soviet Union. The Soviets began to build large infrastructure projects in Afghanistan during Zahir Shah's time, such as the north-south Salang Pass/Tunnel and Bagram airfield. He also accepted agricultural and other development aid from the United States. In part, the countryside was secured during the King's time by local tribal militias called *arbokai*.

Afghanistan's slide into instability began in the 1970s when the diametrically opposed Communist Party and Islamic movements grew in strength. While receiving medical treatment in Italy, Zahir Shah was overthrown by his cousin, Mohammad Daoud, a military leader who established a dictatorship with strong state involvement in the economy. Daoud was overthrown and killed[1] in April 1978 by People's Democratic Party of Afghanistan (PDPA, Communist party) military officers under the direction of two PDPA (Khalq faction) leaders, Hafizullah Amin and Nur Mohammad Taraki, in what is called the Saur (April) Revolution. Taraki became president, but he was displaced in September 1979 by Amin. Both leaders drew their strength from rural ethnic Pashtuns and tried to impose radical socialist change on a traditional society, in part by redistributing land and bringing more women into government. The attempt at rapid modernization sparked rebellion by Islamic parties opposed to such moves. The Soviet Union sent troops into Afghanistan on December 27, 1979, to prevent a seizure of power by the Islamic militias, known as the *mujahedin* (Islamic fighters). Upon their invasion, the Soviets replaced Amin with another PDPA leader perceived as pliable, Babrak Karmal (Parcham faction of the PDPA), who was part of the 1978 PDPA takeover but was exiled by Taraki and Amin.

Soviet occupation forces, which numbered about 120,000, were never able to pacify the outlying areas of the country. The *mujahedin* benefited from U.S. weapons and assistance, provided through the Central Intelligence Agency (CIA) in cooperation with Pakistan's Inter-Service Intelligence directorate (ISI). The *mujahedin* were also relatively well organized and coordinated by seven major parties that in early 1989 formed a Peshawar-based "Afghan Interim Government" (AIG). The seven party leaders were Mohammad Nabi Mohammadi; Sibghatullah Mojaddedi; Gulbuddin Hikmatyar; Burhanuddin Rabbani; Yunus Khalis; Abd-i-Rab Rasul Sayyaf; and Pir Gaylani. Mohammadi and Khalis have died in recent years of natural causes, but the others are still active. Most of those *mujahedin* leaders still active are part of the current government; others, such as Hikmatyar, fight it.

The *mujahedin* weaponry included U.S.-supplied portable shoulder-fired anti-aircraft systems called "Stingers," which proved highly effective against Soviet aircraft. The United States decided in 1985 to provide these weapons to the *mujahedin* after substantial debate within the Reagan Administration and some in Congress over whether they could be used effectively and whether doing so would harm broader U.S.-Soviet relations. The *mujahedin* also hid and stored weaponry in a large network of natural and manmade tunnels and caves throughout Afghanistan. Partly because of the effectiveness of the Stinger in shooting down Soviet helicopters and fixed wing aircraft, the Soviet Union's losses mounted—about 13,400 Soviet soldiers were killed in the war, according to Soviet figures—turning Soviet domestic opinion against the war. In 1986, after the reformist Mikhail Gorbachev became leader, the Soviets replaced Karmal with the director of Afghan intelligence, Najibullah Ahmedzai (known by his first name). Najibullah was a Ghilzai Pashtun, and was from the Parcham faction of the PDPA. Some Afghans say that some aspects of his governing style were admirable, particularly his appointment of a prime minister (Sultan Ali Keshtmand and others) to handle administrative duties and distribute power.

Geneva Accords (1988) and Soviet Withdrawal

On April 14, 1988, Gorbachev agreed to a U.N.-brokered accord (the Geneva Accords) requiring it to withdraw. The withdrawal was completed by February 15, 1989, leaving in place the weak Najibullah government. A warming of relations moved the United States and Soviet Union to try for a political settlement to the Afghan conflict, a trend accelerated by the 1991 collapse of the Soviet Union, which reduced Moscow's capacity for supporting communist regimes in the Third World. On September 13, 1991, Moscow and Washington agreed to a joint cutoff of military aid to the Afghan combatants.

The State Department has said that a total of about $3 billion in economic and covert military assistance was provided by the U.S. to the Afghan *mujahedin* from 1980 until the end of the Soviet occupation in 1989. Press reports say the covert aid program grew from about $20 million per year in FY1980 to about $300 million per year during FY1986-FY1990.[2] The Soviet pullout decreased the perceived strategic value of Afghanistan, causing a reduction in subsequent covert funding. As indicated below in **Table 9**, U.S. assistance to Afghanistan remained at relatively low levels from the time of the Soviet withdrawal, validating the views of many that the United States largely considered its role in Afghanistan "completed" when Soviets troops left, and there was little support for a major U.S. effort to rebuild the country.

Afghanistan

The United States closed its embassy in Kabul in January 1989, as the Soviet Union was completing its pullout, and it remained so until the fall of the Taliban in 2001.

Table 1. Afghanistan Social and Economic Statistics

Population	28 million +. Kabul population is 3 million, up from 500,000 in Taliban era
Ethnicities/Religions	Pashtun 42%; Tajik 27%; Uzbek 9%; Hazara 9%; Aimak 4%; Turkmen 3%; Baluch 2%.
Size of Religious Minorities	Religions: Sunni (Hanafi school) 80%; Shiite (Hazaras, Qizilbash, and Isma'ilis) 19%; other 1%Christians-estimated 500-8,000 persons; Sikh and Hindu-3,000 persons; Bahai's-400 (declared blasphemous in May 2007); Jews-1 person; Buddhist-small numbers, mostly foreigners. No Christian or Jewish schools. One church.
Literacy Rate	28% of population over 15 years of age. 43% of males; 12.6% of females.
Total and Per Capita GDP/Growth Rates	$23.3 billion purchasing power parity. 114th in the world. Per capita: $800 purchasing power parity. 219th in the world. Growth: 3.5%, down from 12% in 2007.
Unemployment Rate	40%
Children in School/Schools Built	5.7 million, of which 35% are girls. Up from 900,000 in school during Taliban era. 8,000 schools built; 140,000 teachers hired since Taliban era. 17 universities, up from 2 in 2002. 75,000 Afghans in universities in Afghanistan; 5,000 when Taliban was in power. 35% of university students in Afghanistan are female.
Afghans With Access to Health Coverage	65% with basic health services access-compared to 8% during Taliban era. Infant mortality down 18% since Taliban to 135 per 1,000 live births. 680 clinics built .
Roads Built	About 2,500 miles paved post-Taliban, including repaving of "Ring Road" (78% complete) that circles the country. Kabul-Qandahar drive reduced to 6 hours.
Judges/Courts	900 sitting judges trained since fall of Taliban; some removed for corruption
Banks Operating	17, including branches in some rural areas, but still about 90% of the population use *hawalas*, or informal money transfer services. Zero banks existed during Taliban era. Some limited credit card use. Some Afghan police now paid by cell phone (E-Paisa).
Access to Electricity	15%-20% of the population.
Gov't Revenues (excl. donor funds)	Expected to be about $1.4 billion in 2010; nearly double the $720 million 2007
Financial Reserves	About $4.4 billion, up from $180 million in 2002. Includes amounts due Central Bank.
Expenditures	About $3 billion in 2009; $2.7 billion in 2008; $1.2 billion in 2007; 900 million in 2006. Budget supported by international donors, including through World Bank-run Afghanistan Reconstruction Trust Fund.

Table 1. (Continued)

External Debt	$8 billion bilateral, plus $500 million multilateral. U.S. forgave $108 million in debt in 2004, and $1.6 billion forgiven by other creditors in March 2010.
Foreign/Private Investment	About $500 million to $1 billion per year. Four Afghan airlines: Ariana (national) plus three privately owned: Safi, Kam, and Pamir.
Agriculture/Major Legal Exports	80% of the population is involved in agriculture. Self-sufficiency in wheat production as of May 2009 (first time in 30 years). Products for export include fruits, raisins, melons, pomegranate juice (Anar), nuts, carpets, lapis lazuli gems, marble tile, timber products (Kunar, Nuristan provinces). July 2010 Afghanistan-Pakistan trade agreement may increase these exports. Vast untapped minerals affirmed by U.S. experts (June 2010).
Oil Proven Reserves	3.6 billion barrels of oil, 36.5 trillion cubic feet of gas. Current oil production negligible. USAID funding project to revive oil and gas facilities in the north.
Import Partners/Imports	Pakistan 38.6%; U.S. 9.5%; Germany 5.5%; India 5.2%.. Main imports are food, petroleum, capital goods, textiles, autos
Cellphones/Tourism	About 12 million cellphones, up from several hundred used by Taliban government officials. Tourism: National park opened June 2009. Increasing tourist visits.

Sources: CIA, The World Factbook; various press and U.S. government official testimony.

With Soviet backing withdrawn, Najibullah rallied the PDPA Army and the party-dominated paramilitary organization called the Sarandoy, and successfully beat back the post-Soviet withdrawal *mujahedin* offensives. Although Najibullah defied expectations that his government would immediately collapse after a Soviet withdrawal, military defections continued and his position weakened in subsequent years. On March 18, 1992, Najibullah publicly agreed to step down once an interim government was formed. That announcement set off a wave of rebellions primarily by Uzbek and Tajik militia commanders in northern Afghanistan—particularly Abdul Rashid Dostam, who joined prominent *mujahedin* commander Ahmad Shah Masud of the Islamic Society, a largely Tajik party headed by Burhannudin Rabbani. Masud had earned a reputation as a brilliant strategist by preventing the Soviets from occupying his power base in the Panjshir Valley of northeastern Afghanistan. Najibullah fell, and the *mujahedin* regime began April 18, 1992.[3] Each year, a public parade is held to mark that day. (Some major *mujahedin* figures did not attend the 2010 celebration because of a perception that they are under Afghan public and international criticism of their immunity from alleged human rights abuses during the anti-Soviet war.)

The *Mujahedin* Government and Rise of the Taliban

The fall of Najibullah exposed the differences among the *mujahedin* parties. The leader of one of the smaller parties (Afghan National Liberation Front), Islamic scholar Sibghatullah Mojadeddi, was president during April-May 1992. Under an agreement among the major parties, Rabbani became President in June 1992 with agreement that he would serve until

December 1994. He refused to step down at that time, saying that political authority would disintegrate without a clear successor. Kabul was subsequently shelled by other *mujahedin* factions, particularly that of nominal "Prime Minister" Gulbuddin Hikmatyar, a Pashtun, who accused Rabbani of monopolizing power. Hikmatyar, who never formally assumed a working prime ministerial role in Kabul because of suspicions of Rabbani, was purportedly backed by Pakistan. Hikmatyar 's radical faction of the Islamist Hizb-e-Islami (Islamic Party) had received a large proportion of the U.S. aid during the anti-Soviet war. (Yunus Khalis led a more moderate faction of Hizb-e-Islami during that war.)

In 1993-1994, Afghan Islamic clerics and students, mostly of rural, Pashtun origin, formed the Taliban movement. Many were former *mujahedin* who had become disillusioned with conflict among *mujahedin* parties and had moved into Pakistan to study in Islamic seminaries ("madrassas") mainly of the "Deobandi" school of Islam.[4] Some say this Islam is similar to the "Wahhabism" that is practiced in Saudi Arabia. Taliban practices were also consonant with conservative Pashtun tribal traditions.

The Taliban viewed the Rabbani government as corrupt and anti-Pashtun, and the four years of civil war (1992-1996) created popular support for the Taliban as able to deliver stability. With the help of defections, the Taliban peacefully took control of the southern city of Qandahar in November 1994. By February 1995, it was approaching Kabul, after which an 18-month stalemate ensued. In September 1995, the Taliban captured Herat province, bordering Iran, and imprisoned its governor, Ismail Khan, ally of Rabbani and Masud, who later escaped and took refuge in Iran. In September 1996, new Taliban victories near Kabul led to the withdrawal of Rabbani and Masud to the Panjshir Valley north of Kabul with most of their heavy weapons; the Taliban took control of Kabul on September 27, 1996. Taliban gunmen subsequently entered a U.N. facility in Kabul to seize Najibullah, his brother, and aides, and then hanged them.

Taliban Rule (September 1996-November 2001)

The Taliban regime was led by Mullah Muhammad Umar, who lost an eye in the anti-Soviet war while fighting as part of the Hizb-e-Islami *mujahedin* party of Yunis Khalis. Umar held the title of Head of State and "Commander of the Faithful," remaining in the Taliban power base in Qandahar and almost never appearing in public, although he did occasionally receive high-level foreign officials. Umar forged a political and personal bond with bin Laden and refused U.S. demands to extradite him. Like Umar, most of the senior figures in the Taliban regime were Ghilzai Pashtuns, which predominate in eastern Afghanistan. They are rivals of the Durrani Pashtuns, who are predominant in the south.

The Taliban progressively lost international and domestic support as it imposed strict adherence to Islamic customs in areas it controlled and employed harsh punishments, including executions. The Taliban authorized its "Ministry for the Promotion of Virtue and the Suppression of Vice" to use physical punishments to enforce strict Islamic practices, including bans on television, Western music, and dancing. It prohibited women from attending school or working outside the home, except in health care, and it publicly executed some women for adultery. In what many consider its most extreme action, and which some say was urged by bin Laden, in March 2001 the Taliban blew up two large Buddha statues carved into hills above Bamiyan city, considering them idols.

The Clinton Administration held talks with the Taliban before and after it took power, but was unable to moderate its policies. The United States withheld recognition of Taliban as the legitimate government of Afghanistan, formally recognizing no faction as the government. The United Nations continued to seat representatives of the Rabbani government, not the Taliban. The State Department ordered the Afghan embassy in Washington, DC, closed in August 1997. U.N. Security Council Resolution 1193 (August 28, 1998) and 1214 (December 8, 1998) urged the Taliban to end discrimination against women. Women's rights groups urged the Clinton Administration not to recognize the Taliban government. In May 1999, the Senate-passed S.Res. 68 called on the President not to recognize an Afghan government that oppresses women.

The Taliban's hosting of Al Qaeda's leadership gradually became the Clinton Administration's overriding agenda item with Afghanistan. In April 1998, then U.S. Ambassador to the United Nations Bill Richardson (along with Assistant Secretary of State Karl Indurfurth and NSC senior official Bruce Riedel) visited Afghanistan, but the Taliban refused to hand over bin Laden. They did not meet Mullah Umar. After the August 7, 1998, Al Qaeda bombings of U.S. embassies in Kenya and Tanzania, the Clinton Administration progressively pressured the Taliban, imposing U.S. sanctions and achieving adoption of some U.N. sanctions as well. On August 20, 1998, the United States fired cruise missiles at alleged Al Qaeda training camps in eastern Afghanistan, but bin Laden was not hit.[5] Some observers assert that the Administration missed several clearer opportunities to strike him, including a purported sighting of him by an unarmed Predator drone at the Tarnak Farm camp in Afghanistan in the fall of 2000.[6] Clinton Administration officials say they did not try to oust the Taliban militarily because domestic and international support for doing so was lacking.

The "Northern Alliance" Congeals

The Taliban's policies caused different Afghan factions to ally with the ousted President Rabbani and Masud and their ally in the Herat area, Ismail Khan—the Tajik core of the anti-Taliban opposition—into a broader "Northern Alliance." In the Alliance were Uzbek, Hazara Shiite, and even some Pashtun Islamist factions discussed in **Table 3**. Virtually all the figures mentioned remain key players in politics in Afghanistan, sometimes allied with and at other times feuding with President Hamid Karzai:

- **Uzbeks/General Dostam**. One major faction was the Uzbek militia (the Junbush-Melli, or National Islamic Movement of Afghanistan) of General Abdul Rashid Dostam. Frequently referred to by some Afghans as one of the "warlords" who gained power during the anti-Soviet war, Dostam first joined those seeking to oust Rabbani during his 1992-1996 presidency, but later joined Rabbani's Northern Alliance against the Taliban. (For more information on Dostam, see CRS Report RS2 1922, *Afghanistan: Politics, Elections, and Government Performance*, by Kenneth Katzman.)
- **Hazara Shiites**. Members of Hazara tribes, mostly Shiite Muslims, are prominent in Bamiyan, Dai Kundi, and Ghazni provinces (central Afghanistan) and are always wary of repression by Pashtuns and other larger ethnic factions. The Hazaras have

tended to serve in working class and domestic household jobs, although more recently they have been prominent in technology jobs in Kabul, raising their economic status. During the various Afghan wars, the main Hazara Shiite militia was Hizb-e-Wahdat (Unity Party, composed of eight different groups). Hizb-e-Wahdat suffered a major setback in 1995 when the Taliban captured and killed its leader Abdul Ali Mazari. One of Karzai's vice president's Karim Khalili, is a Hazara. Another prominent Hazara faction leader is Mohammad Mohaqeq.

- **Pashtun Islamists/Sayyaf.** Abd-I-Rab Rasul Sayyaf, later a post-Taliban parliamentary committee chairman, headed a Pashtun-dominated hardline Islamist *mujahedin* faction called the Islamic Union for the Liberation of Afghanistan during the anti-Soviet war. Even though he is an Islamic conservative, Sayyaf viewed the Taliban as selling out Afghanistan to Al Qaeda and he joined the Northern Alliance to try to oust the Taliban.

Policy Pre-September 11, 2001

Throughout 2001, but prior to the September 11 attacks, Bush Administration policy differed little from Clinton Administration policy—applying economic and political pressure while retaining dialogue with the Taliban, and refraining from militarily assisting the Northern Alliance. The September 11 Commission report said that, in the months prior to the September 11 attacks, Administration officials leaned toward such a step and that some officials also wanted to assist ethnic Pashtuns who were opposed to the Taliban. Other covert options were reportedly under consideration as well.[7] In a departure from Clinton Administration policy, the Bush Administration stepped up engagement with Pakistan to try to reduce its support for the Taliban. At that time, there were allegations that Pakistani advisers were helping the Taliban in their fight against the Northern Alliance. In accordance with U.N. Security Council Resolution 1333, in February 2001 the State Department ordered the Taliban representative office in New York closed, although Taliban representative Abdul Hakim Mujahid continued to operate informally. (Mujahid has reconciled with the current Afghan government, and serves on a Council to oversee broader reconciliation.) In March 2001, Administration officials received a Taliban envoy to discuss bilateral issues.

Even though the Northern Alliance was supplied with Iranian, Russian, and Indian financial and military support—all of whom had different motives for that support—the Northern Alliance nonetheless continued to lose ground to the Taliban after it lost Kabul in 1996. By the time of the September 11 attacks, the Taliban controlled at least 75% of the country, including almost all provincial capitals. The Alliance suffered a major setback on September 9, 2001, two days before the September 11 attacks, when Ahmad Shah Masud was assassinated by Arab journalists who allegedly were Al Qaeda operatives. He was succeeded by his intelligence chief, Muhammad Fahim,[8] a veteran figure but one who lacked Masud's undisputed authority.

September 11 Attacks and Operation Enduring Freedom

After the September 11 attacks, the Bush Administration decided to militarily overthrow the Taliban when it refused to extradite bin Laden, judging that a friendly regime in Kabul was needed to enable U.S forces to search for Al Qaeda activists there. United Nations Security Council Resolution 1368 of September 12, 2001, said that the Security Council

> expresses its readiness to take all necessary steps to respond (implying force) to the September 11 attacks.

This is widely interpreted as a U.N. authorization for military action in response to the attacks, but it did not explicitly authorize Operation Enduring Freedom to oust the Taliban. Nor did the Resolution specifically reference Chapter VII of the U.N. Charter, which allows for responses to threats to international peace and security.

In Congress, S.J.Res. 23 (passed 98-0 in the Senate and with no objections in the House, P.L. 107-40), was somewhat more explicit than the U.N. Resolution, authorizing[9]

> all necessary and appropriate force against those nations, organizations, or persons he determines planned, authorized, committed, or aided the terrorist attacks that occurred on September 11, 2001 or *harbored such organizations or persons.*

Major combat in Afghanistan (Operation Enduring Freedom, OEF) began on October 7, 2001. It consisted primarily of U.S. air-strikes on Taliban and Al Qaeda forces, facilitated by the cooperation between small numbers (about 1,000) of U.S. special operations forces and CIA operatives. The purpose of these operations was to help the Northern Alliance and Pashtun antiTaliban forces by providing information to direct U.S. air strikes against Taliban positions. In part, the U.S. forces and operatives worked with such Northern Alliance contacts as Fahim and Amrollah Saleh, who during November 2001–June 2010 served as Afghanistan's intelligence director, to weaken Taliban defenses on the Shomali plain north of Kabul (and just south of Bagram Airfield, which marked the forward position of the Northern Alliance during Taliban rule). Some U.S. combat units (about 1,300 Marines) moved into Afghanistan to pressure the Taliban around Qandahar at the height of the fighting (October-December 2001), but there were few pitched battles between U.S. and Taliban soldiers. Some critics believe that U.S. dependence on local Afghan militia forces in the war subsequently set back post-war democracy building.

The Taliban regime unraveled rapidly after it lost Mazar-e-Sharif on November 9, 2001, to forces led by Dostam.[10] Other, mainly Tajik, Northern Alliance forces—the commanders of which had initially promised U.S. officials they would not enter Kabul—entered the capital on November 12, 2001, to popular jubilation. The Taliban subsequently lost the south and east to U.S.- supported Pashtun leaders, including Hamid Karzai. The end of the Taliban regime is generally dated as December 9, 2001, when the Taliban surrendered Qandahar and Mullah Umar fled the city, leaving it under tribal law administered by Pashtun leaders such as the Noorzai clan.

Subsequently, U.S. and Afghan forces conducted "Operation Anaconda" in the Shah-i-Kot Valley south of Gardez (Paktia Province) during March 2-19, 2002, against 800 Al Qaeda and Taliban fighters. In March 2003, about 1,000 U.S. troops raided suspected Taliban or Al Qaeda fighters in villages around Qandahar (Operation Valiant Strike). On May 1, 2003, Secretary of Defense Rumsfeld announced an end to "major combat."

Post-Taliban Nation-Building Efforts[11]

With Afghanistan devastated after more than 20 years of warfare, the 2001 fall of the Taliban regime raised questions about the extent of a U.S. and international commitment to Afghanistan. Taking the view that leaving the Afghanistan-Pakistan theater after the 1989 Soviet pullout had led Afghanistan degenerate into chaos, the decision was made by the Bush Administration to try to rebuild try to build a relatively strong central government and to assist Afghanistan's economy, in order to prevent a return of the Taliban, Al Qaeda, and other militants to Afghanistan.

The effort, which many outside experts described as "nation-building,"was supported by major international institutions and U.S. partners in several post-Taliban international meetings. The task has proved slower and more difficult than anticipated, in part because of the devastation that years of war wrought on governing institutions, on the education system, and on the already limited infrastructure. Some observers believe the international community had unrealistic expectations of what could be achieved in a relatively short time frame—particularly in establishing competent, non-corrupt governance and a vibrant democracy.

The Obama Administration's two "Afghanistan strategy reviews," the results of which were announced on March 27, 2009, and on December 1, 2009, narrowed official U.S. goals to preventing terrorism safe haven in Afghanistan and Pakistan. However, the elements of Obama Administration strategy in many ways enhance the nation-building strategy put in place by the Bush Administration. Reforming Afghan governance was emphasized both at the international January 28, 2010, "London Conference" and the July 20, 2010, "Kabul Conference."[12] Although the issue of governance is inseparable from that of securing Afghanistan, the sections below briefly outline Afghan-generated and international community-led efforts to build Afghanistan's governing capacity. These governance issues are discussed in greater detail in CRS Report RS21922, *Afghanistan: Politics, Elections, and Government Performance*, by Kenneth Katzman.

Post-Taliban Political Transition

The 2001 ouster of the Taliban government paved the way for the success of a long-stalled U.N. effort to form a broad-based Afghan government and for the international community to help Afghanistan build legitimate governing institutions. In the formation of the first post-Taliban transition government, the United Nations was viewed as a credible mediator by all sides largely because of its role in ending the Soviet occupation. During the 1990s, a succession of U.N. mediators adopted many of former King Zahir Shah's proposals for a government to be selected by a traditional assembly, or *loya jirga*. However, U.N.-mediated cease-fires between warring factions did not hold. Non-U.N. initiatives made little progress, particularly the "Six Plus Two" multilateral contact group, which began meeting in 1997 (the United States, Russia, and the six states bordering Afghanistan: Iran, China, Pakistan, Turkmenistan, Uzbekistan, and Tajikistan). Other failed efforts included a "Geneva group" (Italy, Germany, Iran, and the United States) formed in 2000; an Organization of Islamic Conference (OIC) contact group; and prominent Afghan exile efforts, including discussion groups launched by Hamid Karzai and his clan, former *mujahedin* commander Abd al-Haq, and Zahir Shah ("Rome process").

Bonn Agreement

Immediately after the September 11 attacks, former U.N. mediator Lakhdar Brahimi was brought back (he had resigned in frustration in October 1999). U.N. Security Council Resolution 1378 (November 14, 2001) called for a "central" role for the United Nations in establishing a transitional administration and inviting member states to send peacekeeping forces to promote stability and aid delivery. After the fall of Kabul in November 2001, the United Nations invited major Afghan factions, most prominently the Northern Alliance and that of the former King—but not the Taliban—to an international conference in Bonn, Germany.

On December 5, 2001, the factions signed the "Bonn Agreement."[13] It was endorsed by U.N. Security Council Resolution 1385 (December 6, 2001). The agreement was reportedly forged with substantial Iranian diplomatic help because Iran had supported the military efforts of the Northern Alliance faction and had leverage to persuade temporary caretaker Rabbani and the Northern Alliance to cede the top leadership to Hamid Karzai as leader of an interim administration. Other provisions of the agreement:

- authorized an international peace keeping force to maintain security in Kabul, and Northern Alliance forces were directed to withdraw from the capital. Security Council Resolution 1386 (December 20, 2001, and renewed yearly thereafter) gave formal Security Council authorization for the international peacekeeping force (International Security Assistance Force, ISAF);
- referred to the need to cooperate with the international community on counter narcotics, crime, and terrorism; and
- applied the constitution of 1964 until a permanent constitution could be drafted.[14]

Permanent Constitution

A June 2002 "emergency" *loya jirga* put a representative imprimatur on the transition; it was attended by 1,550 delegates (including about 200 women). Subsequently, a 35-member constitutional commission drafted the constitution, unveiling it in November 2003. It was debated by 502 delegates, selected in U.N-run caucuses, at a "*constitutional loya jirga* (CLJ)" during December 13, 2003–January 4, 2004. The CLJ, chaired by Sibghatullah Mojadeddi (mentioned above) ended with approval of the constitution with only minor changes. It set up a presidential system, with an elected president and a separately elected National Assembly (parliament). The Northern Alliance failed in its effort to set up a prime ministership (in which the elected parliament would select a prime minister and a cabinet) , but the faction did achieve a limitation on presidential powers by assigning major authorities to the parliament, such as the power to veto senior official nominees. The constitution made former King Zahir Shah honorary "Father of the Nation," a title that is not heritable. Zahir Shah died on July 23, 2007.[15]

Afghanistan

First Post-Taliban Elections in 2004

Security conditions precluded the holding of the first post-Taliban elections simultaneously. The first election, for president, was held on October 9, 2004, missing a June constitutional deadline. Turnout was about 80%. On November 3, 2004, Karzai was declared winner (55.4% of the vote) over his 17 challengers on the first round, avoiding a runoff. Parliamentary and provincial council elections were intended for April-May 2005 but were delayed until September 18, 2005. Because of the difficulty in confirming voter registration rolls and determining district boundaries, elections for the 364 district councils, each of which will likely have contentious boundaries because they will inevitably separate tribes and clans, have not been held to date.

Formation of an Elected National Assembly (Parliament)

The National Assembly (parliament), particularly the elected lower house, has emerged as a relatively vibrant body that creates accountability and has often asserted itself politically. The most notable example has been the 2009-20 10 confirmation process for Karzai's cabinet choices, in which many of Karzai's nominees were voted down, and the lower house's subsequent vote against a Karzai election decree to govern the September 18, 2010, National Assembly election (see "September 18, 2010, Parliamentary Elections"). The Assembly's assertiveness shows, in part, that the better educated "independents" are emerging as pivotal members of parliament, although some interpret the activism as a product of emboldened "Northern Alliance" opposition to Karzai and his plan to reconcile with senior Taliban figures. Substantial detail on the factions in the Afghan parliament is provided in CRS Report RS2 1922, *Afghanistan: Politics, Elections, and Government Performance*, by Kenneth Katzman.

HAMID KARZAI, PRESIDENT OF THE ISLAMIC REPUBLIC OF AFGHANISTAN

Hamid Karzai, born December 24, 1957, was selected to lead Afghanistan at the Bonn Conference because he was a prominent Pashtun leader who had been involved in Taliban-era political talks among exiled Afghans and was viewed as a compromiser rather than a "strongman." However, some observers consider his compromises as Afghanistan's leader a sign of weakness, and criticize him for indulging members of his clan and other allies with appointments. Others view him as overly suspicious of the intentions of the United States and other outside powers, believing they are intent on replacing him or favoring certain groups of Afghans over others.

From Karz village in Qandahar Province, Hamid Karzai has led the powerful Popolzai tribe of Durrani Pashtuns since 1 999, when his father was assassinated, allegedly by Taliban agents, in Quetta, Pakistan. Karzai's grandfather was head of the consultative National Council during King Zahir Shah's reign. He attended university in India and supported the *mujahin* party of Sibghatullah Mojadeddi (still a very close ally) during the ant-Soviet war. He was deputy foreign minister in the *mujahidin* government of Rabbani during 1992-1995, but he left the government and supported the Taliban as a Pashtun alternative to Rabbani.

He broke with the Taliban as its excesses unfolded and forged alliances with other anti-Taliban factions, including the Northern Alliance. Karzai entered Afghanistan after the September 11 attacks to organize Pashtun resistance to the Taliban, supported by U.S. Special Forces. He became central to U.S. efforts after Pashtun commander Abdul Haq entered Afghanistan in October 2001 without U.S. support and was captured and hung by the Taliban. Karzai was slightly injured by an errant U.S. bomb during major combat of Operation Enduring Freedom (late 2001).

His half brother, Ahmad Wali Karzai, is the most powerful political figure in that province, He is key to Karzai's maintenance of support and the cornerstone of his information network in Qandahar but Ahmad Wali has been widely accused of involvement in or tolerating narcotics trafficking. A *New York Times* article on October 28, 2009, said Ahmad Wali is also a paid informant for the CIA and some of his property has been used by U.S. Special Forces. Ahmad Wali was the apparent target of at least two bombings in Qandahar in 2009. Others of Karzai's several brothers have lived in the United States, including Qayyum Karzai. Qayyum Karzai won a parliament seat in the September 2005 election but resigned his seat in October 2008 due to health reasons. Qayyum subsequently represented the government in inconclusive talks, held in several Persian Gulf states, to reconcile with Taliban figures close to Mullah Umar. Another brother, Mahmoud Karzai, is a businessman reportedly under U.S. Justice Department investigation of his business interests in Qandahar and Kabul, including auto dealerships, apartment houses, and a stake in Kabul Bank, which nearly collapsed in September 20 1 0. Other Karzai relatives and associates have formed security companies and other contracting firms that have profited extensively from international reconstruction, transportation, and protection funds, including a $2.2 billion U.S. "Host Nation Trucking" contract.

Karzai also relies heavily for advice from tribal and faction leaders from southern Afghanistan, including Sher Mohammad Akhunzadeh, the former governor of Helmand (until 2005), as well as from well-educated professionals such as his current Foreign Minister Zalmay Rasool, his brother-in-law and key Afghanistan National Security Council official Ibrahim Spinzada, and the former foreign minister, now National Security Adviser, Rangeen Spanta.

With heavy protection, Karzai has survived several assassination attempts since taking office, including rocket fire or gunfire at or near his appearances. His wife, Dr. Zenat Karzai, is a gynecologist by profession. They have been married about 11 years and have a son, Mirwais, born in 2008. In December 2009, he spoke publicly about personal turmoil among relatives in Karz village that resulted in the death of an 18-year-old relative in October 2009.

2009 Presidential and Provincial Elections

The 2009 presidential and provincial elections were expected to further Afghanistan's democratic development. However, because of the widespread fraud identified by Afghanistan's U.N.- appointed "Elections Complaints Commission" (ECC) in the August 20, 2009, first round of the elections, the process did not produce that result. The election fraud difficulty may have contributed to the substantial parliamentary opposition to many of Karzai's nominees for his postelection cabinet. In each of three rounds of cabinet nominations in 2009 and 2010, many, if not most, of Karzai's nominees were voted down by the National Assembly. The latest round of nominations occurred in late June 2010, after Karzai forced Interior Minister Mohammad Hanif

Atmar to resign, ostensibly for failing to prevent insurgent attacks in Kabul itself. Atmar was close to and well respected by U.S. officials. Also resigning on June 6 was National Directorate of Security (NDS, Afghan intelligence) chief Amrollah Saleh, a Tajik and an ally of the United Front leaders. Both were believed to oppose Karzai's efforts to reconcile with senior insurgent leaders. See also: CRS Report RS21922, *Afghanistan: Politics, Elections, and Government Performance*, by Kenneth Katzman.

September 18, 2010, Parliamentary Elections

A key test of Karzai's repeated commitment to reforms were the September 18, 2010, National Assembly elections. That election was held amid significant violence but not sufficient to derail the voting. Final results were expected October 30, 2010 but widespread fraud complaints have delayed finalization of the results. The election is covered in CRS Report RS21922, *Afghanistan: Politics, Elections, and Government Performance*, cited earlier.

Some worry that ethnic differences might resurge once the results are announced. Karzai's allies reportedly want to win enough seats (a majority) to ensure that Pashtun conservative Sayyaf, mentioned above, can replace Yunus Qanooni, an Abdullah supporter, as lower house speaker.

Other Major Governance Issues

Obama Administration policy, as articulated on March 27, 2009, and December 1, 2009, emphasizes expanding and improving Afghan governance as a long-term means of stabilizing Afghanistan. The latter Obama statement specified that there would be "no blank check" for the Afghan government if it does not reduce corruption and deliver services. This emphasis is expressed extensively in the State Department January 2010 document outlining its policy priorities, entitled *Afghanistan and Pakistan Regional Stabilization Strategy*.[16] The corruption has repeatedly been stressed emphasized by international participants at two international meetings in 2010 (London in January and Kabul in July) as well as by U.S. officials, including top commander in Afghanistan General Petraeus. However, the Obama Administration reportedly has decided to mute its public criticism of Karzai on the grounds that public criticism causes Karzai to become suspicious of U.S. intent and to ally with undemocratic elements in Afghanistan.

"Unity of Effort": U.S. and International Policy Management and U.S. Embassy Kabul

In line with the prioritization of Afghanistan policy, in February 2009, the Administration appointed Ambassador Richard Holbrooke as "Special Representative for Afghanistan and Pakistan" (SRAP), reporting to Secretary of State Clinton. His team at the State Department consists mainly of members detailed from several different agencies; several have long experience on Afghanistan and Pakistan affairs. Karl Eikenberry, who served as commander of U.S. forces in Afghanistan during 2004-2005, is U.S. Ambassador. President Obama has said he expects the civilian team to work closely with the U.S. and NATO military structure, and a U.S. civilian-military "joint campaign plan" was developed and released in mid-August 2009.[17]

Table 2. U.N. Assistance Mission in Afghanistan (UNAMA)

The United Nationsl is extensively involved in Afghan governance and national building, primarily in factional conflict resolution and coordination of development assistance. The coordinator of U.N. efforts is the U.N. Assistance Mission in Afghanistan (UNAMA), headed as of March 22, 2010, by Swedish diplomat Staffan de-Mistura, replacing Norwegian diplomat Kai Eide. Mistura formerly played a similar role in Iraq. U.N. Security Council Resolution 1806 of March 20, 2008, expanded UNAMA's authority to coordinating the work of international donors and strengthening cooperation between the international peacekeeping force (ISAF, see below) and the Afghan government. In concert with the Obama Administration's emphasis on Afghan policy, UNAMA is to open offices in as many of Afghanistan's 34 provinces as financially and logistically permissible. (The mandate of UNAMA, reviewed at one-year intervals, ran until March 23, 2010, as provided for by Resolution 1869 of March 23, 2009, and was renewed for another year on March 22, 2010 (Resolution 1917)). Resolution 1917 largely restated UNAMA's expanded mandate and coordinating role with other high-level representatives in Afghanistan, and election support role.

In keeping with its expanding role, in 2008 U.S. Ambassador Peter Galbraith was appointed as Eide's deputy, although he left Afghanistan in early September 2009 in a reported dispute with Eide over how vigorously to insist on investigating fraud in the August 20 Afghan election. Galbraith reportedly pressed Afghan and independent election bodies to be as vigorous as possible in the interests of rule of law and election legitimacy; Eide purportedly was willing to encourage an Afghan compromise to avoid a second round run-off. The split led U.N. Secretary General Ban Ki Moon to remove Galbraith from his post at UNAMA in late September 2009 on the grounds that the disharmony was compromising the UNAMA mission. Several Galbraith supporters subsequently resigned from UNAMA and Galbraith has appealed his firing amid reports he was proposing a plan to replace Karzai had an election runoff been postponed until 2010. The turmoil may have caused Eide to leave his post when his contract with the U.N. expired in March 2010.

UNAMA is co-chair of the joint Afghan-international community coordination body called the Joint Coordination and Monitoring Board (JCMB), and is helping implement the five-year development strategy outlined in a "London Compact," (now called the Afghanistan Compact) adopted at the January 31–February 1, 2006, London conference on Afghanistan. The priorities developed in that document comport with Afghanistan's own "National Strategy for Development," presented on June 12, 2008, in Paris. During his term, Eide urged the furnishing of additional capacity-building resources, and he complained that some efforts by international donors are redundant or tied to purchases by Western countries. In statements and press conferences, Eide continued to note security deterioration but also progress in governance and in reduction of drug cultivation, and he publicly supported negotiations with Taliban figures to end the war. His final speech before leaving criticized the U.S.-led coalition for focusing too much on military success and not enough on governance. UNAMA also often has been involved in local dispute resolution among factions, and it helps organize elections. Under a March 2010 compromise with Karzai, it nominates two international members of the five person Electoral Complaints Commission (ECC), one fewer than the three it selected under the prior election law. UNAMA was a co-convener of the January 28, 2010, and July 20, 2010, London and Kabul Conferences, respectively.

The difficulties in coordinating U.N. with U.S. and NATO efforts were evident in a 2007 proposal to create a new position of "super envoy" that would represent the United Nations, the European Union, and NATO in Afghanistan. The concept advanced and in January 2008, with U.S. support, U.N. Secretary General Ban Ki Moon tentatively appointed British diplomat Paddy Ashdown as the "super envoy." However, Karzai rejected the appointment reportedly over concerns about the scope of authority of such an envoy. Karzai might have also sought to show independence from the international community. Ashdown withdrew his name on January 28, 2008. However, the concept reportedly was floated again in late 2009, but was again suppressed by Karzai and others who say it contradicts U.S. and other efforts to promote Afghan leadership. The NATO senior civilian representative post, held by Amb. Mark Sedwill (UK), appears to represent a step in the direction of improved donor coordination in Afghanistan and streamlining of the foreign representative structure there.

For more information on UNAMA, see CRS Report R40747, *United Nations Assistance Mission in Afghanistan: Background and Policy Issues*, by Rhoda Margesson.

On February 7, 2010, in an effort to improve civilian coordination between the United States, its foreign partners, and the Afghan government, a NATO "Senior Civilian Representative" in Afghanistan, UK Ambassador Mark Sedwill, took office. Ambassador

Sedwill works not only with U.S. military officials but with representatives of the embassies of partner countries and with a special U.N. Assistance Mission–Afghanistan (UNAMA, see **Table 2**).

At U.S. Embassy Kabul, there is a "deputy Ambassador"—senior official Francis Ricciardone. Another Ambassador rank official (William Todd) manages U.S. economic assistance issues. Another Ambassador-rank official, Joseph Mussomeli, handles Embassy management. Ambassador Timothy Carney oversaw U.S. policy for the 2009 elections. Another official of Ambassador rank, Hans Klemm, arrived in June 2010 to coordinate U.S. Embassy rule of law programs

The U.S. Embassy has progressively expanded its personnel and facilities and will expand its facilities further to accommodate some of the additional civilian hires and Foreign Service officers who have been posted to Afghanistan as mentors and advisers to the Afghan government. The tables at the end of this chapter include U.S. funding for State Department and USAID operations, including Embassy construction and running the "Embassy air wing," a fleet of twin- engine turboprops that ferry U.S. officials and contractors around Afghanistan. In a significant development attempting to signal normalization of certain areas of Afghanistan, in early 2010 the United States formally inaugurated U.S. consulates in Herat and Mazar-e-Sharif. In November 2010, contracts were announced for expansion of the U.S. Embassy ($511 million) and to construct the two consulates ($20 million for each facility).

The Afghan Ambassador to the United States, Sayed Tayib Jawad, served as Ambassador from 2004 until his recall in August 2010. He was recalled because of complaints in Kabul about Western-style parties that were being held at the Afghan embassy in the United States. No replacement has been named, to date. There is some discussion on the Afghan side of appointing a special envoy, possibly Ashraf Ghani, to interact on a global basis with the Afghanistan donor community.

U.S. Efforts to Expand and Reform Central Government/Corruption

U.S. policy has been to expand governance throughout the country, a policy that is receiving increased U.S. financial and advisory resources under the Obama Administration. However, in part because building the central government has gone slowly and because official corruption is widespread, there has been a U.S. shift, predating the Obama Administration, away from reliance toward promoting local governance. Some argue that, in addition to offering the advantage of bypassing an often corrupt central government, doing so is more compatible with Afghan traditions of local autonomy.

Several other efforts to build and promote better Afghan governance are discussed below. Several of the various aspects of U.S. efforts to build the capacity of the central and local government institutions are discussed in greater detail in CRS Report RS2 1922, *Afghanistan: Politics, Elections, and Government Performance.*

Marginalization of Regional Strongmen

A key to U.S. strategy, particularly during 2002-2006, was to strengthen the central government by helping Karzai curb key regional strongmen and local militias—whom some refer to as "warlords." These actors controlled much of Afghanistan after the Taliban regime disintegrated in late 2001, but there was a decision by the international community to build up an accountable central government rather than leave Afghanistan in the hands of local militias. These forces often arbitrarily administer justice and use their positions to enrich themselves and their supporters.

Karzai has marginalized some of the largest regional leaders, but he is criticized by some human rights groups and international donors for continuing to tolerate or rely on others to keep order in some areas, particularly in non-Pashtun inhabited parts of Afghanistan (the north and west). Karzai's view is that maintaining ties to ethnic and regional faction leaders has prevented the emergence of ethnic conflict that would detract from the overall effort against the Taliban. Several of these faction leaders are discussed in CRS Report RS21922, *Afghanistan: Politics, Elections, and Government Performance*, by Kenneth Katzman.

Anti-Corruption Efforts

An accelerating trend in U.S. policy—and emphasized in both major Obama Administration strategy reviews as well as by many in Congress—is to press Karzai to weed out official corruption. U.S. officials believe that rife corruption in the Afghan government is undermining U.S. domestic support for the U.S. mission in Afghanistan, and causing the Afghan population to sour on the Karzai government. U.S. anti-corruption and rule of law efforts are discussed extensively in the "Afghanistan and Pakistan Regional Stabilization Strategy" issued by Ambassador Holbrooke's office in January 2010, referenced above. The corruption issue—its sources, U.S. and Afghan efforts to curb corruption, and progress—is discussed in CRS Report R41484, Afghanistan: U.S. Rule of Law and Justice Sector Assistance, by Liana Sun Wyler and Kenneth Katzman and in CRS Report RS21922, *Afghanistan: Politics, Elections, and Government Performance*, by Kenneth Katzman.

In FY2011 legislation, on June 30, 2010, the State and Foreign Operations Subcommittee of House Appropriations Committee marked up its aid bill. The Subcommittee deferred consideration of much of the Administration's Afghanistan request pending a Committee investigation of allegations of governmental corruption and possible diversion of U.S. aid funds by Afghan officials and other elites.

Enhancing Local Governance

As emphasized in the January 2010 SRAP strategy document cited earlier, there has been a major U.S. and Afghan push to build up local governing structures, reflecting a shift in emphasis from the 2001-2007 approach of focusing on building up central authority. However, building local governance has suffered from a deficit of trained and respected local government administrators ready or willing to serve, particularly where hostilities are ongoing. This deficiency has hindered U.S. counter-insurgency efforts in southern Afghanistan, as discussed further below. The U.S. effort to expand local governance is discussed in CRS Report RS2 1922, *Afghanistan: Politics, Elections, and Government Performance*, by Kenneth Katzman

U.S. policy has sought to use local governance promotion efforts to support U.S. security strategy for Afghanistan. Several districts have received special attention to become "models" of district security and governance are Nawa, in Helmand Province, and Baraki-Barak, in Lowgar Province, both cleared of Taliban militants in 2009. With substantial infusions of U.S. development funds that put sometime insurgents to work on projects (offering $5 per day to perform such tasks as cleaning irrigation canals), these districts are, by several accounts, far more stable and secure than they were in 2009. As part of "Operation

Moshtarek" (Operation Together), launched February 13, 2010, to clear the city of Marjah of militants, a district governor (Hajji Zahir) and district administration were selected in advance. Zahir tried to build up his administration after the town was wrested from Taliban control, but governance there was slow to expand. Zahir was replaced in early July 2010. Still, the British civilian representative in Marjah said in October 2010 that central government ministry representation in Marjah is now in place and operating consistently. (Marjah is currently part of Nad Ali district, and is eventually to become its own district, according to Afghan observers.)

Human Rights and Democracy

The Administration and Afghan government claim progress in building a democratic Afghanistan that adheres to international standards of human rights practices. The State Department report on human rights practices for 2009 (released March 11, 2010)[18] said that Afghanistan's human rights record remained "poor," noting in particular that the government or its agents commit arbitrary or unlawful killings. Still, virtually all observers agree that Afghans are freer than they were under the Taliban. The tables at the end of this chapter contain information on U.S. funding for democracy, governance, rule of law and human rights, and elections support since the fall of the Taliban. Of these, by far the largest category was "good governance," discussed above. FY2009 and FY2010 levels, and funding earmarks for programs benefitting women and girls, are also in the tables. Numerous aspects of Afghan performance on human rights are covered in CRS Report RS2 1922, *Afghanistan: Politics, Elections, and Government Performance.*

Narcotics Trafficking/Insurgent Financing[19]

Narcotics trafficking is regarded by some as a core impediment to the U.S. mission in Afghanistan by undermining rule of law and providing funds to the insurgency. However, it is also an area on which there has been progress in recent years. The trafficking generates an estimated $70 million–$100 million per year for the Taliban.

U.S. officials hope that recent progress will be sustained. A UNODC report of September 2010, continued a relatively positive trend in reporting on this issue, noting that all of the 20 provinces (out of 34 provinces in Afghanistan) in the "poppy free" category remain that way. Total production in 2010 is estimated at 3,600 metric tons, a 48% decrease from 2009, although this was due to a crop disease, for the most part. [20]

Obama Administration policy is focusing on promoting legitimate agricultural alternatives to poppy growing and, in conjunction, Ambassador Holbrooke announced in July 2009 that the United States would end its prior focus on eradication of poppy fields. In this view, eradication was driving Afghans into the arms of the Taliban as protectors of their ability to earn a living, even if doing so is from narcotics cultivation. Encouraging alternative livelihoods has always been the preferred emphasis of the Afghan government. The de-emphasis on eradication also put aside the long-standing differences over whether to conduct spraying of fields, particularly by air. That concept was strenuously opposed by Karzai and not implemented. Congress sided with Karzai's view; the FY2008 Consolidated Appropriation (P.L. 110-161) prohibited U.S. counter-narcotics funding from being used for aerial spraying on Afghanistan poppy fields without Afghan concurrence. That provision was reiterated in the FY2010 consolidated appropriation (P.L. 111-117).

Other policies promote incentives; Helmand, for example, received about $10 million in Good Performance funding in 2009 for a 33% cut in poppy cultivation that year. According to Afghan cabinet members, the government also is spending funds on a "social safety net" to help wean landless farmers away from poppy cultivation work.

How consistently to use U.S. and NATO forces to combat narcotics is another facet under debate. Some NATO contributors, such as Britain, have focused on interdicting traffickers and raiding drug labs. The U.S. military, in support of the effort after initial reluctance, is flying Afghan and U.S. counter-narcotics agents (Drug Enforcement Agency, DEA) on missions and identifying targets; it also evacuates casualties from counter-drug operations. The Department of Defense is also playing the major role in training and equipping specialized Afghan counter-narcotics police, in developing an Afghan intelligence fusion cell, and training Afghan border police, as well as assisting an Afghan helicopter squadron to move Afghan counter-narcotics forces around the country. To help break up narcotics trafficking networks, the DEA presence in Afghanistan is has expanded from 13 agents in 2008 to over 80 in 2010, with additional agents in Pakistan.

Ambassador Holbrooke has also placed additional focus on the other sources of Taliban funding, including continued donations from wealthy residents of the Persian Gulf. He has established a multinational task force to combat Taliban financing generally, not limited to narcotics, and U.S. officials are emphasizing with Persian Gulf counterparts the need for cooperation.

Narcotics trafficking control was perhaps the one issue on which the Taliban regime satisfied much of the international community. The Taliban enforced a July 2000 ban on poppy cultivation.[21]

Narcotics-Related Aid Conditionality

The Bush Administration repeatedly named Afghanistan as a major illicit drug producer and drug transit country, but did not include Afghanistan on a smaller list of countries that have "failed demonstrably to make substantial efforts" to adhere to international counter-narcotics agreements and take certain counter-narcotics measures set forth in U.S. law.[22] The Bush Administration exercised waiver provisions to a required certification of full Afghan cooperation that was needed to provide more than congressionally stipulated amounts of U.S. economic assistance to Afghanistan. A similar certification requirement (to provide amounts over $300 million) was contained in the FY2008 appropriation (P.L. 110-161); in the FY2009 regular appropriation, P.L. 111-8 ($200 million ceiling); and the FY20 10 appropriation, P.L. 111-117, ($200 million ceiling). The FY2009 supplemental (P.L. 111-32) withheld 10% of State Department narcotics funding (International Narcotics Control and Law Enforcement, INCLE) pending a report that Afghanistan is removing officials involved in narcotics trafficking or gross human rights violations. No funds for Afghanistan have been held up, and the required certifications have been issued by the Administration or apparently are pending.

SECURITY POLICY AND FORCE CAPACITY BUILDING[23]

The U.S. definition of "success" of the stabilization mission in Afghanistan, articulated since the ouster of the Taliban in late 2001, is to help build up an Afghan government and security force that can defend itself, expand governance, and develop economically. The Obama Administration's policy reviews in 2009 formally narrowed U.S. goals to preventing Al Qaeda from reestablishing a base in Afghanistan. However, the policy and military tools employed by the Obama Administration in most ways continue and even expand a nation-building goal. The December 1, 2009, speech by President Obama stated U.S. goals as: (1) denying Al Qaeda a safe haven [in Afghanistan]; and (2) reversing the Taliban's momentum and denying it the ability to overthrow the government. The statement generally backed the August 30, 2009, recommendations of then-top commander in Afghanistan Gen. Stanley McChrystal's to undertake a fully resourced counter-insurgency mission. The focus of the mission is on 121 districts (out of 364 total districts in Afghanistan) deemed restive and in which support for the Afghan government is lowest. Of those, 80 districts are of the most intense focus, according to Defense Department reports and officials.

The two major U.S. policy reviews in 2009 did not significantly change most of the basic pillars of U.S. and NATO security strategy that have been in place since 2001, although the emphasis of some of these components might have shifted. The main elements include: (1) combat operations and patrols by U.S. forces and a NATO-led International Security Assistance Force (ISAF) to "provide space" for the expansion of Afghan governance, security leadership, and infrastructure and economic development; (2) U.S. and NATO operation of "provincial reconstruction teams" (PRTs) to serve as enclaves to facilitate the strategy; and (3) the equipping, training, and expansion of Afghanistan National Security Forces (ANSF). Some strategy elements that have emerged since 2008, and which are taking precedence as Western public support for the war effort erodes, include establishing local protection forces and backing efforts to reintegrate Taliban fighters and leaders who might want to end armed struggle.

Who are U.S. /NATO Forces Fighting? Taliban, Al Qaeda, and Related Insurgents and Their Strength

As noted in General McChrystal's August 2009 initial assessment and the Defense Department April 2010 report, security is being challenged by a confluence of related armed groups who are increasingly well equipped and sophisticated in their tactics and operations, particularly by using roadside bombs.[24] However, there is not agreement about the relative strength of insurgents in all of the areas where they operate, or their degree of cooperation with each other. Afghan and U.S. assessments are that there are more than 20,000 total insurgents operating in Afghanistan, up from a few thousand in 2003.

Prior to U.S.-led offensives launched since mid-2009, the Karzai government was estimated by to control about 30% of the country, while insurgents controlled 4% (13 out of 364 districts). Insurgents "influenced" or "operated in" another 30% (Afghan Interior Ministry estimates in August 2009). Tribes and local groups with varying degrees of loyalty to the central government control the remainder. Outside groups, such as aid groups that released their own findings in September 2010, sometimes report higher percentages of insurgent control or influence.[25] U.S. military officers in Kabul told CRS in October 2009 that the Taliban had named "shadow governors" in 33 out of 34 of Afghanistan's provinces, although many provinces in northern Afghanistan were assessed as having minimal Taliban presence.

As far as tactics, U.S. commanders increasingly worry about growing insurgent use of improvised explosive devices (IEDs), including roadside bombs. IED's are the leading cause of U.S. combat deaths, and IED attacks nearly doubled again in frequency in the first four months of 2010, according to the U.N. Secretary General's report of June 16, 2010. In January 2010, President Karzai issued a decree banning importation of fertilizer chemicals (ammonium nitrate) commonly used for the roadside bombs, but the material reportedly still comes into Afghanistan from Pakistan . Contrary to press reports quoting leaked material about the war effort, U.S. commanders have said they have not seen insurgent use of surface-to-air missiles.[26]

There were about 310 U.S. soldiers killed in 2009, nearly double the previous year, and U.S. deaths in June and July 2010 (about 55 each of those months) were at or near the highs of the war effort thus far. Including the U.S. losses, there were about 506 total coalition deaths in Afghanistan in 2009. A UNAMA report issue in August 2010, covering the first half of 2010, noted a 30% increase in Afghan civilian deaths over the same period one year ago. It attributed the increase to insurgent attacks, and said that casualties caused by Afghan or pro-government forces had fallen 30% during the same period.

Groups: The Taliban ("Quetta Shura Taliban")

The core of the insurgency remains the Taliban movement centered around Mullah Umar, who led the Taliban regime during 1996-2001. Mullah Umar and many of his top advisers remain at large and are reportedly running their insurgency from their safe haven in Pakistan. They are believed to be in and around the city of Quetta, according to Afghan officials, thus accounting for the term usually applied to Umar and his aides: "Quetta Shura Taliban" (QST).

Some believe that Umar and his inner circle blame their past association with Al Qaeda for their loss of power and want to distance themselves from Al Qaeda. Other experts see continuing close association that is likely to continue were the Taliban movement to return to power.. On September 19, 2009, Umar issued an audiotape criticizing the Afghan elections as fraudulent.

Some believe that the U.S. "surge" in Afghanistan may be causing Umar, or some around him, to mull the concept of a political settlement. Umar 's top deputy, Mullah Bradar, was arrested in a reported joint U.S.-Pakistani operation near the city of Karachi in February 2010 -- Karzai considered his capture set back Afghan government-Taliban reconciliation talks, which Bradar reportedly supports. It was also reported in March 2010 that Pakistan had briefly detained another member of the Quetta Shura, Mullah Kabir, and arrested Agha Jhan Motasim, a son-in-law of Umar.[27] In recent years, other top Taliban figures, including Mullah Dadullah, his son Mansoor, and Mullah Usmani have been killed or captured. Some observers say that informal settlement ideas floated between the Taliban and the Karzai government may envision Umar being granted exile in Saudi Arabia.

To address losses, Umar reportedly replaced Bradar with a young leader, Mullah Abdul Qayyum Zakir, a U.S. detainee in Guantanamo Bay, Cuba, until 2007.[28] Some reports assert that other aides (most notably Mullah Ghul Agha Akhund) may not recognize Zakir and might themselves be seeking the number two spot in the organization. The Taliban has several official spokespersons still at large, including Qari Yusuf Ahmadi and Zabiullah Mujahid, and it operates a clandestine radio station, "Voice of Shariat" and publishes videos.

Two members of the Quetta Shura, Mullah Hassan Rahmani, former Taliban governor of Qandahar, and Mullah Afghan Tayib, another spokesman, are said to have come under some Pakistani pressure.

Al Qaeda/Bin Laden Whereabouts

U.S. commanders say that Al Qaeda militants are more facilitators of militant incursions into Afghanistan rather than active fighters in the Afghan insurgency. Director of Central Intelligence Leon Panetta said on June 27, 2010, that Al Qaeda fighters in Afghanistan itself might number 50-100.[29] Small numbers of Al Qaeda members—including Arabs, Uzbeks, and Chechens—have been captured or killed in battles in Afghanistan itself, according to U.S. commanders. Some of these fighters apparently belong to Al Qaeda affiliates such as the Islamic Movement of Uzbekistan (IMU). Some NATO/ISAF officials said in October 2010, however, that some Al Qaeda cells may be moving back into remote areas of Kunar and Nuristan provinces.[30]

Al Qaeda's top leadership has eluded U.S. forces in Afghanistan and other efforts in Pakistan. In December 2001, in the course of the post-September 11 major combat effort, U.S. Special Operations Forces and CIA operatives reportedly narrowed Osama bin Laden's location to the Tora Bora mountains in Nangarhar Province (30 miles west of the Khyber Pass), but the Afghan militia fighters who were the bulk of the fighting force did not prevent his escape. Some U.S. military and intelligence officers (such as Gary Berntsen and Dalton Fury, who have written books on the battle) have questioned the U.S. decision to rely mainly on Afghan forces in this engagement.

Bin Laden and his close ally Ayman al-Zawahiri are presumed to be on the Pakistani side of the border. CNN reported October 18, 2010, that assessments from the U.S.-led coalition now say the two are likely in a settled area near the border with Afghanistan, and not living in a very remote uninhabited area. A U.S. strike reportedly missed Zawahiri by a few hours in the village of Damadola, Pakistan, in January 2006, suggesting that there was intelligence on his movements.[31] From their redoubt, these leaders are widely believed to continue to be looking for ways to attack the U.S. homeland or U.S. allies and continuing to issue audio statements threatening such attacks. On the ninth anniversary of the September 11 attacks on some U.S. observers said it was still significant to try to capture bin Laden if for no other reason than for symbolic value. Press reports in September 2010 said that Al Qaeda's former spokesman, Kuwait-born Sulayman Abu Ghaith, may have been released from house arrest by Iran and allowed to proceed to Pakistan. Other reports in November 2010 said that another Al Qaeda senior operative, Sayf al Adl, who was believed to be in Iran during 2002-2010, may have left Iran and gone to Pakistan, and reportedly may have been elevated by bin Laden to top Al Qaeda operational commander.

Among other efforts, a strike in late January 2008, in an area near Damadola, killed Abu Laith alLibi, a reported senior Al Qaeda figure who purportedly masterminded, among other operations, the bombing at Bagram Air Base in February 2007 when Vice President Cheney was visiting. In August 2008, an airstrike was confirmed to have killed Al Qaeda chemical weapons expert Abu Khabab al-Masri, and two senior operatives allegedly involved in the 1998 embassy bombings in Africa reportedly were killed by a Predator strike in January 2009.

These strikes have become more frequent under President Obama, indicating that the Administration sees the tactic as effective in preventing attacks. Unmanned vehicle strikes are also increasingly used on the Afghanistan battlefield itself and against Al Qaeda affiliated militants in such countries as Yemen.

Hikmatyar Faction

Another "high value target" identified by U.S. commanders is the faction of former *mujahedin* party leader Gulbuddin Hikmatyar (Hizb-e-Islami Gulbuddin, HIG) allied with Al Qaeda and Taliban insurgents. As noted above, Hikmatyar was one of the main U.S.-backed *mujahedin* leaders during the Soviet occupation era. Hikmatyar's faction received extensive U.S. support against the Soviet Union, but is now active against U.S. and Afghan forces in Kunar, Nuristan, Kapisa, and Nangarhar provinces, north and east of Kabul. On February 19, 2003, the U.S. government formally designated Hikmatyar as a "Specially Designated Global Terrorist," under the authority of Executive Order 13224, subjecting it to financial and other U.S. sanctions. It is not designated as a "Foreign Terrorist Organization" (FTO). **Table 5** contains estimated numbers of HIG.

While U.S. commanders continue to battle Hikmatyar's militia, on March 22, 2010, both the Afghan government and Hikmatyar representatives confirmed they were in talks in Kabul, including meetings with Karzai. Hikmatyar has expressed a willingness to discuss a cease-fire with the Karzai government since 2007, and some of Karzai's key allies in the National Assembly are former members of Hikmatyar 's *mujahedin* party. In January 2010, he outlined specific conditions for a possible reconciliation with Karzai, including elections under a neutral caretaker government following a U.S. withdrawal. These conditions are unlikely to be acceptable to Karzai or the international community, although many of them might be modified or dropped. Some close to Hikmatyar apparently attended the consultative peace *loya jirga* on June 2-4, 2010, which discussed the reconciliation issue, as analyzed further below.

Haqqani Faction

Another militant faction, cited repeatedly as a major threat, is the "Haqqani Network" led by Jalaludin Haqqani and his eldest son, Siraj (or Sirajjudin). Jalaludin Haqqani, who served as Minister of Tribal Affairs in the Taliban regime of 1996-2001, is believed closer to Al Qaeda than to the ousted Taliban leadership in part because one of his wives is purportedly Arab. The group is active around its key objective, Khost city, capital of Khost Province. The Haqqani network may have been responsible for the January 18, 2010, attacks in Kabul that prompted four hours of gun battles with Afghan police in locations near the presidential palace.

U.S. officials say they are continuing to pressure the Haqqani network with military action in Afghanistan and air strikes on the Pakistani side of the border. Haqqani property inside Pakistan has been repeatedly targeted since September 2008 by U.S. aerial drone strikes. Siraj 's brother, Mohammad, was reportedly killed by a U.S. unmanned vehicle strike in late February 2010, although Mohammad was not thought to be a key militant commander. In July 2010, it was reported that Gen. Petraeus, as part of his adjustments to policy as top commander in Afghanistan, wants the Haqqani network to be named as an FTO under the Immigration and Naturalization Act. Secretary of State Clinton said on July 19, 2010, during a visit to Pakistan, that U.S. policy is moving in that direction. Such a move would be intended to signal to Pakistan that it should not see the Haqqani network, as a whole, as part of a reconciled political structure in Afghanistan that would protect Pakistan's interests and work to limit the influence of India. This view was emphasized in a *New York Times* story of June 25, 2010.[32] The Haqqani faction has been thought not amenable to a political settlement, but some reports in November 2010 have said that members of the faction may have participated in exploratory reconciliation meetings with government representatives. **Table 5** contains estimated numbers of Haqqani fighters.

Pakistani Groups

The Taliban of Afghanistan are increasingly linked politically and operationally to Pakistani Taliban militants. These groups might see a Taliban recapture of Afghanistan's government as helpful to the prospects for these groups inside Pakistan or in their Kashmir struggle.

The Pakistani Taliban (Tehrik-e-Taliban Pakistan, TTP) is primarily seeking to challenge the government of Pakistan, but they facilitate the transiting into Afghanistan of Afghan Taliban and support the Afghan Taliban goals of recapturing Afghanistan. The TTP may also be seeking to target the United States, based on a failed bombing in New York in May 2010. The State Department designated the TTP as a Foreign Terrorist Organization (FTO) under the Immigration and Naturalization Act on September 2, 2010, allegedly for having close connections to Al Qaeda.

Another Pakistani group said to be increasingly active inside Afghanistan is Laskhar-e-Tayyiba (LET, or Army of the Righteous). LET is an Islamist militant group that has previously been focused on operations against Indian control of Kashmir.

The U.S. Military Effort

The large majority of U.S. troops in Afghanistan are under NATO/ISAF command. The remainder are part of the post-September 11 anti-terrorism mission Operation Enduring Freedom (OEF). There are also Special Operations Forces in Afghanistan under a separate command. Serving under General Petraeus is Maj. Gen. David Rodriguez, who heads a NATO-approved "Intermediate Joint Command" focused primarily on day-to-day operations and located in a facility adjoining Kabul International Airport. He has been in this position since mid-2009. The ISAF/U.S. Forces-Afghanistan commander reports not only to NATO but, through U.S. channels, to U.S. Central Command (CENTCOM).

Whether under NATO or OEF, many U.S. forces in Afghanistan are in eastern Afghanistan and lead Regional Command East of the NATO/ISAF operation. These U.S. forces belong to Combined Joint Task Force 101 (as of June 2010), which is commanded by Maj. Gen. John Campbell. As of November 2010, the most restive provinces in RC-E are Paktia, Paktika, Khost, Kunar, Nangarhar, and Nuristan.

Helmand, Qandahar, Uruzgan, Zabol, Nimruz, and Dai Kundi provinces constitute "Regional Command South (RC-S)," a command formally transferred to NATO/ISAF responsibility on July 31, 2006. U.S. forces have not led RC-S; the command was rotated among Britain, the Netherlands, and Canada. However, with the Dutch pullout in July 2010 and the growing U.S. troop strength in RC-S prompted a May 23, 2010, NATO decision to bifurcate RC-S, with the United States leading a "southwest" subdivision focused on

Helmand and Nimruz. This is an evolution of the growing U.S. involvement in RC-S since 2008.

Perception of "Victory" in the First Five Post-Taliban Years

During 2001 -mid-2006, U.S. forces and Afghan troops fought relatively low levels of insurgent violence. The United States and Afghanistan conducted "Operation Mountain Viper" (August 2003); "Operation Avalanche" (December 2003); "Operation Mountain Storm" (March-July 2004) against Taliban remnants in and around Uruzgan province, home province of Mullah Umar; "Operation Lightning Freedom" (December 2004–February 2005); and "Operation Pil" (Elephant) in Kunar Province in the east (October 2005). By late 2005, U.S. and partner commanders appeared to believe that the combat, coupled with overall political and economic reconstruction, had virtually ended any insurgency. Anticipating further stabilization, NATO/ISAF assumed lead responsibility for security in all of Afghanistan during 2005-2006.

Contrary to U.S. expectations, violence increased significantly in mid-2006, particularly in the east and the south, where ethnic Pashtuns predominate. Reasons for the deterioration include some of those discussed above in the sections on governance: Afghan government corruption; the absence of governance or security forces in many rural areas. Other factors included the safe haven enjoyed by militants in Pakistan; the reticence of some NATO contributors to actively combat insurgents; a popular backlash against civilian casualties caused by NATO and U.S. military operations; and the slow pace of economic development. Many Afghans are said to have turned to the Taliban as a source of impartial and rapid justice, in contrast to the slow and corrupt processes instituted by the central government.

Perception of Deterioration and Growing Force Levels in 2007 and 2008

Since 2006, the key theater of intensified combat has been eastern and southern Afghanistan. The provinces that are particularly restive include Helmand and Qandahar provinces. NATO counteroffensives in 2006 cleared areas of these provinces, but militants regrouped, following such operations as Operation Mountain Lion, Operation Mountain Thrust, and Operation Medusa (August-September 2006, in Panjwai district of Qandahar Province). Later, British forces—who believe in negotiated local solutions—entered into an agreement with tribal elders in the Musa Qala district of Helmand Province, under which they would secure the main town of the district themselves. That strategy failed when the Taliban took over Musa Qala town in February 2007. A NATO offensive in December 2007 retook it.

As a further response, NATO and OEF forces tried to apply a more integrated strategy involving preemptive combat, increased development work, and a more streamlined command structure. Major combat operations in 2007 included U.S. and NATO attempted preemption of an anticipated Taliban "spring offensive" ("Operation Achilles," March 2007) in the Sangin district of Helmand Province, around the Kajaki dam, and Operation Silicon (May 2007), also in Helmand. (In September 2010, Britain turned over security leadership in Sangin to U.S. forces in the near future; combat in the district has accounted for nearly half of Britain's entire casualties in Afghanistan to date. U.S. strategy for the district is said to try to push out the boundaries of secure area of the district; British efforts focused on better securing the district major city.)

Despite the additional resources put into Afghanistan, throughout 2008, growing concern took hold within the Bush Administration. Pessimism was reflected in such statements as one in September 2008 by Joint Chiefs of Staff chairman Admiral Mike Mullen that "I'm not sure we're winning" in Afghanistan. Several major incidents supported that assessment, including: (1) expanding Taliban operations in provinces where it had not previously been active, particularly Lowgar, Wardak, and Kapisa, close to Kabul; (2) high-profile attacks in Kabul against well-defended targets, such as the January 14, 2008, attack on the Serena Hotel in Kabul and the July 7, 2008, suicide bombing at the Indian Embassy in Kabul, killing more than 50; (3) the April 27, 2008, assassination attempt on Karzai during a military parade celebrating the ouster of the Soviet Union; and (4) a June 12, 2008, Sarposa prison break in Qandahar (several hundred Taliban captives were freed, as part of an emptying of the 1,200 inmates there).

To try to arrest deterioration, the United States and its partners decided to increase force levels. The added forces partly fulfilled a mid-2008 request by Gen. McKiernan for 30,000 additional U.S. troops (beyond the approximately 35,000 there at the time of the request). However, as the November 2008 U.S. presidential election approached, the decision whether to fulfill the entire request was deferred to the next Administration. U.S. troop levels started 2006 at 30,000; climbed slightly to 32,000 by December 2008; and reached 39,000 by April 2009. Partner forces were increased significantly as well, by about 6,000 during this time, to a total of 39,000 at the end of 2009 (rough parity between U.S. and non-U.S. forces). Many of the U.S. forces deployed in 2008 and 2009 were Marines that deployed to Helmand, large parts of which had fallen out of coalition/Afghan control.

Obama Administration Strategy Reviews and Further Buildup

In September 2008, the U.S. military and NATO each began strategy reviews. The primary U.S. review was headed by Lt. Gen. Douglas Lute, the Bush Administration's senior adviser on Iraq and Afghanistan (who was kept on under the Obama Administration with responsibility for Afghanistan). Other U.S. reviews were conducted by the Department of Defense, by CENTCOM, and by the State Department. These reviews were briefed to the incoming Obama Administration. The Obama Administration, which maintained that Afghanistan needed to be given a higher priority than it was during the Bush Administration, integrated the reviews into an overarching 60-day inter-agency "strategy review." It was chaired by South Asia expert Bruce Riedel and co- chaired by Ambassador Holbrooke and Under Secretary of Defense for Policy Michele Flournoy.

March 27, 2009, Policy Announcement and Troop Increase, First Command Change, and McChrystal Assessment

President Obama announced a "comprehensive" strategy on March 27, 2009.[33] In conjunction, he announced the deployment of an additional 21,000 U.S. forces, of which about 4,000 would be trainers. Shortly after the announcement, the Administration decided that U.S. military leadership in Afghanistan was insufficiently innovative. On May 11, 2009, Secretary of Defense Gates and Joint Chiefs of Staff Chairman Michael Mullen announced that Gen. McKiernan would be replaced by Gen. Stanley McChrystal, considered an innovative commander as head of U.S. special operations from 2003 to 2008. He assumed command on June 15, 2009.

Gen. McChrystal, after assuming command, assessed the security situation and suggested a strategy in a report of August 30, 2009, and presented to NATO on August 31, 2009.[34] The main elements are:

- That the goal of the U.S. military should be to protect the population—and to help the Afghan government take steps to earn the trust of the population—rather than to search out and combat Taliban concentrations. Indicators of success such as ease of road travel and normal life for families are more important than are counts of numbers of enemy fighters killed.
- That there is potential for "mission failure" unless a fully resourced, comprehensive counter-insurgency strategy is pursued and reverses Taliban momentum within 12-18 months.
- About 44,000 additional U.S. combat troops (including trainers) would be needed to have the greatest chance for his strategy's success—beyond those approved by the Obama Administration strategy review in March 2009.

Some of the data supporting McChrystal's assessment and recommendations included Taliban gains in Konduz, Farah, and other areas in the north that previously were peaceful. McChrystal's report took particular note of Taliban gains in and around Qandahar. A high-profile attack there on August 25, 2009, killing about 40 persons.

Second High-Level Review and Further Force Increase

The McChrystal assessment set off debate within the Administration. In September 2009, the Administration began a second high-level review of U.S. strategy, taking into account the McChrystal recommendations and the marred August 20, 2009, presidential election. Some senior U.S. officials, such as Secretary of Defense Gates, were concerned that adding many more U.S. forces could create among the Afghan people a sense of "occupation" that could prove counterproductive. Some Members of Congress, including Senate Armed Services Committee Chairman Carl Levin, said that the U.S. focus should be on expanding Afghan security forces capabilities before sending additional U.S. forces.

The high-level review included at least nine high-level meetings, chaired by President Obama, and reportedly concluded on November 19, 2009. The President announced his decisions in a speech at West Point military academy on December 1, 2009.[35] The major features of the December 1 statement included the following:

- That 30,000 additional U.S. forces (plus an unspecified number of additional "enablers") would be sent to "reverse the Taliban's momentum" and strengthen the capacity of Afghanistan's security forces and government in order to pave the way for a transition, beginning in July 2011, to Afghan leadership of the stabilization effort. U.S. force levels did reach their current level of about 104,000 on/about September 4, 2010. (Perhaps reflecting further need, Gen. Petraeus did request an additional 2,000 NATO/ISAF forces on September 6, 2010, of which 750 are to be trainers for the Afghan national security forces.)

- The July 2011 deadline is the policy element that has caused significant controversy, as discussed below. The pace and scope of the transition is to be determined as a consequence of a major review of the battlefield situation to be completed by December 2010.

McChrystal Replaced by Petraeus

On June 23, 2010, President Obama accepted the resignation of Gen. McChrystal after summoning him to Washington, DC, to discuss the comments by him and his staff to a reporter for *Rolling Stone* (article cited earlier) that disparaged virtually all the civilian figures involved in Afghanistan policy. He named Gen. Petraeus as Gen. McChrystal's successor, a move that appeared to reassure President Karzai. In a June 23, 2010, statement in the Rose Garden, President Obama attributed the change purely to the disrespect of civilian authority contained in the *Rolling Stone* comments, and stated that Afghanistan policy would not change. Gen. Petraeus was confirmed by the Senate on June 30, 2010, and assumed command on July 4, 2010.

Summary of Current U.S. Strategy as Implemented by Gen. Petraeus

The major outlines of Obama Administration strategy have taken shape as outlined below, and a wide range of U.S. officials have said that the December 2010 DOD review, and a White House review around that time as well, are not likely to result in major changes to strategy. Gen. Petraeus has not dramatically altered the McChrystal strategy, but he has increased (nearly tripled) Special Operations Force operations and air strikes on concentrations across the border in Pakistan to try to drive insurgents to reconcile with the Karzai government and cease fighting. In November 2010, Gen.Petraeus reportedly approved the deployment of about 16 M1A1 tanks for use by the Marines in southern Afghanistan in order to put further pressure on militants:

- *Key Goals:* (1) disrupt terrorist networks in Afghanistan and Pakistan to degrade their ability to launch international terrorist attacks; (2) promote a more capable, accountable, and effective government in Afghanistan; (3) develop self-reliant Afghan security forces; and (4) involve the international community to actively assist in addressing these objectives. These relatively targeted goals are in line with comments by President Obama that he wants to "finish the job" in Afghanistan during his presidency.
- *Strategy Definition:* The overall counter-insurgency strategy is intended to "clear, hold, build, and transition"—to protect the population and allow time for Afghan governance and security forces to take leadership and for infrastructure and economic development to take root.
- *Limiting Civilian Casualties.* Part of the strategy is to win support of Afghans by sharply limiting air strikes and some types of raids and combat that cause Afghan civilian casualties and resentment[36] Some refer to the rules as the "Karzai 12," referring to the number of points of these rules of engagement. The NATO International Security Assistance Force (ISAF) and the Karzai government want to prevent any recurrence of incident such as the one that occurred near Herat on August 22, 2008, in which a NATO bomb killed up to 90 civilians, as well as the

incident in September 2009 in Konduz in which Germany's contingent called in an airstrike on Taliban fighters who captured two fuel trucks; killing several civilians as well as Taliban fighters. Still, ISAF-caused civilian casualties continue, mainly due to misunderstandings at ISAF checkpoints, and in November 2010 President Karzai publicly called for a reduction of some of the night raids that are causing popular backlash.

- *July 2011 Deadline.* The Obama Administration emphasis on transition to Afghan security leadership beginning in July 2011 has been interpreted by some Administration officials—and by some Afghan and regional leaders—as laying the groundwork for winding down U.S. involvement in coming years.[37] Because the time frame has stimulated considerable debate, it is discussed further below.

- *Resources and Troops:* The Administration and foreign partners asserts that resource "inputs" are, as of October 2010, aligned with mission requirements.

- *Pressing the Afghan Government:* The Administration asserts that the Karzai government is being held to account for its performance, although, as noted, no specific penalties have been imposed on the Afghan government for shortfalls.

- *Civilian "Uplift":* A key strategy component is to develop Afghan institutions, particularly at the provincial and local levels. To be effective, the number of U.S. civilian advisors in Afghanistan reached about 1,000 in early 2010 and is about 1,300 as of November 2010. Of these at least 400 serve outside Kabul as part of initiatives such as the 32 "District Support Teams" and the "District Working Groups." That is up from 67 outside Kabul in early 2009.

- *Civilian-Military Integration:* There is a commitment to civilian-military integration, as outlined in a DOD-State Department joint campaign plan and Ambassador Holbrooke's January 2010 strategy document, referenced earlier. High-level "Senior Civilian Representatives" have been appointed to help the military formulate strategy for the regional commands where they serve. This is part of a new "Interagency Provincial Affairs" initiative that is less military- focused.

- *Reintegration and Reconciliation:* As discussed later, the Administration supports Afghan efforts to provide financial and social incentives to persuade insurgents to lay down their arms and accept the Afghan constitution. The United States was at first skeptical but is now increasingly supporting Karzai's policy of negotiating with senior insurgent leaders.

- *Pakistan:* Engagement with Pakistan and enlisting its increased cooperation is pivotal to U.S. policy. More information is in the section on Pakistan, below, and in CRS Report RL33498, *Pakistan-U.S. Relations*, by K. Alan Kronstadt.

- *International Dimension:* New international diplomatic mechanisms have been formed to better coordinate all "stakeholders" in the Afghanistan issue (NATO, Afghanistan's neighbors, other countries in Afghanistan's region, the United Nations, and other donors). Meetings such as the January 28, 2010, meeting in London and the July 20, 2010, Kabul Conference are part of that effort. To date, at least 25 nations have appointed direct counterparts to Holbrooke, including the UAE, Saudi Arabia, and Turkey, which meet periodically as part of a 44-nation (and growing) "International Contact Group" for Afghanistan. It has met nine times, most recently in Rome on October 18, 2010. (Iran attended it for the first time.)

- *Partner Contributions:* Increased partner contributions of funding and troops were sought and offered. Currently, there is U.S. effort to encourage partner forces to remain in Afghanistan at least until a planned transition to Afghan leadership by 2014.
- *Metrics:* The Administration will continue to measure progress along clear metrics. Many in Congress, pressing for clear metrics to assess progress, inserted into P.L. 111-32 (FY2009 supplemental appropriation) a requirement that the President submit to Congress, 90 days after enactment (by September 23, 2009), metrics by which to assess progress, and a report on that progress every 180 days thereafter. The Administration's approximately 50 metrics were reported at the website of *Foreign Policy*[38] and were submitted. However, the difficulty in formulating useful and clear metrics that would enable Members and officials to assess progress in the war effort was demonstrated by comments by Ambassador Holbrooke on August 12, 2009, saying that on defining success in Afghanistan and Pakistan: "We will know it when we see it."[39] In its September 22, 2009, report on the situation in Afghanistan (A/64/364-S/2009/475), the United Nations developed its own "benchmarks" for progress in Afghan governance and security.

July 2011 "Deadline" Giving Way to 2014 "Transition"

The Obama Administration emphasis on transition to Afghan security leadership beginning in July 2011 has been perhaps the most widely discussed and debated aspect of policy. Debate over whether to announce such a timeframe is covered extensively in the book "Obama's Wars," by Bob Woodward. The 2011 "deadline" was interpreted by some Administration critics—and by some Afghan and regional leaders—as laying the groundwork for winding down U.S. involvement in coming years.[40] The Administration has said it set the time frame to demonstrate to a war-weary public that U.S. military involvement in Afghanistan is not open-ended. In a press conference on June 24, 2010, President Obama said "we didn't say we'd be switching off the lights and closing the door behind us [in July 2011]. What we said is we'd begin a transition phase in which the Afghan government is taking on more and more responsibility." In an August 31, 2010 statement, the President asserted that the pace and scope of any drawdown in 2011 would be subject to conditions on the ground, as assessed by the DOD assessment to be completed by December 2010. These comments appear to modify the July 18, 2010, Vice President Biden amended earlier remarks by saying that only a few thousand U.S. forces might come out at that time as part of a process of transitioning some Afghan provinces to Afghan lead.

Subsequently, in interviews, Gen. Petraeus has said that he would likely recommend to President Obama that any drawdown be limited. At the same time, with European publics tiring of involvement, in July 2010 agreement reportedly was reached on a joint Afghan-NATO board to decide on locations that might be selected for transition to Afghan lead. These locations, most likely whole provinces and districts to transition, beginning in 2011 and running through 2014, are expected to be ratified at the November 19-20, 2010, NATO summit in Lisbon. According to some U.S. commanders, some provinces in the U.S.-led eastern sector, such as Panjshir or Bamiyan, could be turned over in 2011, with Nangarhar considered a candidate for turnover thereafter. Some U.S. officials say that 2014 is not a date certain for a complete international pullout, but rather for a transition to Afghan lead, with some international forces remaining to train and mentor the Afghans.

Implementation of Strategy, Early Results, and Doubts

Going into the November 19-20 NATO summit in Lisbon, U.S. strategy, as implemented by Gen. Petraeus, may be starting to show results, according to statements by Petraeus and other NATO/ISAF commanders. The possible signs of momentum appear to reflect the beginnings of a possible turnaround from more pessimistic assessments of an April 2010 Defense Department report, and a September 30, 2010, White House assessments of the situation. In an interview with ABC News on September 14, 2010, Gen. Peraeus said that, "in some areas, we have already reversed the momentum of the Taliban. In others, we still need to do that and we are intent on doing that." His reference to those areas where the insurgency still has momentum include previously quiet provinces where violence has increased, including Baghlan, Konduz, and Faryab provinces. Other U.S. commanders say they are receiving overtures from local insurgent leaders who seek to discuss possible terms for their surrender and reintegration. Other reports say that insurgent factions are running low on supplies and ammunition.

According to Gen. Petraeus in November 2010, operations in 2010 have ended Taliban control in large parts of Helmand and produced major progress in Qandahar province, as discussed below. The progress is creating a contiguous secure corridor for commerce between Helmand and Qandahar. Markets and other signs of normal life have proliferated in Helmand, according to several U.S. commanders in October 2010. In August 2010, he took NBC News correspondents to Wardak province as a showcase of stability in a province that, in 2008, was considered largely under Taliban influence. The first of the operations in 2009 that produced some of the relatively positive assessments was Operation Khanj ar—intended to expel the Taliban and reestablish Afghan governance in parts of the province. The offensive reportedly ended Taliban control of several districts in Helmand, including Nawa, Now Zad, and Musa Qala.

Operation Moshtarek in Marjah/Nad Ali

The reports of progress in Helmand represent a turnaround from earlier pessimism about the outcome of "Operation Moshtarek" (Operation Together). It consisted of about 15,000 U.S., foreign partner, and Afghan forces (about 8,000 of the total) that, beginning on February 13, 2010, sought to clear Taliban militants from Marjah city (85,000 population) in Helmand. An Afghan governing structure was identified in advance (so-called "government in a box"), the population had substantial warning, and there were meetings with regional elders just before the offensive began—all of which were an apparent effort to cause militants to flee and to limit civilian losses.[41] The city, for the most part, was declared cleared of militants as of February 26, 2010, but some militants continue to fight in and on the outskirts of Marjah and to assassinate and intimidate Afghans cooperating with U.S. and Afghan forces. Some Afghan officials, such as ministry representatives, are now beginning to serve regularly in the city itself, although town governor Hajji Zahir was fired in July 2010.

As part of the U.S. effort, U.S. forces, primarily Marines, have reportedly been disbursing Commanders Emergency Response Program (CERP-funds controlled by U.S. officers) funds to clear rubble from schools, clean canals, repair markets, rebuild bridges, and compensate families who lost members due to the combat. Afghans who work on these projects in Marjah and in the previously cleared Nawa district are reportedly being paid about $5 per day as part of an effort to provide livelihoods to Afghans who might previously have supported the

Taliban for purely financial reasons.[42] Some fear that many of these workers might rejoin insurgent activities when U.S. funding for these "cash for work" programs decline.

Qandahar Effort

As of November 2010, U.S. military assessments of progress in Qandahar province are dramatic, although no one is certain how permanent are the gains. In early 2010, U.S. commanders had emphasized that the Qandahar effort would focus less on combat and more on conducting consultations and shuras with tribal leaders and other notables to enlist their cooperation against Taliban infiltrators. U.S. commanders described the operation as more of a "process," or a slow push into restive districts by setting up Afghan checkpoints to secure the city and districts around it (particularly Arghandab, Zhari, and Panjwai)—and not a classic military offensive. Qandahar's population is far larger (about 2 million in the province), and Qandahar province and city have functioning governments, which Marjah did not. The city hosts numerous businesses and has always remained vibrant, despite some Taliban clandestine activity.

A sense of doubt about the prospects for the operation built in April-August 2010 as Afghan tribal and other residential resistance—expressed at local *shuras* —to any combat to secure Qandahar. However, Gen. Petraeus has increased operations by U.S. Special Operations Forces against key militants near the city that began in April 2010.[43] Subsequently, as U.S. forces have expanded their presence in the province in partnership with Afghan forces in September 2010, Taliban control was ended in some neighborhoods and Afghan checkpoints were established. Further *shuras* have been held to promote Afghan governance. As part of the effort to stabilize Qandahar U.S. officials are also reportedly trying to strengthen Governor Tooryalai Wesa and balance the flow of U.S. and international funds to the various tribes and clans in the province. An unstated objective is also to weaken the influence of Karzai's brother, Ahmad Wali Karzai, chair of the provincial council, who is discussed above.[44]

Security Experiments Under Way

Discussed below are some additional or alternative approaches that are increasing feature of U.S. policy.

"Reintegration" and "Reconciliation" With Insurgents

The issue of reintegration fighters and reconciling with insurgent leaders is an Afghan-led process but one in which the United States and the international community is increasingly involved. The issue has made some in the international community, and within Afghanistan, concerned for the potential to involve compromises with insurgents and perhaps some backsliding on human rights. Most insurgents are highly conservative Islamists who agreed with the limitations in women's rights that characterized Taliban rule. Many leaders of ethnic minorities are also skeptical of the effort because they fear that it might further Pashtun political strength within Afghanistan, and enhance the influence of Pakistan in Afghan politics. Gen. Petraeus has said that the way conflicts like the one in Afghanistan end is through a political settlement. The United States and the Karzai government agree that any settlement must involve fighters and insurgent leaders: (1) cease fighting, (2) accept the Afghan constitution, and (3) sever any ties to Al Qaeda or other terrorist groups.

Reintegration/"Peace *Jirga*"

A January 28, 2010, London conference of international donors backed devoting more emphasis to reintegration of fighters amenable to surrendering. Britain, Japan, and several other countries announced a total of about $160 million in donations to a new fund to support the reintegration process.[45] The United States is to contribute an additional $100 million. Some of the incentives to surrendering insurgents that the international community deemed likely to fund are jobs, amnesty, and protection, and possibly making them part of the security architecture for their communities. These are elements included in a reintegration plan drafted by the Afghan government and presented to the peace *loya jirga* during June 2-4, 2010.[46] In its final declaration, the peace *jirga* backed the plan, but also called for limits in NATO-led raids and further efforts to limit civilian casualties. It also called for the release of some detained insurgents where allegations against them are weak. The day after the *jirga* concluded, Karzai sought to implement that recommendation by calling for a review of the cases of all insurgent detentions. In late June 2010, President Karzai issued a decree to implement the plan, which involves outreach by Afghan local leaders to tribes and others who are in a position to convince insurgents to lay down their arms. The international community gave its support to the effort in the communiqué of the July 20, 2010, Kabul Conference.

Although it reached some substantive conclusions, the peace *jirga* itself received mixed reviews for its inclusiveness or lack thereof. Karzai tried to bring other minority communities along in backing the peace *jirga* and the reintegration process, and to do so he appointed former leader Rabbani to chair the *jirga*. However, "opposition leader" Dr. Abdullah Abdullah, Karzai's rival in the 2009 presidential election, boycotted the *jirga*.

However, despite the international funding for the effort, the Afghan-led reintegration process has moved forward only slowly. Only $200,000 of the donated funds have been spent, as of early September 2010, and only about 100 fighters have surrendered since April 2010. However, press reports in September 2010, citing briefings by Gen. Petraeus for senior U.S. officials, say he anticipates many more surrenders of insurgent fighters between September and the end of 2010. In addition, press reports say that some Taliban fighters sought information on the September 18, 2010, parliamentary election as a possible prelude to joining the political process.

To help the process along from the international perspective, in November 2009, ISAF set up a "force reintegration cell," headed by Britain's Maj. Gen. Richard Barrons, to develop additional programs and policies to accelerate the effort to cause insurgents to change sides. These strategies are similar to what was employed successfully in Anbar Province in Iraq in 2006 and 2007.

The Obama Administration has been separately expanding U.S. efforts to lure lower-level insurgents off the battlefield with job opportunities and infrastructure construction incentives. Another component of the program has been meetings with tribal elders to persuade Taliban and other insurgents in their areas to give up their fight. Some U.S. commanders are reporting some successes with this effort, using Commanders Emergency Response Program (CERP) funds. The National Defense Authorization Act for FY20 10 (P.L. 111-84) authorizes the use of CERP funds to win local support, to "reintegrate" Taliban fighters who renounce violence.

FY20 11 budget language requested by the Administration would authorize U.S. funds to be contributed to the reintegration fund mentioned above.

Karzai has consistently advocated talks with Taliban militants who want to consider ending their fight. Noted above is the "Program for Strengthening Peace and Reconciliation" (referred to in Afghanistan by its Pashto acronym "PTS") headed by *Meshrano Jirga* speaker Sibghatullah Mojadeddi and former Vice President Karim Khalili, and overseen by Karzai's National Security Council. The program is credited with persuading 9,000 Taliban figures and commanders to renounce violence and join the political process.

Reconciliation with Taliban/Insurgent Leaders

A separate Karzai initiative—far more widely debated than reintegration—is to conduct negotiations with senior insurgent leaders. Many in the international community, and within the Obama Administration, had feared that reconciliation has the potential to result in insurgent leaders obtaining senior positions or control over some Afghan territory, and that these figures will retain ties to Al Qaeda and commit abuses similar to those under the Taliban regime. The July 20, 2010, Kabul Conference did not issue unqualified support for high-level reconciliation talks, instead endorsing establishment of an Afghan High Peace Council to build Afghan consensus on the issue. That Council was established on September 5, 2010, and its 68 members met for the first time under the leadership of Tajik leader Rabbani on October 10, 2010. Yet, the direct role of the Council in negotiations is unclear; rather, it might be asked to review and endorse any settlement that is reached.

In an apparent shift, the United States has begun backing the effort more clearly as of October 2010. Earlier, in March 2009, President Obama publicly ruled out negotiations with Mullah Umar and his aides because of their alignment with Al Qaeda. Others still differ on the willingness of senior insurgents to bargain in earnest. CIA director Panetta, in a June 27, 2010 interview cited earlier, and reflecting the reported view of several U.S. intelligence agencies as of late 2010, said he saw no indications that insurgent leaders are contemplating settling with the government.

Senior U.S. commanders have grown more optimistic about reconciliation as contacts between Taliban representatives and the Karzai government appear to have broadened.. Several sets of talks have been reported in October 2010, and some press accounts say that NATO/ISAF forces were in fact facilitation the movement of insurgent representatives to these talks. Representatives of the Quetta Shura Taliban purportedly have participated in talks. As noted above, Mullah Bradar, who is close to Mullah Umar, may have been engaged in talks with the Afghan government prior to his arrest by Pakistan in February 2010. Karzai reportedly believes that Pakistan arrested Bradar in order to be able to influence the course of any Afghan governmentTaliban settlement. Other accounts say that even the Haqqani faction, often viewed as least amenable to settlement, has been represented at some exploratory meetings with Karzai government representatives. However, observers say the discussions to date are about modalities and an agenda for further talks. The Taliban continues to demand that (1) all foreign troops leave Afghanistan; (2) a new "Islamic" constitution be adopted; and (3) Islamic law is imposed. However, those are viewed as opening positions; the Afghan government, for its part, may have softened its position on disallowing any changes to the Afghan constitution as part of a settlement.

The October 2010 reports build on earlier reports of contact. The Taliban as a movement was not invited to the June 2-4, 2010, consultative peace *jirga*, some Taliban sympathizers reportedly were there, and Karzai has said he is open to potential talks to reconcile even high-level leaders such as Mullah Umar. In advance of the peace *jirga*, the Karzai government and representatives of Hikmatyar confirmed peace talks on March 21, 2010, in which Karzai, his brother, Ahmad Wali, and several Northern Alliance figures met with the Hikmatyar representatives. The representatives reportedly presented a 15-point peace plan to Karzai that does not necessarily demand his government step down immediately.

Other talks have taken place over the past few years, although with less apparent momentum than is the case in 2010. Press reports said that Afghan officials (led by Karzai's brother Qayyum) and Taliban members had met each other in Ramadan-related gatherings in Saudi Arabia in September 2008. Another round of talks was held in January 2009 in Saudi Arabia, and there were reports of ongoing contacts in Dubai, UAE. Some of these talks apparently involved Arsala Rahmani, a former Taliban official now in parliament, and the former Taliban Ambassador to Pakistan, Abdul Salam Zaeef, who purportedly is in touch with Umar's inner circle. These same Taliban representatives may have been involved in talks in mid-late 2010 as well.

The consultative peace *jirga*, in its final declaration, supported Karzai's call for the removal of the names of some Taliban figures from U.N. lists of terrorists, lists established pursuant to Resolution 1267 and Resolution 1333 (October 15, 1999, and December 19, 2000, both pre- September 11 sanctions against the Taliban and Al Qaeda) and Resolution 1390 (January 16, 2002). Press reports before the July 20 Kabul Conference said the Afghan government has submitted a list of 50 Taliban figures it wants taken off this list as a confidence-building measure. The Conference called on Afghanistan to engage with the U.N. Security Council to provide evidence to justify such de-listings, and U.N., U.S., and other international officials said they would support considering de-listings on a case-by-case basis. On January 26, 2010, Russia, previously a hold-out against such a process, dropped opposition to removing five Taliban-era figures from these sanctions lists, including Taliban-era foreign minister Wakil Mutawwakil, who ran in 2005 parliamentary elections. Also removed was Abdul Hakim Monib, who has served Karzai as governor of Uruzgan, Abdul Hakim Mujahid, who was Taliban representative in the United States, and three others. Mujahid now serves on the High Peace Council. "Mullah Rocketi," not on the sanctions list, is a former Taliban commander who ran for president in the August 2009 elections.

Local Security Experiments: Afghan Provincial Protection Program (APPP) and Local Defense Initiative

Until mid-2008, U.S. military commanders opposed assisting local militias anywhere in Afghanistan for fear of creating new rivals to the central government who would arbitrarily administer justice. The urgent security needs in Afghanistan caused reconsideration and Gen Petraeus is seeking to expand these type of local security experiments, based on his similar and successful experiences in Iraq. Press reports in July 2010 say he succeeded, after several of his first meetings with Karzai, in overcoming Karzai's reticence to them. Gen. Petraeus reportedly has guaranteed that any local security organs would be under the administration of the Ministry of Interior.

The newest initiative is the Afghan "Local Police Initiative," in which local security organs would be formed from local recruits who want to defend their communities. It was planned that up to 10,000 volunteers will serve in the initiative, but on October 19, 2010, the

Defense Department said it would be expanded to at least 20,000, if possible. The ultimate target level might be 50,000, according to press reports. The Defense Department notified Congress in September 2010 that it will reprogram about $35 million in Afghan security forces funding to support the initiative.

The Local Police Initiative follows on another program begun in 2008, termed the "Afghan Provincial Protection Program" (APPP, commonly called "AP3") and is funded with DOD (CERP) funds. The APPP got under way in Wardak Province (Jalrez district) in early 2009 and 100 local security personnel "graduated" in May 2009. It has been expanded to 1,200 personnel, in a province with a population of about 500,000. (These personnel are expected to be integrated into the local police initiative). U.S. commanders say that no U.S. weapons are supplied to the militias, but this is an Afghan-led program and the Afghan government is providing weapons (Kalashnikov rifles) to the local groups, possibly using U.S. funds. Participants in the program are given $200 per month.

Before the program was placed on hold, it was to be expanded to Ghazni, Lowgar, and Kapisa provinces and eventually include as many as 8,000 Afghans. Gen. Petraeus showcased Wardak in August 2010 as an example of the success of the APPP and similar efforts. As an indication of divisions among Afghan leaders about the concept, the upper house of the Afghan parliament (*Meshrano Jirga*) passed a resolution in November 2008 opposing the concept. The National Defense Authorization Act (P.L. 111-84) calls for a report within 120 days of enactment (October 28, 2009) on the results of the program.

Another program, the Local Defense Initiative, began in February 2010 in Arghandab district of Qandahar Province. U.S. Special Forces organized about 25 villagers into a neighborhood watch group, which is armed. The program has been credited by U.S. commanders as bringing normal life back to the district. A different militia was allowed to operate in Konduz to help secure the northern approaches to that city. Problems arose when the militia began arbitrarily administering justice, fueling concerns of Karzai and Ambassador Eikenberry about these local security approaches.

The local security experiments to date are not arbokai, which are private tribal militias. Still, some believe that the arbokai concept should be revived as a means of securing Afghanistan, as the arbokai did during the reign of Zahir Shah and in prior pre-Communist eras.

Reversal of Previous Efforts: DDR and DIAG programs

As noted, the local security programs appear to reverse the 2002-2007 efforts to disarm local sources of armed force. The main program, run by UNAMA, was called the "DDR" program— Disarmament, Demobilization, and Reintegration—and it formally concluded on June 30, 2006. The program got off to a slow start because the Afghan Defense Ministry did not reduce the percentage of Tajiks in senior positions by a July 1, 2003, target date, dampening Pashtun recruitment. In September 2003, Karzai replaced 22 senior Tajiks in the Defense Ministry officials with Pashtuns, Uzbeks, and Hazaras, enabling DDR to proceed. The major donor for the program was Japan, which contributed about $140 million. Figures for collected weapons are contained in Table 5 and U.S. spending on the program are in the U.S. aid tables at the end of this chapter.

The DDR program was initially expected to demobilize 100,000 fighters, although that figure was later reduced. (Figures for accomplishment of the DDR and DIAG programs are contained in Table 5 below.) Of those demobilized, 55,800 former fighters have exercised reintegration options provided by the program: starting small businesses, farming, and other options. U.N. officials say at least 25% of these found long-term, sustainable jobs. Some studies criticized the DDR program for failing to prevent a certain amount of rearmament of militiamen or stockpiling of weapons and for the rehiring of some militiamen.[47] Part of the DDR program was the collection and cantonment of militia weapons, but generally only poor-quality weapons were collected. As one example, Fahim, still the main military leader of the Northern Alliance faction, continues to turn heavy weapons over to U.N. and Afghan forces (including four Scud missiles), although the U.N. Assistance Mission in Afghanistan (UNAMA) says that large quantities of weapons remain in the Panjshir Valley.

Despite the earlier demobilization, which affected many of the northern minorities, there are indications that some faction leaders may be seeking to revive disbanded militias. The minorities may fear increased Taliban influence as a result of the Karzai reconciliation efforts, and the minorities want to be sure they could combat any Taliban abuses that might result if the Taliban achieves a share of power.

DIAG

Since June 11, 2005, the disarmament effort has emphasized another program called "DIAG"— Disbandment of Illegal Armed Groups. It is run by the Afghan Disarmament and Reintegration Commission, headed by Vice President Khalili. Under the DIAG, no payments are available to fighters, and the program depends on persuasion rather than use of force against the illegal groups. DIAG has not been as well funded as was DDR: it has received $11 million in operating funds. As an incentive for compliance, Japan and other donors have made available $35 million for development projects where illegal groups have disbanded. These incentives were intended to accomplish the disarmament of a pool of as many as 150,000 members of 1,800 different "illegal armed groups": militiamen that were not part of recognized local forces (Afghan Military Forces, AMF) and were never on the rolls of the Defense Ministry. These goals were not met by the December 2007 target date in part because armed groups in the south say they need to remain armed against the Taliban, but UNAMA reports that some progress continues to be achieved. Several U.S.-backed local security programs implemented since 2008, discussed below, appear to reverse the intent and implementation of the DIAG process.

Possible Future Limits on U.S. Operations/Status of Forces Agreement

The issue of a larger Afghan government role in approving NATO-led operations surfaced again at the June 2-4, 2010, peace *jirga*, whose final declaration called for the Afghan government to "be able to lead military operations and coordination" among international forces operating in Afghanistan. Such sentiments arose in 2008, when the Afghan cabinet reacted to some high- profile instances of accidental civilian deaths by demanding negotiation of a formal "Status of Forces Agreement" (SOFA). A SOFA would spell out the combat authorities of non-Afghan forces, and might limit the United States to airstrikes, detentions, and house raids.[48] As noted earlier, differences between Karzai and the U.S. command in Afghanistan erupted again in November 2010 with Karzai calling for a decrease in the number of night raids and other operations that cause civilian unrest.

A draft SOFA—or technical agreement clarifying U.S./coalition authorities in Afghanistan— reportedly has been under discussion between the United States and Afghanistan since 2007. U.S. forces currently operate in Afghanistan under a "diplomatic note" between the United States and the interim government of Afghanistan that was exchanged in November 2002; the agreement gives the United States legal jurisdiction over U.S. personnel serving in Afghanistan and states the Afghan government's acknowledgment that U.S.-led military operations were "ongoing."

Long-Term Security Commitment

As noted, some Afghan leaders perceived the Obama Administration's 2011 deadline to "begin" a transition to Afghan security leadership as a sign the Administration might want to wind down U.S. involvement in Afghanistan. In part to reassure the Afghan government, President Obama, at a May 12, 2010, press conference with visiting President Karzai, stated that the United States and Afghanistan would renew a five-year-old strategic partnership. The target for renewing the partnership is early in 2011.

The strategic partnership was first established on May 23, 2005, when Karzai and President Bush issued a "joint declaration"[49] providing for U.S. forces to have access to Afghan military facilities, in order to prosecute "the war against international terror and the struggle against violent extremism." The joint statement did not give Karzai enhanced control over facilities used by U.S. forces, over U.S. operations, or over prisoners taken during operations. Some of the bases, both in and near Afghanistan, that support combat in Afghanistan, include those in **Table 6**.

Karzai's signing of the partnership had been blessed by Afghan representatives on May 8, 2005, when he summoned about 1,000 delegates to a consultative *jirga* in Kabul on whether to host permanent U.S. bases. That *jirga* supported an indefinite presence of international forces to maintain security but urged Karzai to delay a decision. A FY2009 supplemental appropriation (P.L. 111-32) and the FY20 10 National Defense Authorization Act (P.L. 111-84) prohibit the U.S. establishment of permanent bases in Afghanistan.

Alliance Issues: The NATO-Led International Security Assistance Force (ISAF) and Operation Enduring Freedom[50]

Most U.S. troops in Afghanistan remain under the umbrella of the NATO-led "International Security Assistance Force" (ISAF)—consisting of all 26 NATO members states plus partner countries. President Obama's December 1, 2009, policy speech on Afghanistan was explicit in seeking new partner troop commitments, and pledges met or exceeded what some U.S. officials expected. These contributions temporarily refuted arguments by observers that U.S. partners were unwilling to contribute more combat troops to the Afghanistan effort. However, several key contingents have ended their combat missions, will end those missions, or are setting notional future deadlines for departure and "transition" to Afghan leadership before or at 2014- a time frame that Karzai says will represent the ability of the Afghan security forces to assume a leadership role. Partner forces that continue to bear the brunt of combat in Afghanistan include Britain, Canada, Poland, France, Denmark, Romania, and Australia.

Virtually all the European governments are under pressure from their publics and parliaments to end or reduce the military involvement in Afghanistan. This pressure led Britain, France, and Germany to ask the United Nations to organize the international conference that took place in London on January 28, 2010. The conference did, as these countries sought, endorse the concept of transition to Afghan leadership on security and improvement of its governance, while also encouraging more regional assistance from India, China, and Russia. The transition concept, including specific provinces and districts that are to be handed over to Afghan leadership, is to be discussed in depth at the NATO summit in Lisbon November 19-20, 2010.

Recent Major Contingent Developments

Following the Obama Administration's March 27, 2009, policy announcement, some additional pledges came through at the April 3-4, 2009, NATO summit. Major new force pledges were issued after the December 1 policy statement, and in conjunction with the January 28, 2010, conference in London. However, some of these forces were intended to compensate for the pullouts by the Netherlands and Canada 2010 and 2011, respectively. The major recent pledges are the following:

- April 2009: Deployment of 3,000 non-U.S. troops to secure the Afghan elections and 2,000 trainers for the Afghan security forces. Contributing forces for the election period include Spain (400), Germany (600), Poland (600), and Britain (about 900). Other pledges (from Bulgaria, Estonia, Italy, Greece, Portugal, Turkey, and Slovakia) were for trainers to fill out 61 existing Operational Mentor and Liaison Teams (OMLTs), each of which has about 30 trainers.
- April 2009: NATO agreed to new training missions for the ANSF. A NATO Training Mission—Afghanistan (NTM-A) has been established. Also that month, $500 million in additional civilian assistance to Afghanistan was pledged by several donors.
- November 10, 2009: Ahead of President Obama's visit to Asia, Japan announced a pledge of $5 billion over the next five years for Afghanistan civilian development, although it suspended its naval refueling mission (discussed below).
- July 2009: South Korea announced it would increase its aid contribution to Afghanistan by about $20 million, in part to expand the hospital capabilities at Bagram Air Base. In November 2009, it announced a return of about 150 engineers to Afghanistan for development missions, protected by 300 South Korean forces. The forces deployed to Parwan Province in July 2010. (Until December 2007, 200 South Korean forces at Bagram Air Base, mainly combat engineers, were part of Operation Enduring Freedom (OEF); they left in December 2007 in fulfillment of a decision by the South Korean government the previous year. However, many observers believe South Korea did not further extend its mission beyond that, possibly as part of an agreement in August 2007 under which Taliban militants released 21 kidnapped South Korean church group visitors.[52])
- December 2009-January 2010 (London conference): A total of about 9,000 forces were pledged (including retaining 2,000 sent for the August 2009 election who were due to rotate out). The pledges included Britain (500), Poland (600), Romania (600,

plus about 30 trainers), Italy (1,000), Georgia (900+), Spain (500), Colombia (240, first time contributor of forces), Slovakia (60), Sweden (125), Portugal (120), and Germany (500 plus 350 on reserve, but still only in the north, not heavy combat zones). France pledged 80 trainers but no new combat forces. Several countries pledged police trainers.

- Other Major Civilian Aid Pledges in Context of London Conference:[53] France ($45 million); Saudi Arabia ($150 million over three years); Australia ($40 million); China ($75 million). Japan agreed to pay ANP salaries for another six months (until the end of 2010), a cost of about $125 million in a six month period, to come out of its $5 billion contribution mentioned above. Japan reiterated that commitment during Karzai's June 17, 2010, visit to Tokyo. Other pledges were made for Taliban reintegration, as noted above.
- In July 2010, Malaysia became a new contributor to the Afghanistan effort, furnishing 40 military medics.

Table 3. Background on NATO/ISAF Formation and U.N. Mandate

The International Security Assistance Force (ISAF) was created by the Bonn Agreement and U.N. Security Council Resolution 1386 (December 20, 2001, a Chapter 7 resolution),[51] initially limited to Kabul. In October 2003, after Germany agreed to contribute 450 military personnel to expand ISAF into the city of Konduz, ISAF contributors endorsed expanding its presence to several other cities, contingent on formal U.N. approval—which came on October 14, 2003 in U.N. Security Council Resolution 1510. In August 2003, NATO took over command of ISAF— previously the ISAF command rotated among donor forces including Turkey and Britain.

NATO/ISAF's responsibilities broadened significantly in 2004 with NATO/ISAF's assumption of security responsibility for northern and western Afghanistan (Stage 1, Regional Command North, in 2004 and Stage 2, Regional Command West, in 2005, respectively). The transition process continued on July 31, 2006, with the formal handover of the security mission in southern Afghanistan to NATO/ISAF control. As part of this "Stage 3," a British/Canadian/Dutchled "Regional Command South" (RC-S) was formed. Britain is the lead force in Helmand; Canada is lead in Qandahar, and the Netherlands was lead in Uruzgan until its departure in July 2010; the three rotated the command of RC-S. "Stage 4," the assumption of NATO/ISAF command of peacekeeping in 14 provinces of eastern Afghanistan (and thus all of Afghanistan), was completed on October 5, 2006. As part of the completion of the NATO/ISAF takeover, the United States put about half the U.S. troops then operating in Afghanistan under NATO/ISAF in "Regional Command East" (RC-E).

The ISAF mission was renewed (until October 13, 2011) by U.N. Security Council Resolution 1943 (October 13, 2010), which reiterated previous resolutions' support for the Operation Enduring Freedom mission. Tables at the end of this chapter list contributing forces, areas of operations, and their Provincial Reconstruction Teams.

Upcoming Contingent Withdrawals

The war-weariness in many coalition nations is reflected in drawdown plans announced or contemplated. As noted, the Netherland has completed its combat mission as of the end of July 2010. In November 2010, Canada reaffirmed that it would follow suit by the end of

2011. Both countries are considered likely to deploy mentors or trainers in a non-combat role to partly compensate for their combat troop pullouts.

Britain has steadily increased its troop commitment in Afghanistan—mainly in high combat Helmand Province—to about 9,500 (plus 500 Special Forces). In line with other contributors, British official comments have indicated that Britain might want to end its mission by 2014. Britain has lost over 300 soldiers in Afghanistan. Italy, Poland, and Germany have also indicated an intent to try to wind down their involvement in Afghanistan no later than 2014. As noted above, some of the provinces considered good candidates to transition to Afghan leadership are in the German sector in the north.

Equipment Issues

Some of the pledges address NATO's chronic equipment shortages—particularly helicopters, both for transport and attack—for the Afghanistan mission. In 2007, to try to compensate for the shortage, NATO chartered about 20 commercial helicopters for extra routine supply flights to the south, freeing up Chinooks and Black Hawks for other missions. Some of the Polish troops deployed in 2008 operate and maintain eight helicopters. Germany provides six Tornado combat aircraft to assist with strikes in combat situations in the south. NATO/ISAF also assists the Afghan Ministry of Civil Aviation and Tourism in the operation of Kabul International Airport (where Dutch combat aircraft also are located). In 2009, Belgium sent two more F- 16 fighters.

National "Caveats" on Combat Operations

One of the most thorny issues has been the U.S. effort to persuade other NATO countries to adopt flexible rules of engagement that allow all contributing forces to perform combat missions. NATO and other partner forces have not, as they pledged at the NATO summit in April 2008, removed the so-called "national caveats" on their troops' operations that Lt. Gen. McChrystal says limits operational flexibility. For example, some nations refuse to conduct night-time combat. Others have refused to carry Afghan personnel on their helicopters. Others do not fight after snowfall. These caveats were troubling to those NATO countries with forces in heavy combat zones, such as Canada, which feel they are bearing the brunt of the fighting.

Provincial Reconstruction Teams (PRTs)

U.S. and partner officials have generally praised the effectiveness of "Provincial Reconstruction Teams" (PRTs)—enclaves of U.S. or partner forces and civilian officials that provide safe havens for international aid workers to help with reconstruction and to extend the writ of the Kabul government—in accelerating reconstruction and assisting stabilization efforts. The PRTs, announced in December 2002, perform activities ranging from resolving local disputes to coordinating local reconstruction projects, although most U.S.-run PRTs and most PRTs in combat-heavy areas focus mostly on counter-insurgency. Many of the additional U.S. civilian officials deployed to Afghanistan during 2009 and 2010 are based at PRTs, which have facilities, vehicles, and security.

There are 27 PRTs in operation; the list of PRTs, including lead country, is shown in **Table 22**. Virtually all the PRTs are now under the ISAF mission. Each PRT operated by the

United States has U.S. forces (50-100 U.S. military personnel); Defense Department civil affairs officers; representatives of USAID, State Department, and other agencies; and Afghan government (Interior Ministry) personnel. Most PRTs, including those run by partner forces, have personnel to train Afghan security forces. USAID officers assigned to the PRTs administer PRT reconstruction projects, although USAID observers say there is little Afghan input, either into project decisionmaking or as contractors for facility and other construction. USAID spending on PRT projects is in the table on USAID spending in Afghanistan at the end of this chapter, and there is a database on development projects sponsored by each PRT available to CRS, information from which can be provided on request.

Table 4. Operation Enduring Freedom Partner Forces

Operation Enduring Freedom continues as a separate combat track, led by the United States but joined by a few partners. The caveat issue is less of a factor with OEF, since OEF is known as a combat-intensive mission conducted in large part by Special Forces contingents of contributing nations. The overwhelming majority of non-U.S. forces are under the NATO/ISAF mission. Prior to NATO assumption of command in October 2006, 19 coalition countries— primarily Britain, France, Canada, and Italy contributing approximately 4,000 combat troops to OEF-Afghanistan. Now, that figure is lower as most have been re-badged to ISAF. However, several foreign contingents, composed mainly of special operations forces, including a 200 person unit from the UAE, are still part of OEF-Afghanistan. This includes about 500 British special forces, some German special forces, and other special forces units. In early 2010, U.S. Special Forces operating in Afghanistan were brought under direct command of the top U.S. command in Afghanistan, now Gen. Petraeus.

Under OEF, Japan provided naval refueling capabilities in the Arabian sea, but the mission was suspended in October 2007 following a parliamentary change of majority there in July 2007. The mission was revived in January 2008 when the new government forced through parliament a bill to allow the mission to resume. It was renewed again, over substantial parliamentary opposition, in December 2008, but the opposition party won September 2009 elections in Japan and reportedly has decided on an alternative to continuing the refueling mission—by increasing its financial contributions to economic development in Afghanistan. That led to an October 2009 pledge by Japan—already the third largest individual country donor to Afghanistan, providing about $1.9 billion in civilian reconstruction aid since the fall of the Taliban—to provide another $5 billion over five years. It has been requested to be a major financial donor of an Afghan army expansion, and, in March 2009, it pledged to pay the costs of the Afghan National Police for six months.

As part of OEF outside Afghanistan, the United States leads a multi-national naval anti-terrorist, anti-smuggling, anti- proliferation interdiction mission in the Persian Gulf/Arabian Sea, headquartered in Bahrain. That mission was expanded after the fall of Saddam Hussein to include protecting Iraqi oil platforms in the Gulf.

In the south, most PRTs are heavily focused on security. In August 2005, in preparation for the establishment of Regional Command South (RC-S), Canada took over the key U.S.-led PRT in Qandahar. In May 2006, Britain took over the PRT at Lashkar Gah, capital of Helmand Province. At the same time, the Netherlands took over the PRT at Tarin Kowt, capital of Uruzgan Province. However, the Tarin Kowt PRT has been led by Australia and the United States since the September 2010 Dutch departure.

Some aid agencies say they have felt more secure since the PRT program began, fostering reconstruction,[54] and many of the new civilian advisers arriving in Afghanistan under the new Obama Administration strategy work out of the PRTs. On the other hand, some relief groups do not want to associate with military forces because doing so might taint their perceived neutrality. Others, such as Oxfam International, argue that the PRTs are delaying the time when the Afghan government has the skills and resources to secure and develop Afghanistan on its own.

Evolving Civil-Military Concepts at the PRTs

Representing evolution of the PRT concept, some donor countries—as well as the United States—are trying to enhance the civilian component of the PRTs and change their image from mainly military institutions. There has been long been consideration to turn over the lead in the U.S.-run PRTs to civilians rather than military personnel, presumably State Department or USAID officials. That was first attempted in 2006 with the establishment of a civilian-led U.S.- run PRT in the Panjshir Valley. As noted, in March 2009, the Netherlands converted its PRT to civilian lead, although that alteration has not continued with the assumption of U.S. and Australian PRT command as of July 2010. Turkey opened a PRT, in Wardak Province, on November 25, 2006, to focus on providing health care, education, police training, and agricultural alternatives in that region.

As of November 2009, the "civilianization" of the PRT concept has evolved further with the decision to refer to PRTs as Interagency Provincial Affairs (IPA) offices or branches. In this new concept—a local paralled to the Senior Civilian Representatives now assigned to each regional command—State Department officers enjoy enhanced decision-making status at each PRT.

Afghan National Security Forces

The U.S. "exit strategy" from Afghanistan relies heavily on increasing the capability of the Afghan National Security Forces (ANSF)—the Afghan National Army (ANA) and Afghan National Policy (ANP)—to the point where they can assume the security mission from the international coalition. Obama Administration strategy emphasizes expanding the ANSF and improving it through partnering and more intense mentoring and training. On January 21, 2010, the joint U.N.-Afghan "Joint Coordination and Monitoring Board" (JCMB) agreed that, by the end of 2011, the ANA would expand to 171,600 and the ANP to about 134,000. As of August 11, 2010, both forces reached their interim size of 134,000 and 109,000 respectively (two months earlier than planned). As of November 2010, the forces now total about 140,000 ANA and 125,000 ANP.

U.S. forces along with partner countries and contractors, train the ANSF. In February 2010, the U.S.-run "Combined Security Transition Command-Afghanistan" (CSTC-A) that ran the training was subordinated to the broader NATO Training Mission—Afghanistan (NTM-A).

Afghanistan

Table 5. Major Security-Related Indicators

Force	Current Level
Total Foreign Forces in Afghanistan	About 145.000: About 104,000 U.S. and 41,000 non-U.S. partner forces. (U.S. total was: 25,000 in 2005; 16,000 in 2003; 5,000 in 2002. ISAF totals were: 12,000 in 2005; and 6,000 in 2003.) US. forces deployed at 88 bases in Afghanistan, and include 1 air wing (40 aircraft) and 1 combat aviation brigade (100 aircraft). U.S. number includes only about 2,000 of the new U.S. troop commitments announced December 1.
U.S. Casualties in Afghanistan	1,289 killed, of which 1,060 by hostile action. Additional 94 U.S. deaths in other OEF theaters, including the Philippines and parts of Africa. Over 315 U.S. killed in 2009- highest yet. 150 U.S. killed from October 2001-January 2003. 45 killed in each of July and August 2009,and 50-55 in each of September and October 2009. At least 25 U.S. killed per month in 2010, with over 60 in each of June and July. Over 300 UK forces killed in Afghanistan to date.
NATO Sectors (Regional Commands-South, east, north, west, and central/Kabul)	RC-S- 35,000 (U.K. lead). RC-Southwest - 27,000 (U.S. lead); RC-E- 32,000 (U.S. lead); RC-N- 11,000 (German lead); RC-W- 6,000 (Italy lead) RC-Kabul-5,000 (Turkey, Afghan lead).
Afghan National Army (ANA)	140,000+, more than the interim goal for October 2010. End goal is 171,600 by late 2011. There are 120+ battalions ranging from 300-1,000 soldiers each. About 2,000 trained per month. 4,000 are commando forces, trained by U.S. Special Forces. ANA private paid about $200 per month; generals receive about $750 per month. ANA being outfitted with U.S. M1 6 rifles and 4,000 up-armored Humvees.
Afghan National Police (ANP)	125,000+, exceeding the interim goal of 109,000 by October 2010. End goal is 134,000 by late 2011. Of the force, 14,000 are border police; 3,800+ counter-narcotics police; 5,300 civil order police. 1,000 are female, some serving in very conservative south. Most ANP salaries raised to $240 per month in November 2009, from $120, to counter corruption. Some police paid by E-Paisa system of Roshan cell phone network.
U.S. and Partner Trainers	About 4,000, with target of 4,800.
Legally Armed Fighters disarmed by DDR	63,380; all of the pool identified for the program
Number of Al Qaeda	50-100, according to CIA Director Panetta in June 2010. Also, small numbers of Lashkar-e-Tayyiba, Islamic Movement of Uzbekistan, Pakistan Taliban, others.
Number of Taliban fighters	Over 20,000 (U.S. military and Afghan estimates). Some estimates higher. Plus about 2,500 Haqqani faction and 1,000 Hikmatyar (HIG).
Attacks per day (average)	1,100 per month in 2009; 1,000 per month in 2008; 800 per month in 2007 and 2006; 400 in 2005. 7,000 IEDs in 2009, almost double the 2008 level.
Afghan casualties	For extended discussion, see CRS Report R4 1084, *Afghanistan Casualties: Military Forces and Civilians*, by Susan G. Chesser.

Sources: CRS; testimony and public statements by DOD officials.

NTM-A is commanded by U.S. Maj. Gen. William Caldwell. CSTC-A's mission was reoriented to building the capacity of the Afghan Defense and Interior Ministries, and to provide resources to the ANSF. The total number of required trainers (U.S. and partner) for these institutions is 4,800. There has been an unfilled gap of trainers totaling about 750, although Gen. Petraeus requested forces to fill that gap in September 2010 and partner countries have pledged those amounts. A separate France- led 300-person European Gendarmerie Force (EGF) has been established to train Afghan forces out in the provinces. The European Union is providing a 190-member "EUPOL" training effort, and 60 other experts to help train the ANP. These efforts are subsumed under NTM-A.

The U.S. police training effort was first led by State Department/INL, but the Defense Department took over the lead in police training in April 2005. Much of the training is still conducted through contracts with DynCorp. In addition to the U.S. effort, which includes 600 civilian U.S. police trainers (mostly still Dyncorp contractors) in addition to the U.S. military personnel (see Table 5),

Afghan National Army

The Afghan National Army has been built "from scratch" since 2002—it is not a direct continuation of the national army that existed from the 1 880s until the Taliban era. That national army all but disintegrated during the 1992-1996 *mujahedin* civil war and the 1996-200 1 Taliban period. However, some Afghan military officers who served prior to the Taliban have joined the new military.

U.S. and allied officers say that the ANA is becoming a major force in stabilizing the country and a national symbol. It now has at least some presence in most of Afghanistan's 34 provinces, working with the PRTs, and it deployed outside Afghanistan to assist relief efforts for victims of the October 2005 Pakistan earthquake. According to the Department of Defense, the ANA is able to lead a growing percentage of all combat operations, but there is substantial skepticism within the U.S. defense establishment that it can assume full security responsibility by 2014, which is the target time frame announced by Karzai. Among examples of the ANA taking overall responsibility, in August 2008, the ANA took over security of Kabul city from Italy, and it took formal control of Kabul Province in early 2009. The commando forces of the ANA, trained by U.S. Special Operations Forces, are considered well-trained and are taking the lead in some operations against high-value targets, particularly against HIG elements in Nuristan province.

However, some U.S. military assessments say the force remains poorly led. It still suffers from at least a 20% desertion rate. Many officers are illiterate or poorly motivated.[55] Some accounts say that a typical ANA unit is only at about 50% of its authorized strength at any given time, and there are significant shortages in about 40% of equipment items. The high desertion rate complicates U.S.-led efforts to steadily grow the force. Some recruits take long trips to their home towns to remit funds to their families, and often then return to the ANA after a long absence. Others, according to U.S. observers, often refuse to serve far from their home towns. The FY2005 foreign aid appropriation (P.L. 108-447) required that ANA recruits be vetted for terrorism, human rights violations, and drug trafficking.

ANA battalions, or "Kandaks," are the main unit of the Afghan force. There are over 120 Kandaks. The Kandaks are stiffened by the presence of U.S. and partner embeds, called "Operational Mentor and Liaison Teams" (OMLTs). Each OMLT—of which there are about 61— has about 12-19 personnel, and U.S. commanders say that the ANA will continue to need embeds for the short term, because embeds give the units confidence they will be resupplied, reinforced, and evacuated in the event of wounding.

The Obama Administration strategy is to also partner the ANA with U.S. and other foreign units to enhance effectiveness. Gen. Petraeus and others have attributed the previous lack of progress in the ANSF to the non-systematic use of the partnering concept. Among the other countries contributing training OMLTs (all or in part) are Canada, Croatia, Czech Republic, France, Germany, Italy, the Netherlands, Norway, Poland, Slovenia, Spain, Sweden, Britain, and the United States.

The United States has built five ANA bases: Herat (Corps 207), Gardez (Corps 203), Qandahar (Corps 205), Mazar-e-Sharif (Corps 209), and Kabul (Division HQ, Corps 201, Air Corps). Coalition officers conduct heavy weapons training for a heavy brigade as part of the "Kabul Corps," based in Pol-e-Charki, east of Kabul.

Ethnic and Factional Considerations

At the time the United States first began establishing the ANA, Northern Alliance figures who were then in key security positions weighted recruitment for the national army toward its Tajik ethnic base. Many Pashtuns, in reaction, refused recruitment or left the ANA program. The naming of a Pashtun, Abdul Rahim Wardak, as Defense Minister in December 2004 reduced desertions among Pashtuns (he remains in that position). U.S. officials in Afghanistan say this problem was further alleviated with better pay and more close involvement by U.S. forces, and that the force is ethnically integrated in each unit and representative. With about 41% Pashtuns, 34% Tajiks, 12% Hazaras, and 8% Uzbeks, the force is roughly in line with the broad demographics of the country, according to the April 2010 DOD report. However, U.S. commanders say that those Pashtuns who are in the force are disproportionately eastern Pashtuns (from the Ghilzai tribal confederations) rather than southern Pashtuns (mostly Durrani tribal confederations). The chief of staff was Gen. Bismillah Khan, a Tajik who was a Northern Alliance commander, although as of June 2010 he is Interior Minister.

Afghan Air Force

Equipment, maintenance, and logistical difficulties continue to plague the Afghan National Army Air Corps (Afghan Air Force). The force is a carryover from the Afghan Air Force that existed prior to the Soviet invasion, and is expanding gradually after its equipment was virtually eliminated in the 2001-2002 U.S. combat against the Taliban regime. It now has about over 3,000 personnel, including 400 pilots, as well as a total of about 46 aircraft. Afghan pilots are based at Bagram air base.

The Afghan goal is to have 61 aircraft by 2011, but it remains mostly a support force for ground operations rather than a combat-oriented Air Force. However, the Afghan Air Force has been able to make ANA units nearly self-sufficient in airlift. Afghanistan is seeking the return of 26 aircraft, including some MiG-2s that were flown to safety in Pakistan and Uzbekistan during the past conflicts in Afghanistan. U.S. plans do not include supply of fixed-wing combat aircraft such as F-1 6s, which Afghanistan wants, according to U.S. military officials. In 2010, Russia and Germany supplied MI-8 helicopters to the Afghan Air Force.

Afghan National Police (ANP)

U.S. and Afghan officials believe that building up a credible and capable national police force is at least as important to combating the Taliban insurgency as building the ANA. The April 2010 DOD report reinforces a widespread consensus that the ANP substantially lags the ANA in its development. Outside assessments are widely disparaging, asserting that there is rampant corruption to the point where citizens are openly mistrustful of the ANP. Among other criticisms are a desertion rate far higher than that of the ANA; substantial illiteracy; involvement in local factional or ethnic disputes because the ANP works in the communities its personnel come from; and widespread use of drugs. It is this view that has led to consideration of stepped up efforts to promote local security solutions such as those discussed above.

Some U.S. commanders are more positive, saying that it is increasingly successful in repelling Taliban assaults on villages and that is experiencing fewer casualties from attacks than it was previously. Afghan police in Kabul won praise from the U.S. commanders for putting down, largely on their own and without major civilian casualties, the insurgent attack on Kabul locations near the presidential palace on January 18, 2010, and a similar attack on February 26, 2010. Bismillah Khan, the new Interior Minister, was highly respected as ANA chief of staff and has taken new steps to try to improve the police force, including through unannounced visits to ANP bases and stations around the country. Still, some Pashtuns might resent him for his Tajik ethnicity.

Other U.S. commanders credit a November 2009 raise in police salaries (nearly doubled to about $240 per month for service in high combat areas)—and the streamlining and improvement of the payments system for the ANP—with reducing the solicitation of bribes by the ANP. The raise also stimulated an eightfold increase in the number of Afghans seeking to be recruited. Others note the success, thus far, of efforts to pay police directly (and avoid skimming by commanders) through cellphone-based banking relationships (E-Paisa, run by Roshan cell network).

Retraining and Other Initiatives

Some U.S. officials believe that the United States and its partners still have not centered on a clearly effective police training strategy. The latest training reorganization implemented since 2007 is called *"focused district development,"* which attempts to retrain individual police forces in districts, which is the basic geographic area of ANP activity. (There are about 10 "districts" in each of Afghanistan's 34 provinces.) In this program, a district force is taken out and retrained, its duties temporarily performed by more highly trained police (Afghan National Civil Order Police, or ANCOP, which number about 5,800 nationwide), and then reinserted after the training is complete. As of late 2010, police in at least 100 districts have undergone this process, although the program has had "limited success," according to the DOD April 2010 report, because of continuing governance and other problems in those districts. There has also been some criticism of the ANCOP performance in Marjah, even though the unit is supposed to be elite and well trained. The ANCOP officers are being used to staff the new checkpoints being set up to better secure Qandahar.

Police training now includes instruction in human rights principles and democratic policing concepts, and the State Department human rights report on Afghanistan, referenced above, says the government and outside observers are increasingly monitoring the police force to prevent abuses. In March 2010, then-Interior Minister Atmar signed a "strategic guidance" document for the ANP, which prioritizes eliminating corruption within the ANP and winning public confidence. About 1,000 ANP are women, demonstrating some commitment to gender integration of the force.

There have been few quick fixes for the chronic shortage of equipment in the ANP. Most police are under-equipped, lacking ammunition and vehicles. In some cases, equipment requisitioned by their commanders is being sold and the funds pocketed by the police officers. These activities contributed to the failure of a 2006 "auxiliary police" effort that attempted to rapidly field large numbers of new ANP officers.

Rule of Law/Criminal Justice Sector

Many experts believe that an effective justice sector is vital to Afghan governance. Some of the criticisms and allegations of corruption at all levels of the Afghan bureaucracy have been discussed throughout this chapter. U.S. justice sector programs generally focus on promoting rule of law and building capacity of the judicial system, including police training and court construction. The rule of law issue is covered in greater detail in CRS Report R41484, *Afghanistan: U.S. Rule of Law and Justice Sector Assistance*, by Liana Sun Wyler and Kenneth Katzman

U.S. Security Forces Funding/"CERP"

Because the Afghan government has so few resources, the Afghan security sector is funded almost entirely through international donations. In December 2009, Karzai asserted that the Afghan government could not likely fund its own security forces until 2024. More than half of all U.S. assistance to Afghanistan since 2002 has gone toward building the ANSF. U.S. funds are used to cover ANA salaries as well as to equip and train them. Recent appropriations for the ANA and ANP are contained in the tables at the end of this chapter, which also contain breakdowns for Commanders Emergency Response Program funds, or CERP. CERP is used for projects that build goodwill and presumably reduce the threat to use forces. The tables at the end also list breakdowns for requested ANSF funding for FY20 11 and supplemental FY20 10 funding. As noted in the table, as of FY2005, the security forces funding has been DOD funds, not State Department funds.

International Trust Fund for the ANSF

In 2007, ISAF set up a trust fund for donor contributions to fund the transportation of equipment donated to and the training of the ANSF. U.S. funding for the ANSF is provided separately, not through this fund. The fund is estimated to require $2 billion per year. In April 2009, $100 million in contributions were pledged. Of this, $57 million was pledged by Germany. Japan, as noted, separately pledged to pay the expenses of the Afghan police for six months (about $125 million). As noted above, some additional funds for the fund were pledged at the London conference, including by Greece ($4 million); and Japan ($11 million out of the $5 billion mentioned above).

Law and Order Trust Fund

There is also a separate "Law and Order" Trust Fund for Afghanistan, run by the U.N. Development Program. The fund is used to pay the salaries of the ANP and other police-related functions. Its budget for the two years September 2008 – August 2010 is about $540 million, funded by donors such as Japan (as discussed above)

Policy Alternatives/Support for Reduced U.S. Military Involvement

Although Gen. Petraeus says U.S. strategy is beginning to show results, and that his December 2010 assessment might not recommend any major changes, there is growing discussion of alternatives. Those who support policy alternatives generally believe that the current Afghanistan effort is unwinnable at acceptable cost, and that it is distracting from other priorities on foreign or domestic policy. [56] Others believe that pursuing the suggested alternatives could lead to a collapse of the Afghan government, and would produce an unraveling of the economic, political, and social gains made through the international military involvement in Afghanistan since 2001.

"Counter-Terrorism" Strategy

During the late 2009 strategy review, some, purportedly including Vice President Joseph Biden, favored a more limited mission for Afghanistan designed solely to disrupt Al Qaeda in Afghanistan and Pakistan. This approach envisioned only a small increase in U.S. or other international forces present in Afghanistan. Advocates of this approach asserted that the government of Afghanistan is not a fully legitimate partner, primarily because of widespread governmental corruption. This strategy was not adopted, in favor of the U.S. "surge" that was authorized. However, as noted above, U.S. commanders say that some of the most effective U.S. operations consist of Special Operations forces tracking and killing selected key mid-level insurgent commanders, even though such operations were not intended to be the centerpiece of U.S. strategy that was decided in 2009. Some believe that there could be a decision to pursue this strategy when the July 2011 transition start date arrives.

Critics of the limited counter-terrorism strategy express the view that the Afghan government might collapse and Al Qaeda would have safe haven again in Afghanistan if there are insufficient numbers of U.S. forces there to protect the government.[57] Others believed it would be difficult for President Obama to choose a strategy that could jeopardize the stability of the Afghan government, after having defined Afghan security and stability as a key national interest. Still others say that it would be difficult to identify targets to strike with unmanned or manned aircraft unless there were sufficient forces on the ground to identify targets.

Legislative Initiatives: Drawdown Plans

The policy articulated on December 1, 2009, introduced the concept of transition to Afghan security leadership, and specifically stated that better performance is expected of the Afghan government. To this extent, some Afghan, neighboring, and partner country leaders question whether the December 1, 2009, policy statement foreshadows an eventual Obama Administration effort to wind down the U.S. mission there. Perhaps to address growing unrest about the course of the conflict, during the July 2010 Kabul Conference (and contained in the communiqué), President Karzai pledged that Afghan security forces would "lead and conduct military operations in all provinces by the end of 2014."

Table 6. Afghan and Regional Facilities Used for Operations in and Supply Lines to Afghanistan

Facility	Use
Bagram Air Base	50 miles north of Kabul, the operational hub of U.S. forces in Afghanistan, and base for CJTF-82. At least 2000 U.S. military personnel are based there. Handles many of the 150+ U.S. aircraft (including helicopters) in country. Hospital constructed, one of the first permanent structures there. FY2005 supplemental (P.L. 109-13) provided about $52 million for various projects to upgrade facilities at Bagram, including a control tower and an operations center, and the FY2006 supplemental appropriation (P.L. 109-234) provided $20 million for military construction there. NATO also using the base and sharing operational costs. Bagram can be accessed directly by U.S. military flights following April 2010 agreement by Kazakhstan to allow overflights of U.S. lethal equipment.
Qandahar Air Field	Just outside Qandahar, the hub of military operations in the south. Turned over from U.S. to NATO/ISAF control in late 2006 in conjunction with NATO assumption of peacekeeping responsibilities. Enhanced (along with other facilities in the south) at cost of $1.3 billion to accommodate influx of U.S combat forces in the south.
Shindand Air Base	In Farah province, about 20 miles from Iran border. Used by U.S. forces and combat aircraft since October 2004, after the dismissal of Herat governor Ismail Khan, who controlled it.
Peter Ganci Base: Manas, Kyrgyzstan	Used by 1,200 U.S. military personnel as well as refueling and cargo aircraft for shipments into Afghanistan. Leadership of Kyrgyzstan changed in April 2005 in an uprising against President Askar Akayev and again in April 2010 against Kurmanbek Bakiyev. Previous Kyrgyz governments demanded the U.S. vacate the base but in both cases, (July 2006 and July 2009) agreement to use the base was extended in exchange for large increase in U.S. payments for its use (to $60 million per year in the latter case). Interim government formed in April 2010 first threatened then retracted eviction of U.S. from the base, but the issue remains subject to decisionmaking by a new government elected in Kyrgyzstan on October 11, 2010. Some questions have arisen in Congress over alleged corruption involving fuel suppliers of U.S. aircraft at the base.
Incirlik Air Base, Turkey	About 2,100 U.S. military personnel there; U.S. aircraft supply U.S. forces in Iraq and Afghanistan. U.S. use repeatedly extended for one year intervals by Turkey.
Al Dhafra, UAE	Air base used by about 1,800 U.S. military personnel, to supply U.S. forces and related transport into Iraq and Afghanistan. Could see increasing use if Manas closes.
Al Udeid Air Base, Qatar	Largest air facility used by U.S. in region. About 5,000 U.S. personnel in Qatar. Houses central air operations coordination center for U.S. missions in Iraq and Afghanistan; also houses CENTCOM forward headquarters. Could see increased use if Manas closes.
Naval Support Facility, Bahrain	U.S. naval command headquarters for OEF anti-smuggling, anti-terrorism, and anti-proliferation naval search missions, and Iraq-related naval operations (oil platform protection) in the Persian Gulf and Arabian Sea. About 5,100 U.S. military personnel there.
Karsi-Khanabad Air Base, Uzbekistan	Not used by U.S. since September 2005 following U.S.-Uzbek dispute over May 2005 Uzbek crackdown on unrest in Andijon. Once housed about 1,750 U.S. military personnel (900 Air Force, 400 Army, and 450 civilian) supplying Afghanistan. Uzbekistan allowed German use of the base temporarily in March 2008, indicating possible healing of the rift. U.S. relations with Uzbekistan improved in 2009, but U.S. officials said in 2010 that the use of the air base is still not under active discussion. Some shipments beginning in February 2009 through Navoi airfield in central Uzbekistan, and U.S. signed agreement with Uzbekistan on April 4, 2009, allowing nonlethal supplies for the Afghanistan war. Goods are shipped to Latvia and Georgia, some transits Russia by rail, then to Uzbekistan.
Tajikistan	Some use of air bases and other facilities by coalition partners, including France, and emergency use by U.S. India also uses bases under separate agreement. New supply lines to Afghanistan established in February 2009 ("northern route") make some use of Tajikistan.
Pakistan	As discussed below, most U.S. supplies flow through Pakistan. Heavy equipment docks in Karachi and is escorted by security contractors to the Khyber Pass crossing.

In Congress, H.Con.Res. 248, a resolution introduced by Representative Kucinich to require removal of U.S. forces from Afghanistan not later than December 31, 2010, was defeated in the House by a vote of 65 to 356 on March 10, 2010.) Other Members have introduced legislation to require the Administration to develop, by January 1, 2011, plans to wind down the U.S. military presence in Afghanistan. This provision was voted on in consideration of a FY20 10 supplemental appropriation (H.R. 4899), where it failed in the Senate (May 27, 2010) by a vote of 18-80. On July 1, 2010, the House voted 162-260 to reject a plan in that bill to require the Administration to submit, by April 4, 2011, a plan and timetable to redeploy from Afghanistan. Earlier, in House consideration of a FY20 10 National Defense Authorization Act (H.R. 2647), a similar provision failed on June 25, 2009, by a vote of 138-278.

Concede Parts of Afghanistan to the Taliban

Some experts believe that the Afghanistan conflict is unwinnable and that a preferable strategy would be to work with Pakistan and other regional actors to reach a political settlement relatively favorable to the Taliban. These plans might involve allowing the Taliban to control large parts of the south and east, where the insurgency is most active, and to work with the Northern Alliance to keep other parts of Afghanistan relatively peaceful. Others believe these plans amount to little more than a managed U.S. defeat and that Al Qaeda and other militants would likely take root in Taliban-controlled areas.

REGIONAL DIMENSION

Most of Afghanistan's neighbors believed that the fall of the Taliban would stabilize the region, but Islamist militants have not only continued to challenge the Afghan government but have also battled the government of Pakistan and have conducted acts of terrorism in India and elsewhere in the region. The Obama Administration announcement of a beginning of a "transition" to Afghan leadership in July 2011 has led some regional powers to plan for what they believe might be a post-U.S. presence scramble for influence in Afghanistan—or at least for the ability to deny their rivals influence there. Iran, which shares with India a fear of any return of radical Taliban extremism in Afghanistan, has begun discussing the future of Afghanistan with other regional countries and, to a lesser extent ,with other international actors in Afghanistan. These maneuverings, to some extent, cast doubt on the commitment of Afghanistan's six neighbors to a non-interference pledge (Kabul Declaration) on December 23, 2002. U.S. officials have sought to enlist both regional and greater international support for Afghanistan through a still expanding 44-nation "International Contact Group."

At the same time, Afghanistan has been re-integrating into regional security and economic organizations that reflect an effort to conduct relatively normal commerce and diplomatic relationships. In November 2005, Afghanistan joined the South Asian Association for Regional Cooperation (SAARC), and Afghanistan has observer status in the Shanghai Cooperation Organization, which is discussed below. Several regional summit meeting series have been established involving Afghanistan, including summit meetings between Afghanistan, Pakistan, and Turkey; and between Iran, Afghanistan, and Pakistan.

Afghanistan

Table 7. Major Reporting Requirements

Several provisions require Administration reports on numerous aspects of U.S. strategy, assistance, and related issues:

- P.L. 108-458, The Afghanistan Freedom Support Act Amendments require, through the end of FY2010, an overarching annual report on U.S. strategy in Afghanistan. Other reporting requirements expired, including required reports: (1) on long-term U.S. strategy and progress of reconstruction; (2) on how U.S. assistance is being used; (3) on U.S. efforts to persuade other countries to participate in Afghan peacekeeping; and (4) a joint State and Defense Department report on U.S. counter-narcotics efforts in Afghanistan.
- P.L. 110-181 (Section 1230), FY2008 Defense Authorization Act requires a quarterly DOD report on the security situation in Afghanistan; the first was submitted in June 2008. It is required through FY2011.
- Section 1229 of the same law requires the quarterly report of the Special Inspector General for Afghanistan Reconstruction (SIGAR).
- P.L. 111-8 (Omnibus Appropriation, explanatory statement) requires a State Department report on the use of funds to address the needs of Afghan women and girls (submitted by September 30, 2009).
- P.L. 111-32, FY2009 Supplemental Appropriation (Section 1116), required a White House report, by the time of the FY2011 budget submission, on whether Afghanistan and Pakistan are cooperating with U.S. policy sufficiently to warrant a continuation of Administration policy toward both countries, as well as efforts by these governments to curb corruption, their efforts to develop a counter-insurgency strategy, the level of political consensus in the two countries to confront security challenges, and U.S. government efforts to achieve these objectives. The report was released with a date of September 30, 2010.
- The same law (Section 1117) required a report, by September 23, 2009, on metrics to be used to assess progress on Afghanistan and Pakistan strategy. A progress report measured against those metrics is to be submitted by March 30, 2010, and every six months thereafter, until the end of FY2011.
- Section 1228 of the FY2010 National Defense Authorization Act (P.L. 111-84) requires a report, within 120 days, on the Afghan Provincial Protection Program and other local security initiatives. Section 1235 authorizes a DOD- funded study of U.S. force levels needed for eastern and southern Afghanistan, and Section 1226 requires a Comptroller General report on the U.S. "campaign plan" for the Afghanistan (and Iraq) effort.

Russia has put together two "quadrilateral summits," the latest of which was on August 18, 2010, among Pakistan, Russia, Afghanistan, and Tajikistan, and focused on counter-narcotics and anti-smuggling. As shown in the table below, cooperation from several of the regional countries are crucial to U.S. and ISAF operations and resupply in Afghanistan.

Akistan/Pakistan-Afghanistan Border[58]

Pakistan's apparent determination to retain influence over Afghanistan is heavily colored by fears of historic rival India. Pakistan viewed the Taliban regime as providing Pakistan strategic depth against rival India, and Pakistan apparently remains wary that the current Afghan government may come under the sway of India. Numerous militant groups, such as LET (Laskhar-e-Tayyiba, or Army of the Righteous) were formed in Pakistan to challenge

India's control of part of the disputed territories of Jammu and Kashmir. Some observers believe Pakistan wants to retain the ability to stoke these militants against India, even though these militants may be aiding Islamist groups challenging Pakistan's stability. Pakistan says India is using its Embassy and four consulates in Afghanistan (Pakistan says India has nine such consulates) to train and recruit anti- Pakistan insurgents, and is using its reconstruction funds to build influence there.

The Obama Administration strategy reviews in 2009 both emphasized the linkage between militants present in Pakistan and the difficulty stabilizing Afghanistan. Since the late 2009 review, in which the concept of a start of a U.S. drawdown beginning in July 2011 was stated, Pakistan appears to have tried to position a political deal between the Afghan government and the insurgency. The United States has said that Pakistan could do more to assist the U.S. effort in Afghanistan, but U.S. policy continues to assist and engage extensively with Pakistan as a necessary ally. As part of its efforts to engage Karzai on the shape of any conflict-ending settlement, during 2010 there has been a growing pattern of meetings between Karzai and Pakistan's army chief of staff Gen. Ashfaq Kiyani and with the head of Pakistan's Inter Services Intelligence Directorate (ISI), Gen. Ahmad Shuja Pasha. Through meetings such as these, Pakistan has sought to rebut allegations that its Inter Service Intelligence (ISI) directorate are supporting Afghanistan militants, particularly the Haqqani faction.[59] Haqqani network terrorists were reputedly involved in the July 7, 2008, suicide bombing of India's embassy in Kabul and other attacks in Kabul on India-related targets.

Pakistan has also sought to control Afghanistan's trade, particularly with India, leading to U.S. efforts to persuade Pakistan to forge a "transit trade" agreement with Afghanistan. That effort bore success with the signature of a trade agreement between the two on July 18, 2010, allowing for an easier flow of Afghan products, which are mostly agricultural products that depend on rapid transit. The agreement could also represent a success for the Canada-sponsored "Dubai Process" of talks between Afghanistan and Pakistan on modernizing border crossings, new roads, and a comprehensive border management strategy to meet IMF benchmarks. The trade agreement comes after earlier signs of growing cooperation, including Afghan agreement to send more Afghan graduate students to study in Pakistan, and a June 2010 Afghan agreement to send small numbers of ANA officers to undergo training in Pakistan.[60]

Cooperation against Al Qaeda

During 2001-2006, the Bush Administration praised then President Pervez Musharraf for Pakistani accomplishments against Al Qaeda, including the arrest of over 700 Al Qaeda figures since the September 11 attacks.[61] After the attacks, Pakistan provided the United States with access to Pakistani airspace, some ports, and some airfields for OEF. Others say Musharraf acted against Al Qaeda only when it threatened him directly; for example, after the December 2003 assassination attempts against him. Musharraf resigned in August 2008, and the civilian government is led by the party of the late Pakistani secular leader Benazir Bhutto. Her widower, Asif Ali Zardari, is President.

U.S. criticism of Pakistan's approach increased following a *New York Times* report (February 19, 2007) that Al Qaeda had reestablished some small terrorist training camps in Pakistan, near the Afghan border. This possibly was an outgrowth of a September 5, 2006, compromise between Pakistan and tribal elders in this region. That, and subsequent compromises were criticized, including a 2008 "understanding" with members of the Mehsud tribe, among which is Tehrik-eTaliban (TTP, Pakistan Taliban) leader Baitullah Mehsud (killed in a U.S. strike in August 2009). As noted, the TTP was named a Foreign Terrorist Organization on September 2, and some of its leaders (Hakimullah Mehsud) were named as terrorism supporting entities that day.

Increased Direct U.S. Action[62]

The Obama Administration has tried to combat Afghanistan-focused militants in Pakistan without directly violating Pakistan's restrictions on the U.S. ability to operate "on the ground" in Pakistan. The Obama Administration has significantly increased the use of Predator and Reaper unmanned aircraft to strike militant targets in Pakistan as compared to the Bush Administration. Such a strike reportedly was responsible for the death of Beitullah Mehsud, and some militant websites say the strikes are taking a major toll on their operations and networks. The *New York Times* reported on February 23, 2009, that there are about 70 U.S. military advisers on the ground in Pakistan but they are there to help train Pakistani forces to battle Al Qaeda and Taliban militants. However, a U.S. raid over the border, which killed two Pakistani Frontier Corps soldiers in early October 2010, caused Pakistan to close off for several days the northern border crossing through with much of NATO/ISAF's supplies flow.

Recent History of Pakistan-Afghanistan Relations

The fluctuating nature of Afghanistan-Pakistan relations is not a new feature, and is based on Pakistan's past involvements in Afghanistan's struggles. Afghans fondly remember Pakistan's role as the hub for U.S. backing of the *mujahedin* that forced the Soviet withdrawal in 1988-89. However, some Afghan leaders resent Pakistan as the most public defender of the Taliban movement when it was in power (Pakistan was one of only three countries to formally recognize it as the legitimate government; Saudi Arabia and the United Arab Emirates are the others).

Since 2008, the end of the Musharraf era, there has been a dramatic improvement in Afghanistan- Pakistan relations. Karzai attended the September 9, 2008, inauguration of Zardari. A "peace *jirga*" process—a series of meetings of notables on each side of the border—was launched at a September 28, 2006, dinner hosted by President Bush for Karzai and Musharraf, and meetings of 700 Pakistani and Afghan tribal elders were held in August 2007 and again in October, 2008. The latter, led on the Afghan side by Dr. Abdullah, and resulted in a declaration to endorse efforts to try to engage militants in both Afghanistan and Pakistan to bring them into the political process. Zardari visited Kabul and met with Karzai on January 9, 2009, where the two signed a joint declaration against terrorism that affects both countries. (A September 2010 meeting between them appeared to be a rededication of this declaration.) Additional progress was made during the visit of Afghan and Pakistani ministers to Washington, DC, during February 23-27, 2009, to participate in the Obama Administration strategic review. As noted above, Karzai and Zardari visit Washington, DC, in May 2009 to continue the strategic dialogue.

In April 2008, in an extension of the Tripartite Commission's work, the three countries agreed to set up five "border coordination centers"—which will include networks of radar nodes to give liaison officers a common view of the border area. These centers build on an agreement in May 2007 to share intelligence on extremists' movements. Three have been established to date, including one near the Torkham Gate at the Khyber Pass, one at Nawa, and one at Liwara. In June 2008, Pakistan ended a six-month suspension in attendance at meetings of the Tripartite Commission under which NATO, Afghan, and Pakistani military leaders meet regularly on both sides of the border.

Regarding the long-term relationship, Pakistan wants the government of Afghanistan to pledge to abide by the "Durand Line," a border agreement reached between Britain (signed by Sir Henry Mortimer Durand) and then Afghan leader Amir Abdul Rahman Khan in 1893, separating Afghanistan from what was then British-controlled India (later Pakistan after the 1947 partition). The border is recognized by the United Nations, but Afghanistan continues to indicate that the border was drawn unfairly to separate Pashtun tribes and should be renegotiated. As of October 2002, about 1.75 million Afghan refugees have returned from Pakistan since the Taliban fell, but as many as 3 million might still remain in Pakistan, and Pakistan says it plans to expel them back into Afghanistan in the near future.

Iran

The Obama Administration initially saw Iran as potentially helpful to its strategy for Afghanistan. Ambassador Holbrooke had advocated a "regional" component of the strategy, which focuses primarily on Pakistan but also envisioned cooperation with Iran on Afghanistan issues. However, as Iran-U.S. relations worsened in 2010 over Iran's nuclear program, the Obama Administration became more critical of Iran's activities in Afghanistan. Still, press reports in September 2010 indicated that the view within the Administration that Iran is key to helping stabilizing Afghanistan may be returning to the forefront. The Administration reported to be considering a U.S.-Iran dialogue in Kabul on Afghan issues.[63] Iran's attendance of the October 18, 2010, International Contact Group" meeting in Rome, including a briefing by Gen. Petraeus, might be an indication of more engagement between Iran and the United States on the Afghanistan issue.

Early in the Administration, Secretary of State Clinton made a point of announcing that Iran would be invited to the U.N.-led meeting on Afghanistan at the Hague on March 31, 2009. At the meeting, Special Representative Holbrooke briefly met the Iranian leader of his delegation to the meeting, and handed him a letter on several outstanding human rights cases involving Iranian-Americans. At the meeting, Iran pledged cooperation on combating Afghan narcotics and in helping economic development in Afghanistan—both policies Iran is already pursuing to a large degree. The United States and Iran took similar positions at a U.N. meeting in Geneva in February 2010 that discussed drug trafficking across the Afghan border. Iran did not attend the January 28, 2010, international meeting in London, but it did attend the July 28, 2010, international meeting in Kabul (both discussed above).

Iranian Material Support to Militants in Afghanistan

A U.S.-Iran dialogue on Afghanistan would presumably be intended to address the U.S. concerns about Iran's support for groups that operate against U.S. forces. Iran may be arming groups in Afghanistan to try to pressure U.S. forces that use Afghanistan's Shindand air base,[64] which Iran fears the United States might use to attack or conduct surveillance against Iran.

Table 8. Major International (Non-U.S.) Pledges to Afghanistan Since January 2002 (as of March 2010; $ in millions)

Japan	6,900
Britain	2,897
World Bank	2,803
Asia Development Bank	2,200
European Commission (EC)	1,768
Netherlands	1,697
Canada	1,479
India	1,200
Iran	1,164
Germany	1,108
Norway	977
Denmark	683
Italy	637
Saudi Arabia	533
Spain	486
Australia	440
Total Non-U.S. Pledges (including donors not listed)	**30,800**

Sources: Special Inspector General for Afghanistan Reconstruction. October 2008 report, p. 140; various press announcements. Figures include funds pledged at April 2009 NATO summit and Japan's October 2009 pledge of $5 billion over the next five years.
Note: This table lists donors pledging over $400 million total.

Or, Iran's policy might be to gain broader leverage against the United States by demonstrating that Iran is in position to cause U.S. combat deaths in Afghanistan. Yet, the Iranian aid is not at a level that would make Iran a major player in the insurgency in Afghanistan. U.S. officials, including Gen. Petraeus in his August 2010 press meetings, has called Iranian influence in Afghanistan, including its support for armed groups, "modest." Others are puzzled by Iran's support of Taliban fighters who are Pashtun, because Iran has traditionally supported Persian-speaking non-Pashtun factions in Afghanistan.

The State Department report on international terrorism for 2009, released August 5, 2010, said the Qods Force of the Revolutionary Guard of Iran continues to provide training to the Taliban on small unit tactics, small arms, explosives, and indirect weapons fire, as well as ships arms to "selected Taliban members" in Afghanistan. Weapons provided, according to the State Department report, as well as an April 2010 Defense Department report on Iran's military capabilities, include mortars, 107mm rockets, rocket-propelled grenades, and plastic explosives. Some reports, however, say Iran is actively paying Afghan militants to specifically target U.S. forces. On August 3, 2010, the Treasury Department, acting under Executive Order 13224, named two Qods Force officers as terrorism supporting entities (freezing assets in the United States, if any). They are: Hossein Musavi, Commander of the Qods Force Ansar Corps, which is the key Qods unit involved in Afghanistan, and Hasan Mortezavi, who is a Qods officer responsible for providing funds and materiel to the Taliban, according to the Treasury Department. [65]

Bilateral Afghan-Iranian Relations

Iran, like President Karzai, is concerned about how any reduction in U.S. involvement in Afghanistan might improve the prospects for a Taliban return to power. Iran's interest in a broad relationship with Karzai has not, to date, been affected by Iran's continued support for Taliban and other militants in Afghanistan. Aside from its always tense relations with the United States, Iran perceives its key national interests in Afghanistan as exerting its traditional influence over western Afghanistan, which Iran borders and was once part of the Persian empire, and to protect Afghanistan's Shiite and other Persian-speaking minorities. Karzai has, at times, called Iran a "friend" of Afghanistan, and in March 2010 he met with Iranian President Mahmoud Ahmadinejad on two occasions, possibly to signal to the United States that he might realign with regional actors if the United States continues to criticize his leadership. One of the meetings was just after the departure of visiting Defense Secretary Gates. Previously, Karzai received Ahmadinejad in Kabul in August 2007, and he visited Tehran at the end of May 2009 as part of the tripartite diplomatic process between Iran, Pakistan, and Afghanistan. During his visit to the United States in May 2009, Karzai said he had told both the United States and Iran that Afghanistan must not become an arena for the broader competition and disputes between the United States and Iran.[66]

Iran's pledged assistance to Afghanistan has totaled about $1.1 64 billion since the fall of the Taliban, mainly to build roads, schools, and electricity lines in Herat Province, near the Iranian border.[67] Iranian funds have also been used to construct mosques in the province, as well as pro- Iranian theological seminaries in Shiite districts of Kabul. Iran also offers scholarships to Afghans to study in Iranian universities, and there are consistent allegations that Iran has funded Afghan provincial council and parliamentary candidates who are perceived as pro-Tehran.[68] A controversy arose in late October 2010 when Karzai acknowledged accepting about $2 million per year in cash payments from Iran, via his chief of Staff Mohammad Daudzai.

Many Afghans look fondly on Iran for helping them try to oust the Taliban regime when it was in power. Iran saw the Taliban regime, which ruled during 1996-2001, as a threat to its interests in Afghanistan, especially after Taliban forces captured Herat in September 1995. Iran subsequently drew even closer to the ethnic minority-dominated Northern Alliance than previously, providing its groups with fuel, funds, and ammunition.[69] In September 1998, Iranian and Taliban forces nearly came into direct conflict when Iran discovered that nine of its diplomats were killed in the course of the Taliban's offensive in northern Afghanistan. Iran massed forces at the border and threatened military action, but the crisis cooled without a major clash, possibly out of fear that Pakistan would intervene on behalf of the Taliban. Iran offered search and rescue assistance in Afghanistan during the U.S.-led war to topple the Taliban, and it also allowed U.S. humanitarian aid to the Afghan people to transit Iran. Iran helped construct Afghanistan's first post-Taliban government, in cooperation with the United States—at the December 2001 "Bonn Conference." In February 2002, Iran expelled Karzai-opponent Gulbuddin Hikmatyar, but it did not arrest him. At other times, Afghanistan and Iran have had disputes over Iran's efforts to expel Afghan refugees. About 1.2 million remain, mostly integrated into Iranian society, and a crisis erupted in May 2007 when Iran expelled about 50,000 into Afghanistan. About 300,000 Afghan refugees have returned from Iran since the Taliban fell.

India

The interests and activities of India in Afghanistan are almost the exact reverse of those of Pakistan. India's goal is to deny Pakistan "strategic depth" in Afghanistan, and to deny Pakistan the ability to block India from trade and other connections to Central Asia and beyond. Some believe India is increasingly concerned that any negotiated settlement of the Afghanistan conflict will give Pakistan preponderant influence in Afghanistan, and India, which supported the Northern Alliance against the Taliban in the mid-1990s, is said to be stepping up its contacts with those factions to discuss possible contingencies in the event of an Afghan settlement deal.

Many of the families of Afghan leaders have lived in India at one time or another and, as noted above, Karzai studied there. India saw the Taliban's hosting of Al Qaeda as a major threat to India itself because of Al Qaeda's association with radical Islamic organizations in Pakistan dedicated to ending Indian control of parts of Jammu and Kashmir. Some of these groups have committed major acts of terrorism in India, and there might be connections to the militants who carried out the terrorist attacks in Mumbai in November 2008.

Pakistan accuses India of using its four consulates in Afghanistan (Pakistan says there are nine such consulates) to spread Indian influence in Afghanistan. However, many U.S. observers believe India's role in Afghanistan is constructive, and some would support an Indian decision to deploy more security forces in Afghanistan to protect its construction workers, diplomats, and installations. India reportedly decided in August 2008 to improve security for its officials and workers in Afghanistan, but not to send actual troops there. Yet, Tajikistan, which also supported the mostly Tajik Northern Alliance against the Taliban when it was in power, allows India to use one of its air bases.

India is the fifth-largest single country donor to Afghan reconstruction, funding projects worth over $1.2 billion. Indian officials assert that all their projects are focused on civilian, not military, development and are in line with the development priorities set by the Afghan government. India, along with the Asian Development Bank, financed a $300 million project, mentioned above, to bring electricity from Central Asia to Afghanistan. It has also renovated the well-known Habibia High School in Kabul and committed to a $25 million renovation of Darulaman Palace as the permanent house for Afghanistan's parliament. India financed the construction of a road to the Iranian border in remote Nimruz province, and it is currently constructing the 42 megawatt hydroelectric Selwa Dam in Herat Province at a cost of about $80 million. This will increase electricity availability in the province. India is also helping the IDLG with its efforts to build local governance organizations, and it provides 1,000 scholarships per year for Afghans to undergo higher education in India. Some Afghans want to enlist even more Indian assistance in training Afghan bureaucrats in accounting, forensic accounting, oversight, and other disciplines that will promote transparency in Afghan governance.

Russia, Central Asian States, and China

Some neighboring and nearby states take an active interest not only in Afghan stability, but in the U.S. military posture that supports U.S. operations in Afghanistan.

Table 9. U.S. Assistance to Afghanistan, FY1978-FY1 998 ($ in millions)

Fiscal Year	Devel. Assist.	Econ. Supp. (ESF)	P.L. 480 (Title I and II)	Military	Other (Incl. Regional Refugee Aid)	Total
1978	4.989	— 5.742		0.269	0.789	11.789
1979	3.074	— 7.195		—	0.347	10.616
1980	—	(Soviet invasion-December 1979)			—	—
1981	—	—	—	—	—	—
1982	—	—	—	—	—	—
1983	—	—	—	—	—	—
1984	—	—	—	—	—	—
1985	3.369	—	—	—	—	3.369
1986	—	—	8.9	—	—	8.9
1987	17.8	12.1	2.6	—	—	32.5
1988	22.5	22.5	29.9	—	—	74.9
1989	22.5	22.5	32.6	—	—	77.6
1990	35.0	35.0	18.1	—	—	88.1
1991	30.0	30.0	20.1	—	—	80.1
1992	25.0	25.0	31.4	—	—	81.4
1993	10.0	10.0	18.0	—	30.2	68.2
1994	3.4	2.0	9.0	—	27.9	42.3
1995	1.8	—	12.4	—	31.6	45.8
1996	—	—	16.1	—	26.4	42.5
1997	—	—	18.0	—	31.9[a]	49.9
1998	—	—	3.6	—	49.14[b]	52.74

Source: Department of State.

a. Includes $3 million for demining and $1.2 million for counternarcotics.

b. Includes $3.3 million in projects targeted for Afghan women and girls, $7 million in earthquake relief aid, 100,000 tons of 41 6B wheat worth about $15 million, $2 million for demining, and $1.54 for counternarcotics.

The region to the north of Afghanistan is a growing factor in U.S. efforts to secure new supply lines to Afghanistan. Some of these alternative lines have begun to open, at least to non-lethal supplies.

Russia

Russia wants to reemerge as a great power and to contain U.S. power in Central Asia, including Afghanistan. Its hosting of the "quadrilateral summits"mentioned above, the first in July 2009 and the latest on August 18, could represent stepped up efforts by Russia to exert influence on the Afghanistan issue. Still, Russia supports U.S. efforts to combat militants in the region who have sometimes posed a threat to Russia itself. In February 2009, Russia resumed allowing the United States to ship non-lethal equipment into Afghanistan through Russia (following a suspension in 2008 caused by differences over the Russia-Georgia conflict). In July 2009, following President Obama's visit to Russia, it announced it would allow the transit to Afghanistan of lethal supplies as well. Russia reportedly is being urged by

NATO (as evidenced in a visit by NATO Secretary General Anders Fogh Rasmussen to Russia in December 2009) to provide helicopters and spare parts to the Afghan forces (which still make heavy use of Russian-made Hind helicopters) as well as fuel.

In June 2010, Russia said more economic and social assistance is needed for Afghanistan. Russia reportedly is considering investing $1 billion in Afghanistan to develop its electricity capacity and build out other infrastructure. Since 2002, Russia has been providing some humanitarian aid to Afghanistan, although it keeps a low profile in the country because it still feels humiliated by its withdrawal in 1989 and senses some Afghan resentment of the Soviet occupation. Dr. Abdullah told CRS in October 2009, however, that Afghan resentment of Russia because of that occupation has eased in recent years. During the 1990s, Russia supported the Northern Alliance against the Taliban with some military equipment and technical assistance in order to blunt Islamic militancy emanating from Afghanistan.[70] Although Russia supported the U.S. effort against the Taliban and Al Qaeda in Afghanistan out of fear of Islamic (mainly Chechen) radicals, Russia continues to seek to reduce the U.S. military presence in Central Asia. Russian fears of Islamic activism emanating from Afghanistan may have ebbed since 2002 when Russia killed a Chechen of Arab origin known as "Hattab" (full name is Ibn al-Khattab), who led a militant pro-Al Qaeda Chechen faction. The Taliban government was the only one in the world to recognize Chechnya's independence, and some Chechen fighters fighting alongside Taliban/Al Qaeda forces have been captured or killed.

Central Asian States

These states are becoming increasingly crucial to U.S. strategy in Afghanistan. As discussed in the chart, Uzbekistan, Turkmenistan, Tajikistan and Kazakhstan are pivotal actors in U.S. efforts to secure supply routes into Afghanistan that avoid Pakistan.

During Taliban rule, Russian and Central Asian leaders grew increasingly alarmed that radical Islamic movements were receiving safe haven in Afghanistan. Uzbekistan, in particular, has long asserted that the group Islamic Movement of Uzbekistan (IMU), allegedly responsible for four simultaneous February 1999 bombings in Tashkent that nearly killed President Islam Karimov, is linked to Al Qaeda.[71] One of its leaders, Juma Namangani, reportedly was killed while commanding Taliban/Al Qaeda forces in Konduz in November 2001. Kazakhstan and Kyrgyzstan do not directly border Afghanistan, but IMU guerrillas transited Kyrgyzstan during incursions into Uzbekistan in the late 1990s.

During Taliban rule, Uzbekistan supported Uzbek leader Abdul Rashid Dostam, who was part of that Alliance. It allowed use of Karshi-Khanabad air base by OEF forces from October 2001 until a rift emerged in May 2005 over Uzbekistan's crackdown against riots in Andijon, and U.S.- Uzbek relations remained largely frozen. Uzbekistan's March 2008 agreement with Germany for it to use Karshi-Khanabad air base temporarily, for the first time since the rift in U.S.-Uzbek relations developed in 2005, suggests that U.S.-Uzbek cooperation on Afghanistan and other issues might be rebuilt. Ambassador Holbrooke visited in February 2010, indicating further warming. Renewed U.S. discussions with Uzbekistan apparently bore some fruit with the Uzbek decision in February 2009 to allow the use of Navoi airfield for shipment of U.S./NATO goods into Afghanistan.

Central Asian Activities during Taliban Rule

In 1996, several of the Central Asian states banded together with Russia and China into a regional grouping called the Shanghai Cooperation Organization to discuss the Taliban threat. It includes China, Russia, Uzbekistan, Tajikistan, Kazakhstan, and Kyrgyzstan. Reflecting Russian and Chinese efforts to limit U.S. influence in the region, the group has issued statements, most recently in August 2007, that security should be handled by the countries in the Central Asia region. Despite the Shanghai Cooperation Organization statements, Tajikistan allows access primarily to French combat aircraft, and Kazakhstan allows use of facilities in case of emergency. In April 2010, it also agreed to allow U.S. overflights of lethal military equipment to Afghanistan, allowing the United States to use polar routes to fly materiel directly from the United States to Bagram Airfield. A meeting of the Shanghai Cooperation Organization to discuss Afghanistan was held in Moscow on March 25, 2009, and was observed by a U.S. official, as well as by Iran.

Of the Central-Asian states that border Afghanistan, only Turkmenistan chose to seek close relations with the Taliban leadership when it was in power, possibly viewing engagement as a more effective means of preventing spillover of radical Islamic activity from Afghanistan. It saw Taliban control as facilitating construction of a natural gas pipeline from Turkmenistan through Afghanistan (see above). The September 11 events stoked Turkmenistan's fears of the Taliban and its Al Qaeda guests and the country publicly supported the U.S.-led war. No U.S. forces have been based in Turkmenistan.

China[72]

China's involvement in Afghanistan policy appears to be growing. China reportedly is considering contributing some People's Liberation Army (PLA) forces, possibly in a non-combat role, to helping secure Afghanistan. A communiqué from the Obama visit to China in November 2009 implied a possible larger role for China to help stabilize Afghanistan. In late 2009, China allocated an additional $75 billion in economic aid to Afghanistan, bringing its total to close to $1 billion since 2002. On March 20, 2010, ahead of a visit to China by Karzai, China called for more international support for Afghanistan. During the visit, China stressed that its investments in Afghanistan would continue.

Chinese delegations continue to assess the potential for new investments in such sectors as mining and energy,[73] and a $3.4 billion deal was signed in November 2007 for China Metallurgical Group to develop the Aynak copper mine south of Kabul, and build related infrastructure. The deal represents the largest investment in Afghanistan in history. However, U.S. Embassy officials told CRS in October 2009 that actual work at the mine has been stalled for some time. U.S. forces do not directly protect the project, but U.S. forces are operating in Lowgar province, where the project is located, and provide general stability there. China is also a major contender to develop the Hajji Gak iron ore mine near Kabul.

A major organizer of the Shanghai Cooperation Organization, China has a small border with a sliver of Afghanistan known as the "Wakhan corridor." China had become increasingly concerned about the potential for Al Qaeda to promote Islamic fundamentalism among Muslims in China. In December 2000, sensing China's increasing concern about Taliban policies, a Chinese official delegation met with Mullah Umar. China did not enthusiastically support U.S. military action against the Taliban, possibly because China was wary of a U.S.

military buildup nearby. In addition, China has been allied to Pakistan in part to pressure India, a rival of China.

Persian Gulf States: Saudi Arabia and UAE

The Gulf states are, according to Ambassador Holbrooke, a key part of the effort to stabilize Afghanistan. As noted, Ambassador Holbrooke has focused increasing U.S. attention—and has formed a multilateral task force—to try to curb continuing Gulf resident donations to the Taliban in Afghanistan. Holbrooke has said these donations might be a larger source of Taliban funding than is the narcotics trade.

Saudi Arabia has a role to play in Afghanistan in part because, during the Soviet occupation, Saudi Arabia channeled hundreds of millions of dollars to the Afghan resistance, primarily Hikmatyar and Sayyaf. Drawing on its reputed intelligence ties to Afghanistan during that era, Saudi Arabia worked with Taliban leaders to persuade them to suppress anti-Saudi activities by Al Qaeda. Some press reports indicate that, in late 1998, Saudi and Taliban leaders discussed, but did not agree on, a plan for a panel of Saudi and Afghan Islamic scholars to decide bin Laden's fate. A majority of Saudi citizens practice the strict Wahhabi brand of Islam similar to that of the Taliban, and Saudi Arabia was one of three countries to formally recognize the Taliban government. The Taliban initially served Saudi Arabia as a potential counter to Iran, but Iranian- Saudi relations improved after 1997 and balancing Iranian power ebbed as a factor in Saudi policy toward Afghanistan.

Saudi Arabia has played a role as a go-between for negotiations between the Karzai government and "moderate" Taliban figures. This role was recognized at the London conference on January 28, 2010, in which President Karzai stated in his opening speech that he sees a role for Saudi Arabia in helping stabilize Afghanistan. As noted, some reports say that a political settlement might involve Mullah Umar going into exile in Saudi Arabia.

According to U.S. officials, Saudi Arabia cooperated extensively, if not publicly, with OEF. It broke diplomatic relations with the Taliban in late September 2001 and quietly permitted the United States to use a Saudi base for command of U.S. air operations over Afghanistan, but it did not permit U.S. airstrikes from it.

The United Arab Emirates, the third country that recognized the Taliban regime, is emerging as another major donor to Afghanistan. Its troop contribution was discussed under OEF, above. At a donors conference for Afghanistan in June 2008, UAE pledged an additional $250 million for Afghan development, double the $118 million pledged by Saudi Arabia. That brought the UAE contribution to Afghanistan to over $400 million since the fall of the Taliban. Projects funded include housing in Qandahar, roads in Kabul, a hospital in Zabol province, and a university in Khost. There are several daily flights between Kabul and Dubai emirate.

U.S. AND INTERNATIONAL AID TO AFGHANISTAN AND DEVELOPMENT ISSUES

Many experts have long believed that accelerating economic development would do more to improve the security situation—and to eliminate narcotics trafficking—than intensified antiTaliban combat. This belief appears to constitute a major element of Obama Administration strategy. Afghanistan's economy and society are still fragile after decades of warfare that left about 2 million dead, 700,000 widows and orphans, and about 1 million Afghan children who were born and raised in refugee camps outside Afghanistan. More than 3.5 million Afghan refugees have since returned, although a comparable number remain outside Afghanistan. The U.N. High Commission for Refugees (UNHCR) supervises Afghan repatriation and Afghan refugee camps in Pakistan. The literacy rate is very low and Afghanistan lacks a large pool of skilled labor.

U.S. Assistance to Afghanistan

During the 1990s, the United States became the largest single provider of assistance to the Afghan people. During Taliban rule, no U.S. aid went directly to that government; monies were provided through relief organizations. Between 1985 and 1994, the United States had a cross-border aid program for Afghanistan, implemented by USAID personnel based in Pakistan. Citing the difficulty of administering this program, there was no USAID mission for Afghanistan from the end of FY1 994 until the reopening of the U.S. Embassy in Afghanistan in late 2001.

For all of FY2002-FY2009, the United States has provided about $40 billion in assistance, including military "train and equip" for the ANA and ANP (which is about $21 billion of these funds). The Obama Administration request for FY2010 (regular and supplemental) and for FY2011 are in separate tables below. The figures in the tables do not include costs for U.S. combat operations. Including those costs, the United States spent about $105 billion for FY2010 and expects to spend about $120 billion for FY2011. For further information on combat costs, see CRS Report RL33 110, *The Cost of Iraq, Afghanistan, and Other Global War on Terror Operations Since 9/11*, by Amy Belasco.

There is also a debate over how aid is distributed. Some of the more stable provinces, such as Bamiyan and Balkh, are complaining that U.S. and international aid is flowing mostly to the restive provinces in an effort to quiet them, and ignoring the needs of poor Afghans in peaceful areas. Later in this chapter are tables showing U.S. appropriations of assistance to Afghanistan, and Table 20 lists U.S. spending on all sectors for FY2002-FY2009.

Direct Aid and Budget Support to the Afghan Government

Although the Afghan government has been increasing its revenue (about $1.4 billion for 2010) and is covering about one quarter of its overall budget, USAID provides funding to help the Afghan government meet gaps in its operating budget—both directly and through a U.N.-run multi-donor Afghan Reconstruction Trust Fund (ARTF) account, run by the World Bank. The Obama Administration has requested about $200 million in FY20 11 funds to

Afghanistan

provide direct budget support to Afghan ministries that meet reform benchmarks. Those figures are provided in the U.S. aid tables at the end.

Currently, only about 20% of all donated aid funds disbursed are channeled through the Afghan government. The United States views only four ministries as sufficiently transparent to handle donor funds. However, the Kabul Conference (July 20, 2010) communiqué endorsed a goal of increasing that to about 50%.

Aid Oversight

Still heavily dependent on donors, Karzai has sought to reassure the international donor community by establishing a transparent budget and planning process. Some in Congress want to increase independent oversight of U.S. aid to Afghanistan; the conference report on the FY2008 defense authorization bill (P.L. 110-181) established a "special inspector general" for Afghanistan reconstruction, (SIGAR) modeled on a similar outside auditor for Iraq ("Special Inspector General for Iraq Reconstruction," SIGIR). Funds provided for the SIGAR are in the tables below. On May 30, 2008, Maj. Gen. Arnold Fields (Marine, ret.) was named to the position. He has filed several reports on Afghan reconstruction, which include discussions of SIGAR staffing levels and activities, as well as several specific project audits. However, he acknowledged that criticisms in a July 2010 "peer review" of SIGAR operations by the Inspectors General of several U.S. agencies were valid, attributing many of the shortcomings to slow pace of fully funding his office.[74] One recent SIGAR report noted deficiencies in the ability of the Afghan government's Central Audits Office to monitor how funds are used. Some Members of Congress have criticized the SIGAR for ineffective oversight and have called for his replacement.

Aid Authorization: Afghanistan Freedom Support Act

A key post-Taliban aid authorization bill, S. 2712, the Afghanistan Freedom Support Act (AFSA) of 2002 (P.L. 107-327, December 4, 2002), as amended, authorized about $3.7 billion in U.S. civilian aid for FY2003-FY2006. The law, whose authority has now expired, was intended to create a central source for allocating funds; that aid strategy was not implemented. However, some of the humanitarian, counter-narcotics, and governance assistance targets authorized by the act were met or exceeded by appropriations. No Enterprise Funds authorized by the act have been appropriated. The act authorized the following:

- $60 million in total counter-narcotics assistance ($15 million per year for FY2003-FY2006);
- $30 million in assistance for political development, including national, regional, and local elections ($10 million per year for FY2003-FY2005);
- $80 million total to benefit women and for Afghan human rights oversight ($15 million per year for FY2003-FY2006 for the Afghan Ministry of Women's Affairs, and $5 million per year for FY2003-FY2006 to the Human Rights Commission of Afghanistan);
- $1.7 billion in humanitarian and development aid ($425 million per year for FY2003-FY2006);
- $300 million for an Enterprise Fund;

- $550 million in drawdowns of defense articles and services for Afghanistan and regional militaries. (The original law provided for $300 million in drawdowns. That was increased by subsequent appropriations laws.)

A subsequent law (P.L. 108-458, December 17, 2004), implementing the recommendations of the 9/11 Commission, contained "The Afghanistan Freedom Support Act Amendments of 2004." The subtitle mandated the appointment of a U.S. coordinator of policy on Afghanistan and requires additional Administration reports to Congress.

Afghan Freedom Support Act Reauthorization

In the 110th Congress, H.R. 2446, passed by the House on June 6, 2007 (406-10), would have reauthorized AFSA through FY20 10. A version (S. 3531), with fewer provisions than the House bill, was not taken up by the full Senate. AFSA reauthorization was not reintroduced in the 111th Congress. H.R. 2446 would have authorized about $1.7 billion in U.S. economic aid and $320 in military aid (including drawdowns of equipment) per fiscal year. It also would have authorized a pilot program of crop substitution to encourage legitimate alternatives to poppy cultivation; and a cut off of U.S. aid to any Afghan province in which the Administration reports that the leadership of the province is complicit in narcotics trafficking.

International Reconstruction Pledges/National Development Strategy

International (non-U.S.) donors have pledged over $30 billion since the fall of the Taliban. When combined with U.S. aid, this by far exceeds the $27.5 billion for reconstruction identified as required for 2002-20 10. The major donors, and their aggregate pledges to date, are listed below. These amounts were pledged, in part, at the following donor conferences: (Tokyo), Berlin (April 2004), Kabul (April 2005), the London conference (February 2006), and the June 12, 2008, conference in Paris, discussed below. The January 28, 2010, London conference resulted in further pledges, as noted above. The Afghanistan Compact leaned toward the view of Afghan leaders that a higher proportion of the aid be channeled through the Afghan government, a policy adopted by the United States.

Among multilateral lending institutions, in May 2002, the World Bank reopened its office in Afghanistan after 20 years. Its projects have been concentrated in the telecommunications and road and sewage sectors. The Asian Development Bank (ADB) has also been playing a major role in Afghanistan. One of its projects in Afghanistan was funding the paving of a road from Qandahar to the border with Pakistan, and as noted above, it is contributing to a project to bring electricity from Central Asia to Afghanistan. On the eve of the London conference on January 28, 2010, the IMF and World Bank announced $1.6 billion in Afghanistan debt relief.

Key Sectors

Efforts to build the legitimate economy are showing some results, by accounts of senior U.S. officials, including expansion of roads and education and health facilities constructed.

The following are some key sectors and what has been accomplished with U.S. and international donor funds:

- **Roads.** Road building is considered a U.S. priority and has been USAID's largest project category there, taking up about 25% of USAID spending since the fall of the Taliban. Roads are considered key to enabling Afghan farmers to bring legitimate produce to market in a timely fashion, and former commander of U.S. forces in Afghanistan Gen. Eikenberry (now Ambassador) said "where the roads end, the Taliban begin." The major road, the Ring Road, is nearly all repaved. Among other major projects completed are a road from Qandahar to Tarin Kowt, (Uruzgan province) built by U.S. military personnel, inaugurated in 2005; and a road linking the Panjshir Valley to Kabul. In several provinces, U.S. funds (sometimes CERP funds) are being used to build roads that link up farming communities to the market for their products. Another key priority is building a Khost-Gardez road, under way currently.
- **Bridges.** Afghan officials are said to be optimistic about increased trade with Central Asia now that a new bridge has opened (October 2007) over the Panj River, connecting Afghanistan and Tajikistan. The bridge was built with $33 million in (FY2005) U.S. assistance. The bridge is helping what press reports say is robust reconstruction and economic development in the relatively peaceful and ethnically homogenous province of Panjshir, the political base of the Northern Alliance.
- **Education.** Despite the success in enrolling Afghan children in school since the Taliban era (see statistics above), setbacks have occurred because of Taliban attacks on schools, causing some to close.
- **Health.** The health care sector, as noted by Afghan observers, has made considerable gains in reducing infant mortality and giving about 65% of the population at least some access to health professionals. In addition to U.S. assistance to develop the health sector's capacity, Egypt operates a 65-person field hospital at Bagram Air Base that instructs Afghan physicians. Jordan operates a similar facility in Mazar-e-Sharif.
- **Electricity/Energy/Hydrocarbons.** At least 10% of USAID funds for Afghanistan have been spent on power projects, although that percentage is likely to rise in 2010 and 2011. The Afghanistan Compact states that the goal is for electricity to reach 65% of households in urban areas and 25% in rural areas by 2010. Severe power shortages in Kabul are fewer now than they were two years ago. The power shortages were caused in part by the swelling of Kabul's population to about 3 million, up from half a million when the Taliban was in power. Power to the capital has grown due to the Afghan government's agreements with several Central Asian neighbors to import electricity, as well as construction of new substations. Many shops in Kabul are now lit up at night, as observed by CRS in October 2009. Afghanistan has no hydrocarbons energy export industry and a small refining sector that provides some of Afghanistan's needs for gasoline or other fuels. Russia, Kazakhstan, and Uzbekistan are its main fuel suppliers.

A major USAID and DOD focus is on power projects in southern Afghanistan. The key longterm project is to expand the capacity of the Kajaki Dam, located in unstable Helmand Province. USAID has allocated about $500 million to restore and expand the capacity of the dam. As of October 2009, two turbines were operating—one was always working, and the second was repaired by USAID contractors. This has doubled electricity production in the south and caused small factories and other businesses to come to flourish. USAID plans to further expand capacity of the dam by installing a third turbine (which there is a berth for but which never had a turbine installed.) In an operation involving 4,000 NATO troops (Operation Ogap Tsuka), components of the third turbine were successfully delivered to the dam in September 2008. It was expected to be operational in mid-late 2009 but technical and security problems, such as inability to secure and build roads leading to the dam, have delayed the project and there is no public estimate as to when the third turbine will be completed. In the interim, the U.S. military and USAID have agreed on a plan to focus on smaller substations and generator projects that can bring more electricity to Qandahar and other places in the south quickly. For this and other power projects, the Administration is requesting legislative authority for an "Infrastructure Fund" to be funded by DOD ($400 million - $600 million in FY2011) but controlled jointly by DOD and USAID.

- **Railways.** Afghanistan does not currently have any functioning railway. However, a railway from Mazar-i-Sharif to the border with Uzbekistan, is now under construction with $165 million from the Asian Development Bank. The rail will eventually link up with Herat and will integrate Afghanistan to the former Soviet railway system in Central Asia, increasing Afghanistan's economic integration in the region.

Agriculture Sector

With about 80% of Afghans living in rural areas, the agriculture sector has always been key to Afghanistan's economy and stability. Ambassador Holbrooke, including in his January 2010 strategy document, has outlined U.S. policy to boost Afghanistan's agriculture sector not only to reduce drug production but also as an engine of economic growth. Prior to the turmoil that engulfed Afghanistan in the late 1970s, Afghanistan was a major exporter of agricultural products.

USAID has spent about 15% of its Afghanistan funds on agriculture (and "alternative livelihoods" to poppy cultivation), and this has helped Afghanistan double its legitimate agricultural output over the past five years. One emerging "success story" is growing Afghan exports of high-quality pomegranate juice called Anar. Other countries are promoting not only pomegranates but also saffron rice and other crops that draw buyers outside Afghanistan. Another emerging success story is Afghanistan's November 2010 start of exports of raisins to Britain.[75] Wheat production was robust in 2009 because of healthy prices for that crop, and Afghanistan is again self-sufficient in wheat production. According to the SRAP January 2010 strategy document reference earlier, 89 U.S. agricultural experts (64 from U.S. Department of Agriculture and 25 from USAID) are in Afghanistan. Their efforts include providing new funds to buy seeds and agricultural equipment, and to encourage agri-business.

U.S. strategy has addressed not only crop choice but also trying to construct the entirety of the infrastructure needed for a healthy legitimate agriculture sector, including road building, security of the routes to agriculture markets, refrigeration, storage, transit through Pakistan and other transportation of produce, building legitimate sources of financing, and other aspects of the industry. U.S. officials in Kabul say that Pakistan's restrictions on trade between Afghanistan and India have, to date, prevented a rapid expansion of Afghan pomegranate exports to that market. Dubai is another customer for Afghan pomegranate exports. A key breakthrough on this issue was reached with the July 18, 2010, signing of a transit trade agreement between Afghanistan and Pakistan, reportedly brokered by the United States. It will allow for more rapid transit of Afghan and Pakistani trucks through each others' territories, ending a requirement that goods be offloaded at border crossings.

Table 10. U.S. Assistance to Afghanistan, FY1999-FY2002 ($ in millions)

	FY1 999	FY2000	FY200 1	FY2002 (Final)
U.S. Department of Agriculture (DOA) and USAID Food For Peace (FFP), via World Food Program(WFP)	42.0 worth of wheat (100,000 metric tons under "416(b)" program.)	68.875 for 165,000 metric tons. (60,000 tons for May 2000 drought relief)	131.1 (300,000 metric tons under P.L. 480, Title II, and 416(b))	198.12 (for food commodities)
State/Bureau of Population, Refugees and Migration (PRM) via UNHCR and ICRC	16.95 for Afghan refugees in Pakistan and Iran, and toassist their repatriation	14.03 for the same purposes	22.03 for similar purposes	136.54 (to U.N. agencies)
State Department/ Office of Foreign Disaster Assistance (OFDA)	7.0 to various NGOs to aid Afghans inside Afghanistan	6.68 for drought relief and health, water, and sanitation programs	18.934 for similar programs	113.36 (to various U.N. agencies and NGOs)
State Department/ HDP (Humanitarian Demining Program)	2.6 15	3.0	2.8	7.0 to Halo Trust/other demining
Aid to Afghan Refugees in Pakistan (through various NGOs)	5.44 (2.789 for health, training— Afghan females in Pakistan)	6.169, of which $3.82 went to similar purposes	5.31 for similar purposes	
Counter-Narcotics			1.50	63.0
USAID/Office of Transition Initiatives			0.45 (Afghan women in Pakistan)	24.35 for broadcasting/media
Dept. of Defense				50.9 (2.4 million rations)
Foreign Military Financing				57.0 (for Afghan national army)
Anti-Terrorism				36.4
Economic Support Funds(E.S.F)				105.2
Peacekeeping				24.0
Totals	**76.6**	**113.2**	**182.6**	**815.9**

Source: CRS.

To help Afghanistan develop the agriculture sector, the National Guard from several states (Texas, for example) is deploying "Agribusiness Development Teams" in several provinces to help Afghan farmers with water management, soil enhancement, crop cultivation, and improving the development and marketing of their goods. The timber industry in the northwest is said to be vibrant as well.

Private Sector Initiatives

Some sectors are being developed primarily with private investment funding. There is substantial new construction, particularly in Kabul, such as the Serena luxury hotel (opened in November 2005) and a $25 million Coca Cola bottling factory (opened in September 2006). The bottling factory is located near the Bagrami office park (another private initiative), which includes several other factories. The Serena was built by the Agha Khan foundation, a major investor in Afghanistan; the Agha Khan is a leader of the Isma'ili community, which is prevalent in northern Afghanistan. The foundation has also funded the successful Roshan cellphone company. Some say that private investment could be healthier if not for the influence exercised over it by various faction leaders and Karzai relatives.

- **Telecommunications and Transportation.** Several Afghan telecommunications firms have been formed, including Afghan Wireless (another cell phone service, which competes with Roshan) and Tolo Television. The 52-year-old national airline, Ariana, is said to be in significant financial trouble due to corruption that has affected its safety ratings and left it unable to service a heavy debt load, but there are new privately run airlines, such as Pamir Air, Safi Air (run by the Safi Group, which has built a modern mall in Kabul), and Kam Air. Major new buildings include several marriage halls in Kabul city, as observed by CRS in October 2009.
- **Mining and Gems**. Afghanistan's mining sector has been largely dormant since the Soviet invasion. Some Afghan leaders complain that not enough has been done to revive such potentially lucrative industries as minerals mining, such as of copper and lapis lazuli (a stone used in jewelry). The issue became more urgent in June 2010 when a Defense Department development team announced, based on surveys, that Afghanistan may have untapped minerals worth over $1 trillion.[76] Gen. Petraeus, in an interview with NBC News on August 15, 2010, said the amount could be in the "trillions." Among the most valuable are significant reserves of such minerals as lithium in western Afghanistan; lithium is crucial to the new batteries being used to power electric automobiles.

  Still, in November 2007, the Afghan government signed a deal with China Metallurgical Group for the company to invest $3.4 billion to develop Afghanistan's Aynak copper field in Lowgar Province. The agreement, viewed as generous to the point where it might not be commercially profitable for China Metallurgical Group, includes construction of two coal-fired electric power plant (one of which will supply more electricity to Kabul city); a freight railway (in conjunction with the Asian Development Bank project above); and a road from the project to Kabul. However, work on the mine reportedly has been slowed by the need to clear mines in the area. Bids are being accepted for another large mining project, the Haji Gak iron ore mine (which may contain 60 billion tons of iron ore) near Kabul. China Metallurgy, as well as companies from India, are said to be finalists for the project.

- **Hydrocarbons and Pipelines.** As noted, Afghanistan has virtually no operational hydrocarbon energy sector. Afghanistan's prospects in this sector appeared to brighten by the announcement in March 2006 of an estimated 3.6 billion barrels of oil and 36.5 trillion cubic feet of gas reserves. Experts believe these amounts, if proved, could make Afghanistan relatively self-sufficient in energy and able to export energy to its neighbors. USAID is funding a test project to develop gas resources in northern Afghanistan.

Another major energy project remains under consideration. During 1996-1998, the Clinton Administration supported proposed natural gas and oil pipelines through western Afghanistan as an incentive for the warring factions to cooperate. A consortium led by Los Angeles-based Unocal Corporation proposed a $2.5 billion Central Asia Gas Pipeline, estimated to cost $3.7 billion to construct, that would originate in southern Turkmenistan and pass through Afghanistan to Pakistan, with possible extensions into India.[77] The deterioration in U.S.-Taliban relations after 1998 largely ended hopes for the pipeline projects. Prospects for the project have improved in the post-Taliban period. In a summit meeting in late May 2002 between the leaders of Turkmenistan, Afghanistan, and Pakistan, the three countries agreed to revive the project. Sponsors held an inaugural meeting on July 9, 2002, in Turkmenistan, signing a series of preliminary agreements. Turkmenistan's leadership (President Gurbanguly Berdimukhamedov, succeeding the late Saparmurad Niyazov) favors the project as well. Some U.S. officials view this project as a superior alternative to a proposed gas pipeline from Iran to India, transiting Pakistan.

National Solidarity Program

The United States and the Afghan government are also trying to promote local decision making on development. The "National Solidarity Program" (NSD) largely funded by U.S. and other international donors—but implemented by Afghanistan's Ministry of Rural Rehabilitation and Development—seeks to create and empower local governing councils to prioritize local reconstruction projects. It is widely hailed as a highly successful, Afghan-run program. The assistance, channeled through donors, provides block grants of about $60,000 per project to the councils to implement agreed projects, most of which are water projects. The U.S. aid to the program is part of the World Bank-run Afghanistan Reconstruction Trust Fund (ARTF) account.

A FY2009 supplemental request asked about $85 million for the ARTF account, of which much of those funds would be used to fill a $140 million shortfall in the NSP program. P.L. 111-32, the FY2009 supplemental discussed above, earmarks $70 million to defray the shortfall. The FY20 10 consolidated appropriation (P.L. 111-117) earmarked another $175 million in ESF for the program. The FY20 10 National Defense Authorization Act (P.L. 111-84) authorizes the use of some CERP funds, controlled by the U.S. military, to supplement the funding for the NSP. However, this authorization, if implemented, is likely to incur opposition from some international NGOs who are opposed to combining military action with development work.

Table 11. U.S. Assistance to Afghanistan, FY2003
($ in millions, same acronyms as Table 10)

FY2003 Foreign Aid Appropriations (P.L. 108-7)	
Development/Health	90
P.L. 480 Title II (Food Aid)	47
Peacekeeping	10
Disaster Relief	94
ESF	50
Non-Proliferation, De-mining, Anti-Terrorism (NADR)	5
Refugee Relief	55
Afghan National Army (ANA) train and equip (FM F)	21
Total from this law:	**372**
FY2003 Supplemental (P.L. 108-1 1)	
Road Construction (ESF, Kabul-Qandahar road)	100
Provincial Reconstruction Teams (ESF)	10
Afghan government support (ESF)	57
ANA train and equip (FMF)	170
Anti-terrorism/de-mining	28
(NADR, some for Karzai protection)	
Total from this law:	**365**
Total for FY2003	**737**

Source: CRS.

Note: Earmarks for programs benefitting women and girls totaled: $65 million. Of that amount, $60 million was earmarked in the supplemental and $5 million in the regular appropriation.

Trade Initiatives/Reconstruction Opportunity Zones

The United States is trying to build on Afghanistan's post-war economic rebound with trade initiatives. In September 2004, the United States and Afghanistan signed a bilateral trade and investment framework agreement (TIFA). These agreements are generally seen as a prelude to a broader and more complex bilateral free trade agreement, but negotiations on an FTA have not yet begun. On December 13, 2004, the 148 countries of the World Trade Organization voted to start membership talks with Afghanistan. Another initiative supported by the United States is the establishment of joint Afghan-Pakistani "Reconstruction Opportunity Zones" (ROZ's) which would be modeled after "Qualified Industrial Zones" run by Israel and Jordan in which goods produced in the zones receive duty free treatment for import into the United States. For FY2008, $5 million in supplemental funding was requested to support the zones, but P.L. 110-252 did not specifically mention the zones.

Bills in the 110th Congress, S. 2776 and H.R. 6387, would have authorized the President to proclaim duty-free treatment for imports from ROZ's to be designated by the President. In the 111th Congress, a version of these bills was introduced (S. 496 and H.R. 1318). President Obama specifically endorsed passage of these bills in his March 2009 strategy announcement. H.R. 1318 was incorporated into H.R. 1886, a Pakistan aid appropriation that is a component of the new U.S. strategy for the region, and the bill was passed by the House on June 11,

2009, and then appended to H.R. 2410. However, another version of the Pakistan aid bill, S. 1707, did not authorize ROZ's; it was passed and became law (P.L. 111-73).

**Table 12. U.S. Assistance to Afghanistan, FY2004
($ in millions, same acronyms as previous tables)**

Afghan National Police (FMF)	160
Counter-Narcotics	125.52
Afghan National Army (FMF)	719.38
Presidential Protection (NADR)	52.14
DDR Program (disarming militias)	15.42
MAN PAD destruction	1.5
Terrorist Interdiction Program	0.41
Border Control (WMD)	0.23
Good Governance Program	113.57
Political Competition, Consensus Building(Elections)	24.41
Rule of Law and Human Rights	29.4
Roads	348.68
Education/Schools	104.11
Health/Clinics	76.85
Power	85.13
PRTs	57.4
CERP (DOD funds to build good will)	39.71
Private Sector Development/Economic Growth	63.46
Water Projects	28.9
Agriculture	50.5
Refugee/IDPs	82.6
Food Assistance	88.25
De-Mining	12.61
State/USAID Program Support	203.02
Total Aid for FY2004	**2,483.2**

Laws Derived: FY2004 supplemental (P.L. 108-106); FY2004 regular appropriation (P.L. 108- 199). Regular appropriation earmarked $5 million for programs benefitting women and girls.

Table 13. U.S. Assistance to Afghanistan, FY2005 ($ in millions)

Afghan National Police (State Dept. funds, FMF, and DOD funds, transition to DOD funds to Afghan security forces	624.46
Counter-Narcotics	775.31
Afghan National Army (State Dept. funds, FMF, and DOD funds)	1,633.24
Presidential (Karzai) Protection (NADR funds)	23.10
DDR	5.0
Detainee Operations	16.9
MANPAD Destruction	0.75

Table 13. (Continued)

Small Arms Control	3.0
Terrorist Interdiction Program	0.1
Border Control (WMD)	0.85
Good Governance	137.49
Political Competition/Consensus-Building/Election Support	15.75
Rule of Law and Human Rights	20.98
Roads	334.1
Afghan-Tajik (Nizhny Panj) Bridge	33.1
Education/Schools	89.63
Health/Clinics	107.4
Power	222.5
PRTs	97.0
CERP	136.0
Civil Aviation (Kabul International Airport)	25.0
Private Sector Development/Economic Growth	77.43
Water Projects	43.2
Agriculture	74.49
Refugee/IDP Assistance	54.6
Food Assistance (P.L. 480, Title II)	108.6
Demining	23.7
State/USAID Program Support	142.84
Total Aid for FY2005	**4,826.52**

Laws Derived: FY2005 Regular Appropriations (P.L. 1 08-447); Second FY2005 Supplemental (P.L. 109-13). The regular appropriation earmarked $50 million to be used for programs to benefit women and girls.

Source: CRS.

Note: In FY2005, funds to equip and train the Afghan national security forces was altered from State Department funds (Foreign Military Financing, FMF) to DOD funds.

Table 14. U.S. Assistance to Afghanistan, FY2006 ($ in millions)

Afghan National Police (DOD funds)	1,217.5
Counter-narcotics	419.26
Afghan National Army (DOD funds)	735.98
Presidential (Karzai) protection (NADR funds)	18.17
Detainee Operations	14.13
Small Arms Control	2.84
Terrorist Interdiction	.10
Counter-terrorism Finance	.28
Border Control (WMD)	.40
Bilateral Debt Relief	11.0
Budgetary Support to the Government of Afghanistan	1.69
Good Governance	10.55

Table 14. (Continued)

Afghanistan Reconstruction Trust Fund	47.5
Political Competition/Consensus Building/Elections	1.35
Civil Society	7.77
Rule of Law and Human Rights	29.95
Roads	235.95
Education/Schools	49.48
Health/Clinics	51.46
Power	61.14
PRTs	20.0
CERP Funds (DOD)	215.0
Private Sector Development/Economic Growth	45.51
Water Projects	.89
Agriculture	26.92
Food Assistance	109.6
De-mining	14.32
Refugee/IDP aid	36.0
State/USAID program support	142.42
Total	**3,527.16**
Laws Derived: FY2006 Regular Foreign Aid Appropriations (P.L. 109-102); FY06 supplemental (P.L. 109-234). The regular appropriation earmarked $50 million for programs to benefit women and girls.	

Source: CRS.

Table 15. U.S. Assistance to Afghanistan, FY2007 ($ in millions)

Afghan National Police (DOD funds)	2,523.30
Afghan National Army (DOD funds)	4,871.59
Counter-Narcotics	737.15
Presidential (Karzai) Protection (NADR)	19.9
Detainee Operations	12.7
Small Arms Control	1.75
Terrorist Interdiction Program	0.5
Counter-Terrorism Finance	0.4
Border Control (WMD)	0.5
Budget Support to Afghan Government	31.24
Good Governance	107.25
Afghanistan Reconstruction Trust Fund (incl. National Solidarity Program)	63
Political Competition/Election support (ESF)	29.9
Civil Society (ESF)	8.1
Rule of Law/Human Rights (ESF)	65.05
Roads (ESF)	303.1
Education/Schools (ESF)	62.75
Health/Clinics	112.77

Table 15. (Continued)

Power (ESF)	194.8
PRTs (ESF)	126.1
CERP (DOD funds)	206
Private Sector Development/Economic Growth	70.56
Water Projects (ESF)	2.3
Agriculture (ESF)	67.03
Refugee/ID P Assistance	72.61
Food Assistance	150.9
Demining	27.82
State/USAID Program Support	88.7
Total	**9,984.98**

Laws Derived: Regular Appropriation P.L. 110-5; DOD Appropriation P.L. 109-289; and FY2007 Supplemental Appropriation P.L. 110-28. The regular appropriation earmarked $50 million for programs to benefit women/ girls. Providing ESF in excess of $300 million subject to certification of Afghan cooperation on counter-narcotics.

Sources: CRS; Special Inspector General for Afghanistan Reconstruction, October 2008 report.

Table 16. U.S. Assistance to Afghanistan, FY2008 (appropriated, $ in millions)

Afghan National Army (DOD funds)	1,724.68
Afghan National Police (DOD funds)	1,017.38
Counter-Narcotics (INCLE and DOD funds)	619.47
NADR (Karzai protection)	6.29
Radio Free Afghanistan	3.98
Detainee operations	9.6
Small Arms Control	3.0
Terrorist Interdiction Program	.99
Counter-Terrorism Finance	.60
Border Control (WMD)	.75
Commanders Emergency Response Program (CERP, DOD funds)	269.4
Direct Support to Afghan Government	49.61
Good Governance	245.08
Afghanistan Reconstruction Trust Fund (incl. National Solidarity program)	45.0
Election Support	90.0
Civil Society Building	4.01
Rule of Law and Human Rights	125.28
Special Inspector General for Afghanistan Reconstruction(SIGAR)	2.0
Roads	324.18
Education/Schools	99.09
Health/Clinics	114.04
Power (incl. Kajaki Dam rehabilitation work)	236.81
PRT programs	75.06

Afghanistan

Table 16. (Continued)

Economic Growth/Private Sector Development	63.06
Water Projects	1 6.4q
Agriculture	34.44
Refugee/ID P Assistance	42.1
Food Aid	101.83
De-Mining	15.0
State/USAID Program Support	317.4
Total	**5,656.53**

Appropriations Laws Derived: Regular FY2008 (P.L. 110-161); FY2008 Supplemental (P.L. 110-252). The regular appropriation earmarked $75 million for programs to benefit woman and girls. ESF over $300 million subject to narcotics cooperation certification.

Sources: Special Inspector General Afghanistan Reconstruction, October 2008 report; CRS.

Table 17. U.S. Assistance to Afghanistan, FY2009 ($ in millions)

	Regular Appropriation (P.L. 111-8)	Bridge Supplemental (P.L. 110-252)	FY2009 Supplemental (P.L. 111-32)	Total
ANSF Funding		2,000	3,607	5,607
CERP (DOD funds)		683		683
Detainee ops (DOD)		4		4
Counternarcotics (C-N) (DOD)	24	150	57	232
C-N (DEA)	19			19
C-N--Alternative. Livelihoods (INCLE)	100	70	87	257
C-N--Eradication, Interdiction (INCLE)	178	14	17	209
IMET	1.4			1.4
ARTF (Incl. National Solidarity Program)	45	20	85	150
Governance building	100	68	115	283
Civil Society promotion	8	4		12
Election Support	93	56	25	174
Strategic Program Development			50	50
Rule of Law Programs (USAID)	8	15	20	43
Rule of Law (INCLE)	34	55	80	169
Roads (ESF)	74	65		139
Power (ESF)	73	61		134
Agriculture (ESF and DA)	25		85	110
PRTs/Local Governance (ESF)	74	55	159	288
Education	88	6		94
Health	61	27		88
Econ Growth/"Cash for Work"	49	37	220	306
Water, Environment, Victims Comp.	31	3		34
Karzai Protection (NADR)	32		12	44
Food Aid (P.L. 480, Food for Peace)	14	44		58
Migration, Refugee Aid		50	7	57
State Ops/Embassy Construction	308	131	450	889
USAID Programs and Ops	18	2	165	185
State/USAID IG/SIGAR	3	11	7	20
Cultural Exchanges, International Orgs	6	10		16
Totals	**1,463**	**3,640**	**5,248**	**10,352**

Notes: P.L. 111-32 (FY2009 supplemental): provides requested funds, earmarks $70 million for National Solidarity Program; $150 million for women and girls (all of FY2009); ESF over $200 million subject to narcotics certification; 1 0% of supplemental INCLE subject to certification of Afghan government moves to curb human rights abuses, drug involvement.

Table 18. FY20 10 Assistance (Includes Supplemental) ($ in millions)

Afghan Security Forces Funding (DOD funds)	9,162 (6,563 appropriated plus 2,600 supplemental request)
CERP (DOD funds)	1,000
Counternarcotics (DOD)	361
INCLE: all functions: interdiction, rule of law, alternative livelihoods	620 (420 regular approp. plus 200 supplemental request)
IMET	1.5
Global Health/Child Survival	92.3
Afghanistan Reconstruction Trust Fund (Incl. National Solidarity Program) (ESF)	200
Governance building (ESF)	191
Civil Society promotion (ESF)	10
Election Support (ESF)	90
Strategic Program Development (ESF)	100
USAID Rule of Law Programs (ESF)	50
Roads (ESF)	230
Power (ESF)	230
Agriculture (ESF)	230
PRT programs/Local governance (ESF)	251
Education (ESF)	95
Health (ESF)	102
Econ Growth/"Cash for Work" (ESF)	274
Water, Environment, Victim Comp. (ESF)	15
Karzai Protection (NADR)	58
Food Aid (P.L. 480, Food for Peace)	16
Refugees and Migration	11
State Ops/Embassy Construction	697 (486 regular plus 211 supplemental)
Cultural Exchanges	6
SIGAR	37 (23 regular plus 14 supp request)
FY20 10 supplemental ESF request (for ESF programs above)	1,576
Total Appropriated (Incl. Supplemental)	**15,700**

Laws derived: FY20 10 foreign aid appropriation in Consolidated Appropriation (P.L. 111 - 11 7), which earmarks: $175 million (ESF and INCLE) for programs for women and girls, and $175 million (ESF) for the National Solidarity Program. The FY20 10 Defense Appropriation (P.L. 111-118), which cut $900 million from the requested amount for the ANSF (regular defense appropriation). FY20 10 supplemental funds appropriated by H.R. 4899 (P.L. 111-212)

Source: CRS.

Table 19. FY2011 Regular Request ($ in millions)

Program/Area	Request
Afghan National Security Forces (DOD funds)	11,600
CERP	1,100
Economic Support Funds (ESF)	3,316.3
Global Health/ Child Survival	71.1
INCLE	450
Karzai Protection (NADR funds)	69.3
IMET	1.5
State Dept. Operations (not incl. security)	754
SIGAR	35.3
Total	**17,398**

In FY20 11 legislation, on June 30, 2010, the State and Foreign Operations Subcommittee of House Appropriations Committee marked up its aid bill, deferring consideration of much of the Administration request for Afghanistan

Afghanistan

pending a Committee investigation of allegations of governmental corruption in Afghanistan and of possible diversion of U.S. aid funds by Afghan officials and other elites. The Administration has requested legislation to authorize an "Afghanistan Infrastructure Fund," to contain mostly DOD funds, beginning with $400 million in FY20 11, possibly supplemented by an additional $200 million later in the fiscal year. The fund will be used mostly for electricity projects, including an ongoing major electricity project for Qandahar, but could be used for other infrastructure projects later on, such as roads.

Table 20. Total Obligations for Major Programs: FY2001 -FY2009 ($ millions)

Security Related Programs (mostly DOD funds)	
Afghan National Security Forces	21,297
Counter-Narcotics	3,436
Karzai Protection (NADR funds)	226
DDR (Disarmament, Demobilization, Reintegration of militias)	20.42
Detainee Operations	57.33
MAN PAD Destruction (Stingers left over from anti-Soviet war)	2.25
Small Arms Control	10.59
Commander Emergency Response Program (CERP)	1,976
De-Mining Operations (Halo Trust, other contractors)	98.53
International Military Education and Training Funds (IMET)	3
Humanitarian-Related Programs	
Food Aid (P.L. 480, other aid)	958
Refugee/IDP aid	743
Debt Relief for Afghan government	11
Democracy and Governance Programs (mostly ESF)	
Support for Operations of Afghan Government	80.86
Good Governance (incentives for anti-corruption, anti-narcotics)	1,044
Afghanistan Reconstruction Trust Fund (funds National Solidarity Program)	305.5
Civil Society (programs to improve political awareness and activity)	31.88
Elections Support	600
Rule of Law and Human Rights (USAID and INCLE funds)	552.66
Economic Sector-Related Programs (mostly ESF)	
Roads	1,908
PRT-funded projects (includes local governance as well as economic programs)	698.11
Education (building schools, teacher training)	535.93
Health (clinic-building, medicines)	620.59
Power	934.38
Water (category also includes some funds to compensate Afghan victims/Leahy)	128.02
Agriculture (focused on sustainable crops, not temporary alternatives to poppy)	441
Private Sector Development/Economic Growth (communications, IT, but includes some cash-for-work anti-narcotics programs)	627.52
State Dept. operations/Embassy construction/USAID operations/educational and cultural exchanges/SIGAR operations	2,445
Total (including minor amounts not included in table)	**39,730**

Table 21. NATO/ISAF Contributing Nations (As of November 15, 2010; http://www. isaf.nato.int/images 1 5%20NOV.Placemat%20page 1 -3.pdf)

NATO Countries		Non-NATO Partners	
Belgium	491	Albania	258
Bulgaria	516	Armenia	40
Canada	2,922	Austria	3
Czech Republic	468	Australia	1,550
Denmark	750	Azerbaijan	94
Estonia	140	Bosnia-Herzegovina	45
France	3,850	Croatia	299
Germany	4,341	Finland	150
Greece	80	Georgia	924
Hungary	502	Ireland	7
Iceland	4	Jordan	0
Italy	3,688	Macedonia	163
Latvia	189	Malaysia	30
Lithuania	219	Mongolia	47
Luxemburg	9	Montenegro	31
Netherlands	242	New Zealand	234
Norway	353	Singapore	38
Poland	2,519	South Korea	246
Portugal	95	Sweden	500
Romania	1,648	Ukraine	16
Slovakia	250	United Arab Emirates	35
Slovenia	78	Tonga	0
Spain	1,576		
Turkey	1,790		
United Kingdom	9,500		
United States	90,000		
Total Listed ISAF: 130,930			

Note: As noted elsewhere in this chapter, U.S. force totals in Afghanistan are approximately 104,000. Non-U.S. forces in the table total 41,000. In addition, the NATO/ISAF site states that troop numbers in this table are based on broad contribution and do not necessarily reflect the exact numbers on the ground at any one time.

Table 22. Provincial Reconstruction Teams

Location (City)	Province/Command
U.S.-Lead (all under ISAF banner)	
1. Gardez	Paktia Province (RC-East, E)
2. Ghazni	Ghazni (RC-E). with Poland.
3. Jalalabad	Nangarhar (RC-E)
4. Khost	Khost (RC-E)
5. Qalat	Zabol (RC-South, S). with Romania.
6. Asadabad	Kunar (RC-E)

Afghanistan

Location (City)	Province/Command
7. Sharana	Paktika (RC-E). with Poland.
8. Mehtarlam	Laghman (RC-E)
9. Jabal o-Saraj	Panjshir Province (RC-E), State Department lead
10. Qala Gush	Nuristan (RC-E)
11. Farah	Farah (RC-SW)

Partner Lead (most under ISAF banner)

PRT Location	Province	Lead Force/Other forces
12. Qandahar	Qandahar (RC-S)	Canada (seat of RC-S)
13. Lashkar Gah	Helmand (RC-S)	Britain. with Denmark and Estonia
14. Tarin Kowt	Uruzgan (RC-S)	Australia (and U.S.) (Replaced Netherlands in August 2010)
15. Herat	Herat (RC-W)	Italy (seat of RC-W)
16. Qalah-ye Now	Badghis (RC-W)	Spain
17. Mazar-e-Sharif	Balkh (RC-N)	Sweden
18. Konduz	Konduz (RC-N)	Germany (seat of RC-N)
29. Faizabad	Badakhshan (RC-N)	Germany. with Denmark, Czech Rep.
20. Meymaneh	Faryab (RC-N)	Norway. with Sweden.
21. Chaghcharan	Ghowr (RC-W)	Lithuania. with Denmark, U.S., Iceland
22. Pol-e-Khomri	Baghlan (RC-N)	Hungary
23. Bamiyan	Bamiyan (RC-E)	New Zealand (not NATO/ISAF).
24. Maidan Shahr	Wardak (RC-C)	Turkey
25. Pul-i-Alam	Lowgar (RC-E)	Czech Republic
26. Shebergan	Jowzjan (RC-N)	Turkey
27. Charikar	Parwan (RC-E)	South Korea (Bagram, in Parwan Province, is the base of RC-E)

Note: RC = Regional Command.

Table 23. Major Factions/Leaders in Afghanistan

Party/ Leader	Leader	Ideology/ Ethnicity	Regional Base
Taliban	Mullah (Islamic cleric) Muhammad Umar (still at large possibly in Afghanistan). Jalaludin and Siraj Haqqani allied with Taliban and Al Qaeda. Umar, born in Tarin Kowt, Uruzgan province, is about 65 years old.	Ultra-orthodox Islamic, Pashtun	Insurgent groups, mostly in the south and east.
Islamic Society (leader of "Northern Alliance")	Burhannudin Rabbani/ Yunus Qanooni (speaker of lower house)/Muhammad Fahim/Dr. Abdullah Abdullah (Foreign Minister 2001-2006). Ismail Khan, a so-called "warlord," heads faction of the grouping in Herat area. Khan, now Minister of Energy and Water, visited United States in March 2008 to sign USAID grant for energy projects.	Moderate Islamic, mostly Tajik	Much of northern and western Afghanistan, including Kabul

Table 23 (Continued)

National Islamic Movement of Afghanistan	Abdul Rashid Dostam. During OEF, impressed U.S. commanders with horse-mounted assaults on Taliban positions at Shulgara Dam, south of Mazar-e-Sharif, leading to the fall of that city and the Taliban's subsequent collapse. About 2,000 Taliban prisoners taken by his forces were held in shipping containers, died of suffocation, and were buried in mass grave. Grave excavated in mid-2008, possibly an effort by Dostam to destroy evidence of the incident. Was Karzai rival in October 2004 presidential election, then his top "security adviser" but now in exile in Turkey.	Secular, Uzbek	Jowzjan, Balkh, Faryab, Sar-i-Pol, and Samangan provinces.
Hizb-e-Wahdat	Composed of Shiite Hazara tribes from central Afghanistan. Karim Khalili is Vice President, but Mohammad Mohaqiq is Karzai rival in 2004 presidential election and parliament. Generally pro-Iranian. Was part of Rabbani 1992-1996 government, and fought unsuccessfully with Taliban over Bamiyan city. Still revered by Hazara Shiites is the former leader of the group, Abdul Ali Mazari, who was captured and killed by the Taliban in March 1995.	Shiite, Hazara tribes	Bamiyan, Ghazni, Dai Kundi province
Pashtun Leaders	Various regional governors and local leaders in the east and south; central government led by Hamid Karzai.	Moderate Islamic, Pashtun	Dominant in the south and east
Hizb-e-Islam Gulbuddin (HIG)	*Mujahedin* party leader Gulbuddin Hikmatyar. Was part of Soviet-era U.S.-backed "Afghan Interim Government" based in Peshawar, Pakistan. Was nominal "prime minister" in 1992-1996 *mujahedin* government but never actually took office. Lost power base around Jalalabad to the Taliban in 1994, and fled to Iran before being expelled in 2002. Still allied with Taliban and Al Qaeda in operations east of Kabul, but open to ending militant activity. Leader of a rival Hizb-e-Islam faction, Yunus Khalis, the mentor of Mullah Umar, died July 2006.	Orthodox Islamic, Pashtun	Small groups in Nangarhar, Nuristan, and Kunar provinces
Islamic Union	Abd-I-Rab Rasul Sayyaf. Islamic conservative, leads a pro-Karzai faction in parliament. Lived many years in and politically close to Saudi Arabia, which shares his "Wahhabi" ideology. During anti-Soviet war, Sayyaf's faction, with Hikmatyar, was a principal recipient of U.S. weaponry. Criticized the U.S.-led war against Saddam Hussein after Iraq's invasion of Kuwait.	orthodox Islamic, Pashtun	Paghman (west of Kabul)

Source: CRS.

RESIDUAL ISSUES FROM PAST CONFLICTS

A few issues remain unresolved from Afghanistan's many years of conflict, such as Stinger retrieval and mine eradication.

Stinger Retrieval

Beginning in late 1985 following internal debate, the Reagan Administration provided about 2,000 man-portable "Stinger" anti-aircraft missiles to the *mujahedin* for use against Soviet aircraft. Prior to the U.S.-led ouster of the Taliban, common estimates suggested that 200-3 00 Stingers remained at large, although more recent estimates put the number below 100.[78] The Stinger issue resurfaced in conjunction with 2001 U.S. war effort, when U.S. pilots reported that the Taliban fired some Stingers at U.S. aircraft during the war. No hits were reported. Any Stingers that survived the anti-Taliban war are likely controlled by Afghans now allied to the United States and presumably pose less of a threat, in part because of the deterioration of the weapons' batteries and other internal components.

In 1992, after the fall of the Russian-backed government of Najibullah, the United States reportedly spent about $10 million to buy the Stingers back, at a premium, from individual *mujahedin* commanders. The *New York Times* reported on July 24, 1993, that the buy back effort failed because the United States was competing with other buyers, including Iran and North Korea, and that the CIA would spend about $55 million in FY1994 in a renewed buy-back effort. On March 7, 1994, the *Washington Post* reported that the CIA had recovered only a fraction (maybe 50 or 100) of the at-large Stingers. In February 2002, the Afghan government found and returned to the United States "dozens" of Stingers.[79] In late January 2005, Afghan intelligence began a push to buy remaining Stingers back, at a reported cost of $150,000 each.[80]

The danger of these weapons has become apparent on several occasions, although U.S. commanders have not reported any recent active firings of these devices. Iran bought 16 of the missiles in 1987 and fired one against U.S. helicopters; some reportedly were transferred to Lebanese Hizballah. India claimed that it was a Stinger, supplied to Islamic rebels in Kashmir probably by sympathizers in Afghanistan, that shot down an Indian helicopter over Kashmir in May 1999.[81] It was a Soviet-made SA-7 "Strella" man-portable launchers that were fired, allegedly by Al Qaeda, against a U.S. military aircraft in Saudi Arabia in June 2002 and against an Israeli passenger aircraft in Kenya on November 30, 2002. Both missed their targets. SA-7s were discovered in Afghanistan by U.S. forces in December 2002.

Mine Eradication

Land mines laid during the Soviet occupation constitute one of the principal dangers to the Afghan people. The United Nations estimates that 5 million to 7 million mines remain scattered throughout the country, although some estimates are lower. U.N. teams have destroyed one million mines and are now focusing on de-mining priority-use, residential and commercial property, including lands around Kabul. As shown in the U.S. aid table for FY1999-FY2002 (**Table 10**), the U.S. de-mining program was providing about $3 million per year for Afghanistan, and the amount increased to about $7 million in the post-Taliban period. Most of the funds have gone to HALO Trust, a British organization, and the U.N. Mine Action Program for Afghanistan. The Afghanistan Compact adopted in London in February 2006 states that by 2010, the goal should be to reduce the land area of Afghanistan contaminated by mines by 70%.

APPENDIX. U.S. AND INTERNATIONAL SANCTIONS LIFTED

Virtually all U.S. and international sanctions on Afghanistan, some imposed during the Soviet occupation era and others on the Taliban regime, have now been lifted.

- P.L. 108-458 (December 17, 2004, referencing the 9/11 Commission recommendations) repealed bans on aid to Afghanistan outright. On October 7, 1992, President George H.W. Bush had issued Presidential Determination 93-3 that Afghanistan is no longer a Marxist-Leninist country, but the determination was not implemented before he left office. Had it been implemented, the prohibition on Afghanistan's receiving Export-Import Bank guarantees, insurance, or credits for purchases under Section 8 of the 1986 Export-Import Bank Act, would have been lifted. In addition, Afghanistan would have been able to receive U.S. assistance because the requirement would have been waived that Afghanistan apologize for the 1979 killing in Kabul of U.S. Ambassador to Afghanistan Adolph "Spike" Dubs. (Dubs was kidnapped in Kabul in 1979 and killed when Afghan police stormed the hideout where he was held.)
- U.N. sanctions on the Taliban imposed by Resolution 1267 (October 15, 1999), Resolution 1333 (December 19, 2000), and Resolution 1363 (July 30, 2001) have now been narrowed to penalize only Al Qaeda (by Resolution 1390, January 17, 2002). Resolution 1267 banned flights outside Afghanistan by Ariana, and directed U.N. member states to freeze Taliban assets. Resolution 1333 prohibited the provision of arms or military advice to the Taliban (directed against Pakistan); ordered a reduction of Taliban diplomatic representation abroad; and banned foreign travel by senior Taliban officials. Resolution 1363 provided for monitors in Pakistan to ensure that no weapons or military advice was provided to the Taliban.
- On January 10, 2003, President Bush signed a proclamation making Afghanistan a beneficiary of the Generalized System of Preferences (GSP), eliminating U.S. tariffs on 5,700 Afghan products. Afghanistan had been denied GSP on May 2, 1980, under Executive Order 12204 (45 F.R. 20740).
- On April 24, 1981, controls on U.S. exports to Afghanistan of agricultural products and phosphates were terminated. Such controls were imposed on June 3, 1980, as part of the sanctions against the Soviet Union for the invasion of Afghanistan, under the authority of Sections 5 and 6 of the Export Administration Act of 1979 [P.L. 96-72; 50 U.S.C. app. 2404, app. 2405].
- In mid-1992, the George H.W. Bush Administration determined that Afghanistan no longer had a "Soviet-controlled government." This opened Afghanistan to the use of U.S. funds made available for the U.S. share of U.N. organizations that provide assistance to Afghanistan.

Afghanistan

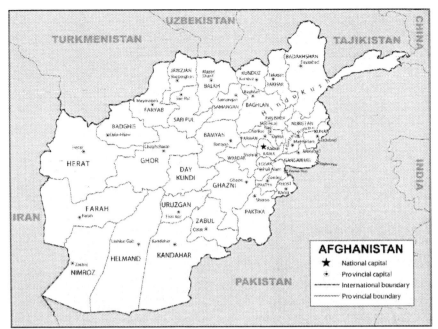

Source: Map Resources. Adapted by CRS.

Figure A-1. Map of Afghanistan.

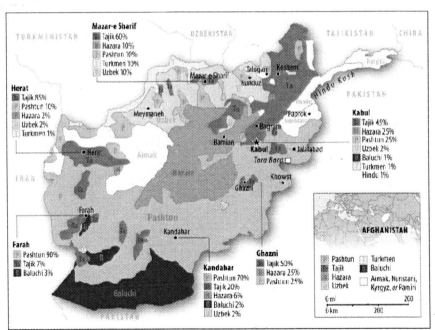

Source: 2003 National Geographic Society. http://www.afghan-network.net/maps/Afghanistan. Adapted by Amber Wilhelm, CRS Graphics.

Notes: This map is intended to be illustrative of the approximate demographic distribution by region of Afghanistan. CRS has no way to confirm exact population distributions.

Figure A-2. Map of Afghan Ethnicities.

- On March 31, 1993, after the fall of Najibullah in 1992, President Clinton, on national interest grounds, waived restrictions provided for in Section 481 (h) of the Foreign Assistance Act of 1961 mandating sanctions on Afghanistan, including bilateral aid cuts and suspensions, including denial of Ex-Im Bank credits; the casting of negative U.S. votes for multilateral development bank loans; and a non-allocation of a U.S. sugar quota. Discretionary sanctions included denial of GSP; additional duties on exports to the United States; and curtailment of air transportation with the United States. Waivers were also granted in 1994 and, after the fall of the Taliban, by President Bush.

- On May 3, 2002, President Bush restored normal trade treatment to the products of Afghanistan, reversing the February 18, 1986, proclamation by President Reagan (Presidential Proclamation 5437) that suspended most-favored nation (MFN) tariff status for Afghanistan (51 F.R. 4287). The Foreign Assistance Appropriations for FY1986 [Section 552, P.L. 99-190] had authorized the denial of U.S. credits or most-favored-nation (MFN) status for Afghanistan.

- On July 2, 2002, the State Department amended U.S. regulations (22 C.F.R. Part 126) to allow arms sales to the new Afghan government, reversing the June 14, 1996, addition of Afghanistan to the list of countries prohibited from importing U.S. defense articles and services. Arms sales to Afghanistan had also been prohibited during 1997-2002 because Afghanistan had been designated under the Antiterrorism and Effective Death Penalty Act of 1996 (P.L. 104-132) as a state that is not cooperating with U.S. anti-terrorism efforts.

- On July 2, 2002, President Bush formally revoked the July 4, 1999, declaration by President Clinton of a national emergency with respect to Taliban because of its hosting of bin Laden. The Clinton determination and related Executive Order 13129 had blocked Taliban assets and property in the United States, banned U.S. trade with Taliban-controlled areas of Afghanistan, and applied these sanctions to Ariana Afghan Airlines, triggering a blocking of Ariana assets (about $500,000) in the United States and a ban on U.S. citizens' flying on the airline. (The ban on trade with Taliban-controlled territory had essentially ended on January 29, 2002, when the State Department determination that the Taliban controls no territory within Afghanistan.).

End Notes

[1] Daoud's grave was discovered outside Kabul in early 2008. He was reburied in an official ceremony in Kabul in March 2009.

[2] For FY1991, Congress reportedly cut covert aid appropriations to the *mujahedin* from $300 million the previous year to $250 million, with half the aid withheld until the second half of the fiscal year. See "Country Fact Sheet: Afghanistan," in *U.S. Department of State Dispatch*, vol. 5, no. 23 (June 6, 1994), p. 377.

[3] After failing to flee, Najibullah, his brother, and aides remained at a U.N. facility in Kabul until the Taliban movement seized control in 1996 and hanged them.

[4] The Deobandi school began in 1867 in a seminary in Uttar Pradesh, in British-controlled India, that was set up to train Islamic clerics and to counter the British educational model.

[5] A pharmaceutical plant in Sudan (Al Shifa) believe to be producing chemical weapons for Al Qaeda also was struck that day, although U.S. reviews later corroborated Sudan's assertions that the plant was strictly civilian in nature.

[6] http://www.msnbc.msn.com/id/4540958.

[7] Drogin, Bob. "U.S. Had Plan for Covert Afghan Options Before 9/11." *Los Angeles Times*, May 18, 2002.

[8] Some Afghan sources refer to him by the name "Fahim Khan," or "Marshal Fahim."

[9] Another law (P.L. 107-148) established a "Radio Free Afghanistan" under RFE/RL, providing $17 million in funding for it for FY2002.

[10] In the process, Dostam captured Taliban fighters and imprisoned them in freight containers, causing many to suffocate. They were buried in a mass grave at *Dasht-e-Laili*. This issue is covered in CRS Report RS2 1922, *Afghanistan: Politics, Elections, and Government Performance*, by Kenneth Katzman.

[11] See also CRS Report RS21922, *Afghanistan: Politics, Elections, and Government Performance*, by Kenneth Katzman.

[12] A draft of the final communiqué of the Kabul Conference is at http://news.yahoo.com/s/ap /20100720.ap_on_re_as/as_afghanistan/print.

[13] Text of Bonn agreement at http://www.ag-afghanistan.de/files/petersberg.htm.

[14] The last pre-Karzai *loya jirga* that was widely recognized as legitimate was held in 1964 to ratify a constitution. Najibullah convened a *loya jirga* in 1987 to approve pro-Moscow policies, but that gathering was widely viewed by Afghans as illegitimate.

[15] Text of constitution: http://arabic.cnn.com/afghanistan/ConstitutionAfghanistan.pdf.

[16] Released by the Office of the Special Representative for Afghanistan and Pakistan, January 2010. http://www.state

[17] For a copy of the joint campaign plan, see: http://info.publicintelligence.net/0908eikenberryandmcchrystal.pdf.

[18] For text, see http://www.state

[19] For a detailed discussion and U.S. funding on the issue, see CRS Report RL32686, *Afghanistan: Narcotics and U.S. Policy*, by Christopher M. Blanchard.

[20] UNDOC. Opium Survey 2010. http://www.unodc.org/documents/cropmonitoring/ Afghanistan

[21] Crossette, Barbara. "Taliban Seem to Be Making Good on Opium Ban, U.N. Says." *New York Times*, February 7, 2001.

[22] Afghanistan had been so designated every year during 1987-2002.

[23] Some of the information in this section is taken from: Department of Defense. "Report on Progress Toward Security and Stability in Afghanistan." April 2010. http://www.defense.gov/pubs/pdfs/ Report_Final_SecDef_04_26_10.pdf.

[24] http://www.defense.gov/pubs/pdfs/Report_Final_SecDef_04_26_10.pdf.

[25] http://www.nytimes.com/2010/09/12/world/asia/12afghan.html?_r=1

[26] Maj. Gen. John Campbell, commander of RC-E, July 28, 2010, press briefing.

[27] Filkins, Dexter and Pir Zubair Shah. "After Arrests, Taliban Promote a Fighter." *New York Times*, March 25, 2010.

[28] Ibid.

[29] Text of the Panetta interview with ABC News is at http://abcnews.go.com/print?id=11025299.

[30] Dreazen, Yochi. "Al Qaida Returning to Afghanistan for New Attacks." Nationaljournal.com. October 18, 2010.

[31] Gall, Carlotta and Ismail Khan. "U.S. Drone Attack Missed Zawahiri by Hours." *New York Times*, November 10, 2006.

[32] Jane Perlez, Eric Schmitt, and Carlotta Gall, "Pakistan Is Said to Pursue Foothold in Afghanistan," *The New York Times*, June 24, 2010.

[33] "White Paper": http://www.whitehouse.gov/assets

[34] Commander NATO International Security Assistance Force, Afghanistan, and U.S. Forces, Afghanistan. "Commander's Initial Assessment." August 30, 2009, available at http://media documents/Ass essment_Redacted_092109.pdf?

[35] President Obama speech, op. cit. Testimony of Secretary Gates, Secretary Clinton, and Admiral Mullen before the Senate Armed Services Committee and the House Foreign Affairs Committee. December 2, 2009.

[36] See CRS Report R41084, *Afghanistan Casualties: Military Forces and Civilians*, by Susan G. Chesser.

[37] Commander NATO International Security Assistance Force, Afghanistan, and U.S. Forces, Afghanistan. "Commander's Initial Assessment." August 30, 2009, available at http://media documents/As sessment_Redacted_092109.pdf. White House. Remarks by the President In Address to the Nation on the Way Forward in Afghanistan and Pakistan. December 1, 2009; Chandrasekaran, Rajiv. "Differing Views of New Afghanistan Strategy." *Washington Post*, December 26, 2009.

[38] http://www.foreignpolicy.com/articles/2009/09/16/evaluating_progress_in_afghanistan_pakistan.

[39] Schmitt, Eric. "White House Is Struggling to Measure Success in Afghanistan". *New York Times*, August 7, 2009. Comments by Ambassador Holbrooke at seminar hosted by the Center for American Progress. August 12, 2009.

[40] Commander NATO International Security Assistance Force, Afghanistan, and U.S. Forces, Afghanistan. "Commander's Initial Assessment." August 30, 2009, available at http://media documents/Assessmen t_Redacted_092109.pdf. White House. Remarks by the President In Address to the Nation on the Way Forward in Afghanistan and Pakistan. December 1, 2009; Chandrasekaran, Rajiv. "Differing Views of New Afghanistan Strategy." *Washington Post*, December 26, 2009.

[41] Holbrooke interview on CNN, March 14, 2010, op. cit.

[42] Nissenbaum, Dion. "Marine Forward Operating Base Marjah Takes Root." McClatchy Newspapers, March 16, 2010.

[43] "U.S. Elite Units Step Up Effort in Afghan City." *New York Times*, April 26, 2010.

[44] Partlow, Joshua. "U.S. Seeks to Bolster Kandahar Governor, Upend Power Balance." *Washington Post*, April 29, 2010.

[45] See: http://afghanistan.hmg.gov.uk/en/conference

[46] Afghanistan National Security Council. "Afghanistan Peace and Reintegration Program." April 2010.

[47] For an analysis of the DDR program, see Christian Dennys. *Disarmament, Demobilization and Rearmament?*, June 6, 2005, http://www.jca.apc.org/~jann/Documents/Disarmament%20demobilization%20rearmament.pdf.

[48] Gall, Carlotta. Two Afghans Lose Posts Over Attack. *New York Times*, August 25, 2008.

[49] See http://merln.ndu.edu/archivepdf/afghanistan/WH/20050523-2.pdf.

[50] Twelve other countries provide forces to both OEF and ISAF.

[51] Its mandate was extended until October 13, 2006, by U.N. Security Council Resolution 1623 (September 13, 2005); and until October 13, 2007, by Resolution 1707 (September 12, 2006).

[52] Two were killed during their captivity. The Taliban kidnappers did not get the demanded release of 23 Taliban prisoners held by the Afghan government.

[53] For more information, see http://afghanistan.hmg.gov.uk/en/conference

[54] Kraul, Chris. "U.S. Aid Effort Wins Over Skeptics in Afghanistan." *Los Angeles Times*, April 11, 2003.

[55] Report by Richard Engel. NBC Nightly News. December 29, 2009.

[56] This argument is presented by State Dept. director of Policy Planning during the Bush Administration, now President of the Council on Foreign Relations Richard Haass in July 2010.http://www.newsweek.com/2010/07/18/we-re-notwinning-it-s-not-worth-it.html.

[57] Ibid.

[58] For extensive analysis of U.S. policy toward Pakistan, and U.S. assistance to Pakistan in conjunction with its activities against Al Qaeda and the Taliban, see CRS Report RL3 3498, *Pakistan-U.S. Relations*, by K. Alan Kronstadt.

[59] Mazzetti, Mark and Eric Schmitt. "CIA Outlines Pakistan Links With Militants." *New York Times*, July 30, 2008.

[60] Partlow, Joshua. "Afghans Build Up Ties With Pakistan." *Washington Post*, July 21, 2010.

[61] Among those captured by Pakistan are top bin Laden aide Abu Zubaydah (captured April 2002); alleged September 11 plotter Ramzi bin Al Shibh (September 11, 2002); top Al Qaeda planner Khalid Shaikh Mohammed (March 2003); and a top planner, Abu Faraj al-Libbi (May 2005).

[62] CRS Report RL34763, *Islamist Militancy in the Pakistan-Afghanistan Border Region and U.S. Policy*, by K. Alan Kronstadt and Kenneth Katzman.

[63] Ignatius, David. "A Chance to Engage Iran?" *Washington Post*, September 17, 2010.

[64] Rashid, Ahmed. "Afghan Neighbors Show Signs of Aiding in Nation's Stability." *Wall Street Journal*, October 18, 2004.

[65] Treasury Department. Fact Sheet: U.S. Treasury Department Targets Iran's Support for Terrorism. August 3, 2010.

[66] Comments by President Karzai at the Brookings Institution. May 5, 2009.

[67] Iranian economic and political influence efforts in Herat were discussed in a CRS visit to Herat in October 2009.

[68] King, Laura. "In Western Afghan City, Iran Makes Itself Felt." *Los Angeles Times*, November 14, 2010.

[69] Steele, Jonathon, "America Includes Iran in Talks on Ending War in Afghanistan." *Washington Times*, December 15, 1997.

[70] Risen, James. "Russians Are Back in Afghanistan, Aiding Rebels." *New York Times*, July 27, 1998.

[71] The IMU was named a foreign terrorist organization by the State Department in September 2000.

[72] For more information, see CRS Report RL33001, *U.S.-China Counterterrorism Cooperation: Issues for U.S. Policy*, by Shirley A. Kan.

[73] CRS conversations with Chinese officials in Beijing. August 2007.

[74] http://www.sigar.mil/pdf/peer_review/Section5.pdf.

[75] Lemmon, Gayle Tzemach. "New Hope for Afghan Raisin Farmers." New York Times, October 9, 2010.

[76] Risen, James. "U.S. Identifies Mineral Riches in Afghanistan." *New York Times*, June 14, 2010.

[77] Other participants in the Unocal consortium include Delta of Saudi Arabia, Hyundai of South Korea, Crescent Steel of Pakistan, Itochu Corporation and INPEX of Japan, and the government of Turkmenistan. Some accounts say Russia's Gazprom would probably receive a stake in the project. *Nezavisimaya Gazeta* (Moscow), October 30, 1997, p. 3.

[78] Saleem, Farrukh. "Where Are the Missing Stinger Missiles? Pakistan," *Friday Times*. August 17-23, 2001.

[79] Fullerton, John. "Afghan Authorities Hand in Stinger Missiles to U.S." Reuters, February 4, 2002.

[80] "Afghanistan Report," Radio Free Europe/Radio Liberty. February 4, 2005.

[81] "U.S.-Made Stinger Missiles—Mobile and Lethal." Reuters, May 28, 1999.

In: Fragile Mideast Countries: Afghanistan and Yemen
Editors: Robert P. Deen and Allison D. Burken

ISBN: 978-1-61209-709-1
© 2011 Nova Science Publishers, Inc.

Chapter 2

AFGHANISTAN: POLITICS, ELECTIONS, AND GOVERNMENT PERFORMANCE

Kenneth Katzman

SUMMARY

The limited capacity and widespread corruption of all levels of Afghan governance are growing factors in debate over the effectiveness of U.S. strategy in Afghanistan, although Afghan governing capacity has increased significantly since the Taliban regime fell in late 2001. In a December 1, 2009, policy statement on Afghanistan, which followed the second major Afghanistan strategy review in 2009, President Obama stated that "the days of providing a blank check [to the Afghan government] are over." During 2010, the Administration has been pressing President Hamid Karzai to move more decisively to address corruption within his government, with mixed success. Karzai has agreed to cooperate with U.S.-led efforts to build the capacity of several emerging anti-corruption institutions, but these same institutions have sometimes caused a Karzai backlash when they have targeted his allies or relatives. Purportedly suspicious that U.S. and other donors are trying to undermine his leadership, Karzai has strengthened his bonds to ethnic and political faction leaders who are often involved in illicit economic activity and who undermine rule of law. Some of the effects of corruption burst into public view in August 2010 when major losses were announced by the large Kabul Bank, in part due to large loans to major shareholders, many of whom are close to Karzai. Addressing U.S. public complaints that U.S. lives are being lost in part to defend a corrupt government, some in Congress have sought to link further U.S. aid to clearer progress on the corruption issue.

The disputes with Karzai over corruption compound continuing international concerns about Afghan democracy and political transparency. In the August 20, 2009, presidential election, there were widespread charges of fraud, many substantiated by an Electoral Complaints Commission (ECC). The ECC invalidated nearly one-third of President Karzai's votes, although Karzai's main challenger dropped out of a runoff and Karzai was declared the winner. He subsequently faced opposition to many of his cabinet nominees by the elected lower house of parliament, and seven permanent ministerial posts remain unfilled. Many of the flaws that plagued the 2009 election recurred in the parliamentary elections held September 18, 2010. However, the alleged fraud is purportedly being addressed more openly and transparently. Final results were to be announced October 30, but have been delayed by complaint investigation requirements. The security situation complicated campaigning and the voting, to some extent, but did not derail the election.

Electoral competition aside, there is growing ethnic and political fragmentation over the terms of a potential settlement to the conflict in Afghanistan. Some leaders of minority communities boycotted a June 24, 2010, "consultative peace *jirga* (assembly)" in Kabul that endorsed Karzai's plan to reintegrate into society insurgents willing to end their fight against the government. However, Karzai has named a senior Tajik leader as chair of the 68-member High Peace Council that is to approve any settlement, if one is reached. Women, who have made substantial gains (including appointment to cabinet posts and governorships and election to parliament) fear their rights may be eroded under any "deal" that might put the Taliban in control of territory or agree to change Afghanistan's constitution and erode protections for women. For more information, see CRS Report RL30588, *Afghanistan: Post-Taliban Governance, Security, and U.S. Policy*, by Kenneth Katzman; CRS Report R40747, *United Nations Assistance Mission in Afghanistan: Background and Policy Issues*, by Rhoda Margesson; and CRS Report R41484, *Afghanistan: U.S. Rule of Law and Justice Sector Assistance*, by Liana Sun Wyler and Kenneth Katzman

POST-TALIBAN TRANSITION AND POLITICAL LANDSCAPE

In implementing policy to stabilize Afghanistan, a U.S. policy priority has been to increase the capabilities of and extend the authority of Afghanistan's government. The policy was predicated on the observation that weak governance was causing some Afghans to acquiesce to, or even support, Taliban insurgents as providers of security and traditional justice. Since 2007, in line with the perception that weak and corrupt governance was contributing to insurgent gains, the U.S. and Afghan focus has been on reforming and reducing corruption within the central government, and on expanding local governance. Then-head of the U.N. Assistance Mission Afghanistan (UNAMA) Kai Eide said in a departing news conference on March 4, 2010, that improving governance and political processes are "indispensable" for resolving the conflict in Afghanistan, and that U.S. and partner efforts have focused too much on military approaches. Eide was succeeded by Staffan de Mistura in March 2010; his substantive position on the issue is similar.

Overview of Afghan Politics and Governance

Through differing regimes of widely varying ideologies, Afghanistan's governing structure has historically consisted of weak central government unwilling or unable to enforce significant financial or administrative mandates on the 80% of Afghans who live in rural areas. The tribal, clan, village, and district political structures that provided governance and security until the late 1970s were weakened by over 20 years of subsequent war. Some traditional local authority figures fled or were killed; others were displaced by *mujahedin* commanders, militia leaders, and others. These local power brokers are widely accused of selectively applying Afghan law and have resisted ceding any influence. In other cases, traditional tribal councils have remained intact, and continue to exercise their writ rather than accept the authority of local government. Still other community authorities prefer to accommodate local insurgent commanders (who are seen as wayward members of the community) rather than help the government secure their areas.

At the national level, Afghanistan had few, if any, Western-style democratic institutions prior to the international intervention that took place after the September 11, 2001, attacks on the United States. Karzai is the first directly elected president in Afghan history. There were parliamentary elections during the reign of King Zahir Shah (the last were in 1969, before his reign was ended in a 1973 military coup), but the parliament during that era was not the check on presidential power that the post-Taliban National Assembly has. The elected institutions and the 2004 adoption of a constitution were part of a post-Taliban transition roadmap established by a United Nations-sponsored agreement of major Afghan factions signed in Bonn, Germany, on December 5, 2001, ("Bonn Agreement"),[1] after the Taliban had fallen. The political transition process is depicted in **Table 1**.

Some believe that the elements of Western-style democracy introduced since 2001 are supported by traditional Afghan patterns of decision making that have some democratic and representative elements. On the other hand, some see the traditional patterns as competing mechanisms that resist change and modernization, generally minimize the role of women, and do not meet international standards of democratic governance. At the national level, the convening of a loya *jirga*, or traditional Afghan assembly consisting of about 1,500 delegates from all over Afghanistan, has been used on several occasions. In the post-Taliban period, *Loya jirgas* have been convened to endorse Karzai's leadership, to adopt a constitution, and to back long-term defense relations with the United States. A major peace *jirga* was held on June 2-4, 2010, to review government plans to offer incentives for insurgent fighters to end their armed struggle and rejoin society. At the local level, shuras, or *jirga*s (consultative councils)[2] composed of local notables, are key mechanisms for making authoritative community decisions or dispensing justice. Some of these mechanisms are practiced by Taliban members in areas under their control.

Affiliations Based on Ethnicity, Tribal, and Personal Relations

Patterns of political affiliation by family, clan, tribe, village, ethnicity, region, and other relationships remain. These patterns were evident in the August 20, 2009, presidential campaign in Afghanistan. Many presidential candidates, Karzai included, pursued campaign strategies designed primarily to assemble blocs of ethnic and geographic votes, rather than advance specific new ideas. These patterns were more pronounced in campaigns for the provincial councils, which were elected concurrently, and appear to have been evident again in the September 18, 2010, parliamentary election. In these cases, electorates (the eligible voters of a specific province) are small and candidates can easily appeal to clan and familial relationships.

While Afghans continue to follow traditional patterns of affiliation, there has been a sense among Afghans that their country now welcomes members of all political and ethnic groups and factions. There have been very few incidents of ethnic-based violence since the fall of the Taliban, but jealousies over relative economic and political positions of the different ethnic communities have sporadically manifested as clashes or political disputes.

Ethnic Pashtuns (sometimes referred to as Pathans—pronounced pah-TAHNS), as the largest single ethnicity, have historically asserted a right to rule. Pashtuns are about 42% of the population and, with few exceptions, have governed Afghanistan. The sentiment of the "right to lead" is particularly strong among Pashtuns of the Durrani tribal confederation, which predominates in the south and is a rival to the Ghilzai confederation, which predominates in the east. One recent exception was the 1992-1996 presidency of the *mujahedin* government of Burhanuddin Rabbani, a Tajik. Karzai is a Durrani Pashtun, and his cabinet and inner advisory circle has come to be progressively dominated by Pashtuns and to exclude members of the other communities. The Taliban government was and its insurgency is composed almost completely of Pashtuns, although there have been non-Pashtun rebel factions with given names such as "Tajik Taliban" to denote that they are working against the Karzai government. A table on major Pashtun clans is provided below (see Table 2), as is a map showing the distribution of Afghanistan's various ethnicities (see Figure 1).

The Ethnic Politics of the Security Sector/Security Issues

Although they largely concede Pashtun rule, non-Pashtuns want to be and are represented at high levels of the central government. Non-Pashtuns also have achieved a large measure of control over how government programs are implemented in their geographic regions. The security organs are considered an arena where Pashtuns and Tajiks have worked together relatively well. The National Directorate for Security (NDS, the intelligence directorate) was headed by a nonPashtun (Amrollah Saleh, a Tajik) during 2006-2010, although he was dismissed on June 6, 2010, by Karzai for disagreements over whether and how to engage insurgent leaders in political settlement negotiations. He was replaced by a Pashtun, Rehmat Nabil, who has no previous intelligence experience but is perceived as more consultative than was Saleh. Still, he inherited a service dominated by Tajiks (although some left when Saleh was ousted) and by a mix of personnel that served during the Soviet occupation era (the service was then called Khad), and in the *mujahedin* government of 1992-1996, as well as more recent recruits. During 2002-2007, the Central Intelligence Agency reportedly paid for all of the NDS budget.[3]

Perhaps to restore the tradition of ethnic balance in the security sector of government, the chief of staff of the Afghan National Army, Bismillah Khan (a Tajik), was named interior minister on June 26, 2010. He replaced Mohammad Hanif Atmar, a Pashtun, who was fired the same day and on roughly the same grounds as Saleh. The security ministries tend to have key deputies who are of a different ethnicity than the minister or top official.

There is also a National Security Council that is located in the palace complex and advises Karzai. As of February 2010, it has been headed by former Foreign Minister Rangin Spanta, a Pashtun who was in the government during the Soviet occupation era and is said to retain leftwing views. The NSC is dominated by Pashtuns; two high officials trusted by Karzai there are Ibrahim Spinzadeh, first deputy NSC adviser, and Shaida Mohammad Abdali, the second deputy NSC adviser (both are Pashtuns).

Karzai's chief of staff is Mohammad Umar Daudzai, who is considered an Islamic conservative. During the anti-Soviet war, he fought in the Pashtun Islamist faction of Gulbuddin Hikmatyar. Daudzai is said to be a skeptic of Western/U.S. influence over Afghan decision making. On October 23, 2010, the *New York Times* asserted that he has been the presidential office's liaison with Iran for accepting the approximately $2 million per year in Iranian assistance that is provided as cash. Karzai acknowledged this financial arrangement.

Some observers take a different view, asserting that Tajiks continue to control many of the command ranks of the Afghan security institutions, giving Pashtuns only a veneer of control of these organizations. U.S. commanders in Afghanistan say the composition of the national security forces—primarily the Afghan National Army and Afghan National Police—has recently been brought more into line with the population, although Pashtuns from the south (Durranis) remain underrepresented.

Others believe that ethnic differences may be on the verge of erupting over a key security issue— Karzai's plan to try to induce both low-level and leading insurgent figures to end their fight and rejoin society (reintegration and reconciliation), perhaps even in prominent posts. Tajik leaders, in particular, as the most prominent group after the Pashtuns, fear that Karzai's plans will increase the Pashtun predominance in government and lead to marginalization of the Tajiks and other nonPashtun minorities. They also assert—and ousted NDS chief Saleh has reportedly been giving speeches in Tajik areas making this point extensively—that Karzai is now willing to turn over Afghanistan to undue influence from Pakistan. In part to mollify this ethnic unrest on this issue, in September 2010 Karzai appointed a 68-member broad based High Peace Council that would oversee any negotiations with Taliban leaders. Former President Burhanuddin Rabbani, the most senior Tajik faction leader, was appointed Council chairman on October 10, 2010.

Pakistan supports Afghanistan's Pashtun community, and purportedly wants some insurgent factions to come into a post-settlement government. The growing rift over the reconciliation issue has alarmed Pakistan's rival India and, to a lesser extent, Iran, who traditionally support the Tajik, Uzbek, and Hazara communities and see Afghanistan's Pashtuns as surrogates of Pakistan. (For more information on the topic of reconciliation talks with insurgent leaders, see CRS Report RL30588, *Afghanistan: Post-Taliban Governance, Security*, and U.S. Policy, by Kenneth Katzman.)

Lack of Affiliation by Party

The major factions in Afghanistan identify only loosely with Afghanistan's 110 registered political parties. There is a popular aversion to formal "parties" as historically tools of neighboring powers—a perception stemming from the war against the Soviet Union when seven *mujahedin* parties were funded by and considered tools of outside parties. Partly because parties are viewed with suspicion, Karzai has not formed his own party. Others say that parties are weak because the Single, Non-Transferable Vote (SNTV) system—in which each voter casts a ballot for only one candidate—favors candidates running as independents rather than as members of parties. Moreover, Western-style parties are generally identified by specific ideologies, ideas, or ideals, while most Afghans, as discussed above, retain their traditional affiliations. The larger parties that do exist, for example the Junbush Melli of Abdul Rashid Dostam, tend to be identified with specific ethnic (in his case, Uzbeks) or sectarian factions, rather than overarching themes.

Politics: Karzai, His Allies, and His Opponents

In post-Taliban Afghanistan, the National Assembly (parliament)—particularly the 249-seat elected lower house (*Wolesi Jirga*, House of the People)—has been the key institution for nonPashtuns and political independents to exert influence on Karzai. The process of confirming Karzai's second-term cabinet—in which many of Karzai's nominees were voted down in several nomination rounds—demonstrates that the Assembly is an increasingly strong institution that is pressing for honest, competent governance. These principles are advocated most stridently, although not exclusively, by the younger, more technocratic independent bloc in the lower house. These independents were key to the lower house vote on March 31, 2010, to reject an election decree that would structure the holding of September 18, 2010, National Assembly elections.

This institutional development has come despite the fact that about one-third of the seats in the lower house are held by personalities and factions prominent in Afghanistan's recent wars, many of whom are non-Pashtuns from the north and the west. Karzai and his allies were hoping that the September 18, 2010, parliamentary elections would produce an increase in pro-Karzai members. Both houses of parliament, whose budgets are controlled by the Ministry of Finance, are staffed by about 275 Afghans, reporting to a "secretariat." There are 18 oversight committees, a research unit, and a library.

Pro-Karzai Factions in the Outgoing Parliament

Karzai's core supporters in the outgoing *Wolesi Jirga*, which he and his aides hoped to increase in the September 18, 2010, elections, have been about 50 former members of the conservative Pashtun-based Hizb-e-Islam party (the same party as that headed by insurgent leader Gulbuddin Hikmatyar); and supporters of Abd-i-Rab Rasul Sayyaf—a prominent Islamic conservative *mujahedin* era party leader.[4] Karzai's allies reportedly hope that they would win enough additional seats in the September 18 election to enable Sayyaf to become lower house Speaker, displacing Yunus Qanooni (Tajik); see below. However, it is not certain that pro-Karzai deputies will increase in the newly elected Assembly.

Another base of Karzai's support have been figures from Qandahar (Karzai's home province) and Helmand provinces, including several Karzai clan members. One clan member in the parliament is his cousin Jamil Karzai, and another is relative by marriage Aref Nurzai, who was prominent in Karzai's 2009 election campaign. Karzai's elder brother, Qayyum, was in the lower house representing Qandahar until his October 2008 resignation, although he retains continued influence in Afghanistan. Other pro-Karzai Pashtuns in the outgoing parliament are former militia and Taliban leaders, including Hazrat Ali (Nangarhar Province), who led the Afghan component of the failed assault on Osama bin Laden's purported redoubt at Tora Bora in December 2001; Pacha Khan Zadran (Paktia) who, by some accounts, helped Osama bin Laden escape Tora Bora; and Mullah Abdul Salam ("Mullah Rocketi"), from Zabol. (Salam ran unsuccessfully for president in 2009.) A key Karzai brother, discussed further below, is Ahmad Wali Karzai, who purportedly worked to try to ensure that pro-Karzai Assembly candidates were elected in Qandahar Province, but it is not clear that this effort succeeded.

The Opposition: Dr. Abdullah and His Lower House Supporters

Although the political opposition to Karzai is fluid and often joins him on some issues, those who can be considered opposition (putting aside Taliban and other insurgents) are mainly ethnic minorities (Tajik, Uzbek, and Hazara) who were in an anti-Taliban grouping called the "Northern Alliance." Leaders of these groups, and particularly Tajiks, view as a betrayal Karzai's firing of many of the non-Pashtuns from the cabinet and, as noted, are increasingly concerned about Karzai's outreach to Taliban figures and to Pakistan (including his meetings with Pakistan's military leader and the director of its intelligence service).

The overall "leader of the opposition" is former Foreign Minister Dr. Abdullah Abdullah, who is about 50 years old and whose mother is Tajik and father is Pashtun. His identity as a key aide to the slain Tajik *mujahedin* commander Ahmad Shah Masoud causes him to be identified politically as a Tajik. He was dismissed from that post by Karzai in March 2006 and now heads a private foundation named after Masoud. He emerged as Afghanistan's opposition leader after his unsuccessful challenge against Karzai for president in the August 2009 election in which widespread fraud was demonstrated. He visited Washington, DC, one week after Karzai's May 10-14, 2010, visit, criticizing Karzai's governance at various think tanks and in a meeting with the State Department. Dr. Abdullah subsequently declined to attend the June 2-4, 2010, peace *jirga* in Kabul on the grounds that the 1,600 delegates were not representative of all Afghans, implying that it would be overwhelmingly run and dominated by Pashtuns. He announced in late May 2010 that he has begun laying groundwork to create a formal, national democratic opposition organization called the "Hope and Change Movement."

Dr. Abdullah's main base of support within the National Assembly is called the United Front (UF), although some accounts refer to it as the "National Front" or "United National Front." It was formed in April 2007 by *Wolesi Jirga* Speaker Yunus Qanooni (Karzai's main challenger in the 2004 presidential election) and former Afghan President Burhanuddin Rabbani (both also prominent ethnic Tajik Northern Alliance figures and former associates of the legendary *mujahedin* commander Ahmad Shah Masood. Rabbani remains titular head of the *mujahedin* party to which Masoud belonged—*Jamiat Islami*, or Islamic Society).

Although not aimed at mass appeal as is Dr. Abdullah's Hope and Change Movement, the United Front is nonetheless broader than the "Northern Alliance" in that the Front includes some Pashtuns. Examples include Soviet-occupation era security figures Sayed Muhammad Gulabzoi and Nur ul-Haq Ulumi, who has chaired the defense committee. Even before the debate over the terms of any settlement with the Taliban escalated in 2010, the UF advocated amending the constitution to give more power to parliament and to empower the elected provincial councils (instead of the president) to select governors and mayors. Such steps would ensure maximum autonomy from Kabul for non-Pashtun areas, and serve as a check and balance on Pashtun dominance of the central government. Running in the September 18, 2010, elections under Dr. Abdullah's Hope and Change Movement banner, Abdullah supporters sought to nearly double their numbers in the new Assembly from about 50 in the outgoing one. The bloc seeks to hold a commanding position that would enable it to block Karzai initiatives and possibly even obtain passage of its own alternative proposals. However, it is not clear that this objective was achieved.

Even before the formation of the UF, the opposition in the *Wolesi Jirga* first showed its strength in March 2006, following the December 19, 2005, inauguration of parliament, by requiring Karzai's cabinet to be approved individually, rather than *en bloc*, increasing opposition leverage. However, Karzai rallied his support and all but 5 of the 25 nominees were confirmed. In May 2006, the opposition compelled Karzai to change the nine-member Supreme Court, the highest judicial body, including ousting 74-year-old Islamic conservative Fazl Hadi Shinwari as chief justice. The proximate justification for the ouster was Shinwari's age, which was beyond the official retirement age of 65. (Shinwari later went on to head the Ulema Council, Afghanistan's highest religious body.) Parliament approved Karzai's new court choices in July 2006, all of whom are trained in modern jurisprudence.

Lower House Independents

Karzai and the UF have often competed for the support of the "independents" in the lower house. Among them are several outspoken women, intellectuals, and business leaders, such as the 43- year-old Malalai Joya (Farah Province), a leading critic of war-era faction leaders. In May 2007 the lower house voted to suspend her for this criticism for the duration of her term. Others in this camp include Ms. Fauzia Gailani (Herat Province); Ms. Shukria Barekzai, editor of *Woman Mirror* magazine; and Mr. Ramazan Bashardost, a former Karzai minister who champions parliamentary powers and has established a "complaints tent" near the parliament building to highlight and combat official corruption. (He ran for president in the 2009 elections on an anticorruption platform and drew an unexpectedly large amount of votes.) U.S.-based International Republican Institute (IRI) has helped train the independents; the National Democratic Institute (NDI) has assisted the more established factions.

The Upper House

Karzai has relatively fewer critics in the 102-seat *Meshrano Jirga* (House of Elder, upper house), partly because of his bloc of 34 appointments (one-third of that body). He engineered the appointment of an ally as speaker: Sibghatullah Mojadeddi, a noted Islamic scholar and former *mujahedin* party leader (Afghanistan National Liberation Front, ANLF), who headed the post- Communist *mujahedin* government for one month (May 1992). However, because it is composed of more elderly, established, notable Afghans who are traditionalist in their political outlook, the upper house has tended to be more Islamist conservative than the lower house, advocating a legal system that accords with Islamic law, and restrictions on press and Westernized media broadcasts. As an example of the upper house's greater support for Karzai, it voted on April 3, 2010, not to act on the election decree that the lower house had rejected on March 31, 2010, meaning that the decree applied to the September 18 parliamentary election.

Karzai also has used his bloc of appointments to the upper house to co-opt potential antagonists or reward his friends. He appointed Northern Alliance military leader Muhammad Fahim to the upper body, perhaps to compensate for his removal as defense minister, although he resigned after a few months and later joined the UF. (He was Karzai's primary running mate in the 2009 elections and is now a vice president.) Karzai named a key ally, former Helmand governor Sher Mohammad Akhunzadeh, to the body. There is one Hindu, and 23 women; 17 are Karzai appointees and six were selected in their own right.

A new upper house will be named after the results of the lower house elections are finalized. Karzai will appoint 34 members, and the provincial councils that were elected in 2009 will appoint a total of 68 members (two per province).

ENHANCING GOVERNMENT CAPACITY AND PERFORMANCE[5]

Since 2001, U.S. policy has been to help expand the capacity of Afghan institutions, which were nearly non-existent during Taliban rule. At the time of the fall of the Taliban in late 2001, Afghan government offices were minimally staffed, and virtually none had computer or other modern equipment, according to observers in Kabul. Since 2007, but with particular focus during the Obama Administration, U.S. policy has been to not only try to expand Afghan governing capacity—at the central and local levels—but to push for its reform and oversight. In two major Afghanistan policy addresses—March 27, 2009, and December 1, 2009—President Obama stressed that more needed to be done to promote the legitimacy and effectiveness of the Afghan government at both the Kabul and local levels. In the latter statement, he said: "The days of providing a blank check [to the Afghan government] are over."

U.S.-Karzai Relations

U.S. relations with President Hamid Karzai, and U.S. assessments of his performance, are key to U.S. efforts to implement its stabilization strategy. During 2010, Obama Administration criticism of the shortcomings of the Karzai government, particularly its corruption, have caused substantial frictions in U.S.-Karzai relations. Continuing U.S. concerns prompted President Obama to make anti-corruption efforts a particular focus of his talks with President Karzai in Kabul on March 28, 2010. Karzai's frustrations at what he sees as U.S. and international pressure on him to reform emerged in his comments on April 1, 2010, and April 4, 2010, both to groups of Afghans. On both occasions, and the latter of which was to National Assembly members, Karzai expressed frustration with what he claims was international meddling in the August 20, 2009, presidential election and, more generally, what he sees as his subordination to the decisions of Afghanistan's international partners. The April 4, 2010, comments were more specifically critical of the United States and suggested that Western meddling in Afghanistan was fueling support for the Taliban as a legitimate resistance to foreign occupation. (An exact English translation of his April 4 comments, in which he purportedly said that even he might consider joining the Taliban if U.S. pressure on him continues, is not available.) White House spokesperson Robert Gibbs said on April 6, 2010, that the May 10-14, 2010, Karzai visit to Washington, DC, might be called off if Karzai continued to make similar remarks. The visit did go forward and was widely considered productive, including a decision to review, renew, and expand a 2005 "strategic partnership" that would reflect a long-term U.S. commitment to Afghanistan.[6] Karzai also has taken exception to U.S. press reports that he is on mood-altering or other medication designed to treat psychological ailments; he denies the reports categorically.

At each downturn in the relationship, top Obama Administration officials, including Secretary of Defense Gates, Secretary of State Clinton, and General David Petraeus, have tended to issue comments apparently designed to restore the relationship.[7] Administration officials praised Karzai for holding the June 2-4, 2010, *loya jirga* on reintegration of insurgents and for recommitting to specific reform steps at the international conference in Kabul on July 20, 2010.

Still, press reports assert that differences remain within the Administration over whether to confront Karzai more forcefully to implement reform pledges. A perception has persisted that Karzai's closest U.S. interlocutors are the top U.S. military representatives in Afghanistan (then- top commander in Afghanistan, General Stanley McChrystal, and now, General David Petraeus). Karzai reiterated that he has had very good relations with these two top U.S. and NATO commanders in an interview with Larry King on October 11, 2010. Karzai's relations with Special Representative for Afghanistan and Pakistan (SRAP) Richard Holbrooke, and with Ambassador Eikenberry, are widely assessed as severely strained, although Holbrooke denied this in an October 22, 2010, State Department briefing. The perception has been fed by numerous reports and comments by observers that said that Holbrooke and Eikenberry, reportedly backed by Vice President Biden and, to a certain extent, President Obama, believe in the efficacy of public U.S. pressure on Karzai. In public statements, General Petraeus has stressed that Karzai is president of a sovereign country and his support and partnership is required in order to successfully implement U.S. strategy.

The Influences of Regional Faction Leaders/"Warlords

A significant international concern about Afghan governance is Karzai's willingness to sometimes ally with unelected or well-armed faction leaders. Most of these leaders are from the north and west, where non-Pashtun minorities predominate, but there are some major Pashtun faction leaders that Karzai has become dependent upon as well. The Obama Administration's March 27, 2009, and December 1, 2009, strategy statements did not outline new measures to sideline these strongmen, who are sometimes referred to by experts and others as "warlords." General McChrystal's August 2009 "initial assessment," cited below, indicated that some of these faction leaders—most of whom the United States and its partners regularly deal with and have good working relations with—cause resentment among some sectors of the population and complicate U.S. stabilization strategy. A number of them are alleged to own or have equity in security or other Afghan firms that have won business from various U.S. and other donor agencies and fuel allegations of nepotism and other forms of corruption. On the other hand, some Afghans and outside experts believe that the international community's strategy of dismantling local power structures, particularly in northern Afghanistan, and instead to empower the central government, has caused the security deterioration noted since 2006.

Some assert that the Obama Administration's criticism of Karzai has caused him to become ever more reliant on these factional power brokers. Karzai's position is that confronting faction leaders outright would likely cause their followers—who usually belong to ethnic or regional minorities—to go into armed rebellion. Even before the Obama Administration came into office, Karzai argued that keeping the faction leaders on the government side is needed in order to keep the focus on fighting "unrepentant" Taliban insurgents (who are almost all ethnic Pashtuns).

In February 2007, both houses passed a law giving amnesty to faction leaders and others who committed abuses during Afghanistan's past wars. Karzai altered the draft to give victims the right to seek justice for any abuses; Karzai did not sign a modified version in May 2007, leaving the status unclear. However, in November 2009, the Afghan government

Afghanistan: Politics, Elections, and Government Performance 99

published the law in the official gazette (a process known as "gazetting"), giving it the force of law.

The following sections analyze some of the main faction leaders who often attract criticism and commentary from U.S. and international partners in Afghanistan.

Vice President Muhammad Fahim

Karzai's choice of Muhammad Fahim, a Tajik from the Panjshir Valley region who is military chief of the Northern Alliance/UF faction, as his first vice presidential running mate in the August 2009 elections might have been a manifestation of Karzai's growing reliance on faction leaders. Dividing the United Front/ Northern Alliance might have been another. The Fahim choice was criticized by human rights and other groups because of Fahim's long identity as a *mujahedin* commander/militia faction leader. A *New York Times* story of August 27, 2009, said that the Bush Administration continued to deal with Fahim when he was defense minister (2001-2004) despite reports that he was involved in facilitating narcotics trafficking in northern Afghanistan. Other allegations suggest he has engineered property confiscations and other benefits to feed his and his faction's business interests. During 2002-2007, he also reportedly withheld turning over some heavy weapons to U.N. disarmament officials who have been trying to reduce the influence of local strongmen such as Fahim. Obama Administration officials have not announced any limitations on dealings with Fahim now that he is vice president. In August 2010, NDS director Nabil appointed a Fahim relative to a senior NDS position. As of August 2010, Fahim has been undergoing treatment in Germany for a heart ailment. His ailment coincides with the accusations that his brother was a beneficiary of concessionary loans from Kabul Bank, a major bank that has faced major losses due to its lending practices and may need to be recapitalized (see below).

Abdurrashid Dostam: Uzbeks of Northern Afghanistan—Jowzjan, Faryab, Sar-i-Pol, and Balkh Provinces

Some observers have cited Karzai's handling of prominent Uzbek leader Abdurrashid Dostam as evidence of political weakness. Dostam commands numerous partisans in his redoubt in northern Afghanistan (Jowzjan, Faryab, Balkh, and Sar-I-Pol provinces), where he was, during the Soviet and Taliban years, widely accused of human rights abuses of political opponents. To try to separate him from his armed followers, in 2005 Karzai appointed him to the post of chief of staff of the armed forces. On February 4, 2008, Afghan police surrounded Dostam's villa in Kabul in response to reports that he attacked an ethnic Turkmen rival, but Karzai did not order his arrest for fear of stirring unrest among Dostam's followers. To try to resolve the issue without stirring unrest, in December 2008 Karzai purportedly reached an agreement with Dostam under which he resigned as chief of staff and went into exile in Turkey in exchange for the dropping of any case against him.[8]

Dostam returned to Afghanistan on August 16, 2009, and subsequently held a large pro-Karzai election rally in his home city of Shebergan. Part of his intent in supporting Karzai has been to potentially oust a strong rival figure in the north, Balkh Province governor Atta Mohammad, see below. Mohammad is a Tajik but, under a 2005 compromise with Karzai, is in control of a province that is inhabited by many Uzbeks—a source of irritation for Dostam and other Uzbeks. Dostam's support apparently helped Karzai carry several provinces in the north, including Jowzjan, Sar-i-Pol, and Faryab, although Dr. Abdullah won Balkh and

Samangan. Dostam was not nominated to the post-election cabinet, but two members of his "Junbush Melli" (National Front) party were—although they were voted down by the National Assembly because the Assembly insisted on competent officials rather than party loyalists in the new cabinet. Dostam returned to Afghanistan in January 2010 and was restored to his previous, primarily honorary, position of chief of staff of the armed forces.

Dostam's reputation is further clouded by his actions during the U.S.-backed war against the Taliban. On July 11, 2009, the New York Times reported that allegations that Dostam had caused the death of several hundred Taliban prisoners during the major combat phase of OEF (late 2001) were not investigated by the Bush Administration. In responding to assertions that there was no investigation of the "*Dasht-e-Laili*" massacre because Dostam was a U.S. ally,[9] President Obama said any allegations of violations of laws of war need to be investigated. Dostam responded to Radio Free Europe/Radio Liberty (which carried the story) that only 200 Taliban prisoners died and primarily because of combat and disease, not intentional actions of his forces.

Atta Mohammad Noor: Balkh Province

Atta Mohammad Noor, who is about 47 years old, has been the governor of Balkh Province, whose capital is the vibrant city of Mazar-e-Sharif, since 2005. He is an ethnic Tajik and former *mujahedin* commander who openly endorsed Dr. Abdullah in the 2009 presidential election. However, Karzai has kept Noor in place because he has kept the province secure, allowing Mazar-e-Sharif to become a major trading hub, and because displacing him could cause ethnic unrest. Observers say that Noor exemplifies the local potentate, brokering local security and business arrangements that enrich Noor and his allies while ensuring stability and prosperity.[10]

Isma'il Khan: Western Afghanistan/Herat

Another strongman that Karzai has sought to simultaneously engage and weaken is prominent Tajik political leader and former Herat governor Ismail Khan. In 2006, Karzai appointed him minister of energy and water, taking him away from his political base in the west. However, Khan remains influential there, and maintaining ties to Khan has won Karzai election support. Khan apparently was able to deliver potentially decisive Tajik votes in Herat Province that might otherwise have gone to Dr. Abdullah. Certified results showed Karzai winning that province, indicating that the deal with Khan was helpful to Karzai.

Still, Khan is said to have several opponents in Herat, and a bombing there on September 26, 2009, narrowly missed his car. U.S. officials purportedly preferred that Khan not be in the cabinet because of his record as a local potentate, although some U.S. officials credit him with cooperating with the privatization of the power sector of Afghanistan. Karzai renominated Khan in his ministry post on December 19, 2009, causing purported disappointment by parliamentarians and western donor countries who want Khan and other faction leaders weakened. His renomination was voted down by the National Assembly and no new nominee for that post was presented on January 9, 2010. Khan remains as head of the ministry but in an acting capacity. Khan is on the High Peace Council that is to oversee negotiations with insurgent leaders. However, new questions about Khan were raised in November 2010 when Afghan television broadcast audio files purporting to contain Khan insisting that election officials alter the results of the September 18, 2010, parliamentary elections.[11]

Sher Mohammad Akhundzadeh and "Koka:" Southern Afghanistan/Helmand Province

Karzai's relationship with another Pashtun strongman, Sher Mohammad Akhundzadeh, demonstrates the dilemmas facing Karzai in governing Afghanistan. Akhunzadeh was a close associate of Karzai when they were in exile in Quetta, Pakistan, during Taliban rule. Karzai appointed him governor of Helmand after the fall of the Taliban, but in 2005, Britain demanded he be removed for his abuses and reputed facilitation of drug trafficking, as a condition of Britain taking security control of Helmand. Karzai reportedly wants to reappoint Akhundzadeh, who Karzai believes was more successful against militants in Helmand using his local militiamen than Britain has been with its more than 9,500 troops there. Akhunzadeh said in a November 2009 interview that many of his followers joined the Taliban insurgency after Britain insisted on his ouster. However, Britain and the United States have strongly urged Karzai to keep the existing governor, Ghulab Mangal, who is winning wide praise for his successes establishing effective governance in Helmand (discussed further under "Expanding Local Governance," below) and for reducing poppy cultivation there. Akhunzadeh attempted to deliver large numbers of votes for Karzai in Helmand, although turnout in that province was very light partly due to Taliban intimidation of voters.

An Akhunzadeh ally, Abdul Wali Khan (nicknamed "Koka"), was similarly removed by British pressure in 2006 as police chief of Musa Qala district of Helmand. However, Koka was reinstated in 2008 when that district was retaken from Taliban control. The Afghan government insisted on his reinstatement and his militia followers subsequently became the core of the 220-person police force in the district. Koka is mentioned in a congressional report as accepting payments from security contractors who are working under the Defense Department's "Host National Trucking" contract that secures U.S. equipment convoys. Koka allegedly agrees to secure the convoys in exchange for the payments.[12]

Ahmad Wali Karzai: Southern Afghanistan/Qandahar Province

Governing Qandahar, a province of about 2 million, of whom about half live in Qandahar city, is a sensitive issue in Kabul because of President Karzai's active political interest in his home province. Qandahar governance is particularly crucial to an ongoing 2010 U.S. military-led operation to increase security in surrounding districts. In Qandahar, Ahmad Wali Karzai, Karzai's elder brother, is chair of the provincial council. He has always been more powerful than any appointed governor of Qandahar, and President Karzai has frequently rotated the governors of Qandahar to ensure that none of them will impinge on Ahmad Wali's authority. Perceiving him as the key power broker in the province, many constituents and interest groups meet him each day, requesting his interventions on their behalf. Numerous press stories have asserted that he has protected narcotics trafficking in the province, and some press stories say he is also a paid informant and helper for CIA and Special Forces operations in the province.[13] Some Afghans explain Ahmad Wali Karzai's activities as an effort to ensure that his constituents in Qandahar have financial means to sustain themselves, even if through narcotics trade, before there are viable alternative sources of livelihood. On October 11, 2010, President Karzai said (Larry King interview) Ahmad Wali's attorney had shown President Karzai a letter from the U.S. Department of Justice to the effect that no investigation of him was under way. Observers report that President Karzai has repeatedly rebuffed U.S. and other suggestions to try to convince his brother to step down as provincial council chairman for Qandahar, and U.S. officials reportedly had ceased making those suggestions as of August 2010.

Still, U.S. officials say that policy is to try to bolster the clout in Qandahar of the appointed governor, Tooryalai Wesa. The U.S. intent to is empower Wesa to the point where petitioners seek his help on their problems, not that of Ahmad Wali. Karzai appointed Wesa—a Canadian-Afghan academic—in December 2008, perhaps hoping that his ties to Canada would convince Canada to continue its mission in Qandahar beyond 2011. The United States and its partners are trying to assist Wesa with his efforts to equitably distribute development funds and build local governing structures out of the tribal councils he has been holding. U.S. officials reportedly have sought to keep Ahmad Wali from interfering in Wesa's efforts.[14]

Ghul Agha Shirzai: Eastern Afghanistan/Nangarhar

A key gubernatorial appointment has been Ghul Agha Shirzai as governor of Nangarhar. He is a Pashtun from Qandahar, and is generally viewed in Nangarhar as an implant from the south. However, much as has Noor in Balkh, Shirzai has exercised effective leadership, particularly in curbing poppy cultivation there. At the same time, Shirzai is also widely accused of arbitrary action against political or other opponents, and he reportedly does not remit all the customs duties collected at the Khyber Pass/Torkham crossing to the central government. He purportedly uses the funds for the benefit of the province, not trusting that funds remitted to Kabul would be spent in the province. Shirzai had considered running against Karzai in 2009 but then opted not to run as part of a reported "deal" with Karzai that yielded unspecified political and other benefits for Shirzai.

Building Central Government Capacity

In the nearly nine years of extensive international involvement in Afghanistan, Afghan ministries based in Kabul have been slowly but steadily increasing their staffs and technological capabilities (many ministry offices now have modern computers and communications, for example), although the government still faces a relatively small recruitment pool of workers with sufficient skills. Afghan-led governmental reform and institution-building programs under way, all with U.S. and other donor assistance, include training additional civil servants, instituting merit-based performance criteria, basing hiring on qualifications rather than kinship and ethnicity, and weeding out widespread governmental corruption. Corruption is fed, in part, by the fact that government workers receive very low salaries (about $200 per month, as compared to the pay of typical contractors in Afghanistan that might pay as much as $6,500 per month).

Some observers assert that the Afghan government requires not only more staff and transparency, but also improved focus and organization, most notably in the presidential office. One idea that surfaced in 2009, and which some Afghans are again raising to help overcome administrative bottlenecks in the palace, was to prod Karzai to create a new position akin to a "chief administration officer." Several potential officials reportedly negotiated with Karzai about playing that role, including one of Karzai's 2009 election challengers, Ashaf Ghani. Ghani has not been given this role but he is advising Karzai on government reform and institution building after reconciling with him in November 2009 (after the election was settled). Ghani was part of Karzai's advisory team during the January 28, 2010, London conference and the July 20, 2010, Kabul conference. Some observers say Ghani might be in line for a "special envoy" role abroad.

The Obama Administration has developed about 45 different metrics to assess progress in building Afghan governance and security, as it was required to do (by September 23, 2009) under P.L. 111-32, an FY2009 supplemental appropriation. [15] To date, and under separate authorities such as provisions of supplemental appropriations and foreign aid appropriations, only small amounts of U.S. aid have been made conditional on Afghanistan's performance on such metrics, and no U.S. aid has been permanently withheld.

The Afghan Civil Service

The low level of Afghan bureaucratic capacity is being addressed in a number of ways, although slowly. The United States and its partners do not have in place a broad program to themselves train Afghan government officials, but instead fund Afghan institutions to conduct such training. Issues of standardizing job descriptions, salaries, bonuses, benefits and the like are being addressed by Afghanistan's Civil Service Commission. According to the April 2010 version of a mandated Defense Department report on Afghanistan, [16] the commission has thus far redefined more than 80,000 civil servant job descriptions.

Under a program called the Civilian Technical Assistance Plan, the United States is providing technical assistance to Afghan ministries and to the commission. From January 2010 until January 2011, the United States is giving $85 million to programs run by the commission to support the training and development of Afghan civil servants. One of the commission's subordinate organizations is the Afghan Civil Service Institute, which envisions training over 16,000 additional bureaucrats by the end of 2010, according to USAID.

Many Afghan civil service personnel undergo training in India, building on growing relations between Afghanistan and India. Japan and Singapore also are training Afghan civil servants on good governance, anti-corruption, and civil aviation. Some of these programs are conducted in partnership with the German Federal Foreign Office and the Asia Foundation. In order to address the problem of international donors luring away Afghan talent with higher salaries, the July 20, 2010, Kabul conference included a pledge by the Afghan government to reach an understanding with donors, within six months, on a harmonized salary scale for donor-funded salaries of Afghan government personnel.

Curbing Government Corruption and Promoting Rule of Law[17]

As noted throughout, there is a consensus within the Administration—not disputed by Karzai—on the wide scope of the corruption in Afghan governance. The Administration has wrestled throughout 2010 with the degree to which to press an anti-corruption agenda with the Karzai government, but press accounts in October 2010 suggest the Administration has decided to focus on reducing low-level corruption, and less so on investigations of high-level allies of Karzai. The anti-corruption effort has sometimes come into conflict with other U.S. objectives—not only obtaining Afghan government cooperation on the security mission but also in cultivating allies within the Afghan government who can help stabilize areas of the country. Some of these Afghans are said to be paid by the CIA for information and other support, and the National Security Council reportedly has issued guidance to U.S. agencies to review which Afghans are receiving any direct U.S. funding.[18]

Yet, U.S. officials believe that an anti-corruption effort must be pursued because corruption is contributing to a souring of Western publics on the mission as well as causing some Afghans to embrace Taliban insurgents. Official corruption was identified as a key problem in the August 30, 2009, assessment by General Stanley McChrystal, then overall commander of U.S. and international forces there. His successor in the post, General Petraeus, the top U.S. and NATO commander in Afghanistan, has said he is making anti-corruption a top priority to support his counter-insurgency strategy. In September 2010, he issued guidance throughout the theater for subordinate commanders to review their contracting strategies so as to enhance Afghan capacity and reduce the potential for corruption.

The Obama Administration's March 2009 and December 2009 strategy announcements highlighted the issue but did not specifically make U.S. forces or assistance contingent on progress on this issue. However, the December 2009 stipulation of July 2011 as the beginning of a "transition" process to Afghan leadership implied that U.S. support is not open-ended or unconditional. In the December 1, 2009, statement, the President said "We expect those [Afghan officials] who are ineffective or corrupt to be held accountable." As noted, pressing Karzai on corruption reportedly was a key component of President Obama's brief visit to Afghanistan on March 28, 2010. Attorney General Eric Holder visited Afghanistan during June 2010 to discuss anti-corruption efforts with his Afghan counterparts, including Afghan Attorney General Mohammad Ishaq Aloko.

Scope of the Problem

Partly because many Afghans view the central government as "predatory," many Afghans and international donors have lost faith in Karzai's leadership. A U.N. Office of Drugs and Crime report released in January 2010 said 59% of Afghans consider corruption as a bigger concern than the security situation and unemployment. NATO estimates that about $2.5 billion in total bribes are paid by Afghans each year. Transparency International, a German organization that assesses governmental corruption worldwide, ranked Afghanistan in 2008 as 176th out of 180 countries ranked in terms of government corruption.

At the upper levels of government, some observers have asserted that Karzai deliberately tolerates officials who are allegedly involved in the narcotics trade and other illicit activity, and supports their receipt of lucrative contracts from donor countries, in exchange for their support. Another of Karzai's brother, Mahmoud Karzai, has apparently grown wealthy through real estate and auto sales ventures in Qandahar and Kabul, purportedly by fostering the impression he can influence his brother. Mahmoud Karzai held a press conference in Washington, DC, on April 16, 2009, denying allegations of corruption and, in mid-2010, he hired attorney Gerald Posner to counter corruption allegations against him by U.S. press articles. However, in October 2010 it was reported that a Justice Department investigation of Mahmoud Karzai's dealings (he holds dual U.S.-Afghan citizenship) had begun. Mahmoud

Karzai subsequently announced that he has determined that he does owe back taxes to the United States and would clear up the arrearage.

Several other high officials, despite very low official government salaries, have acquired ornate properties in west Kabul since 2002, according to Afghan observers. This raises the further question of the inadequacy of and possible corruption within Afghanistan's land titling system. Other observers who have served in Afghanistan say that Karzai has appointed some provincial governors to "reward them" and that these appointments have gone on to "prey" economically on the populations of that province.

Kabul Bank Difficulties

The near collapse of Kabul Bank is another example of how well-connected Afghans can avoid regulations and other restrictions in order to garner personal profit. Mahmoud Karzai is a major (7+%) shareholder in the large Kabul Bank, which is used to pay Afghan civil servants and police, and he reportedly received large loans from the bank to buy his position in it. Another big shareholder is the brother of First Vice President Fahim. The insider relationships were exposed in August and September 2010 when Kabul Bank reported large losses from shareholder investments in Dubai properties, prompting President Karzai to appoint a Central Bank official to run the Kabul Bank. However, the moves did not prevent large numbers of depositors from moving their money out of it. As of early November, the bank is still operating, but some doubt whether it can survive long term. U.S. officials have asserted that no U.S. funds will be used to recapitalize the bank, if that is needed. The Afghan government has said it has ample funds (about $800 million in gold, among other assets) to recapitalize it, which may require several hundred million dollars.

Lower-Level Corruption

Aside from the issue of high-level nepotism, observers who follow the issue say that most of the governmental corruption takes place in the course of performing mundane governmental functions, such as government processing of official documents (ex. passports, drivers' licenses), in which processing services routinely require bribes in exchange for action.[19] Other forms of corruption include Afghan security officials' selling U.S./ internationally provided vehicles, fuel, and equipment to supplement their salaries. In other cases, local police or border officials may siphon off customs revenues or demand extra payments to help guard the U.S. or other militaries' equipment shipments. Other examples security commanders' placing "ghost employees" on official payrolls in order to pocket their salaries. As noted, it is this low-level corruption that the Obama Administration reportedly has decided to focus on.

Because of corruption, only about 20% of U.S. aid is channeled through the Afghan government, although a target figure of 50% of total donor funds to be channeled through the government was endorsed at the July 20, 2010, Kabul conference. Currently, the Ministry of Public Health, the Ministry of Communications, the Ministry of Finance, and the World Bank-run Afghan Reconstruction Trust Fund (which the U.S. contributes to for Afghan budget support) qualify to have U.S. funds channeled through them. The FY20 11 Obama Administration aid request expressed the goal that six ministries would qualify for direct funding by the end of 2010. Among those potentially ready, according to criteria laid out by SRAP Holbrooke and USAID Director Shah on July 28, 2010, three others are nearly ready to receive direct funding: the Ministry of Education; the Ministry of Agriculture, Irrigation and

Livestock, run by the widely praised Minister Asif Rahimi; and the Ministry of Rural Rehabilitation and Development (MRRD), which runs the widely praised National Solidarity Program. That program awards local development grants for specific projects. The MRRD has developed a capability, widely praised by Britain and other observers, to account for large percentages of donated funds to ensure they are not siphoned off by corruption.

Karzai Responses

Karzai has taken note of the growing U.S. criticism, and Obama Administration officials have credited him with taking several steps, tempered by congressional and some Administration criticism of slow implementation and allegations that he continues to shield his closest allies from investigation or prosecution. At the January 28, 2010, London conference, the Afghan government committed to 32 different steps to curb corruption; many of them were pledged again at the July 20, 2010, Kabul conference. Only a few of the pledges have been completed outright, others have had their deadlines extended or been modified. The following are measures pledged and the status of implementation, if any:

- *Assets Declarations and Verifications.* During December 15-17, 2009, Karzai held a conference in Kabul to combat corruption. It debated, among other ideas, requiring deputy ministers and others to declare their assets, not just those at the ministerial level. That requirement was imposed. Karzai himself earlier declared his assets on March 27, 2009. On June 26, 2010, Karzai urged anti-corruption officials to monitor the incomes of government officials and their families, including his, to ensure their monies are earned legally. The July 20, 2010, Kabul conference communiqué[20] included an Afghan pledge to verify and publish these declarations annually, beginning in 2010. This will presumably be accomplished by a Joint Monitoring and Evaluation Committee, which, according to the Kabul conference communiqué, is to be established within three months of the conference.
- *Establishment of High Office of Oversight.* In August 2008 Karzai, with reported Bush Administration prodding, set up the "High Office of Oversight for the Implementation of Anti-Corruption Strategy" (commonly referred to as the High Office of Oversight, HOO) with the power to identify and refer corruption cases to state prosecutors, and to catalogue the overseas assets of Afghan officials. On March 18, 2010, Karzai, as promised during the January 28, 2010, international meeting on Afghanistan in London, issued a decree giving the High Office direct power to investigate corruption cases rather than just refer them to other offices. The United States gave the High Office about $1 million in assistance during FY2009 and its performance was audited by the Special Inspector General for Afghanistan Reconstruction (SIGAR), in an audit released in December 2009.[21] USAID will provide the HOO $30 million during FY2011-FY2013 to build capacity at the central and provincial level, according to USAID officials. USAID pays for salaries of 6 HOO senior staff and provides some information technology systems as well.
- *Establishment of Additional Investigative Bodies: Major Crimes Task Force and Sensitive Investigations Unit.* Since 2008, several additional investigative bodies have been established under Ministry of Interior authority. The most prominent is the "Major Crimes Task Force," tasked with investigating public corruption, organized

crime, and kidnapping. A headquarters for the MCTF was inaugurated on February 25, 2010. According to the FBI press release that day, the MTCF is Afghan led, but it is funded and mentored by the FBI, the DEA, the U.S. Marshal Service, Britain's Serious Crimes Organized Crime Agency, the Australian Federal Police, EUPOL (European police training unit in Afghanistan), and the U.S.-led training mission for Afghan forces. The MCTF currently has 169 investigators working on 36 cases, according to Ambassador Holbrooke's July 28, 2010, testimony.

A related body is the Sensitive Investigations Unit (SIU), run by several dozen Afghan police officers, vetted and trained by the DEA.[22] This body led the arrest in August 2010 of a Karzai NSC aide, Mohammad Zia Salehi, on charges of soliciting a bribe from the large New Ansari money trading firm in exchange for ending a money-laundering investigation of the firm. The middle-of-the-night arrest prompted Karzai, by his own acknowledgment on August 22, 2010, to obtain Salehi's release and to say he would establish a commission to place the MCTF and SIU under more thorough Afghan government control. Following U.S. criticism that Karzai is protecting his aides (Salehi reportedly has been involved in bringing Taliban figures to Afghanistan for conflict settlement talks), Karzai pledged to visiting Senate Foreign Relations Committee Chairman John Kerry on August 20, 2010, that the MCTF and SIU would be allowed to perform their work without political interference. In November 2010, the Attorney General's office said it had ended the prosecution of Salehi.

- *Anti-Corruption Unit," and an "Anti-Corruption Tribunal."* These investigative and prosecutory bodies have been established by decree. Eleven judges have been appointed to the tribunal. The tribunal, under the jurisdiction of the Supreme Court, tries cases referred by an Anti-Corruption Unit of the Afghan Attorney General's office. According to testimony before the House Appropriations Committee (State and Foreign Operations Subcommittee) by Ambassador Richard Holbrooke on July 28, 2010, the Anti-Corruption Tribunal has received 79 cases from the Anti-Corruption Unit and is achieving a conviction rate of 90%. President Obama said on September 10, 2010, that 86 Afghan judges have been indicted in 2010 for corruption, up from 11 four years ago. (The July 20, 2010, Kabul conference included a pledge by the Afghan government to establish a statutory basis for the Anti-Corruption Tribunal and the Major Crimes Task Force with laws to be passed by parliament and signed by July 20, 2011.)

- *Implementation: Prosecutions and Investigations of High-Level Officials.* According to the Afghanistan Attorney General's office on November 9, 2010, there are ongoing investigations of at least 20 senior officials, including two sitting members of the cabinet. The two are believed to be Minister of Mining Sharani, and his father, who is a cabinet-rank adviser to Karzai on religious affairs. Two former ministers under investigation currently are former Commerce Minister Amin Farhang for allegedly submitting inflated invoices for reimbursement, and former Transportation Minister Hamidullah Qadri. There have also been investigations of former Minister of Mines Mohammad Ibrahim Adel, who reportedly accepted a $30 million bribe to award a key mining project in Lowgar Province (Aynak Copper Mine) to China;[23] and former Minister of the Hajj Mohammad Siddiq Chakari, under investigation for accepting bribes to steer Hajj-related travel business to certain foreign tourist agencies. Chakari was able to flee Afghanistan to Britain. Karzai publicly criticized the December 2009 embezzlement conviction of then Kabul Mayor Abdul Ahad Sahibi. On December 13, 2009, the deputy Kabul mayor (Wahibuddin Sadat) was arrested at Kabul airport for alleged misuse of authority.

- *Salary Levels.* The government has tried to raise salaries of security forces in order to reduce their inclination to solicit bribes. In November 2009, the Afghan government also has announced an increase in police salaries (from $180 per month to $240 per month).

- *Bulk Cash Transfers.* At the July 2010 Kabul conference, the government pledged to adopt regulations and implement within one year policies to govern the bulk transfers of cash outside the country. This is intended to grapple with issues raised by reports, discussed below, of officials taking large amounts of cash out of Afghanistan (an estimated $1 billion per year taken out). U.S. officials say that large movements of cash are inevitable in Afghanistan because only about 5% of the population use banks and 90% use informal cash transfers ("hawala" system). Ambassador Holbrooke testified on July 28, 2010 (cited earlier), that the Afghan Central Bank has begun trying to control hawala transfers; 475 hawalas have been licensed, to date. None were licensed as recently as three years ago. In June 2010, U.S. and Afghan officials announced establishment of a joint task force to monitor the flow of money out of Afghanistan, including monitoring the flow of cash out of Kabul International Airport. On August 21, 2010, it was reported that Afghan and U.S. authorities would implement a plan to install U.S.-made currency counters at Kabul airport to track how officials had obtained their cash (and ensure it did not come from donor aid funds).[24]

- *Auditing Capabilities.* The U.S. Special Inspector General for Afghanistan Reconstruction (SIGAR) has assessed that the mandate of Afghanistan's Control and Audit Office is too narrow and lacks the independence needed to serve as an effective watch over the use of Afghan government funds.[25] At the Kabul conference, the government pledged to submit to parliament an Audit Law within six months, to strengthen the independence of the Control and Audit Office, and to authorize more auditing by the Ministry of Finance.

- *Legal Review.* The Kabul conference communiqué commits the government to establish a legal review committee, within six months, to review Afghan laws for compliance with the U.N. Convention Against Corruption. Afghanistan ratified the convention in August 2008.

- *Local Anti-Corruption Bodies.* Some Afghans have taken it upon themselves to oppose corruption at the local level. Volunteer local inspectors, sponsored originally by Integrity Watch Afghanistan, are reported to monitor and report on the quality of donor-funded, contractor implemented construction projects.

However, these local "watchdog" groups do not have an official mandate, and therefore their authority and ability to rectify inadequacies are limited.

Moves to Penalize Lack of Progress on Corruption

Several of the required U.S. "metrics" of progress, cited above, involve Afghan progress against corruption. A FY2009 supplemental appropriation (P.L. 111-32) mandated the withholding of 10% of about $90 million in State Department counter-narcotics funding subject to a certification that the Afghan government is acting against officials who are corrupt or committing gross human rights violations. No U.S. funding for Afghanistan has been withheld because of this or any other legislative certification requirement. On the other hand, in FY2011 legislation, in June 2010, the Foreign Operations Subcommittee of the House Appropriations Committee deferred consideration of some of the nearly $4 billion in civilian aid to Afghanistan requested for FY2011, pending the outcome of a committee investigation of the issue. The subcommittee's action came amid reports that Afghan leaders are impeding investigations by the Afghan justice system of some politically well-connected Afghans, and following reports that as much as $3 billion in funds have been allegedly embezzled by Afghan officials over the past several years.[26] Others note that some of the funds might have been legal earnings from contracts or other work, and not represent U.S. aid funds.

Rule of Law Efforts

U.S. efforts to curb corruption go hand-in-hand with efforts to promote rule of law. As of July 2010, the U.S. Embassy has an Ambassador rank official, Hans Klemm, as a rule of law coordinator. U.S. funding supports training and mentoring for Afghan justice officials, direct assistance to the Afghan government to expand efforts on judicial security, legal aid and public defense, gender justice and awareness, and expansion of justice in the provinces. At the July 20, 2010, Kabul conference, the Afghan government committed to:

- Enact its draft Criminal Procedure Code into law within six months.
- Improve legal aid services within the next 12 months.
- Strengthen judicial capabilities to facilitate the return of illegally seized lands.
- Align strategy toward the informal justice sector (discussed below) with the National Justice Sector Strategy.
- Separate from the Kabul conference issues, USAID has provided $56 million during FY2005-2009 to facilitate property registration. An additional $140 million is being provided from FY2010-2014 to inform citizens of land processes and procedures, and to establish a legal and regulatory framework for land administration.

One concern is how deeply the international community should become involved in the informal justice sector. Afghans turn often to local, informal mechanisms (shuras, *jirga*s) to adjudicate disputes, particularly those involving local property, familial or local disputes, or personal status issues, rather than use the national court system. Some estimates say that 80% of cases are decided in the informal justice system. In the informal sector, Afghans can usually expect traditional practices of dispute resolution to prevail, including those practiced by Pashtuns. Some of these customs, including traditional forms of apology ("*nanawati*" and "*shamana*") and compensation for wrongs done, are discussed at http://www.khyber.org/ articles/2004/ JirgaRestorativeJustice.shtml.

However, the informal justice system is dominated almost exclusively by males. Some informal justice *shuras* take place in Taliban-controlled territory, and some Afghans may prefer Talibanrun *shuras* when doing so means they will be judged by members of their own tribe or tribal confederation. The rule of law issue is discussed in substantially greater depth in: CRS Report R41484, *Afghanistan: U.S. Rule of Law and Justice Sector Assistance*, by Liana Sun Wyler and Kenneth Katzman

Expanding Local Governance/U.S. Civilian "Uplift"

As U.S. concerns about corruption in the central government have increased since 2007, U.S. policy has increasingly emphasized building local governance. The U.S. shift in emphasis complements those of the Afghan government, which asserts that it has itself long sought to promote local governance as the next stage in Afghanistan's political and economic development. A key indicator of the Afghan intent came in August 2007 when Karzai placed the selection process for local leaders (provincial governors and down) in a new Independent Directorate for Local Governance (IDLG)—and out of the Interior Ministry. As noted above, the IDLG is headed by Jelani Popal, a member of Karzai's Popolzai tribe and a close ally. Some international officials say that Popal packed local agencies with Karzai supporters, where they were able to fraudulently produce votes for Karzai in the August 2009 presidential elections.

Provincial Governors and Provincial Councils

Many believe that the key to effective local governance is the appointment of competent governors in all 34 Afghan provinces. U.N., U.S., and other international studies and reports all point to the beneficial effects (reduction in narcotics trafficking, economic growth, lower violence) of some of the strong Afghan civilian appointments at the provincial level. However, many of the governors are considered weak, ineffective, or corrupt. Others, such as Ghul Agha Shirzai and Atta Mohammad Noor, discussed above in the section on faction leaders, are considered effective but also relatively independent of central authority.

One of the most widely praised gubernatorial appointments has been the March 2008 replacement of the weak and ineffective governor of Helmand with Gulab Mangal, who is from Laghman Province. The U.N. Office of Drugs and Crime (UNODC) praised Mangal in its September 2009 report for taking effective action to convince farmers to grow crops other than poppy. The UNODC report said his efforts account for the 33% reduction of cultivation in Helmand in 2009, as compared with 2008. Mangal has played a key role in convening tribal *shuras* and educating local leaders on the benefits of the U.S.-led offensive to remove Taliban insurgents from Marjah town and install new authorities there ("Operation Moshtarek," which began in February 2010.)

Still, there are widespread concerns about provincial governing capacity. For example, out of over 200 job slots available for the Qandahar provincial and Qandahar city government, only about 30% are filled. In four key districts around Qandahar city, there are 44 significant jobs, including district governors, but only about 12 officials are routinely present for work.[27] Similar percentages are reported in neighboring Helmand Province, the scene of substantial U.S.-led combat during 2010.

Provincial Councils

One problem noted by governance experts is that the role of the elected provincial councils is unclear. The elections for the provincial councils in all 34 provinces were held on August 20, 2009, concurrent with the presidential elections. The previous provincial council elections were held concurrent with the parliamentary elections in September 2005. The 2009 election results for the provincial councils were certified on December 29, 2009. In most provinces, the provincial councils do not act as true legislatures, and they are considered weak compared to the power and influence of the provincial governors.

Still, the provincial councils will play a major role in choosing the upper house of the National Assembly (*Meshrano Jirga*). The next selection process is to occur in December 2010, after certification of results of the lower house elections. In the absence of district councils (no elections held or scheduled), the provincial councils elected in 2009 will choose two-thirds (68 seats) of the 102-seat *Meshrano Jirga*.

District-Level Governance

District governors are appointed by the president, at the recommendation of the IDLG. Only about half of all district governors (there are 364 districts) have any staff or vehicles. Efforts to expand village local governance have been hampered by corruption and limited availability of skilled Afghans. In some districts of Helmand that had fallen under virtual Taliban control until the July 2009 U.S.-led offensives in the province, there were no district governors in place at all. Some of the district governors, including in Nawa and Now Zad district, returned after the U.S.-led expulsion of Taliban militants.

The ISAF campaign plan to retake the Marjah area of Helmand (Operation Moshtarak), which began on February 14, 2010, and succeeded in ousting Taliban control of the town by February 25, 2010, included recruiting, in advance, civilian Afghan officials who would govern the district once military forces had expelled Taliban fighters from it. Haji Zahir, a businessman who was in exile in Germany during Taliban rule, took up his position to become the chief executive in Marjah (which is to become its own district). He held meetings with Marjah residents, one of which included hosting a visit to Marjah by President Karzai (March 7, 2010). He had planned to expand his staff to facilitate the "build phase" of the ISAF counter-insurgency plan for the area. However, the expansion of that staff—and the building of governance in Marjah more generally—has been slow and some officials assigned to the city refused to serve in it for fear of Taliban assassination. As an example of the difficulties in building up local governance, Zahir was replaced in early July 2010, apparently because of his inability to obtain cooperation from Marjah tribal leaders. However, British civilian representatives in Marjah reported in October 2010 that many central government ministries now have personnel in place in Marjah and they live there and are showing up daily. Still, as noted, many slots are unfilled.

As far as the relationship between local representatives of the central government ministries and district governments, some difficulties have been noted. Local officials sometimes disagree on priorities or on implementation mechanisms. As is the case with the staffing of district government offices, the presence of Kabul representatives throughout Afghanistan is expanding very slowly and unevenly throughout the country.

District Councils and Municipal and Village Level Authority

No elections for district councils have been held due to boundary and logistical difficulties. However, in his November 19, 2009, inaugural speech, Karzai said the goal of the government is to hold these elections along with the 2010 parliamentary elections. However, subsequently, Afghan officials have said that there will not be district elections in September 2010 when the parliamentary elections were to be held.

As are district governors, mayors of large municipalities are appointed. There are about 42 mayors nationwide, many with deputy mayors. Karzai pledged in his November 2009 inaugural that "mayoral" elections would be held "for the purpose of better city management." However, no municipal elections have been held and none is scheduled.

The IDLG, with advice from India and other donors, is also in the process of empowering localities to decide on development priorities by forming Community Development Councils (CDC's). Thus far, there are about 30,000 CDC's established, and they are eventually to all be elected.

U.S. Local Governance Advisory Capacity

As a consequence of the March 2009 Obama Administration review, to help build local governing capacity, the Administration recruited about 500 U.S. civilian personnel from the State Department, USAID, the Department of Agriculture, and several other agencies—and many additional civilians from partner countries will join them—to advise Afghan ministries, and provincial and district administrations. That effort raised the number of U.S. civilians in Afghanistan to about 975 by early 2010. Of these, nearly 350 are serving outside Kabul, up from 67 in early 2009. USAID Director Rajiv Shah testified on July 28, 2010, that 55% of USAID's 420 personnel in Afghanistan are serving outside Kabul. A strategy document released by the office of Ambassador Holbrook in January 2010 said that the number of U.S. civilians is slated to grow by another 30% (to about 1,300) in 2010.[28]

Although many U.S. civilian officials now work outside Kabul, there are about 1,100 employees at the U.S. Embassy in Kabul, rising to about 1,200 by the end of 2010. To accommodate the swelling ranks, in early November 2010 a $511 million contract was let to Caddell Construction to expand it, and two contracts of $20 million each were let to construct U.S. consulates in Herat and Mazar-e-Sharif.

Senior Civilian Representative Program

The Administration also has instituted appointments of "Senior Civilian Representatives" (SCR),[29] who are counterparts to the military commanders of each NATO/ISAF regional command (there are currently five of them). Each Senior Civilian Representative is to have 10-30 personnel on their team. For example, Ambassador Frank Ruggiero, who is serving in Qandahar as the SCR for Regional Command South, is based at Qandahar airfield and interacts closely with the military command of the southern sector. He testified before the Senate Foreign Relations Committee on May 6, 2010. USAID official Dawn Liberi is SCR for Regional Command East (RC-E), which is U.S.-run. She was mentioned specifically by President Obama in his address to U.S. forces at Bagram Airfield (headquarters of RC-E) on March 28, 2010.

Promoting Human Rights

None of the Obama Administration strategy reviews in 2009 specifically changed U.S. policy on Afghanistan's human rights practices. U.S. policy has been to build capacity in human rights institutions in Afghanistan and to promote civil society and political participation. On human rights issues, the overall State Department judgment is that the country's human rights record remains poor, according to the department's report for 2009 (issued March 11, 2010).[30] The latest State Department report was similar in tone and substance to that of previous years, citing Afghan security forces and local faction leaders for abuses, including torture and abuse of detainees.

One of the institutional human rights developments since the fall of the Taliban has been the establishment of the Afghanistan Independent Human Rights Commission (AIHRC). It is headed by a woman, Sima Simar, a Hazara Shiite from Ghazni Province. It acts as an oversight body but has what some consider to be too cozy relations with Karzai's office and is not as aggressive as some had hoped. The July 20, 2010, Kabul conference communiqué contained a pledge by the Afghan government to begin discussions with the AIHRC, within six months, to stabilize its budgetary status. USAID has given the AIHRC about $10 million per year since the fall of the Taliban.

Media and Freedom of Expression/Social Freedoms

Afghanistan's conservative traditions have caused some backsliding in recent years on media freedoms, which were hailed during 2002-2008 as a major benefit of the U.S. effort in Afghanistan. A press law was passed in September 2008 that gives some independence to the official media outlet, but also contains a number of content restrictions, and requires that new newspapers and electronic media be licensed by the government. Backed by Islamic conservatives in parliament, such as Sayyaf (referenced above), and Shiite clerics such as Ayatollah Asif Mohseni, Afghanistan's conservative Council of Ulema (Islamic scholars) has been ascendant. With the council's backing, in April 2008 the Ministry of Information and Culture banned five Indian-produced soap operas on the grounds that they are too risque, although the programs were restored in August 2008 under a compromise that also brought in some Islamic-oriented programs from Turkey. At the same time, according to the State Department there has been a growing number of arrests or intimidation of journalists who criticize the central government or local leaders.

Ulema Council

Press reports in September 2010 note that the Ulema Council, a network of 3,000 clerics throughout Afghanistan, has increasingly taken conservative positions more generally. Each cleric in the council is paid about $100 per month and, in return, is expected to promote the government line. However, in August 2010, 350 members of the Council voted to demand that Islamic law (Sharia) be implemented. If the government were inclined to adopt that recommendation, either on its own or as part of a peace agreement with major Taliban leaders, it is likely that doing so would require amending the Afghan constitution, which does not implement Sharia. Some believe the Ulema Council is drifting out of government control in part because of the incapacity of its chairman, former Supreme Court Chief Justice Fazl

Hadi Shinwari, who has been in a coma in India for several months. No replacement for him has been named by the government.

In September 2010, some Ulema Council figures organized protests against plans by a Florida pastor to burn Qurans on the anniversary of the September 11 attacks (plans which were abandoned). As another example of the growing power of harder line Islamists, alcohol is increasingly difficult to obtain in restaurants and stores, although it is not banned for sale to non- Muslims. There were reports in April 2010 that Afghan police had raided some restaurants and prevented them from selling alcoholic beverages at all.

Harsh Punishments

In October 2007, Afghanistan resumed enforcing the death penalty after a four-year moratorium, executing 15 criminals. In August 2010, the issue of stoning to death as a punishment arose when Taliban insurgents ordered a young couple who had eloped stoned to death in a Taliban-controlled area of Konduz Province. Although the punishment was not meted out by the government, it was reported that many residents of the couple's village supported the punishment. The stoning also followed one week after the national Council of Ulema issued a statement (August 10, 2010), following a meeting with government religious officials, calling for more application of Shariah punishments (including such punishments as stoning, amputations, and lashings) in order to better prevent crime.

Religious Freedom

The October 2009 International Religious Freedom report (released October 26, 2009) says the Afghan government took limited steps during the year to increase religious freedom, but that "serious problems remain." Members of minority religions, including Christians, Sikhs, Hindus, and Baha'i's, often face discrimination; the Supreme Court declared the Baha'i faith to be a form of blasphemy in May 2007. Northeastern provinces have a substantial population of Islamailis, a Shiite Muslim sect often called "Seveners" (believers in the Seventh Imam as the true Imam). Many Ismailis follow the Agha Khan IV (Prince Qarim al-Husseini), who chairs the large Agha Khan Foundation that has invested heavily in Afghanistan.

One major case that drew international criticism was a January 2008 death sentence, imposed in a quick trial, against 23-year-old journalist Sayed Kambaksh for allegedly distributing material critical of Islam. On October 21, 2008, a Kabul appeals court changed his sentence to 20 years in prison, a judgment upheld by another court in March 2009. He was pardoned by Karzai and released on September 7, 2009.

A positive development is that Afghanistan's Shiite minority, mostly from the Hazara tribes of central Afghanistan (Bamiyan and Dai Kundi provinces) can celebrate their holidays openly, a development unknown before the fall of the Taliban. Some Afghan Shiites follow Iran's clerical leaders politically, but Afghan Shiites tend to be less religious and more socially open than their co-religionists in Iran. The Hazaras are also advancing themselves socially and politically through education in such fields as information technology.[31] The former Minister of Justice, Sarwar Danesh, is a Hazara Shiite, the first of that community to hold that post. He studied in Qom, Iran, a center of Shiite theology. (Danesh was voted down by the parliament for reappointment on January 2, 2010, and again on June 28 when nominated for Minister of Higher Education.) The justice minister who was approved on

January 16, 2010, Habibullah Ghalib, is part of Dr. Abdullah's faction, but not a Shiite Muslim. Ghaleb previously (2006) was not approved by the *Wolesi Jirga* for a spot on the Supreme Court. There was unrest among some Shiite leaders in late May 2009 when they learned that the Afghan government had dumped 2,000 Iranian-supplied religious texts into a river when an Afghan official complained that the books insulted the Sunni majority.

A previous religious freedom case earned congressional attention in March 2006. An Afghan man, Abd al-Rahman, who had converted to Christianity 16 years ago while working for a Christian aid group in Pakistan, was imprisoned and faced a potential death penalty trial for apostasy—his refusal to convert back to Islam. Facing international pressure, Karzai prevailed on Kabul court authorities to release him (March 29, 2006). His release came the same day the House passed H.Res. 736 calling on protections for Afghan converts. In May 2010, the Afghan government suspended the operations of two Christian-affiliated international relief groups claiming the groups were attempting to promote Christianity among Afghans—an assertion denied by the groups (Church World Service and Norwegian Church Aid).

Human Trafficking

Afghanistan was placed in Tier 2: Watch List in the State Department report on human trafficking issued on June 14, 2010 (Trafficking in Persons Report for 2010). The placement was a downgrade from the Tier 2 placement of the 2009 report. The Afghan government is assessed in the report as not complying with minimum standards for eliminating trafficking, but making significant efforts to do so. However, the downgrade was attributed to the fact that the government did not prosecute any human traffickers under a 2008 law. The State Department report says that women from China, some countries in Africa, Iran, and some countries in Central Asia are being trafficked into Afghanistan for sexual exploitation. Other reports say some are brought to work in night clubs purportedly frequented by members of many international NGOs. In an effort to also increase protections for Afghan women, in August 2008 the Interior Ministry announced a crackdown on sexual assault—an effort to publicly air a taboo subject. The United States has spent about $500,000 to eliminate human trafficking in Afghanistan since FY2001.

Advancement of Women

Freedoms for women have greatly expanded since the fall of the Taliban with their elections to the parliament and their service at many levels of government. According to the State Department human rights report for 2009, numerous abuses, such as denial of educational and employment opportunities, continue primarily because of Afghanistan's conservative traditions. Other institutions, such as Human Rights Watch, report backsliding due in part to the lack of security.[32] Many Afghan women are concerned that the efforts by Karzai and the international community to persuade insurgents to end their fight and rejoin the political process ("reintegration and reconciliation" process) could result in backsliding on women's rights. Most insurgents are highly conservative Islamists who oppose the advancement of women that has occurred. They are perceived as likely to demand some reversals of that trend if they are allowed, as part of any deal, to control territory, assume high-level government positions, or achieve changes to the Afghan constitution. Karzai has said that these concessions are not envisioned, but skepticism remains, and some Afghan officials close to Karzai do not rule out the possibility of amending the constitution to accommodate some Taliban demands. Women have been a target of attacks by Taliban supporters, including attacks on girls' schools and athletic facilities.

A major development in post-Taliban Afghanistan was the formation of a Ministry of Women's Affairs dedicated to improving women's rights, although numerous accounts say the ministry's influence is limited. It promotes the involvement of women in business ventures, and it plays a key role in trying to protect women from domestic abuse by running a growing number of women's shelters across Afghanistan. Husn Banu Ghazanfar remains minister in an acting capacity, having been voted down by the lower house for reappointment.

The Afghan government tried to accommodate Shiite leaders' demands in 2009 by enacting (passage by the National Assembly and signature by Karzai in March 2009) a "Shiite Personal Status Law," at the request of Shiite leaders. The law was intended to provide a legal framework for members of the Shiite minority in family law issues. However, the issue turned controversial when international human rights groups and governments—and Afghan women in a demonstration in Kabul—complained about provisions that would appear to sanction marital rape and which would allow males to control the ability of females in their family to go outside the home. President Obama publicly called these provisions "abhorrent." In early April 2009, taking into account the outcry, Karzai sent the law back to the Justice Ministry for review, saying it would be altered if it were found to conflict with the Afghan constitution. The offending clauses were substantially revised by the Justice Ministry in July 2009, requiring that wives "perform housework," but also apparently giving the husband the right to deny a wife food if she refuses sex. The revised law was passed by the National Assembly in late July 2009, signed by Karzai, and published in the official gazette on July 27, 2009, although it remains unsatisfactory to many human rights and women's rights groups.

On August 6, 2009, perhaps in an effort to address some of the criticisms of the Shiite law, Karzai issued, as a decree, the "Elimination of Violence Against Women" law. Minister of Women's Affairs Ghazanfar told CRS in October 2009 that the bill was long contemplated and not related to the Shiite status law.[33] However, it is subject to review and passage by the National Assembly, where some Islamic conservatives, such as Sayyaf (cited above) have been blocking final approval. Sayyaf and others reportedly object to the provisions of the law criminalizing child marriages.

Women in Key Positions

Despite conservative attitudes, women have moved into prominent positions in all areas of Afghan governance, although with periodic setbacks. Three female ministers were in the 2004- 2006 cabinet: former presidential candidate Masooda Jalal (Ministry of Women's Affairs), Sediqa Balkhi (Ministry for Martyrs and the Disabled), and Amina Afzali (Ministry of Youth). Karzai nominated Soraya Sobhrang as minister of women's affairs in the 2006 cabinet, but she was voted down by Islamist conservatives in parliament. He eventually appointed another female, Husn Banu Ghazanfar, as minister. Ghazanfar, who is a Russian-speaking Uzbek from northern Afghanistan, has been the only woman in the cabinet for several years. She was renominated on December 19, 2009, was voted down on January 2, 2010, but remains in an acting capacity. Karzai subsequently named three women in new selections presented on January 9, 2010, including Afzali (to Labor and Social Affairs). Of the three, however, only Afzali was confirmed on January 16, 2009; the other two were opposed by Islamic conservatives. In March 2005, Karzai appointed a former minister of women's affairs, Habiba Sohrabi, as governor of Bamiyan province, inhabited mostly by Hazaras. (She hosted then First Lady Laura Bush in Bamiyan in June 2008.)

The constitution reserves for women at least 17 of the 102 seats in the upper house and about one quarter of the 249 seats in the lower house of parliament. There are 23 serving in the outgoing upper house, 6 more than Karzai's mandated bloc of 17 female appointees. There are 68 women in the outgoing lower house (when the quota was 62), meaning 6 were elected without the quota. The ratio is ensured by reserving an average of two seats per province (34 provinces) for women—the top two female vote getters per province. Kabul province reserves 9 female seats. Two women ran for president for the August 20, 2009, election, as discussed below, although each received less than one-half of 1%. Some NGOs and other groups believe that the women elected by the quota system are not viewed as equally legitimate parliamentarians.

For the September 18, 2010, parliamentary elections, about 400 women ran (about 16% of all candidates). About 350 women were delegates to the 1,600-person *"peace jirga"* that was held during June 2-4, 2010, which endorsed an Afghan plan to reintegrate insurgents who want to end their fight. The High Peace Council to oversee the reconciliation process, which met for the first time on October 10, 2010, has eight women out of 68 members.

More generally, women are performing jobs that were rarely held by women even before the Taliban came to power in 1996, including in the new police force. There are over 200 female judges and 447 female journalists working nationwide. The most senior Afghan woman in the police force was assassinated in Qandahar in September 2008. Press reports say Afghan women are increasingly learning how to drive. Under the new government, the wearing of the full body covering called the *burqa* is no longer obligatory, and fewer women are wearing it than was the case a few years ago.

U.S. and International Posture on Women's Rights

U.S. officials have had some influence in persuading the government to codify women's rights. After the Karzai government took office, the United States and the new Afghan government set up a U.S.-Afghan Women's Council to coordinate the allocation of resources to Afghan women. Some believe that, in recent years, the U.S. government has dropped women's issues as a priority for Afghanistan. Some criticized President Obama's speech on December 1, 2009, for its absence of virtually any mention of women's rights. Promoting women's rights was discussed at the January 28, 2010, London conference but primarily in the context of the reintegration issue.

Specific earmarks for use of U.S. funds for women's and girls' programs in Afghanistan are contained in recent annual appropriations, and these earmarks have grown steadily. The United States provided $153 million to programs for Afghan women in FY2009, and expects to provide $175 million for FY2010, in line with these earmarks.[34] According to State Department reports on U.S. aid to women and girls, covering FY2001-2008, and then FY2008-2009, the United States has numerous, multi-faceted projects directly in support of Afghan women, including women's empowerment, maternal and child health and nutrition, funding the Ministry of Women's Affairs, and micro-finance projects. Some programs focus on training female police officers.[35] Some donors, particularly those of Canada, have financed specific projects for Afghan women farmers.

The Afghanistan Freedom Support Act of 2002 (AFSA, P.L. 107-327) authorized $15 million per year (FY2003-FY2006) for the Ministry of Women's Affairs. Those monies are donated to the Ministry from Economic Support Funds (ESF) accounts controlled by USAID. S. 229, the Afghan Women Empowerment Act of 2009, introduced in the 111th Congress, would authorize $45 million per year in FY20 1 0-FY20 12 for grants to Afghan women, for the ministry of Women's Affairs ($5 million), and for the AIHRC ($10 million).

Democracy, Governance, and Elections Funding Issues

U.S. funding for democracy, governance, and rule of law programs has grown, in line with the Obama Administration strategy for Afghanistan. During FY2002-FY2008, a total of $1.8 billion was spent on democracy, governance, rule of law and human rights, and elections support. Of these, by far the largest category was "good governance," which, in large part, are grant awards to provinces that make progress against narcotics.

The following was spent in FY2009:

- $881 million for all of democracy and governance, including
  - $283 million for good governance;
  - $150 million for National Solidarity Program and direct budget support to Afghan government;
  - $174 million for election support;
  - $50 million for strategic program development; and
  - $212 million for rule of law, funded by both USAID and State Department Bureau of International Narcotics Control and Law Enforcement (INCLE).

Planned for FY20 10 (regular appropriation and FY20 10 supplemental request):

- $1.7 billion for all democracy and governance, including
  - $1.15 billion for "good governance";
  - $411 million for rule of law and human rights (ESF funds controlled by USAID and INCLE funds);
  - $113 million for "civil society" building programs; and
  - $25 million for political competition and consensus building (elections).

Key Components of FY2011 request:
- $ 1.388 billion for all democracy and governance funds, including:
  - $1.01 billion for good governance. This program is used to build the financial and management oversight capability of the central government.
  - $248 million for rule of law and human rights;
  - $80 million for civil society building; and
  - $50 million for political competition and consensus building.

For comprehensive tables on U.S. aid to Afghanistan, by fiscal year and by category and type of aid, see CRS Report RL30588, *Afghanistan: Post-Taliban Governance, Security, and U.S. Policy*, by Kenneth Katzman.

ELECTIONS IN **2009** AND **2010**

As noted throughout, the 2009 presidential and provincial elections were anticipated to be a major step in Afghanistan's political development. They were the first post-Taliban elections run by the Afghan government itself in the form of the Afghanistan Independent Electoral Commission. Donors, including the United States, invested almost $500 million in 2009 to improve the capacity of the Afghan government to conduct the elections.[36]

Nonetheless, there were assertions of a lack of credibility of the IEC, because most of its commissioners, including then-Chairman Azizullah Ludin, were selected by and politically close to Karzai. As a check and balance to ensure electoral credibility, there was also a U.N.-appointed Elections Complaints Commission (ECC) that reviews fraud complaints. Under the 2005 election law, there were three seats for foreign nationals, appointed by the Special Representative of the U.N. Secretary General/head of U.N. Assistance Mission–Afghanistan, UNAMA. The two Afghans on the ECC governing council[37] were appointed by the Supreme Court and Afghanistan Independent Human Rights Commission, respectively.

2009 Presidential Election

Special Representative Holbrooke said at a public forum on August 12, 2009, that the August 20, 2009, presidential elections were key to legitimizing the Afghan government, no matter who won. Yet, because of the widespread fraud identified by Afghanistan's U.N.-appointed Elections Complaints Commission (ECC) in the first round of the elections, the process did not produce full legitimacy. The marred elections process was a major factor in a September-November 2009 high-level U.S. strategy reevaluation because of the centrality of a credible, legitimate partner Afghan government to U.S. strategy.[38]

Problems with the election began in late 2008 with a dispute over the election date. On February 3, 2009, Afghanistan's Independent Election Commission (IEC) set August 20, 2009, as the election date (a change from a date mandated by Article 61 of the Constitution as April 21, 2009, in order to allow at least 30 days before Karzai's term expired on May 22, 2009). The IEC decision on the latter date cited Article 33 of the Constitution as mandating universal accessibility to the voting—and saying that the April 21 date was precluded by difficulties in registering voters, printing ballots, training staff, advertising the elections, and the dependence on international donor funding, in addition to the security questions.[39]

In response to UF insistence that Karzai's presidency ended May 22, and that a caretaker government should run Afghanistan until elections, Karzai issued a February 28, 2009, decree directing the IEC to set the elections in accordance with all provisions of the constitution. The IEC reaffirmed on March 4, 2009, that the election would be held on August 20, 2009. Karzai argued against his stepping down, saying that the Constitution does not provide for any transfer of power other than in case of election or death of a President. The Afghan Supreme Court backed that decision on March 28, 2009, and the Obama Administration publicly backed these rulings.

Election Modalities and Processes

Despite the political dispute between Karzai and his opponents, enthusiasm among the public appeared high in the run-up to the election. Registration, which updated 2005 voter rolls, began in October 2008 and was completed as of the beginning of March 2009. About 4.5 million new voters registered, and about 17 million total Afghans were registered. However, there were widespread reports of registration fraud (possibly half of all new registrants), with some voters registering on behalf of women who do not, by custom, show up at registration sites. U.S. and other election observers found instances of fraudulent registration cards and evidence that cards had been offered for sale. U.S./NATO military operations in some areas, including in Helmand in January 2009, were conducted to secure registration centers; however, some election observers noted that there was insufficient international assistance to the IEC, which ran the election, to ensure an untainted registration process.

Candidates filed to run during April 24-May 8, 2009. A total of 44 registered to run for president, of which three were disqualified for various reasons, leaving a field of 41 (later reduced to 32 after several dropped out).

In the provincial elections, 3,200 persons competed for 420 seats nationwide. Those elections were conducted on a "Single Non-Transferable Vote" (SNTV) system, in which each voter votes for one candidate in a multi-member constituency. That system encourages many candidacies and is considered to discourage the participation of political parties. Although about 80% of the provincial council candidates ran as independents, some of Afghanistan's parties, including Hezbi-Islam, which is a prominent grouping in the National Assembly, fielded multiple candidates in several different provinces.

The provincial elections component of the election received little attention, in part because the role of these councils is unclear. Of the seats up for election, about 200 women competed for the 124 seats reserved for women (29%) on the provincial councils, although in two provinces (Qandahar and Uruzgan) there were fewer women candidates than reserved seats. In Kabul Province, 524 candidates competed for the 29 seats of the council.

The European Union, supported by the Organization for Security and Cooperation in Europe (OSCE) sent a few hundred observers, and the International Republican Institute and National Democratic Institute sent observers as well. About 8,000 Afghans assisted the observation missions, according to the U.N. Nations Development Program. Because much of Afghanistan is inaccessible by road, ballots were distributed (and were brought for counting) by animals in addition to vehicles and fixed and rotary aircraft.

Security was a major issue for all the international actors supporting the Afghan elections process, amid open Taliban threats against Afghans who vote. In the first round, about 7,000 polling centers were to be established (with each center having multiple polling places, totaling about 29,000), but, of those, about 800 were deemed too unsafe to open, most of them in restive Helmand and Qandahar provinces. A total of about 6,200 polling centers opened on election day.

The total cost of the Afghan elections in 2009 were about $300 million. Other international donors contributing funds to close the gap left by the U.S. contribution of about $175 million.

The Political Contest and Campaign

The presidential competition took shape in May 2009. In the election-related political deal-making,[40] Karzai obtained an agreement from Fahim to run as his first vice presidential running mate. Karzai, Fahim, and incumbent second Vice President Karim Khalili (a Hazara) registered their ticket on May 4, 2009, just before Karzai left to visit the United States for the latest round of three-way strategic talks (U.S.-Pakistan-Afghanistan).

Karzai convinced several prominent Pashtuns not to run. Ghul Agha Shirzai, a member of the powerful Barakzai clan, reportedly reached an arrangement with Karzai the week of the registration period that headed off his candidacy. Anwar al-Haq Ahady, the former finance minister and Central Bank governor, did not run. (He did receive a cabinet nomination in the December 19 ministry list but was voted down by the parliament.)

Anti-Karzai Pashtuns did not coalesce around one challenger. Former Interior Minister Ali Jalali (who resigned in 2005 over Karzai's compromises with faction leaders), and former Finance Minister (2002-2004) and Karzai critic Ashraf Ghani did not reach agreement to forge a single ticket. In the end, Ghani, the 56-year-old former World Bank official, registered his candidacy, but without Jalali or prominent representation from other ethnicities in his vice presidential slots.

The UF had difficulty forging a united challenge to Karzai. Burhanuddin Rabbani (Afghanistan President during 1992-1996), the elder statesman of the UF bloc, reportedly insisted that an ethnic Tajik (the ethnic core of the UF) head the UF ticket. Former Foreign Minister Dr. Abdullah Abdullah, the 50-year-old former ophthalmologist and foreign envoy of the legendary Tajik *mujahedin* leader Ahmad Shah Masoud, registered to run with UF backing. His running mates were Dr. Cheragh Ali Cheragh, a Hazara who did poorly in the 2004 election, and a little known Pashtun, Homayoun Wasefi. However, the presence of a key Tajik, Fahim, on Karzai's ticket showed the UF to be split. Another problem for the UF was that Ahmad Zia Massoud (a vice president) did not win support of the bloc to head its ticket. Massoud is the brother of Ahmad Shah Masoud (see above), who was killed, purportedly by Al Qaeda, two days before the September 11 attacks on the United States.

The Campaign

Karzai went into the election as a clear favorite, but the key question was whether he would win in the first round (more than 50% of the vote). IRI and other pre-election polls showed him with about 45% support. Dr. Abdullah polled about 25% and emerged as the main challenger. The conventional wisdom has always been that the two-round format favors a Pashtun candidate.

Although Karzai's public support was harmed by perceptions of ineffectiveness and corruption, many Afghan voters apparently see many of Afghanistan's problems as beyond Karzai's control. He used some U.S. policy setbacks to bolster his electoral prospects, for example by railing against civilian casualties resulting from U.S./NATO operations, and by proposing new curbs on international military operations in Afghanistan. Karzai said he would hold a *loya jirga*, if elected, including Taliban figures, to try to reach a settlement with the insurgency. He restated that intent in his November 19, 2009, inaugural speech and has moved on that front, as noted.

Karzai was criticized for a campaign that relied on personal ties to ethnic faction leaders rather than a retail campaign based on public appearances. Karzai agreed to public debates with rivals, although he backed out of a scheduled July 23 debate with Abdullah and Ghani (on the private Tolo Television network) on the grounds that the event was scheduled on short notice and was limited to only those three. Abdullah and Ghani debated without Karzai, generating additional criticism of Karzai. Karzai did attend the next debate (on state-run Radio-Television Afghanistan) on August 16, debating Ghani and Bashardost, but without Abdullah. Karzai was said to benefit from his ready access to media attention, which focuses on his daily schedule as president.

Dr. Abdullah stressed his background of mixed ethnicity (one parent is Pashtun and one is Tajik) to appeal to Pashtuns, but his experience and background has been with other Tajik leaders and he campaigned extensively in the north and west, which are populated mainly by Tajiks. However, he also campaigned in Qandahar, in Pashtun heartland. Both Karzai and Abdullah held large rallies in Kabul and elsewhere.

OTHER CANDIDATES

Abd al-Salam Rocketi ("Mullah Rocketi"). A Pashtun, reconciled Taliban figure, member of the lower house of parliament. Was expected to do well if Taliban sympathizers participated, but received less than 1% (preliminary totals), putting him in 9th place out of 32.

Hedayat Amin Arsala. A Pashtun, was a vice president during 2001-2004. He was Foreign Minister in the 1992-96 Rabbani-led *mujahedin* government. He is a prominent economist and perceived as close to the former royal family. Finished 30th out of 32.

Abd al Jabbar Sabit. A Pashtun, was fired by Karzai in 2007 for considering a run against Karzai in the election. Finished in 19th place.

Shahnawaz Tanai. A Pashtun. Served as defense minister in the Communist government of Najibullah (which was left in place after the Soviets withdrew in 1989) but led a failed coup against Najibullah in April 1990. Finished an unexpectedly strong sixth place and did well in several Pashtun provinces.

Mirwais Yasini. Another strong Pashtun candidate, was viewed as a dark horse possible winner. 48-year-old deputy speaker of the lower house of parliament, but also without well-known non-Pashtun running mates. Finished fifth.

Frozan Fana and Shahla Ata. The two women candidates in the race. Fana is the wife of the first post-Taliban aviation minister, who was killed during an altercation at Kabul airport in 2002. These two candidates are widely given almost no chance of winning, but attracted substantial media attention as trail-blazers. Fana finished seventh but Ata finished in 14th place.

Ghani polled at about 6% just before the election, according to surveys. Ghani appeared frequently in U.S. and Afghan media broadcasts criticizing Karzai for failing to establish democratic and effective institutions, but he has previously spent much time in the United

States and Europe and many average Afghans viewed him as out of touch with day-to-day problems in Afghanistan. Ghani made extensive use of the Internet for advertising and fundraising, and he hired political consultant James Carville to advise his campaign.[41]

Another candidate who polled unexpectedly well was 54-year-old anti-corruption parliamentarian Ramazan Bashardost, an ethnic Hazara. He was polling close to 10% just before the election. He ran a low-budget campaign with low-paid personnel and volunteers, but attracted a lot of media. This suggests that, despite most Hazara ethnic leaders, such as Mohammad Mohaqiq, endorsing Karzai, Bashardost would do well among Hazaras, particularly those who are the most educated. Some believe the Shiite personal status law, discussed above, was an effort by Karzai to win Hazara Shiite votes. According to the preliminary results, Bashardost carried several Hazara provinces, including Ghazni and Dai Kondi, but Mohaqiq's backing apparently helped Karzai carry the Hazara heartland of Bamiyan province. Other significant candidates are shown above.

The Election Results

Taliban intimidation and voter apathy appears to have suppressed the total turnout to about 5.8 million votes cast, or about a 35% turnout, far lower than expected. Twenty-seven Afghans, mostly security forces personnel, were killed in election-day violence. Turnout was said by observers and U.S. and other military personnel based there to have been very low in Helmand Province, despite the fact that Helmand was the focus of a U.S. military-led offensive.

Some observers said that turnout among women nationwide was primarily because there were not sufficient numbers of female poll workers recruited by the IEC to make women feel comfortable enough to vote. In general, however, election observers reported that poll workers were generally attentive and well trained, and the voting process appeared orderly.

In normally secure Kabul, turnout was said to be far lighter than in the 2004 presidential election. Turnout might have been dampened by a suicide bombing on August 15, 2009, outside NATO/ISAF military headquarters and intended to intimidate voters not to participate. In addition, several dozen provincial council candidates, and some workers on the presidential campaigns, were killed in election-related violence. A convoy carrying Fahim (Karzai vice presidential running mate, see below) was bombed, although Fahim was unharmed.

Clouding the election substantially were the widespread fraud allegations coming from all sides. Dr. Abdullah held several news conferences after the election, purporting to show evidence of systematic election fraud by the Karzai camp. Karzai's camp made similar allegations against Abdullah as applied to his presumed strongholds in northern Afghanistan. The ECC, in statements, stated its belief that there was substantial fraud likely committed, and mostly by Karzai supporters. However, the low turnout in the presumed Karzai strongholds in southern Afghanistan led Karzai and many Pashtuns to question the election's fairness as well, on the grounds that Pashtuns were intimidated from voting in greater proportions than were others.

The IEC released vote results slowly. Preliminary results were to be announced by September 3. However, the final, uncertified total was released on September 16, 2009. It showed Karzai at 54.6% and Dr. Abdullah at 27.7%. Bashardost and Ghani received single-digit vote counts (9% and 3% respectively), with trace amounts for the remainder of the field.

Vote Certified/Runoff Mandated

The constitution required that a second-round runoff, if needed, be held two weeks after the results of the first round are certified. Following the release of the vote count, the complaints evaluation period began which, upon completed, would yield a "certified" vote result. On September 8, 2009, the ECC ordered a recount of 10% of polling stations (accounting for as many as 25% total votes) as part of its investigations of fraud. Polling stations were considered "suspect" if: the total number of votes exceeded 600, which was the maximum number allotted to each polling station; or where any candidate received 95% or more of the total valid votes cast at that station (assuming more than 100 votes were cast there). Perhaps reflecting political sensitivities, the recount consisted of a sampling of actual votes.[42] Throughout the investigation period (September 16-October 20), the ECC said it was not "in a rush" to finish.

On October 20, 2009, the ECC determined, based on its investigation, that about 1 million Karzai votes, and about 200,000 Abdullah votes, were considered fraudulent and were deducted from their totals. The final, certified, results of the first round were as follows: Karzai—49.67% (according to the IEC; with a slightly lower total of about 48% according to the ECC determination); Abdullah—30.59%; Bashardost—1 0.46%; Ghani—2.94%, Yasini—1 .03%, and lower figures for the remaining field.[43]

During October 16-20, 2009, U.S. and international officials, including visiting Senator John Kerry, met repeatedly with Karzai to attempt to persuade him to acknowledge that his vote total did not legitimately exceed the 50%+ threshold to claim a first-round victory. On October 21, 2009, the IEC accepted the ECC findings and Karzai conceded the need for a runoff election. A date was set as November 7, 2009. Abdullah initially accepted.

In an attempt to produce a fair second round, UNAMA, which provided advice and assistance to the IEC, requested that about 200 district-level election commissioners be replaced. In addition, it recommended there be fewer polling stations—about 5,800, compared to 6,200 previously—to eliminate polling stations where very few votes are expected to be cast. Still, there were concerns that some voters may be disenfranchised because snow had set in some locations. Insurgents were expected to resume their campaign to intimidate voters from casting ballots.

After a runoff was declared, no major faction leader switched support of either candidate, making it difficult to envision an Abdullah victory. Prior to the ECC vote certification, Dr. Abdullah told CRS at a meeting in Kabul on October 15, 2009, that he might be willing to negotiate with Karzai on a "Joint Program" of reforms—such as direct election of governors and reduced presidential powers—to avoid a runoff. Abdullah told CRS he himself would not be willing to enter the cabinet, although presumably such a deal would involve his allies doing so. However, some said the constitution does not provide for a negotiated settlement and that the runoff must proceed. Others said that a deal between the two, in which Abdullah dropped his candidacy, could have led the third-place finisher, Ramazan Bashardost, to assert that he must face Karzai in a runoff. Still others say the issue could have necessitated resolution by Afghanistan's Supreme Court.

Election Conclusion

The various pre-runoff scenarios were mooted on November 1, 2009, when Dr. Abdullah refused to participate in the runoff on the grounds that the problems that plagued the first round were likely to recur. He asserted that Karzai, in negotiations during October 2009, was

Afghanistan: Politics, Elections, and Government Performance 125

refusing to replace the IEC head, Azizullah Ludin, to fire several cabinet ministers purportedly campaigning for Karzai, or to address several other election-related complaints. The IEC refused to follow a UNAMA recommendation to reduce the number of polling stations. Some believe Abdullah pulled out because of his belief that he would not prevail in the second round.

On November 2, 2009, the IEC issued a statement saying that, by consensus, the body had determined that Karzai, being the only candidate remaining in a two-person runoff, should be declared the winner and the second round not held. The Obama Administration accepted the outcome as "within Afghanistan's constitution," on the grounds that the fraud had been investigated. On that basis, the United States, as well as U.N. Secretary General Ban Ki Moon (visiting Kabul), and several governments, congratulated Karzai on the victory. U.S. officials, including Secretary of State Clinton, praised Dr. Abdullah for his relatively moderate speech announcing his pullout, in particular his refusal to call for demonstrations or violence. Dr. Abdullah denied that his pullout was part of any "deal" with Karzai for a role for his supporters in the next government. Amid U.S. and international calls for Karzai to choose his next cabinet based on competence, merit, and dedication to curbing corruption, Karzai was inaugurated on November 19, 2009, with Secretary of State Clinton in attendance.

As noted above, the election for the provincial council members were not certified until December 29, 2009. The council members have taken office.

Fallout for UNAMA

The political fallout for UNAMA was significant. During the complaint period, a dispute between UNAMA head Kai Eide and the American deputy, Ambassador Peter Galbraith, broke out over how vigorously to press for investigation of the fraud. This led to the September 29, 2009, dismissal by Secretary General Ban Ki Moon of Galbraith, who had openly accused UNAMA head Kai Eide of soft-pedaling on the fraud charges and siding with Karzai. Galbraith appealed his dismissal, amid press reports that he had discussed a plan with some U.S. officials to replace Karzai with an interim government, if the second round could not be held until after the winter. In December 2009, Eide announced he would not seek to renew his two year agreement to serve as UNAMA chief. The replacement named at the January 28, 2010, London conference was Staffan de Mistura, who previously played a similar U.N. role in Iraq. He arrived in Kabul in mid-March 2010.

Post-Election Cabinet

U.S. officials stated they would scrutinize the post-election cabinet for indications that Karzai would professionalize his government and eliminate corruption. Complicating Karzai's efforts to obtain confirmation of a full cabinet was the need to present his choices as technically competent while also maintaining a customary and expected balance of ethnic and political factions. In the parliamentary confirmation process that has unfolded, National Assembly members, particularly the well-educated independents, have objected to many of his nominees as "unknowns," as having minimal qualifications, or as loyal to faction leaders who backed Karzai in the 2009 election. Karzai's original list of 24 ministerial nominees (presented December 19) was generally praised by the United States for retaining the highly praised economic team (and most of that team was confirmed). However, overall, only 7 of the first 24 nominees were confirmed (January 2, 2010), and only 7 of the 17 replacement nominees were confirmed (January 16, 2010), after which the Assembly went into winter recess. Another five (out of seven nominees) were confirmed on June 28, 2010, although one was a replacement for the ousted Interior Minister Atmar. Seven permanent posts remain unfilled. Although then UNAMA head Kai Eide called the vetoing of many nominees a "setback" to Afghan governance, Pentagon Press Secretary Geoff Morrell said on January 6, 2010, that the vetoing by parliament reflected a "healthy give and take" among Afghanistan's branches of government. Outside experts have said the confirmation process—and the later parliamentary review of a 2010 election decree, discussed below—reflects the growing institutional strength of the parliament and the functioning of checks and balances in the Afghan government. Of the major specific developments in the cabinet selection process to date (and with seven ministries remaining unfilled by permanent appointees, as of September 2010):

The main security ministers—Defense Minister Abdal Rahim Wardak and Interior Minister Mohammad Hanif Atmar—were renominated by Karzai and confirmed on January 2, 2010. They work closely with the U.S. military to expand and improve the Afghan national security forces. (Atmar was later dismissed, as discussed below.)

- Three key economic/civilian sector officials who work very closely with USAID and U.S. Embassy Kabul—Finance Minister Omar Zakhiwal, Agriculture Minister Mohammad Rahimi, and Education Minister Ghulam Faruq Wardak— were renominated and also were confirmed on January 2. The highly praised Minister of Rural Rehabilitation and Development (Ehsan Zia), who runs the widely touted and effective National Solidarity Program, was not renominated, to the chagrin of U.S. officials. His named replacement (Wais Barmak, a Fahim and Dr. Abdullah ally) was voted down. The second replacement, Jarullah Mansoori, was confirmed on January 16.
- The U.S.-praised Commerce Minister Wahidollah Sharani was selected to move over to take control of the Mines Ministry from the former minister, who is under investigation for corruption. Sharani was confirmed on January 2, 2010. However, as noted, Sharani is reportedly under investigation for corruption as of November 2010. Also confirmed that day was Minister of Culture Seyyed Makhdum Raheen. He had been serving as Ambassador to India.
- The clan of former moderate *mujahedin* party leader Pir Gaylani rose to prominence in the December 19 list. Gaylani son-in-law Anwar al Haq Al Ahady (see above) was named as economy minister and Hamid Gaylani (Pir Gaylani's son) was named as minister of border and tribal affairs. However, neither was confirmed and neither was renominated.
- Ismail Khan was renominated as minister of energy and water on December 19, disappointing U.S. officials and many Afghans who see him as a faction leader (Tajik leader/*mujahedin* era commander, Herat Province) with no technical expertise. He was voted down but remains in an acting capacity.
- Karzai initially did not nominate a permanent foreign minister, leaving Spanta in place as a caretaker. However, in the second nomination round, Karzai selected his close ally Zalmay Rassoul, who has been national security adviser since 2004, to the post. Rassoul was confirmed on January 16. Spanta is head of the National Security Council.

- Minister of Women's Affairs Ghazanfar was renominated to remain the only female minister, but was voted down (January 2). In the cabinet renominations, Karzai named three women—Suraiya Dalil to Public Health, Pelwasha Hassan to Women's Affairs, and Amina Afzali (minister of youth in an earlier Karzai cabinet) to Labor and Social Affairs. Of those, only Afzali was confirmed on January 16. Ghazanfar and Dalil are heading those ministries in an acting capacity. In the December 16, 2009, list, Karzai proposed a woman to head a new Ministry of Literacy, but parliament did not vote on this nomination because it had not yet acted to approve formation of the ministry

- Of the other nominees confirmed on January 16, 2010, at least one has previously served in high positions. The Assembly confirmed that day: Zarar Moqbel (who previously was interior minister) as Counternarcotics Miinister; Economy Minister Abdul Hadi Arghandiwal, who belongs to the party linked with proTaliban insurgent leader Gulbuddin Hikmatyar (although the faction in the government has broken with Hikmatyar and rejects violence); Yousaf Niazi, minister of Hajj and Waqf (religious endowments) affairs; and Habibullah Ghalib, Minister of Justice.

- The following 10 were voted down on January 16: (1) Palwasha Hassan, nominated to head the Ministry of Women's Affairs; (2) Dalil, Public Health, now acting minister, mentioned above; (3) Muhammad Zubair Waheed, minister of commerce; (4) Muhammad Elahi, minister of higher education; (5) Muhammad Laali, Public Works; (6) Abdul Rahim, who was telecommunications minister in the first Karzai cabinet, as minister of refugee affairs (acting); (7) Arsala Jamal, formerly the governor of Khost Province who was widely praised in that role by Secretary Gates, as minister of border and tribal affairs (and now is acting minister); (8) Abdul Qadus Hamidi, minister of communications; (9) Abdur Rahim Oraz, minister of transport and aviation; and (10) Sultan Hussein Hesari, minister of urban development (acting).

- On June 28, 2010, Karzai obtained parliamentary approval for five positions out of seven nominees. Approved were Bismillah Khan as interior minister (replacing Atmar, who was fired on June 6); Al Ahady as commerce minister; former Qandahar governor Asadullah Khalid as minister of border and tribal affairs; Hamidi (see above) as minister of public works; and Jamahir Anwari as minister of refugees and repatriation. Voted down were two Hazara Shiites: Sarwar Danesh as minister of higher education, and former IEC chief Daud Ali Najafi as minister of transportation. Their rejection caused Hazara members in the Assembly to demonstrate their disapproval of the vote, and Karzai called for Hazaras to be approved in the future to ensure all-ethnic participation in government.

September 18, 2010, Parliamentary Elections

Some, including the referenced report by the SIGAR, feared that the difficulties that plagued the 2009 presidential election were not adequately addressed to ensure that the September 18, 2010, parliamentary elections were fully free and fair. Many of these fears apparently were realized. A dispute over a new election decree that governed the election, which weakened the international voice on the ECC, is discussed below. The July 20, 2010, Kabul conference final communiqué included an Afghan government pledge to initiate, within six months, a strategy for long-term electoral reform.

Election Timing

On January 2, 2010, the IEC had initially set National Assembly elections for May 22, 2010. The IEC view was that this date was in line with a constitutional requirement for a new election to be held well prior to the expiry of the current Assembly's term. However, U.S., ECC, UNAMA, and officials of donor countries argued that Afghanistan's flawed institutions would not be able to hold free and fair elections under this timetable. Among the difficulties noted were that the IEC lacks sufficient staff, given that some were fired after the 2009 election; that the IEC lacks funds to hold the election under that timetable; that the U.S. military buildup will be consumed with securing still restive areas at election time; and that the ECC's term expired at the end of January 2010. A functioning ECC was needed to evaluate complaints against registered parliamentary candidates because there are provisions in the election law to invalidate the candidacies of those who have previously violated Afghan law or committed human rights abuses.

The international community pressed for a delay of all of these elections until August 2010 or, according to some donors, mid-2011.[44] Bowing to funding and the wide range of other considerations mentioned, on January 24, 2010, the IEC announced that the parliamentary elections would be postponed until September 18, 2010. Other experts said that the security issues, and the lack of faith in Afghanistan's election institutions, necessitated further postponement.[45]

About $120 million was budgeted by the IEC for the parliamentary elections, of which at least $50 million came from donor countries, giving donors leverage over when the election might take place. The remaining $70 million was funds left over from the 2009 elections. Donors had held back the needed funds, possibly in an effort to pressure the IEC to demonstrate that it is correcting the flaws identified in the various "after-action" reports on the 2009 election. With the compromises and Karzai announcements below, those funds were released as of April 2010.

Election Decree/Reform

With the dispute between the Karzai government and international donors continuing over how to ensure a free and fair election, the Afghan government drafted an election decree that would supersede the 2005 election law and govern the 2010 parliamentary election.[46] Karzai signed the decree in February 2010. The Afghan government argues that the decree supersedes the constitutional clause that any new election law not be adopted less than one year prior to the election to which that law will apply.

Substantively, some of the provisions of the election decree—particularly the proposal to make the ECC an all-Afghan body—caused alarm in the international community. Another controversial element was the registration requirements of a financial deposit (equivalent of about $650), and that candidates obtain signatures of at least 1,000 voters. On March 14, 2010, after discussions with outgoing UNAMA head Kai Eide, Karzai reportedly agreed to cede to UNAMA two "international seats" on the ECC, rather than to insist that all five ECC members be Afghans. Still, the majority of the ECC seats were Afghans.

Afghanistan: Politics, Elections, and Government Performance 129

The election decree became an issue for Karzai opponents and others in the National Assembly who seek to assert parliamentary authority. On March 31, the *Wolesi Jirga* voted to reject the election decree, leaving its status unclear. However, on April 3, 2010, the *Meshrano Jirga* decided not to act on the election decree, meaning that it was not rejected by the Assembly as a whole and will likely stand to govern the September 18, 2010, National Assembly elections. Karzai upheld his pledge to implement the March 2010 compromise with then UNAMA head Eide by allowing UNAMA to appoint two ECC members and for decisions to require that at least one non-Afghan ECC member concur.

Among other steps to correct the mistakes of the 2009 election, the Afghan Interior Ministry planned instituted a national identity card system to curb voter registration fraud. However, observers say that registration fraud still occurred. On April 17, 2010, Karzai appointed a new IEC head, Fazel Ahmed Manawi, who drew praise from many factions (including "opposition leader" Dr. Abdullah) for impartiality. The IEC also barred 6,000 poll workers who served in the 2009 election from working the 2010 election.

Preparations and The Vote

Preparations for the September 18 election went relatively well, according to reports by the IEC. Candidates registered during April 20-May 6, 2010. A list of candidates was circulated on May 13, 2010, including 2,477 candidates for the 249 seats.[47] These figures included 226 candidates who registered but whose documentation was not totally in order; and appeal restored about 180 of them. On May 30, 2010, in a preliminary ruling, 85 candidates others were disqualified as members of illegal armed groups. However, appeals and negotiations restored all but 36 in this latter category. A final list of candidates, after all appeals and decisions on the various disqualifications, was issued June 22. The final list included 2,577 candidates, including 406 women. Since then, 62 candidates were invalidated by the ECC, mostly because they did not resign their government positions, as required.

Voter registration was conducted June 12-August 12. According to the IEC, over 375,000 new voters were registered, and the number of eligible voters was about 11.3 million. Campaigning began June 23. Many candidates, particularly those who are women, said that security difficulties have prevented them from conducting active campaigning. At least three candidates and 13 candidate supporters were killed by insurgent violence.

On August 24, 2010, the IEC announced that the Afghan security forces say they would only be able to secure 5,897 of the planned 6,835 polling centers. To prevent so-called "ghost polling stations" (stations open but where no voters can go, thus allowing for ballot-stuffing), the 938 stations considered not secure were not opened. The IEC announcement stated that further security evaluation could lead to the closing of still more stations and, on election day, a total of 5,355 centers opened, 304 of those slated to open did not, and for 157 centers there was no information available. In part to compensate, the IEC opened extra polling stations in centers in secure areas near to those that were closed.

On election day, about 5.6 million votes were cast out of about 11.3 million eligible voters. Turnout was therefore about 50%. A major issue was security. At first, it appeared as though election-day violence was lower than in the 2009 presidential election. However, on September 24, NATO/ISAF announced that there were about 380 total attacks, about 100 more than in 2009. However, voting was generally reported as orderly and the attacks did not derail the election.

Outcomes

Preliminary results were announced on October 20, 2010, and final, certified results were to be announced by October 30, 2010, but have been delayed due to investigation of fraud complaints. While the information below illustrates that there was substantial fraud, the IEC and ECC have been widely praised for their handling of the fraud allegations. Among the key outcomes, both in terms of process and results, are:

- Of the 5.6 million votes cast, the ECC has invalidated 1.3 million (about 25%) after investigations of fraud complaints. The ECC prioritized complaints filed as follows: 2,142 as possibly affecting the election, 1,056 as unable to affect the result, and 600 where there will be no investigation. Causes for invalidation most often included ballot boxes in which all votes were for one candidate.
- About 1,100 election workers have been questioned, and 413 candidates have been referred by the ECC to the Attorney General for having allegedly committed election fraud.
- There have been at least three demonstrations against the fraud by about 300 candidates who felt deprived of victory, under a banner called the "Union of Afghan *Wolesi Jirga* Candidates 2010,"

Political Results

Without finally certified results, it is difficult to judge the political impact of the elections. However, the following have become apparent.

- The IEC has said that the new lower house will have approximately 50% new membership, meaning that many incumbents apparently have lost their seats.
- The camps of both Karzai as well as those of Dr. Abdullah and the opposition appear to have failed to meet their objectives, according to observers and press reports. Each camp sought to hold commanding blocs of about 100 seats in the next lower house, and it is not clear that either achieved that result. This apparent result also complicates any effort to pin blame for fraud clearly on one camp or another. It also makes in unlikely that Karzai's allies would be apply to install Sayyaf as next lower house speaker, replacing Abdullah ally Qanooni.
- Karzai's allies fared poorly apparently due to several pro-Karzai candidates losing in Qandahar Province, and because many Pashtuns did not vote, due to security reasons, in mixed Ghazni Province.
- The poor Pashtun turnout in Ghazni has apparently led to a much greater than expected showing for Hazara candidates, who live in more secure areas of Ghazni and voted in large numbers. Some assessments say that Hazaras may win 20% (about 50 seats) in the next lower house.
- It is likely that the next lower house will be more diverse politically than the outgoing one, and less predictable in whether it supports or opposes Karzai on certain issues. The Hazara strength, which has prompted a Pashtun political backlash, has no clear impact because many Hazaras support Karzai while many also oppose him as a representative of the political strength of the Pashtuns (who have a reputation of repressing or discriminating against the Hazaras).

Afghanistan: Politics, Elections, and Government Performance

Table 1. Afghanistan Political Transition Process

Interim Administration	Formed by Bonn Agreement. Headed by Hamid Karzai, an ethnic Pashtun, but key security positions dominated by mostly minority "Northern Alliance." Karzai reaffirmed as leader by June 2002 "emergency loya *jirga*." (A *jirga* is a traditional Afghan assembly).
Constitution	Approved by January 2004 "Constitutional Loya *Jirga*" (CLJ). Set up strong presidency, a rebuke to Northern Alliance that wanted prime ministership to balance presidential power, but gave parliament significant powers to compensate. Gives men and women equal rights under the law, allows for political parties as long as they are not "un-Islamic"; allows for court rulings according to Hanafi (Sunni) Islam (Chapter 7, Article 15). Set out electoral roadmap for simultaneous (if possible) presidential, provincial, and district elections by June 2004. Named ex-King Zahir Shah to non-hereditary position of "Father of the Nation;" he died July 23, 2007.
Presidential Election	Elections for President and two vice presidents, for 5-year term, held Oct. 9, 2004. Turnout was 80% of 10.5 million registered. Karzai and running mates (Ahmad Zia Masud, a Tajik and brother of legendary *mujahedin* commander Ahmad Shah Masud, who was assassinated by Al Qaeda two days before the Sept. 11 attacks, and Karim Khalili, a Hazara) elected with 55% against 16 opponents. Second highest vote getter, Northern Alliance figure (and Education Minister) Yunus Qanooni (16%). One female ran, got about 1%. Hazara leader Mohammad Mohaqiq got 11.7%; and Dostam won 10%. Funded with $90 million in international aid, including $40 million from U.S. (FY2004 supplemental, P.L. 108-106).
First Parliamentary Elections	Elections held Sept. 18, 2005, on "Single Non-Transferable Vote" System; candidates stood as individuals, not part of party list. Parliament consists of a 249 elected lower house (*Wolesi Jirga*, House of the People) and a selected 102 seat upper house (Meshrano *Jirga*, House of Elders). Voting was for one candidate only, although number of representatives varied by province, ranging from 2 (Panjshir Province) to 33 (Kabul Province). Herat has 17; Nangahar, 14; Qandahar, Balkh, and Ghazni, 11 seats each. The body is 28% female (68 persons), in line with the legal minimum of 68 women—two per each of the 34 provinces. Upper house appointed by Karzai (34 seats, half of which are to be women), by the provincial councils (34 seats), and district councils (remaining 34 seats). There are 23 women in it, above the 17 required by the constitution. Because district elections (400 district councils) were not held, provincial councils selected 68 on interim basis. 2,815 candidates for *Wolesi Jirga*, including 347 women. Turnout was 57% (6.8 million voters) of 12.5 million registered. Funded by $160 million in international aid, including $45 million from U.S. (FY2005 supplemental appropriation, P.L. 109-13).
First Provincial Elections/ District Elections	Provincial elections held Sept. 18, 2005, simultaneous with parliamentary elections. Exact powers vague, but now taking lead in deciding local reconstruction Provincial council sizes range from 9 to the 29 seats on the Kabul provincial council. Total seats are 420, of which 121 held by women. 13,185 candidates, including 279 women. Some criticize the provincial election system as disproportionately weighted toward large districts within each province. District elections not held due to complexity and potential tensions of drawing district boundaries.
Second Presidential and Provincial Elections	Presidential and provincial elections were held Aug. 20, 2009, but required a runoff because no candidate received over 50% in certified results issued October 20. Second round not held because challenger, Dr. Abdullah, pulled out of a second-round runoff vote. Election costs about $300 million.
Parliamentary Elections	Originally set for May 22, 2010; held September 18, 2010.

Table 2. Major Pashtun Tribal Confederations

Clan/Tribal Confederations	Location	Example
Durrani	Mainly southern Afghanistan: Qandahar, Helmand, Zabol, Uruzgan,Nimruz	
Popalzai (Zirak branch of Durrani Pashtun)	Qandahar	Hamid Karzai, President of Afghanistan; Jelani Popal, head of the Independent Directorate of Local Governance; Mullah Bradar, the top aide to Mullah Umar, captured in Pakistan in Feb. 2010. Two-thirds of Qandahar's provincial government posts held by Zirak Durrani Pashtuns
Alikozai	Qandahar	Mullah Naqibullah (deceased, former anti-Taliban faction leader in Qandahar)
Barakzai	Qandahar, Helmand	Ghul Agha Shirzai (Governor, Nangarhar Province)
Achakzai	Qandahar, Helmand	Abdul Razziq, Chief of Staff, Border Police, Qandahar Province
Alozai	Helmand (Musa Qala district)	Sher Mohammad Akhunzadeh (former Helmand governor); Hajji Zahir, former governor of Marjah
Noorzai	Qandahar	Noorzai brothers, briefly in charge of Qandahar after the fall of the Taliban in November 2001
Ghilzai	Eastern Afghanistan: Paktia, Paktika, Khost, Nangarhar, Kunar	
Ahmadzai		Mohammed Najibullah (pres. 1986-1992); Ashraf Ghani, Karzai adviser, Finance Minister 2002-2004
Hotak		Mullah Umar, but hails from Uruzgan, which is dominated by Durranis
Taraki		Nur Mohammed Taraki (leader 1978-1979)
Kharoti		Hafizullah Amin (leader September-December1979); Gulbuddin Hekmatyar, founder of Hezb-e-Islami (Gulbuddin), former *mujahedin* party leader now anti-Karzai insurgent.
Zadran	Paktia, Khost	Pacha Khan Zadran; Insurgent leader Jalaluddin Haqqani
Kodai		
Mangal	Paktia, Khost	Ghulab Mangal (Governor of Helmand Province)
Orkazai		
Shinwari	Nangarhar province	Fasl Ahmed Shinwari, former Supreme Court Chief Justice
Mandezai		
Sangu Khel		
Sipah		
Wardak (Pashtu-speaking non-Pashtun)	Wardak Province	Abdul Rahim Wardak (Defense Minister)
Afridis	Tirah, Khyber Pass, Kohat	
Zaka khel		

Table 2. (Continued)

Clan/Tribal Confederations	Location	Example
Jawaki		
Adam khel		
Malikdin, etc		
Yusufzais	Khursan, Swat, Kabul	
Akozais		
Malizais		
Loezais		
Khattaks	Kohat, Peshawar, Bangash	
Akorai		
Terai		
Mohmands	Near Khazan, Peshawar	
Baizai		
Alimzai		
Uthmanzais		
Khawazais		
Wazirs	Mainly in Waziristan	
Darwesh khel		
Bannu		

Source: This table was prepared by Hussein Hassan, Information Research Specialist, CRS.
Note: N/A indicates no example is available.

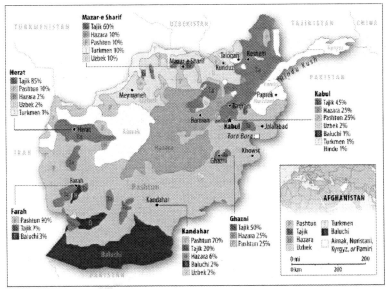

Source: 2003 National Geographic Society, http://www.afghan-network.net/maps/Afghanistan. Adapted by Amber Wilhelm, CRS

Notes: This map is intended to be illustrative of the approximate demographic distribution by region of Afghanistan. CRS has no way to confirm exact population distributions.

Figure 1. Map of Afghan Ethnicities.

Implications for the United States of the Afghan Elections

U.S. officials express clear U.S. neutrality in all Afghan elections. However, in the 2009 presidential election, Karzai reportedly believed the United States was hoping strong candidates might emerge to replace him. This perception was a function of the strained relations between Karzai and some Obama Administration officials, particularly Ambassadors Holbrooke and Eikenberry. Ambassador Timothy Carney was appointed to head the 2009 U.S. election support effort at U.S. Embassy Kabul, tasked to ensure that the United States was even-handed.

The legitimacy of the Afghan partner of the United States was a major factor in the Administration's consideration of the McChrystal initial assessment of August 2009, [48] which recommended pursuing a classic counterinsurgency strategy to protect the Afghan population. If there is no legitimate Afghan partner available, then some might argue that the recommended strategy might not succeed because U.S. forces are not authorized or able to reform the Afghan government. According to the DOD report of April 2010, cited earlier, the strategy is focused on 120 restive districts (of the 364 total Afghan districts). Administration officials clarified that any July 2011 deadline to begin transitioning to Afghan security leadership would be subject to evaluation of conditions that would be determined in a December 2010 review. That review is likely to take into account an assessment of the credibility of the September 18, 2010, parliamentary elections, particularly the public perception of whether the problems of the 2009 presidential election were corrected. A provision of an FY20 10 supplemental appropriation (P.L. 111-212) makes U.S. aid to the IEC and ECC contingent on certification by the Secretary of State that those Afghan officials who committed fraud in the 2009 presidential election are not involved in the September 2010 parliamentary election.

END NOTES

[1] For text, see http://www.un.org/News/dh/latest/afghan/afghan-agree.htm.

[2] *Shura* is the term used by non-Pashtuns to characterize the traditional assembly concept. *Jirga* is the Pashtun term.

[3] Filkins, Dexter, and Mark Mazzetti. "Key Karzai Aide in Graft Inquiry is Linked to C.I.A." *New York Times*, August 26, 2010.

[4] Sayyaf led the *Ittihad Islami* (Islamic Union) *mujahedin* party during the war against the Soviet occupation.

[5] Some information in this section is from the State Department reports on human rights in Afghanistan for 2009, March 11, 2010; for text, see http://www.state and the International Religious Freedom Report, released October 26, 2009, http://www.state.gov/g/drl/rls/irf/2009/127362.htm.

[6] Interview with Admiral Mike Mullen, Chairman of the Joint Chiefs of Staff. CNN, May 30 2010.

[7] Dreazen, Yochi, and Sarah Lynch. "U.S. Seeks to Repair Karzai Tie." *Wall Street Journal*, April 12, 2010.

[8] CRS e-mail conversation with a then National Security aide to President Karzai, December 2008.

[9] This is the name of the area where the Taliban prisoners purportedly died and were buried in a mass grave.

[10] Gall, Carlotta. "In Afghanistan's North, Ex-Warlord Offers Security." *New York Times*, May 17, 2010.

[11] Partlow, Joshua. "Audio Files Raise New Questions About Afghan Elections." *Washington Post*, November 11, 2010.

[12] House of Representatives. Subcommittee on National Security and Foreign Affairs, Committee on Oversight and Government Reform. "Warlord, Inc.: Extortion and Corruption Along the U.S. Supply Chain in Afghanistan." Report of the Majority Staff, June 2010.

[13] Filkins, Dexter, Mark Mazetti and James Risen, "Brother of Afghan Leader Is Said to be on C.I.A. Payroll," *New York Times*, October 28, 2009.

[14] Partlow, Joshua, "U.S. Seeks to Bolster Kandahar Governor, Upend Power Balance," *Washington Post*, April 29, 2010.

[15] "Evaluating Progress in Afghanistan-Pakistan" Foreign Policy website, http://www.foreignpolicy.com/articles/2009/ 09/16/evaluating_progress_in_afghanistan_pakistan.

[16] Department of Defense. "Report on Progress Toward Security and Stability in Afghanistan." April 2010. http://www.defense.gov/pubs/pdfs/report_final_secdef_04_26_10.pdf.

[17] For more information, particularly on Rule of Law programs, see: CRS Report R41484, *Afghanistan: U.S. Rule of Law and Justice Sector Assistance*, by Liana Sun Wyler and Kenneth Katzman.

[18] Chandrasekaran, Rajiv. "A Subtler Take to Fight Afghan Corruption." Washington Post, September 13, 2010.

[19] Filkins, Dexter, "Bribes Corrode Afghan's Trust in Government," *New York Times*, January 2, 2009.

[20] Communique text at http://www.nytimes.com/2010/07/21/world/asia/21kabultext.html.

[21] http://www.sigar.mil/reports/pdf/audits

[22] Nordland, Ron and Mark Mazzetti. "Graft Dispute in Afghanistan Is Test for U.S." *New York Times*, August 24, 2010.

[23] Partlow, Joshua, "Afghanistan Investigating 5 Current and Former Cabinet Members," *Washington Post*, November 24, 2009.

[24] Miller, Greg and Joshua Partlow. "Afghans, U.S. Aim to Plug Cash Drain." *Washington Post*, August 21, 2010.

[25] Madhani, Aamer. "U.S. Reviews Afghan Watchdog Authority." *USA Today*, May 12, 2010.

[26] Rosenberg, Matthew. "Corruption Suspected in Airlift of Billions in Cash From Kabul." Wall Street Journal, June 28, 2010.

[27] Partlow, Joshua and Karen DeYoung. "Afghan Government Falters in Kandahar." Washington Post, November 3, 2010.

[28] For text, see http://www.state

[29] For more information, see the Defense Department report on Afghanistan stability, April 2010, cited earlier. pp. 19-20.

[30] Department of State. 2009 Human Rights Report: Afghanistan, March 11, 2010.

[31] Oppel, Richard Jr. and Abdul Waheed Wafa, "Hazara Minority Hustles to Head of the Class in Afghanistan," *New York Times*, January 4, 2010.

[32] "We Have the Promises of the World:Women's Rights in Afghanistan," Human Rights Watch, December 2009, http://www.wluml.org/sites/wluml.org/files/hrw_report_2009.pdf.

[33] CRS meeting with the Minister of Women's Affairs, October 13, 2009.

[34] For prior years, see CRS Report RL3 0588, *Afghanistan: Post-Taliban Governance, Security, and U.S. Policy*, by Kenneth Katzman, in the section on aid to Afghanistan, year by year.

[35] Department of State and U.S. Agency for International Development, "Report on U.S. Government Activities 2008- 2009 For Women and Girls in Afghanistan," October 20, 2009.

[36] Report by the Special Inspector General for Afghanistan Reconstruction (SIGAR). September 9, 2010.

[37] ECC website, http://www.ecc.org.af/en/.

[38] Fidler, Stephen and John W. Miller, "U.S. Allies Await Afghan Review," *Wall Street Journal*, September 25, 2009.

[39] Statement of the Independent Election Commission Secretariat, February 3, 2009, provided to CRS by a Karzai national security aide.

[40] Some of the information in this section obtained in CRS interviews with a Karzai national security aide, December 2008.

[41] Mulrine, Anna, "Afghan Presidential Candidate Takes a Page From Obama's Playbook," *U.S. News and World Report*, June 25, 2009.

[42] "Afghan Panel to Use Sampling in Recount," *USA Today*, September 22, 2009.

[43] See IEC website for final certified tallies, http://www.iec.org.af/results.

[44] Trofimov, Yaroslav, "West Urges Afghanistan to Delay Election," *Wall Street Journal*, December 11, 2009.

[45] Rondeaux, Candace. "Why Afghanistan's September Elections Ought to Be Postponed." *Washington Post*, July 11, 2010.

[46] Partlow, Joshua, "Afghanistan's Government Seeks More Control Over Elections," *Washington Post*, February 15, 2010.

[47] The seat allocation per province is the same as it was in the 2005 parliamentary election—33 seats up for election in Kabul; 17 in Herat province; 14 in Nangarhar, 11 each in Qandahar, Balkh, and Ghazni; 9 in Badakhshan, Konduz, and Faryab, 8 in Helmand, and 2 to 6 in the remaining provinces. Ten are reserved for Kuchis (nomads).

In: Fragile Mideast Countries: Afghanistan and Yemen
Editors: Robert P. Deen and Allison D. Burken

ISBN: 978-1-61209-709-1
© 2011 Nova Science Publishers, Inc.

Chapter 3

AFGHANISTAN: NARCOTICS AND U.S. POLICY

Christopher M. Blanchard

SUMMARY

Opium poppy cultivation and drug trafficking have eroded Afghanistan's fragile political and economic order over the last 30 years. In spite of ongoing counternarcotics efforts by the Afghan government, the United States, and their partners, Afghanistan remains the source of over 90% of the world's illicit opium. Since 2001, efforts to provide viable economic alternatives to poppy cultivation and to disrupt drug trafficking and related corruption have succeeded in some areas. However, insecurity, particularly in the southern province of Helmand, and widespread corruption fueled a surge in cultivation in 2006 and 2007, pushing opium output to all-time highs.

In 2008 and 2009, poppy cultivation decreased in north-central and eastern Afghanistan, while drug activity became more concentrated in the south and west. National poppy cultivation and opium production totals dropped in 2009 for the second straight season, as pressure from provincial officials, higher wheat prices, drought, and lower opium prices altered the cultivation decisions of some Afghan poppy farmers. Preliminary estimates for the 2010 season suggest that poor weather conditions, disease, and military operations in key poppy growing areas will limit production to 2009 levels, in spite of backsliding in some areas. Some experts continue to question the sustainability of rapid changes in cultivation patterns and recommend reinforcing recent reductions to replace poppy cultivation in local economies over time.

Across Afghanistan, insurgents, criminal organizations, and corrupt officials exploit narcotics as a reliable source of revenue and patronage, which has perpetuated the threat these groups pose to the country's fragile internal security and the legitimacy of its elected government. The trafficking of Afghan drugs appears to provide financial and logistical support to a range of extremist groups that continue to operate in and around Afghanistan. Although coalition forces may be less frequently relying on figures involved with narcotics for intelligence and security support, many observers have warned that drug-related corruption among appointed and elected Afghan officials creates political obstacles to progress.

As of April 2010, Congress had appropriated approximately $4.2 billion in regular and supplemental foreign assistance and defense funding for counternarcotics programs in Afghanistan from FY2001 through FY2010. The Obama Administration is pursuing a two-pronged interdiction and development policy in support of the government of Afghanistan's implementation of its National Drug Control Strategy. At present, U.S. military and law enforcement personnel are assisting Afghan forces and judicial authorities in targeting drug trafficking organizations while State Department, USAID, and USDA personnel are implementing expanded agricultural development assistance programs. The Administration ended U.S. support for eradication after deciding previous efforts were inefficient and potentially counterproductive. Afghan authorities continue to implement targeted eradication efforts.

This chapter provides current statistical information, profiles the narcotics trade's participants, explores linkages between narcotics, insecurity, and corruption, and reviews U.S. and international policy responses since late 2001. The report also considers ongoing policy debates regarding the counternarcotics role of coalition military forces, poppy eradication, alternative livelihoods, and funding issues for Congress. See also CRS Report RL30588, *Afghanistan: PostTaliban Governance, Security, and U.S. Policy*, by Kenneth Katzman, CRS Report R40699, *Afghanistan: U.S. Foreign Assistance*, by Curt Tarnoff, and CRS Report R40 156, *War in Afghanistan: Strategy, Military Operations, and Issues for Congress*, by Steve Bowman and Catherine Dale.

OVERVIEW

In spite of ongoing international efforts to combat Afghanistan's narcotics trade, U.N. officials estimate that Afghanistan supplies over 90% of the world's illicit opium.[1] Afghan, U.S., and international officials have stated that opium poppy cultivation and drug trafficking constitute serious strategic threats to the security and stability of Afghanistan and jeopardize the success of post-9/11 counterterrorism and reconstruction efforts. Since 2001, counternarcotics policy has emerged as a focal point in broader, recurring debates in the executive branch and in Congress about the United States' strategic objectives and policies in Afghanistan.

Relevant concerns include the role of U.S. military personnel and strategies for continuing the simultaneous pursuit of counterterrorism and counternarcotics goals, which may be complicated by practical necessities and political realities. Coalition forces pursuing regional counterinsurgency and counterterrorism objectives may rely on the cooperation of security commanders, tribal leaders, and local officials who may be involved in the narcotics trade. Counterinsurgency operations in key poppy growing areas have presented U.S. forces and officials with challenging decisions about the relative merits and risks inherent in simultaneously seeking to limit poppy cultivation and maintain positive relationships with local farmers. U.S. officials and many observers also believe that the introduction of a democratic system of government to Afghanistan has been accompanied by the election and appointment of many narcotics-associated and corrupt individuals to positions of public office.

Efforts to combat the opium trade in Afghanistan face the challenge of ending a highly profitable enterprise fueled by international demand that has become deeply interwoven with the economic, political, and social fabric of a war-torn country. Afghan, U.S., and international authorities are engaged in a campaign to reverse the unprecedented upsurge of opium poppy cultivation and heroin production that occurred following the fall of the Taliban. U.S. officials continue to implement a multifaceted counternarcotics initiative that includes public awareness campaigns, judicial reform measures, economic and agricultural development assistance, support for Afghan demand reduction programs, and drug interdiction operations. Questions regarding the likely effectiveness, resource requirements, and implications of counternarcotics strategies in Afghanistan continue to arise as Members of the 111th Congress review and debate the Obama Administration's policies.

AFGHANISTAN'S OPIUM ECONOMY

Opium production has become an entrenched negative element of Afghanistan's fragile political and economic order over the last 30 years in spite of ongoing local, regional, and international efforts to reverse its growth. At the time of Afghanistan's pro-Communist coup in 1978, narcotics experts estimated that Afghan farmers produced 300 metric tons (MT) of opium annually, enough to satisfy most local and regional demand and to supply a handful of heroin production facilities whose products were bound for Western Europe.[2] From the early 1980s through 2007, a trend of increasing opium poppy cultivation and opium production unfolded during successive periods of insurgency, civil war, fundamentalist government, and recently, international engagement (**Figures 1** and **2**). During the 2006-2007 poppy growing season, Afghanistan produced a world record opium poppy crop that yielded 8,200 MT of illicit opium—an estimated 93% of the world's supply.

A slight reduction in national poppy cultivation and opium output was recorded in 2007-2008, and many international officials attributed the changes to more effective counternarcotics approaches, including governor-enforced poppy cultivation bans and eradication. United Nations and Afghan government officials announced that further reductions in national cultivation and output statistics were recorded for the 2008-2009 season, due in part to bad weather, interdiction efforts, market prices, and improved agricultural assistance in some key poppy growing areas. Estimates for 2010, suggest that production will remain relatively static, with crop disease and poor weather conditions exerting downward pressure on output.

Overall, practitioners and observers remained focused on Afghan government, United Nations, and other field reporting that shows reductions in poppy cultivation in some northern, central, and eastern provinces, while large-scale cultivation continues in conflict-ridden southern provinces and remote areas of the east and west. By nearly all accounts, opiate trafficking and related corruption remain nationwide problems. With regard to so-called "poppy free" provinces, experts and practitioners continue to debate the causes and durability of recent reductions in poppy cultivation, with some analysts calling for more targeted development assistance to capitalize on and consolidate what they argue are still-reversible reductions in many areas. Parallel debates focus on the advisability and targeting of interdiction and eradication and the relative importance of and appropriate methods for sustainably replacing poppy cultivation and opium industry labor as income sources for Afghan households.

The concentration of poppy cultivation in insecure and remote areas has raised doubts in the minds of some observers about the likelihood of further gains in the absence of more fundamental improvements in security and stability. In the most volatile areas of the country, insecurity and corruption create a climate in which poppy cultivators and drug-trafficking groups remain largely free to operate. Violence and criminality stifle licit economic activity and prevent effective eradication, interdiction, outside investment, or the provision of development assistance. Reports suggest that the drug trade provides financial support to corrupt officials, criminal groups, and insurgents who in turn protect traffickers and perpetuate the chaotic environments that allow illicit trade to thrive.

In light of these challenges, current U.S. policy is designed to: break self-reinforcing cycles of insecurity, crime, and violence through direct action against traffickers, insurgents, and corrupt officials; understand, consolidate, and sustain reductions in poppy cultivation where they have occurred; and, reproduce sustainable reductions in cultivation nationwide.

2009 Production Statistics

According to the 2009 Afghanistan Opium Survey conducted by the Afghan Ministry of Counternarcotics (MCN) and the United Nations Office on Drugs and Crime (UNODC):[3]

- Opium poppy cultivation took place in 14 of 34 Afghan provinces in 2008-2009 (see Figure 3). The land area under poppy cultivation fell by 22% to 123,000 hectares (equal to 1.6% of Afghanistan's arable land). Cultivation remains overwhelmingly concentrated in conflict-ridden Helmand province, where farmers cultivated over 69,833 hectares of poppy—a 33% decline in the province from the prior season. MCN-UNODC estimates for 2010 suggest that three provinces may lose their poppy-free status while several others could become poppy-free depending on Afghan government responses and international support (see below).
- The 2008-2009 opium poppy crop had the potential to produce 6,900 MT of illicit opium, a 10% decline from the prior season. However, crop yields once again improved 15% due to better weather conditions in some areas. A range of accepted opium-to-heroin conversion rates indicate that an estimated opium yield of 6,900 MT could produce 690 to 985 MT of refined heroin.[4]
- Approximately 254,000 Afghan households cultivated opium poppy in 2008-2009, equal to roughly 1.6 million people or 6.4% of the Afghan population. Thousands of laborers, traffickers, warlords, and officials continue to participate.
- The estimated $438 million farmgate value (equal to volume multiplied by the price of non-dried opium paid to farmers) of the 2008-2009 opium harvest is equivalent in value to approximately 4% of the country's licit GDP. The export value of the 2008 crop may have exceeded $3.4 billion, equivalent to approximately 33% of the

country's licit 2008 GDP. Many licit and emerging industries have been financed or supported by profits from narcotics trafficking.[5]

As noted above, some experts and practitioners consider provincial and district level data to be a more accurate and informative reflection of counternarcotics challenges and successes. Recent UNODC/MCN reports attribute sustainable declines in poppy cultivation to political stability, economic integration, alternative livelihood assistance, and effective law enforcement. Other variables such as weather, raw opium prices (see **Table 1**), and the prices of licit crops, including wheat, have significant and difficult to quantify effects on farmers' decisions to grow poppy. At present, changes in opium and wheat price trends have led some expert observers and officials to express concern that prevailing price relationships that have undermined poppy cultivation may be slowing or entering a period of reversal. At the same time, weather conditions and disease patterns that have favored high opium yields in recent years appear to have reversed, amid widespread reports of blight from infection and drought.

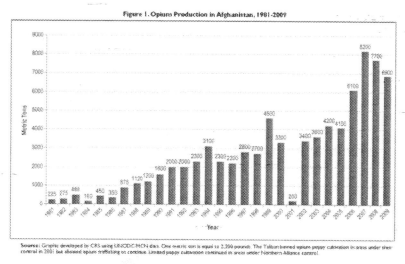

Source: Graphic developed by CRS using UNODC/MCN data. One metric ton is equal to 2,200 pounds. The Taliban banned opium poppy cultivation in areas under their control in 2001 but allowed opium trafficking to continue. Limited poppy cultivation continued in areas under Northern Alliance control.

Figure 1. Opium Production in Afghanistan, 1981-2009.

Table 1. Opium Prices in Afghanistan (regionally weighted fresh opium farmgate[a] price, current US$/kilogram).

	2000	2001[b]	2002	2003	2004	2005	2006	2007	2008	2009
Opium Price	$28	$301	$350	$283	$92	$102	$94	$86	$70	$48

Source: United Nations Office on Drugs and Crime, Afghanistan Opium Surveys 2004-2009.
a. Farmgate price for fresh opium is the price paid to farmers for non-dried opium.
b. Dry opium prices increase following the Taliban ban on poppy cultivation and skyrocketed to nearly $700/kg immediately following the September 11, 2001 terrorist attacks. According to UNODC, prices temporarily fell to $93/kg after U.S. airstrikes began.

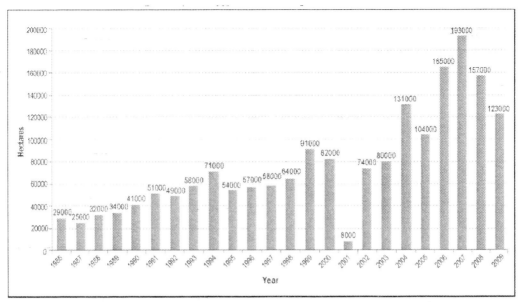

Source: Graphic developed by CRS using UNODC/MCN data. One hectare is equal to 10,000 square meters. The Taliban banned opium poppy cultivation in areas under their control in 2001 but allowed opium trafficking to continue. Limited poppy cultivation continued in areas under Northern Alliance control.

Figure 2. Opium Poppy Cultivation in Afghanistan, 1986-2009.

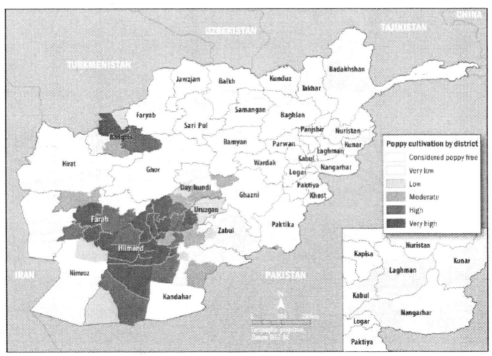

Source: Adapted by CRS from UNODC/MCN Afghanistan Opium Survey 2009, p. 17.
Notes: District boundaries approximate.

Figure 3. Estimated Opium Poppy Cultivation by District, 2009.

UNODC Projections and U.S. Assessments, 2010[6]

The December 2009 UNODC/Afghan Government opium survey reported further consolidation of poppy cultivation in the southern and western provinces of Helmand, Kandahar, Nimroz, Farah, Dai Kundi, Uruzgan, and Zabol. According to the U.S. State Department, 97% of Afghanistan's opium is produced in six of these seven provinces. Overall, UNODC monitoring found a significant decrease in national cultivation levels in 2009, due primarily to an over 33% reduction in cultivation in Helmand province. According to UNODC estimates, three provinces, Kapisa, Baghlan, and Faryab, became "poppy-free" in the last year, while limited production in remote and less secure areas of upper Nangarhar stripped the province of the poppy free designation it earned in 2008.

Although wheat prices declined from their 2008 high, they remained at roughly double their 2007 levels during 2009 and thus remained attractive relative to declining prices in Afghanistan's oversupplied opium market. Survey information from early 2010 suggests this price relationship may be shifting, as wheat prices begin to decline at a faster rate than opium prices. Survey data suggests that government intervention remains less influential in insecure southern and western provinces, with the exception of the Food Zone area of Helmand province, where a specially targeted interdiction and development program is credited with contributing significantly to the large drop in poppy cultivation observed in 2009. Farmers surveyed suggest that the effectiveness of alternative development programs varies across the country, and many reportedly emphasize the need for programs to extend beyond district centers to more remote or "grass roots" areas. Security remains a decisive factor in the ability of the Afghan government and its international partners to do so.

The March 2010 State Department International Narcotics Control Strategy Report for Afghanistan states that:

> "the Government of the Islamic Republic of Afghanistan (GIRoA) generally relies on the international community for assistance in implementing its national counternarcotics strategy. However, more political will, greater institutional capacity, and more robust efforts at the central and provincial levels are required to decrease cultivation in the south and west, maintain cultivation reductions in the rest of the country, and combat trafficking in coming years."[7]

The report also concludes that during 2009, "several governors were unwilling or unable to implement successful poppy reduction programs due to the lack of security and high levels of insurgent activity in their provinces." The 2010 INCSR report concludes that "many Afghan government officials are believed to profit from the drug trade, particularly at the provincial and district levels of government." The report also includes accounts of corruption among officials in national security forces, such as a Afghan National Police commander from Kandahar province. In April 2009, Secretary of State Hillary Clinton called corruption in Afghanistan "a cancer" that "eats away at the confidence and the trust of the people in their government."[8]

Obama Administration Policy and Funding Requests

The Obama Administration is implementing new counternarcotics policies in conjunction with its strategic reviews of U.S. policy in Afghanistan and Pakistan. The Administration's strategic review white paper, released March 27, 2009, called for "a complete overhaul of our civilian assistance strategy" and identified "agricultural sector job creation" as "an essential first step to undercutting the appeal of al Qaeda and its allies." The review document states that the Obama Administration believes crop substitution and alternative livelihood programs in Afghanistan "have been disastrously underdeveloped and under-resourced." It further indicates that interdiction and eradication operations will continue, but targeting will shift toward "higher level drug lords." These goals were echoed in the Afghanistan-Pakistan Regional Stabilization plan released in February 2010, which outlines a two-pronged approach of more robust interdiction and law enforcement efforts supported by agricultural development assistance and existing demand reduction and communications programs. A new National Security Council-approved counternarcotics strategy document summarizes the Administration's goals as follows: "Goal 1: Counter the link between narcotics and the insurgency and significantly reduce the support the insurgency receives from the narcotics industry. Goal 2: Address the narcotics corruption nexus and reinforce the Government of Afghanistan."[9]

In support of these objectives, the Administration requested civilian staff funding, development assistance, and enforcement funding in the FY2009 supplemental and its FY20 10 budget and supplemental proposals. The FY2009 supplemental request included Diplomatic and Consular Program (D&CP) funding requests for $84.8 million to support new U.S. Embassy and provincial reconstruction team (PRT) personnel from the State Department, USAID, and the U.S. Department of Agriculture (USDA). In addition, the D&CP account request included $137.6 million to support expanded interagency staffing in the areas of agriculture, justice, customs and border management, health, finance, and aviation. Some of the staffing funding requests would directly increase the number of U.S. personnel devoted to counternarcotics programs in Afghanistan. The Administration also requested $129 million in International Narcotics Control and Law Enforcement (INCLE) account funding to "support counternarcotics and law enforcement efforts primarily in the south and east of Afghanistan" and $214 million in Economic Support Fund (ESF) account funding to support "counternarcotics and stabilization programs, especially in the south and east." The Administration's FY20 10 request did not dramatically expand economic assistance specifically earmarked for counternarcotics purposes, in spite of official statements about those programs having been "under-resourced" in the past. However, ESF assistance requests for agricultural programs were significantly larger for FY20 10.

Table 2 details appropriations and requests for the main funding accounts supporting U.S. counternarcotics programming in Afghanistan for FY2009 through FY20 11. Drug Enforcement Administration (DEA) funds are not included: in July 2009, the Special Inspector General for Afghanistan Reconstruction (SIGAR) reported that Congress had appropriated $127.37 million for DEA activities in Afghanistan from FY2002 to FY2009. SIGAR also reported that Congress had appropriated approximately $3 billion for counternarcotics programs in Afghanistan from 2001 through 2008. Since 2006, Congress has placed conditions on some amounts of U.S. economic assistance to Afghanistan by requiring the President to certify that the Afghan government is cooperating fully with counternarcotics efforts prior to the obligation of funds or to issue a national security waiver (see "Certification Requirements" below).

ISSUES FOR CONGRESS

Experts and government officials have warned that narcotics trafficking jeopardizes international efforts to secure and stabilize Afghanistan. U.S. officials believe that efforts to reverse the related trends of opium cultivation, drug trafficking, corruption, and insecurity must expand if broader strategic objectives are to be achieved. A broad U.S. interagency initiative to assist Afghan authorities in combating the narcotics trade has been developed, and some officials argue that the U.S. efforts have been effective in areas where all elements of the strategy have been advanced simultaneously. However, in many areas, regional insecurity and corruption continue to prevent or complicate counternarcotics initiatives and thus present formidable challenges.

Table 2. Counternarcotics Appropriations and Requests, Afghanistan FY2009-FY20 1 1 (Current $, millions)

Account[a]	FY2009 Actual	FY2010 Estimate		FY2011 Request
		Base	Supplemental Request	
International Narcotics Control and Law Enforcement (INCLE)[b]	296.50	257.60	25.00	250.60
Economic Support Funds (ESF)	164.60	209.93	135.00	185.00
Department of Defense Counterdrug Activities[c]	215.67	324.60	94.00	457.10
Total	**$676.77**	**$1,046.13**		**$892.70**

Source: Congressional Budget Justifications for Foreign Operations Requests; Office of the Undersecretary of Defense (Comptroller), Justification Materials; and, CRS communications with Office of the Secretary of Defense and Department of State Bureau of Legislative Affairs, 2007 through March 2010.

Notes

a. Figures for State Department administered accounts (INCLE, ESF, DA) reflect amounts designated for the 'Counternarcotics' program area, under the 'Peace and Security' objective in the State Department's foreign assistance framework. Other funds appropriated in those and other accounts also may contribute to the achievement of U.S. counternarcotics objectives. For more information on the State Department foreign assistance framework, see CRS Report R402 13, *Foreign Aid: An Introduction to U.S. Programs and Policy*, by Curt Tarnoff and Marian Leonardo Lawson.

b. Includes INCLE funds for counternarcotics, police, and justice programs.

c. Figures for FY 2009 Department of Defense Counterdrug Activities denote funds used for programs in Afghanistan, Pakistan, Turkmenistan, Kyrgyzstan, Tajikistan, and "other regional support" in the CENTCOM area of responsibility. Figures for FY2010 and FY2011 denote Defense counterdrug requests for Overseas Contingency Operations.

Primary issues of interest to Congress include program funding, the role of the U.S. military, and the scope and nature of eradication, interdiction, and development assistance initiatives. During the term of the 110th Congress, the Bush Administration argued that insecurity in key opium poppy producing areas, delays in building and reforming Afghan institutions, and widespread Afghan corruption continued to prevent full implementation of U.S. and Afghan counternarcotics strategies. The Obama Administration and the 111th Congress have devoted new resources to counternarcotics efforts as part of an expanded civilian and military effort to bring stability to Afghanistan. The shift toward a civilian-military counterinsurgency strategy has created new challenges and opportunities for Afghan and U.S. counternarcotics efforts.

Breaking the Narcotics-Insecurity Cycle

Narcotics trafficking and political instability remain intimately linked in Afghanistan. U.S. officials have identified narcotics trafficking as a primary barrier to the establishment of security and consider insecurity to be a primary barrier to successful counternarcotics operations. The narcotics trade fuels three corrosive trends that have undermined the stability of Afghan society and limited progress toward reconstruction since 2001. First, narcotics proceeds can corrupt police, judges, and government officials and prevent the establishment of basic rule of law in many areas. Second, the narcotics trade can provide the Taliban and other insurgents with funding and arms that support their violent activities. Third, corruption and violence can prevent reform and development necessary for the renewal of legitimate economic activity. In the most conflict- prone areas, symbiotic relationships between narcotics producers, traffickers, insurgents, and corrupt officials can create self-reinforcing cycles of violence and criminality (see **Figure 4**) Across Afghanistan, the persistence of these trends undermines Afghan civilians' confidence in their local, provincial, and national government institutions.

Critics of counternarcotics efforts to date have argued that Afghan authorities and their international partners have been reluctant to directly confront prominent individuals and groups involved in the opium trade because of their fear that confrontation will lead to internal security disruptions or expand armed conflict to include drug-related groups.[10] Indeed, conflict and regional security disruptions have accompanied some efforts to expand crop eradication programs and to implement interdiction and alternative livelihood policies.

The Obama Administration has incorporated more robust interdiction efforts and targeted major drug trafficking figures as a component of an expanded counterinsurgency strategy. For years, U.S. officials have identified rural security and national rule of law as prerequisites for effective counternarcotics policy implementation, while simultaneously identifying narcotics as a primary threat to security and stability. As early as 2005, the State Department was arguing that:

> "Poppy cultivation is likely to continue until responsible governmental authority is established throughout the country and until rural poverty levels can be reduced via provision of alternative livelihoods and increased rural incomes.... Drug processing and trafficking can be expected to continue until security is established and drug law enforcement capabilities can be increased."[11]

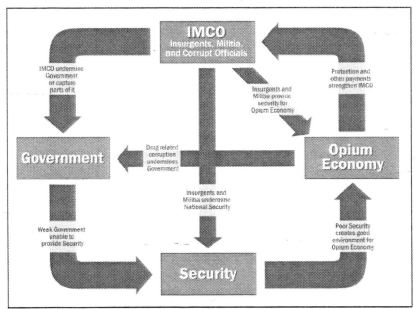

Source: Adapted and updated by CRS from World Bank, Afghanistan: State Building, Sustaining Growth, and Reducing Poverty, Country Economic Report No. 29551-AF September 9, 2004, p. 87.

Figure 4. Narcotics, Corruption, and Security in Afghanistan.

Although an increasing number of Afghan police, security forces, and counternarcotics authorities have been trained by U.S. and coalition officials, the limited size and capability of Afghan forces rendered them unable to effectively and independently challenge entrenched drug-trafficking groups and insurgents. For years, Afghan security and counternarcotics forces alone proved unable to establish the security conditions necessary for the more robust interdiction and alternative livelihood programs planned by U.S. and Afghan officials. Current coalition military operations in areas like central Helmand province—the poppy growing heartland of Afghanistan—seek to establish security conditions for the Afghan government to assert its authority and, working in conjunction with U.S. and other international partners, to disrupt reinforcing relationships between insurgents and narcotics traffickers.

Balancing Counterterrorism, Counterinsurgency, and Counternarcotics

In pursuing counterterrorism and counterinsurgency objectives, Afghan and coalition authorities consider difficult political choices when confronting corrupt officials, militia leaders, narcotics traffickers, and poppy farmers. These choices have changed over time as the conflict in Afghanistan has evolved and differ from region to region. Regional and local militia commanders with alleged links to the opium trade played significant roles in initial post-9/11 coalition efforts to undermine the Taliban regime and capture Al Qaeda operatives, particularly in southern and southeastern Afghanistan.[12] Some of these figures and their political allies were subsequently incorporated into government and security structures, including positions of responsibility for enforcing counternarcotics policies.[13] For example, the current governor of Nangarhar province, Gul Agha Sherzai, is now credited with effectively enforcing bans on poppy cultivation and supporting anti-drug-trafficking efforts. However, in 2001 and 2002, as governor of his native Kandahar province, he was alleged to have maintained a close relationship with an alleged Taliban-associated narcotics kingpin that has been indicted on drug-trafficking charges in the United States.[14]

In areas that enjoyed relative security prior to the more recent Taliban resurgence, Afghan government officials, provincial leaders, and international partners faced difficult decisions about implementing counternarcotics enforcement policies. Forced eradication, whether by central government or provincial government forces, risked antagonizing local populations with marginal economic alternatives and created opportunities for patronage and corruption on the part of those choosing eradication targets and enforcing the policy. Similarly, interdiction targets multiplied as the country's opium economy erupted and expanded, but corruption and the strengthening of trafficking groups created significant potential political and security costs for officials contemplating interdiction and anti-corruption responses. Pragmatic decisions taken since 2001 to prioritize counterterrorism operations and maintain relationships with figures known to benefit from the drug trade compounded these challenges in some areas, as tactical coalition allies inhibited the ability of the central government to extend its authority and enforce its counternarcotics policies.[15]

U.S. and Afghan officials have been increasingly adamant in stating that the Taliban resurgence that has unfolded since early 2006 has been supported in part by narcotics proceeds and that narcotics-related corruption undermines the effectiveness of Afghan security forces. However, current plans to employ counterinsurgency tactics against the Taliban and enforce counternarcotics policies more strictly also may conflict with each other, forcing Afghan and coalition authorities to manage competing priorities. Coalition military operations in Helmand province, and specifically U.S. Marine operations in Marjah and the surrounding districts of Nade Ali and Garm Ser (see below), have illustrated these challenges. One senior Defense Department official has argued that U.S. counternarcotics strategy in Afghanistan must recognize "the impact the drug trade has on our other policy objectives, while complementing (and not competing with) our other efforts in furtherance of those objectives."[16] Striking such a balance may continue to create challenges for the United States and its allies.

Defining the Role of the U.S. Military and ISAF

Debate over the role of the U.S. military and coalition forces in the International Security Assistance Force has shifted as the roles and missions of those forces have changed. The initial focus on counterterrorism (CT) led military forces to view the narcotics trade as a contingent priority, while the shift toward a counterinsurgency (COIN) approach has dictated an increased role for the military in eliminating narcotics targets providing support for the Taliban and other anti-government forces.

Targeting and Enforcement

For years, some observers argued that U.S., coalition, and NATO military forces should play an active, direct role in targeting the leaders and infrastructure of the opiate trade. For example, following the announcement of record poppy cultivation and opium production in 2005-200 6, UNODC Director Antonio Maria Costa called for direct NATO military involvement in counternarcotics enforcement operations in Afghanistan. Arguments in favor of coalition involvement in counternarcotics enforcement activities often cited the limited capabilities of Afghan security forces and held that coalition forces able to take action against narcotics traffickers should do so in the interest of Afghanistan's national security and coalition goals.

In general, opponents of a direct enforcement role for U.S., coalition, or NATO forces claimed that such a role would alienate forces from the Afghan population, jeopardize ongoing counterterrorism missions that require local Afghan intelligence support, and divert limited coalition military resources from direct counter-insurgent and counterterrorism operations. Others in the U.S. government and in Congress opposed direct military involvement in counternarcotics enforcement activities based on concerns about maintaining distinct authorities and capabilities among agencies. For example, the House report on the FY2007 Defense authorization bill argued that the Defense Department "must not take on roles in which other countries or other agencies of the U.S. Government have core capabilities" with regard to counternarcotics in Afghanistan.

During the George W. Bush Administration, U.S. Central Command (CENTCOM) officials indicated that Defense Department counternarcotics programs in Afghanistan were "a key element of our campaign against terrorism."[17] However, U.S. military officials largely resisted the establishment of a direct counternarcotics enforcement role for U.S. forces owing to limited resources and concerns about exacerbating security threats. As late as 2006, former NATO Commander and current National Security Adviser General James Jones advanced the idea that counternarcotics enforcement was "not a military mission," and stated that "having NATO troops out there burning crops" was "not going to significantly contribute to the war on drugs."[18]

Until October 2008, NATO International Security Assistance Force (ISAF) directives precluded direct military action against narcotics targets such as traffickers and laboratories.[19] Changes in authorization agreed to in Budapest during an October 2008 meeting and subsequent consultations now allow ISAF forces to take action against insurgency-linked narcotics targets if they so choose and if authorized under their own domestic laws.[20]

According to the Department of Defense, U.S. military forces have long been authorized to seize narcotics and related supplies encountered during the course of normal stability and counterterrorism operations. Those basic rules of engagement have been changed, but the Defense Department does not publicly disclose details on the content of the changes.[21] Defense Department policy guidance issued in December 2008 states that Department personnel "will not directly participate in searches, seizures, arrests, or similar activity unless such personnel are otherwise authorized by law" with the exception of the provision of force protection "up to and including on the objective."[22] According to the guidance, Department personnel may accompany U.S. or host nation law enforcement and security forces on counternarcotics field operations within presidentially declared combat zones. Executive Order 13239 (issued December 12, 2001, effective as of September 19, 2001) designated Afghanistan and the airspace above it as combat zones.[23]

In August 2009, the Senate Foreign Relations Committee released a report containing statements from unnamed U.S. military officers and officials that provides an unconfirmed account of how the new U.S. military policy on counternarcotics enforcement may be being applied in Afghanistan. According to the report

> two U.S. generals in Afghanistan said that the ROE [rules of engagement] and the internationally recognized Law of War have been interpreted to allow them to put drug traffickers with proven links to the insurgency on a kill list, called the joint integrated prioritized target list. The military places no restrictions on the use of force with these selected targets, which means they can be killed or captured on the battlefield; it does not, however, authorize targeted assassinations away from the battlefield. The generals said standards for getting on the list require two verifiable human sources and substantial additional evidence. Currently, there are roughly 50 major traffickers who contribute funds to the insurgency on the target list.[24]

The Defense Department has declined to comment on the specific statements included in the Senate report. However, a Pentagon spokesman said that "there is a positive, well-known connection between the drug trade and financing for the insurgency and terrorism," and, it is "important to clarify that we are targeting terrorists with links to the drug trade, rather than targeting drug traffickers with links to terrorism."[25] Thus far, U.S. and ISAF officials have declined to offer further public comment on the specific criteria currently used for targeting individuals associated with both the drug trade and insurgency.

Some observers have questioned the legal basis for the targeting of so-called "nexus targets" based on international humanitarian law (IHL), which generally prohibits the direct use of force against civilians unless and for so long as they are directly participating in hostilities.[26] Under this view, drug traffickers could be subject to direct military attack only if they are considered to be active members of the armed forces of a party to the conflict or if they are considered to be civilians directly participating in hostilities. In July 2009, the International Committee of the Red Cross (ICRC) released nonbinding interpretive guidance on the notion of direct participation in hostilities under IHL.[27] The guidance states that individuals involved with the "purchase, production, smuggling and hiding of weapons; general recruitment and training of personnel; and financial, administrative or political support to armed actors" retain the protected status against direct military attack that all civilians enjoy unless such acts qualify as "preparatory measures aiming to carry out a specific hostile act" and are "specifically designed to [inflict harm] in support of a party to an armed conflict and to the detriment of another."[28] Press reports, field surveys, and coalition military statements suggest that some individuals and groups involved in narcotics trafficking provide varying levels of support to some anti-Afghan government forces, which may or may not include direct participation in hostilities on a case-by-case basis.

Expanded counternarcotics roles for the U.S. military, whether under U.S. command, or as a component of ISAF, may lead to requests for more resources. The January 2009 Defense Department report on stability and security in Afghan argued that:

> Use of limited forces in Afghanistan is a zero-sum endeavor. A shift in force application from one mission set to another comes with a cost of a reduction of available forces for the former mission set. A shift of limited assets may result in a degradation of the [counterinsurgency] COIN mission. At the same time, the COIN mission cannot be addressed

effectively without engaging in the [counternarcotics] CN mission. Additional resources, targeted to the CN mission, would be needed to expand direct DoD support to counternarcotics operations.[29]

OPERATION MOSHTARAK AND MARJA ACCELERATED AGRICULTURAL TRANSITION PROGRAM

U.S. military operations in Helmand province have brought U.S. forces into direct contact with communities and individuals at the epicenter of the poppy cultivation and opiate trafficking economies in Afghanistan. Adapting military operations and counternarcotics policies to fit the needs of the overarching civilian-military counterinsurgency campaign plan in Helmand have proven challenging and have required flexibility and ingenuity on the part of Afghan and U.S. personnel. U.S.-assisted counternarcotics raids in central Helmand province during 2009 disrupted narcotics trafficking operations and netted large seizures of opiates and pre-cursor chemicals used in the production of morphine and heroin. The Department of Defense reports that, in advance of the planned Operation MOSHTARAK in early 2010, narcotics traffickers "began buying significant amounts of stocks, settling debts, and closing and moving their businesses to avoid risk of impending interdiction."[30] The Administration observed that "buyers and transporters have demonstrated that they are unwilling to absorb sustained risk and the narcotics business has significantly decreased in the corresponding operational areas." The Administration believes that the "suppressing effect" of military operations in key poppy growing and opiate trafficking areas "creates a window of opportunity to further separate the insurgent criminal nexus from the population."

Managing the economic and political effects of recent military interventions in a major poppy growing area of Helmand like Marja underscored the competing priorities inherent to the simultaneous pursuit of counterinsurgency and counternarcotics goals. As 2nd Marine Expeditionary Brigade commander Brig. Gen. Lawrence Nicholson stated, "When we went into Marja, we didn't declare war on the poppy farmer."[31] Nevertheless, ISAF strategic planners, the Marines, and State Department advisers all recognized that Operation MOSHTARAK "disrupted the economic cycle of Marja" by halting the cultivation of poppy. Amid pressure from the Afghan government to introduce forced eradication measures, U.S. personnel implemented a temporary program known as the Marja Accelerated Agricultural Transition Program that would compensate farmers that destroyed their crops and committed not to cultivate in the future in exchange for a payment of $300 per hectare derived from U.S. Commanders Emergency Response Program (CERP) funds.[32] The program is an experiment in balancing the overarching desire to extend government authority with a recognition of the negative economic and political consequences of counterinsurgency operations in key poppy growing areas. Critics of similar compensation programs have argued that payments create perverse incentives for others to grow poppy in pursuit of self-eradication payments. U.S. forces and officials have been strenuous in asserting that the Marja program was a unique response to a unique situation and have committed to carefully monitoring its results as an indication of the program's potential value and costs for future operations.

The July 2009 report echoed this assessment, arguing that "care must be taken in shifting limited assets out of CT COIN or the CT-COIN nexus into purely CN activities. Such a shift would detract from the former mission and likely result in detrimental effects on the population as military force is applied to purely civilian-criminal narcotics activities." Administration officials have not clearly defined the distinction between so called "nexus targets" that support the insurgency and what it considers "purely civilian-criminal narcotics activities," particularly with regard to narcotics-related government corruption. According to the April 2010 report to Congress on current U.S. strategy and operations in Afghanistan, "The Government of Afghanistan has the lead in all CN operations and partners with ANSF, U.S., and international forces to target narcotics traffickers and facilities known to support the insurgency."

Defense Authorization and the Provision of Equipment and Weaponry

From 2002 through 2009, Congress and the Bush Administration gradually expanded the role for U.S. military forces in training, equipping, and providing intelligence and airlift support for Afghan counternarcotics teams. To date, Defense Department authorizations for counternarcotics activities in Afghanistan have been provided via reference to Section 1033 of the Defense Authorization Act for FY1 998 (P.L. 105-85, as amended) and Section 1004 of the Defense Authorization Act for FY1 991 (P.L. 101-510, as amended). Both acts have been amended on a semiannual basis to extend existing authorizations into subsequent fiscal years, to expand the authorities to include new countries, and, as written, to require reauthorization to extend beyond the end of FY2006. Since 2005, other legislative proposals to expand Defense Department counternarcotics authorities in Afghanistan have been considered, but not adopted. [33] The FY2009 Defense Authorization Act (P.L. 110-417) restated the existing authorizations and reauthorized the Secretary of Defense to provide non-lethal counternarcotics assistance to Afghanistan and a number of its neighbors (and other countries) through FY2009. The FY2010 authorization (P.L. 111-84) extended the authorization through FY2010 and requires the submission of an counter- drug plan for each fiscal year support is provided.

Section 1021 of the Defense Authorization Act for FY2004 (P.L. 108-136) added Afghanistan to the list of countries eligible for transfers of non-lethal Defense Department counternarcotics equipment authorized under Section 1033 of the Defense Authorization Act for FY1 998 (P.L. 105-85). The FY2005 and FY2006 supplemental appropriations acts (P.L. 109-13 and P.L. 109- 234) further authorized the provision of individual and crew-served weapons, ammunition, vehicles, aircraft, and detection, interception, monitoring and testing equipment to Afghan counternarcotics forces. To date, .50-caliber machine guns have been provided along with night vision equipment and a range of other supplies. Afghan counternarcotics forces have requested further weaponry in response to attacks by well armed and supplied trafficking groups. The FY2009 Defense Authorization Act (P.L. 110-417) reauthorized provision of .50-caliber and lighter crew-served weaponry and ammunition through FY2009. The FY2010 authorization (P.L. 111-84) extended the authorization through FY20 10. The House version of the FY2011 defense authorization (H.R. 5136), would extend existing authorities and reporting requirements through FY2011.

Alternative Livelihoods and Development

As noted above, the Obama Administration has highlighted alternative livelihood and agricultural development assistance as a key component of its new strategic priorities in Afghanistan. USAID's current alternative livelihood programs are based on a two-track approach. In areas that have reduced poppy cultivation in the north, east, and west of the country, USAID and its contracting partners are seeking to provide broad-based agricultural development assistance designed to consolidate positive changes in poppy cultivation patterns. The $150 million Incentives Driving Economic Alternatives for the North East, and West (IDEA-NEW) program is planned to run through FY2014. In southern and eastern areas of the country where counterinsurgency operations are ongoing amid continued poppy cultivation and drug production, USAID and its contracting partners plan to provide more targeted, quick-impact agricultural and development assistance as a means of reinforcing efforts to secure newly cleared areas.[34] The $300 million Afghanistan Vouchers for Increased Production in Agriculture (AVIPA-Plus) program is scheduled to run through FY20 10 and includes initiatives coordinated with U.S. counterinsurgency operations in Helmand and Kandahar provinces.

Obama Administration officials have stated that "part of making the counternarcotics strategy more effective will be working a lot harder on crop substitution," which has been an area of congressional interest in the past.[35] The U.S. Department of Agriculture (USDA) has expanded its presence in country in support of new USAID programs, and USDA officials now serve as part of a consolidated interagency agriculture policy team based in Kabul.[36]

HELMAND: FOOD ZONE PROGRAM

Helmand Governor Gulab Mangal, USAID, and the United Kingdom have developed a targeted alternative development effort in Helmand province known as the "Food Zone" program. The initiative is geared toward low income farmers in a series of zones in the fertile poppy producing areas along the Helmand river covering a 27,000 hectare area that stretches from Gareshk in the north through the provincial capital of Lashkar Gah to Garm Ser in the south. The program includes the distribution of improved seeds and fertilizer along with technical assistance during planting, tending, and harvest periods. Beneficiary farmers are required to sign pledges to not grow poppy, and strong eradication efforts have been introduced to areas not participating in the program. Governor Mangal is credited with having led an effective administration as the governor of Laghman Province and is viewed by U.S. officials as committed to achieving counternarcotics goals in Afghanistan's main poppy producing province. The UNODC 2009 Opium Survey cites independent survey data that suggests that the significant decrease in poppy cultivation in Helmand during 2009 occurred mostly in the Food Zone, whereas cultivation was observed to increase by as much as 8% outside of the Zone.

Eradication

Central Government and Governor-Led Eradication

The Obama Administration has "phased out" U.S. support for poppy eradication efforts in Afghanistan in line with its strategic review and the judgment of Administration officials that eradication programs were not cost efficient and that eradication activities often proved counterproductive. The policy change comes after years of debate in Washington, DC, Kabul, and across Europe about the relative merits and drawbacks of supporting Afghan government poppy eradication efforts.

Proponents of forced eradication have long argued that destroying large portions of Afghanistan's opium poppy crops is necessary in order to establish and maintain a credible deterrent for farmers and landowners in line with Afghan law. Critics of forced eradication argued in response that eradication in the absence of existing alternative livelihood options for Afghan farmers contributes to the likelihood that farmers will continue to cultivate opium poppy in the future and may encourage some farmers and landowners to support anti-government elements, including the Taliban.

To date, U.S. and Afghan authorities have maintained that the Central Poppy Eradication Force and governor-led eradication programs have been effective in deterring and reducing some opium poppy cultivation. However, given recurrent clashes between eradication forces and farmers and accounts of selective, politicized eradication efforts by local authorities, other observers and officials have expressed concern about the safety and effectiveness of current ground-based eradication efforts. The Bush Administration sought to improve eradication results by embedding "poppy elimination" teams (now referred to as Counternarcotics Advisory Teams or CNATs) in key opium poppy growing provinces to monitor and advise on early season, locally executed eradication activities. The strategy was designed to minimize violent farmer resistance to central government forces and give farming families time to plant replacement cash crops.

The Obama Administration redirected roughly $150 million in FY2009 INCLE funding from support to central poppy eradication efforts to other initiatives, including interdiction operations, public information campaigns, and advisory efforts by CNAT personnel.[37] Air assets previously used for air support and medivac purposes may be redirected to support Afghan-DEA interdiction operations. The 600-person Central Poppy Eradication Force has been disbanded and its personnel were redirected to other activities—initially election security—but may resume some counternarcotics security functions. The Counternarcotics Infantry Kandak (CNIK) created to secure poppy eradication operations may be redirected to support other counternarcotics or security operations. Accounts suggest that the Obama Administration's decision to "phase out" U.S. support to eradication efforts has not eliminated the Afghan government's commitment to continue to support eradication efforts by Afghan governors. The April 2010 Administration report to Congress on security and stability in Afghanistan notes that "the Afghan Government managed to eradicate 647 hectares of poppy in Helmand and Farah during the first quarter of 2010" through operations planned and implemented by the Ministry of Counter Narcotics and provincial governors.

Manual or Aerial Herbicide-based Eradication

Afghan and U.S. authorities discussed the introduction of aerial herbicide-based eradication to Afghanistan in late 2004, but decided against initiating a program in early 2005 due to financial, logistical, and political considerations. Since 2006, ground-based eradication results have varied drastically based on location and local political and security conditions. This has led some to renew their calls for the introduction of stronger eradication methods, including the use of herbicides to kill poppy plants. With the Obama Administration's policy changes in place, the prospects for such a program look increasingly unlikely. Nevertheless, policy makers and Members of Congress may engage in further debate concerning options for using herbicides for manual or aerial poppy eradication and their possible risks and rewards.

In the past, Afghan President Hamid Karzai has expressed categorical opposition to the use of aerial eradication, citing public health and environmental safety concerns.[38] The 2006 Afghan national drug control strategy also stated that the Afghan government "has also decided that eradication must only be delivered by manual or mechanical ground based means."[39] Bush Administration officials argued for more widespread and non-negotiated eradication operations and stated that while herbicides may be efficient and safe, U.S. officials would follow the decisions of Afghan officials concerning their potential use. Since FY2005, Congress has sought to prohibit or condition the use of appropriated funds to support aerial herbicide spraying in Afghanistan. In the 111th Congress, the Omnibus Appropriations Act, 2009 (H.R. 1105; P.L. 111- 8) specifies that:

> "...none of the funds appropriated under this heading for assistance for Afghanistan may be made available for eradication programs through the aerial spraying of herbicides unless the Secretary of State determines and reports to the Committees on Appropriations that the President of Afghanistan has requested assistance for such aerial spraying programs for counternarcotics or counterterrorism purposes."

The Act further requires the Secretary of State to consult with the Committees on Appropriations prior to the obligation of funds for an aerial eradication programs in the event that such a determination is made.

Counternarcotics Assistance Certification and Reporting Requirements

Since 2002, funding for U.S. counternarcotics operations in Afghanistan has consisted of U.S. program costs and financial and material assistance to Afghan counternarcotics organizations. Although poppy cultivation and drug trafficking were widespread prior to the fall of the Taliban regime, U.S. counternarcotics programs in the region were limited, and focused on eliminating poppy cultivation and supporting interdiction activities in neighboring countries. U.S. funding for counternarcotics programs in Afghanistan did not increase dramatically until FY2005, when the Bush Administration submitted requests to Congress for funding to support the introduction of its five pillar counternarcotics strategy (See Table 2).

Certification Requirements

Since 2006, Congress has placed conditions on some amounts of U.S. economic assistance to Afghanistan by requiring the President to certify that the Afghan government is cooperating fully with counternarcotics efforts prior to the obligation of funds or to issue a national security waiver. The conditions serve as signal of congressional views that U.S. assistance should not be given to a government not fully cooperating with U.S. counternarcotics efforts unless U.S. national security would be jeopardized if assistance were withheld. The 2006 Foreign Operations Appropriations Act (P.L. 109-102) stated that no more than $225 million in Economic Support Fund (ESF) assistance could be obligated until the President certified to Congress that the Afghan government "at both the national and local level is cooperating fully with United States funded poppy eradication and interdiction efforts." The Act provided waiver authority to the President if he deemed it necessary to preserve the vital national security interests of the United States. The Bush Administration issued a waiver of the certification requirement for FY2006 ESF appropriations for Afghanistan on May 22, 2006.[40]

Subsequent appropriations legislation also has included these provisions. For FY2007, the FY2006 conditions were carried forward based on the provisions of the Revised Continuing Appropriations Resolution, 2007 (P.L. 110-5).[41] The certification and justification report were completed in June 2007. The FY2008 Consolidated Appropriations Act (P.L. 110-161, H.R. 2764) limited the obligation of FY2008 ESF assistance to Afghanistan to $300 million until the Secretary of State certified to the Appropriations committees that the Afghan government "at both the national and local level" was fully cooperating with U.S.-funded poppy eradication and drug interdiction efforts. The Act provided for a presidential waiver of this provision, subject to a reporting requirement. The Bush Administration waived the certification requirement for FY2008 ESF appropriations for Afghanistan on May 9, 2008, and issued a detailed report to Congress justifying its decision and describing U.S. and Afghan counternarcotics efforts and remaining challenges.[42]

In the 111th Congress, the Omnibus Appropriations Act, 2009, states that $200,000,000 in ESF funding may be obligated "only after the Secretary of State certifies to the Committees on Appropriations that the Government of Afghanistan at both the national and provincial level is cooperating fully with United States-funded poppy eradication and interdiction efforts in Afghanistan." The Act provides for a presidential waiver based on national security determination. Section 707 6(d) of the Consolidated Appropriations Act, 2010 states that $200,000,000 in ESF funding may not be obligated "unless the Secretary of State certifies to the Committees on Appropriations that the Government of Afghanistan is cooperating fully with United States efforts against the Taliban and Al Qaeda and to reduce poppy cultivation and illicit drug trafficking." The Act provides for waiver authority to the Secretary of State based on national security interests determination.[43]

Reporting Requirements

Since 2002, Congress has required the executive branch to submit a number of detailed reports on its counternarcotics strategies and the use of appropriated funds to support counternarcotics programs in Afghanistan. Among these reports are worldwide annual surveys of Defense Department counterdrug activities, required reports justifying the waiver of conditions on U.S. ESF assistance, and specific reports on the opiate trade in and around Afghanistan and Administration plans to combat it. The following list highlights a number of recent reports that may be of interest to Congress for oversight purposes. It is not exhaustive:

- Section 7104 of the Intelligence Reform and Terrorism Prevention Act of 2004 (P.L. 108-458) required the submission of an interagency report that described current progress toward the reduction of poppy cultivation and heroin production in Afghanistan and provided detail on the extent to which drug profits support terrorist groups and anti-government elements in and around Afghanistan. The report was completed in October 2005.[44]
- P.L. 110-28 required the DEA Administrator to submit a report by July 31, 2007 that included a plan to target and arrest Afghan drug kingpins in Helmand and Kandahar provinces.
- House report on H.R. 2764 (H.Rept. 110-197) required the Administration to report on "the use of aerial assets to include fixed and rotary wing aircraft in coordination with and in support of Drug Enforcement Administration (DEA) counternarcotics operations," and, "the extradition status of Afghan drug kingpins and narco terrorists, the destruction of Afghan heroin laboratories, local Afghan prosecutions of heroin-related crimes, and illegal border crossings by foreign nationals from Pakistan into Afghanistan."
- The National Defense Authorization Act, 2008 (Section 1230, P.L. 110-181) requires the executive branch to submit a report on the comprehensive strategy of the United States for security and stability in Afghanistan every 180 days through FY20 10. The reports issued to date have included sections devoted to counternarcotics policy as well as other issues such as police training and judicial reform relevant to U.S. and Afghan counternarcotics goals.
- The FY2009 Duncan Hunter National Defense Authorization Act (P.L. 110-417) extended the requirement for annual Defense Department reporting on its overseas counterdrug activities through 2009, and Section 1026 of the Act requires the Secretary of Defense to submit by June 30, 2009, "a comprehensive strategy of the Department of the Defense with regard to counternarcotics efforts in the South and Central Asian regions, including the countries of Afghanistan, Turkmenistan, Tajikistan, Kyrgyzstan, Kazakhstan, Pakistan, and India, as well as the countries of Armenia, Azerbaijan, and China."
- The FY2010 Defense Authorization Act (P.L. 111-84) requires the submission of a counter-drug plan for each fiscal year that Defense Department support is provided.

End Notes

[1] United Nations Office on Drugs and Crime (UNODC)/Government of Afghanistan Ministry of Counternarcotics (MCN), Afghan Opium Survey 2009, December 2009.

[2] See Jonathan C. Randal, "Afghanistan's Promised War on Opium," *Washington Post*, November 2, 1978, and Stuart Auerbach, "New Heroin Connection: Afghanistan and Pakistan Supply West With Opium," *Washington Post*, October 11, 1979.

[3] United Nations Office on Drugs and Crime, Afghanistan Opium Survey 2009. Available at: http://www.unodc.org/documents/crop

[4] Methodology described in UNODC/Afghan Gov., Afghanistan Opium Survey 2004, November 2004, pp. 105-7.

[5] Edouard Martin and Steven Symansky, "Macroeconomic Impact of the Drug Economy and Counter-Narcotics Efforts," in Doris Buddenberg and William A. Byrd (eds.), *Afghanistan's Drug Industry: Structure, Functioning, Dynamics, and Implications for Counter-Narcotics Policy*, World Bank/UNODC, November 2006.

[6] Based on UNODC/MCN, Afghanistan Opium Survey, September 2009.

[7] Available at: http://www.state

[8] Radio Free Europe/Radio Liberty, Full Transcript Of Interview With Hillary Clinton, April 6, 2009.

[9] U.S. Department of Defense, Report on Progress Toward Security and Stability in Afghanistan, Report to Congress in accordance with section 1230 of the National Defense Authorization Act for Fiscal Year 2008 (P.L. 110-181), April 2010, p. 73.

[10] In the past, Afghan authorities have expressed their belief that "the beneficiaries of the drugs trade will resist attempts to destroy it," and have argued that "the political risk of internal instability caused by counternarcotics measures" must be balanced "with the requirement to project central authority nationally" for counternarcotics purposes. See National Drug Control Strategy, Transitional Islamic State of Afghanistan, May 18, 2003.

[11] Department of State, INCSR, March 2005.

[12] According to Afghanistan scholar Barnett Rubin, "the empowerment and enrichment of the warlords who allied with the United States in the anti-Taliban efforts, and whose weapons and authority now enabled them to tax and protect opium traffickers," have provided the opium trade "with powerful new protectors." Rubin, "Road to Ruin: Afghanistan's Booming Opium Industry," October 7, 2004.

[13] See Syed Saleem Shahzad, "U.S. Turns to Drug Baron to Rally Support," *Asia Times*, December 4, 2001; Charles Clover and Peronet Despeignes, "Murder Undermines Karzai Government," *Financial Times*, July 8, 2002; Susan B. Glasser, "U.S. Backing Helps Warlord Solidify Power," *Washington Post*, February 18, 2002; Ron Moreau and Sami Yousafzai, with Donatella Lorch, "Flowers of Destruction," *Newsweek*, July 14, 2003; Andrew North, "Warlord Tells Police Chief to Go," *BBC News*, July 12, 2004; Steven Graham, "Group: Warlords to Hinder Afghan Election," *Associated Press*, September 28, 2004; and Anne Barnard and Farah Stockman, "U.S. Weighs Role in Heroin War in Afghanistan," *Boston Globe*, October 20, 2004.

[14] *CBS Evening News*, "Newly Arrived US Army Soldiers Find it Difficult to Adjust...," February 7, 2002; Mark Corcoran, "America's Blind Eye," Australian Broadcasting Corporation, *Foreign Correspondent*, April 10, 2002; and, Steve Inskeep, "Afghanistan's Opium Trade," National Public Radio, April 26, 2002.

[15] The 2007 UNODC Afghanistan Opium Survey argued that "in the provinces bordering with Pakistan, tacit acceptance of opium trafficking by foreign military forces as a way to extract intelligence information and occasional military support in operations against the Taliban and Al-Qaida undermines stabilization efforts."

[16] Testimony of Mary-Beth Long, then-Deputy Assistant Secretary of Defense for Counternarcotics before the House Committee on International Relations, March 17, 2005.

[17] "U.S. CENTCOM views narcotrafficking as a significant obstacle to the political and economic reconstruction of Afghanistan... Local terrorist and criminal leaders have a vested interest in using the profits from narcotics to oppose the central government and undermine the security and stability of Afghanistan." Major Gen. John Sattler, USMC, Dir. of Operations-US CENTCOM before the House Committee on Government Reform Subcommittee on Criminal Justice, Drug Policy, and Human Resources, April 21, 2004.

[18] Lolita C. Baldor, "NATO to Provide More Afghanistan Troops," *Associated Press*, September 20, 2006.

[19] In response, Pentagon press secretary Geoff Morrell stated that, "Secretary Gates is extremely pleased that, after two days of thoughtful discussion, NATO has decided to allow ISAF forces to take on the drug traffickers who are fueling the insurgency, destabilizing Afghanistan, and killing our troops." Judy Dempsey, "NATO allows strikes on Afghan drug sites Ministers agree to major strategic shift," *International Herald Tribune*, October 11, 2008.

[20] In conjunction with the decision, ISAF released the following statement: "Based on the request of the Afghan government, consistent with the appropriate United Nations Security Council resolutions, under the existing operational plan, ISAF can act in concert with the Afghans against facilities and facilitators supporting the insurgency, in the context of counternarcotics, subject to authorization of respective nations." NATO Press Release, "NATO steps up counter-narcotics efforts in Afghanistan," October 10, 2008.

[21] Rules of engagement generally are outlined in classified documents. Author consultations with Department of Defense officials, February and September 2009.

[22] U.S. Department of Defense, Memorandum: Department of Defense International Counternarcotics Policy, December 24, 2008.

[23] The other combat zone with potential relevance to counternarcotics operations in Afghanistan was created January 17, 1991, in Executive Order 12744. The order designated the following areas (including air space and adjacent waters) as combat zones: Persian Gulf; Red Sea; Gulf of Oman; Gulf of Aden; that portion of the Arabian Sea that lies north of 10 degrees N. Lat., and west of 68 degrees E. Long.; and the total land areas of Iraq, Kuwait, Saudi Arabia, Oman, Bahrain, Qatar, and the United Arab Emirates.

[24] "Afghanistan's Narco-War: Breaking the Link Between Drug Traffickers and Insurgents," Report to the Committee on Foreign Relations, United States Senate, August 10, 2009.

[25] James Risen, "U.S. to Hunt Down Afghan Drug Lords Tied to Taliban," *New York Times*, August 10, 2009

[26] See, for example, the concerns expressed in February 2009 when purported NATO operational guidance addressing narcotics targets was leaked. Susanne Koelbl, "Battling Afghan Drug Dealers: NATO High Commander Issues Illegitimate Order to Kill," *Speigel Online*, January 28, 2009; and Matthias Gebauer and

Susanne Koelbl, "Battling Drugs In Afghanistan: Order to Kill Angers German Politicians," *Speigel Online*, January 29, 2009.

[27] Available at: [http://www.icrc.org/Web/eng/siteeng0.nsf/htmlall/direct-participation-report_res/$File/direct-participation-guidance

[28] Ibid. For a discussion of the ICRC's three core criteria - threshold of harm, direct causation and belligerent nexus - see pages 46-64. According to the guidance, "Acts amounting to direct participation in hostilities must meet three cumulative requirements: (1) a threshold regarding the harm likely to result from the act, (2) a relationship of direct causation between the act and the expected harm, and (3) a belligerent nexus between the act and the hostilities conducted between the parties to an armed conflict." The guidance argues that, "In line with the distinction between direct and indirect participation in hostilities, it could be said that preparatory measures aiming to carry out a specific hostile act qualify as direct participation in hostilities, whereas preparatory measures aiming to establish the general capacity to carry out unspecified hostile acts do not."

[29] U.S. Department of Defense, Progress toward Security and Stability in Afghanistan, Report to Congress pursuant to Section 1230 of the 2008 National Defense Authorization Act (P.L. 110-181), January 2009, p. 99.

[30] U.S. Department of Defense, Progress toward Security and Stability in Afghanistan, Report to Congress pursuant to Section 1230 of the 2008 National Defense Authorization Act (P.L. 110-181), April 2010, p. 76.

[31] U.S. Marine Corps, Press Release, "Marines Try Unorthodox Tactics To Disrupt Afghan Opium Harvest," April 14, 2010.

[32] C.J. Chivers, "In Afghan Fields, a Challenge to Opium's Luster," *New York Times*, May 23, 2010.

[33] The conference report (H.Rept. 109-360) on the Defense Authorization Act for FY2006 (P.L. 109-163) did not include a provision that was included in the Senate version of the bill (S. 1042, Section 1033) that would have authorized the Defense Department to provide a range of technical and operational support to Afghan counternarcotics authorities under Section 1004 of the Defense Authorization Act for FY1991 (P.L. 101-5 10). The Senate version would have authorized "the use of U.S. bases of operation or training facilities to facilitate the conduct of counterdrug activities in Afghanistan" in response to the Defense Department's request "to provide assistance in all aspects of counterdrug activities in Afghanistan, including detection, interdiction, and related criminal justice activities." (S.Rept. 109-69) This would have included transportation of personnel and supplies, maintenance and repair of equipment, the establishment and operation of bases and training facilities, and training for Afghan law enforcement personnel.

[34] Author consultation with USAID Afghanistan Desk, September 2009.

[35] Remarks By Undersecretary of Defense for Policy Michele Flournoy, Brookings Institution, Washington, D.C., Federal News Service, March 27, 2009. The House report on H.R. 2765 (H.Rept. 110-197) directed the Secretary of State to initiate a pilot crop substitution program in "an area in which poppy production is prevalent."

[36] Author consultation with USAID Afghanistan Desk, September 2009. Basic information on current USDA activities in Afghanistan is available at: http://www.fas.usda.gov/ICD/drd/afghanistan.asp.

[37] Author consultations with State and Defense Department personnel, September 2009.

[38] Office of the Spokesperson to the President—Transitional Islamic State of Afghanistan, "About the Commitment by the Government of Afghanistan to the Fight Against Narcotics and Concerns About the Aerial Spraying of Poppy Fields." In January 2007, President Karzai announced that any herbicide-based eradication efforts would be delayed, and presidential spokesmen have since repeated their criticism of herbicides on numerous occasions. It was unlikely that President Karzai would have approved a controversial measure such as aerial eradication in the run up to the 2009 presidential election and he has not indicated support for such a policy since his reelection.

[39] Afghanistan Ministry of Counternarcotics, Updated NDCS, January 2006, p. 21.

[40] U.S. Department of State Public Notice 5486, "Determination To Waive the Certification Requirement that the Government of Afghanistan Is Cooperating Fully with U.S.-Funded Poppy Eradication and Interdiction Efforts in Afghanistan," May 22, 2006. *Federal Register*, Volume 71, Number 153, August 9, 2006.

[41] The House version of the FY2007 Foreign Operations Appropriations Act (H.R. 5522) would have limited the obligation of Economic Support Fund (ESF) assistance to Afghanistan to $225 million until the Secretary of State certified to the Appropriations committees that the Afghan government "at both the national and local level" was fully cooperating with U.S.-funded poppy eradication and drug interdiction efforts. The Senate version of the FY2007 foreign operations bill did not contain this provision.

[42] U.S. Department of State, Justification for the Waiver and the Status of Cooperation by the Government of Afghanistan with the United States Funded Poppy Eradication and Interdiction Efforts in Afghanistan, April 2008, transmitted to Congress May 12, 2008.

[43] The House version of the FY2010 Foreign Operations Appropriations bill (H.R. 3081) stated that $300,000,000 in ESF funding may be obligated "only after the Secretary of State certifies to the Committees on Appropriations that the Government of Afghanistan at both the national and provincial level is cooperating fully with United States-funded poppy eradication and interdiction efforts in Afghanistan." The House version provided for a presidential waiver based on national security determination. The Senate version of the bill (S. 1434) stated that $55 million in International Narcotics Control and Law Enforcement (INCLE) funds for Afghanistan may

not be obligated "unless the Secretary of State certifies to the Committees on Appropriations that the Government of Afghanistan is cooperating fully with United States efforts against the Taliban and Al Qaeda and to reduce poppy cultivation and illicit drug trafficking." The Senate version provided for a waiver authority based on a national security interests determination.

[44] Report on Counter Drug Efforts in Afghanistan—October 18, 2005, as required by Sec. 7104, Section 207 (b) of the Intelligence Reform and Terrorism Prevention Act, 2004 (P.L. 108-458); House Committee on International Relations, Ex. Comm. 4575.

In: Fragile Mideast Countries: Afghanistan and Yemen
Editors: Robert P. Deen and Allison D. Burken

ISBN: 978-1-61209-709-1
© 2011 Nova Science Publishers, Inc.

Chapter 4

YEMEN: BACKGROUND AND U.S. RELATIONS

Jeremy M. Sharp

SUMMARY

With limited natural resources, a crippling illiteracy rate, and high population growth, Yemen faces an array of daunting development challenges that some observers believe make it at risk for becoming a failed state. In 2009, Yemen ranked 140 out of 182 countries on the United Nations Development Program's Human Development Index, a score comparable to the poorest sub- Saharan African countries. Over 43% of the population of nearly 24 million people lives below the poverty line, and per capita GDP is estimated to be between $650 and $800. Yemen is largely dependent on external aid from Persian Gulf countries, Western donors, and international financial institutions, though its per capita share of assistance is below the global average.

As the country's population rapidly rises, resources dwindle, terrorist groups take root in the outlying provinces, and a southern secessionist movement grows, the Obama Administration and the 111th Congress are left to grapple with the consequences of Yemeni instability. Traditionally, U.S.-Yemeni relations have been tepid, as the lack of strong military-to-military partnership, trade relations, and cross cultural exchanges has hindered the development of close bilateral ties. During the early years of the Bush Administration, relations improved under the rubric of the war against Al Qaeda, though Yemen's lax policy toward wanted terrorists and U.S. concerns about governance and corruption have stalled large-scale U.S. support.

Over the past several fiscal years, Yemen has received on average between $20 million and $25 million annually in total U.S. foreign aid. In FY2010, Yemen is receiving $58.4 million in aid. The Defense Department also is providing Yemen's security forces with $150 million worth of training and equipment for FY20 10. For FY20 11, the Obama Administration requested $106 million in U.S. economic and military assistance to Yemen.

As President Obama and the 111th Congress reassess U.S. policy toward the Arab world, the opportunity for improved U.S.-Yemeni ties is strong, though tensions persist over counterterrorism cooperation. In recent years, the broader U.S. foreign policy community has not adequately focused on Yemen, its challenges, and their potential consequences for U.S. foreign policy interests beyond the realm of counterterrorism.

The failed bomb attack against Northwest Airlines Flight 253 on Christmas Day 2009 once again highlighted the potential for terrorism emanating from Yemen, a potential that periodically emerges to threaten U.S. interests both at home and abroad. Whether terrorist groups in Yemen, such as Al Qaeda in the Arabian Peninsula (AQAP), have a long-term ability to threaten U.S. homeland security may determine the extent of U.S. resources committed to counterterrorism and stabilization efforts there. Some believe these groups lack such capability and fear the United States might overreact; others assert that Yemen is gradually becoming a failed state and safe haven for Al Qaeda operatives and as such should be considered an active theater for U.S. counterterrorism operations. Given Yemen's contentious political climate and its myriad development challenges, most long-time Yemen watchers suggest that security problems emanating from Yemen may persist in spite of increased U.S. or international efforts to combat them.

LATEST DEVELOPMENTS: POSSIBLE AQAP BOMB PLOT

On October 28, 2010, after receiving a warning from Saudi Arabian intelligence,[1] British, U.S., and other international authorities began searching cargo flights for the presence of explosive devices believed, but not confirmed, to be the work of Al Qaeda in the Arabian Peninsula (AQAP) terrorists. The next morning, two separate packages containing explosives and addressed to fictitious people in Chicago associated with Jewish synagogues were discovered at Dubai Airport in the United Arab Emirates and at East Midlands Airport in Britain.[2] Both devices were concealed inside desktop printers with PETN (Pentaerythritol tetranitrate) explosives packed into the printer toner cartridges (in order to escape detection) and with cell phone circuit boards, but no SIM cards, connected to the printer head and explosive to serve as detonators.[3] At this time, it appears that the devices were intended to explode in midair.[4] U.S. officials are not ruling out the possibility that more devices may still be undetected. Major cargo firms have already suspended shipments from Yemen.

As of Monday, November 1, 2010, authorities have not announced a prime suspect, but most U.S. officials suspect that AQAP is behind the thwarted attack. Specifically, officials believe that Ibrahim Hassan al Asiri, AQAP's top bombmaker, may be the primary culprit along with other senior AQAP figures, including Anwar al Awlaki. Al Asiri is believed to have created the explosive devices used in last year's Christmas Day attempted bombing of Northwest Airlines Flight 253 and in a 2009 attack against Saudi Arabia's intelligence chief Mohammed bin Nayef. To date, a young Yemeni woman whose identity was reportedly stolen and used as a return address for at least one of the packages was detained and subsequently released.

For the past several months, numerous reports have indicated the Obama Administration is contemplating how to properly increase assistance and intelligence cooperation with Yemen without overly militarizing the U.S. presence there and causing a backlash from the local population. Some reports suggest that the CIA may increase its use of drones inside Yemen or place military units overseen by the Defense Department under its control.[5] The Defense Department also has proposed increasing its 1206 aid to Yemen to $1.2 billion over a five- or six- year period.[6] In the past, the Yemeni government has cautioned the United States against overreacting to the terrorist threat there, though in recent months, Yemeni forces have launched several large-scale campaigns against suspected AQAP strongholds in Abyan and Shabwah governorates.

COUNTRY OVERVIEW

Located at the southwestern tip of the Arabian Peninsula, Yemen is an impoverished Arab country with a population of 23.8 million. The country's rugged terrain and geographic isolation, strong tribal social structure, and sparsely settled population have historically made it difficult to centrally govern (and conquer), a feature that has promoted a more pluralistic political environment, but that also has hampered socioeconomic development. Outside of the capital of Sana'a, tribal leaders often exert more control than central and local government authorities. Kidnappings of Yemeni officials and foreign tourists have been carried out mainly by dissatisfied tribal groups pressing the government for financial largesse or for infrastructure projects in their districts.

A series of Zaydi[7] Islamic dynasties ruled parts of Yemen both directly and nominally from 897 until 1962. The Ottoman Empire occupied a small portion of the Western Yemeni coastline between 1849 and 1918. In 1839, the British Empire captured the port of Aden, which it held, including some of its surrounding territories, until 1967.

The 20th century political upheavals in the Arab world driven by anti-colonialism and Arab nationalism tore Yemen apart in the 1 960s. In the north, a civil war pitting royalist forces backed by Saudi Arabia against a republican movement backed by Egypt ultimately led to the dissolution of the Yemeni Imamate and the creation of the Yemen Arab Republic (YAR). In the south, a Yemeni Marxist movement became the primary vehicle for resisting the British occupation of Aden. Communist insurgents eventually succeeded in establishing their own socialist state (People's Democratic Republic of Yemen or PDRY) that over time developed close ties to the Soviet Union and supported what were then radical Palestinian terrorist organizations. Throughout the cold war, the two Yemeni states frequently clashed, and the United States assisted the YAR, with Saudi Arabian financial support, by periodically providing it with weaponry.

By the mid-1980s, relations between North and South Yemen improved, aided in part by the discovery of modest oil reserves. The Republic of Yemen was formed by the merger of the formerly separate states of North Yemen and South Yemen in 1990. However, Yemen's support for Iraq during Operation Desert Storm crippled the country economically, as Saudi Arabia and other Gulf states expelled an estimated 850,000 expatriate Yemeni workers (the United States also cut off ties to the newly unified state). In 1994, government forces loyal to President Ali Abdullah Saleh put down an attempt by southern-based dissidents to secede. Many southerners still resent what they perceive as continued northern political economic and cultural domination of daily life.

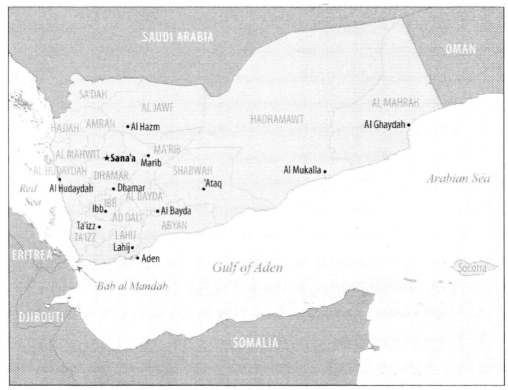

Source: Map Resources. Adapted by CRS (July 2010).

Figure 1. Map of Yemen.

President Saleh, a former YAR military officer, has governed Yemen since the unified state came into being in 1990; prior to this, he had headed the former state of North Yemen from 1978 to 1990. In Yemen's first popular presidential election, held in 1999, President Saleh won 96.3% of the vote amidst allegations of ballot tampering. In 2006, Saleh stood for reelection and received 77% of the vote. The president's current and last term expires in 2013, barring any future constitutional amendments.

A Perpetually Failing State: Yemen and the Dilemma for U.S. National Security Policy

Throughout his decades of rule, President Saleh has balanced various political forces—tribes, political parties, military officials, and radical Islamists—to create a stable ruling coalition that has kept his regime intact. He has also managed relations with a changing coterie of international supporters, including other Arab states, the Soviet Union, the United States, European countries, and numerous international organizations, seeking support in times of crisis and leveraging external assistance to meet internal challenges. Throughout this period, experts have periodically warned about the impending collapse of the Yemeni state and its potential consequences for regional or international security. President Saleh has consistently overcome obstacles to his continued rule, even as Yemen's overall political and economic situation has deteriorated. In recent years, a series of events, including more numerous and sophisticated Al Qaeda attacks, an insurgency in the north, and civil unrest in the south, have led some experts to conclude that Yemen may be on the verge of collapse, particularly given its increasingly precarious economic condition.

As the country's population rapidly rises, water and oil resources dwindle, terrorist groups take root in the outlying provinces, and the southern population becomes increasingly restless, the Obama Administration and Congress are left to grapple with the consequences of Yemeni instability. Some experts suggest that the United States should focus more attention on Yemen because of the risks that state failure would pose to U.S. national security. Some advocates also note that instability in Yemen would affect more than just U.S. interests—it would affect global energy security, due to Yemen's strategic location astride the Bab al Mandab strait between the Red Sea and the Indian Ocean. Others assert that, while increased lawlessness in Yemen most likely will lead to more terrorist activity, U.S. involvement in Yemen should stem from basic humanitarian concerns for a poverty-stricken population desperately in need of development assistance. Still other analysts suggest that Yemen is not of major significance to U.S. interests and is far more important to the Gulf Arab states, notably Saudi Arabia. U.S.-Yemeni trade is marginal, Russia and China are its major arms suppliers, and many of its conservative, tribal leaders are suspicious of U.S. policy in the region.

With so many other pressing issues in the region to address (Iraq, Iran, the Israeli-Palestinian conflict, Somalia), Yemen is often overlooked by U.S. policymakers and opinion leaders. However, the failed bomb attack against Northwest Airlines Flight 253 on Christmas Day 2009 thrust Yemen back into the public spotlight and heightened its relevance for global U.S. counterterrorism operations in a way that other attacks, including failed attacks on the U.S. Embassy in Sana'a during 2008, did not. Whether the United States can or should remain focused on Yemen over the long term remain open questions, even as some observers criticize policymakers for overlooking the country and underestimating the terrorist threat there.

Many analysts suggest that policymakers focus on whether terrorist groups in Yemen, such as Al Qaeda in the Arabian Peninsula (AQAP), have a sustainable ability to directly threaten U.S. homeland security. Such a determination, some argue, should dictate the extent of U.S. resources committed to counterterrorism and stabilization efforts there. Some argue that these groups lack such a capability or can be denied such a capability with relatively limited U.S. support, and contend that the United States might overreact and jeopardize the Yemeni government's stability through increased direct assistance. Others assert that Yemen is a failing state, and suggest that since security problems emanating from Yemen may persist for some time that the U.S. government should adequately prepare for Yemen to become another theater for continuing U.S. counterterrorism operations. For many analysts, the reliability of the Yemeni government as a partner for the United States remains an open question.

By all accounts, U.S. policymakers would benefit from taking into consideration the Yemeni government's views of its own interests and goals when considering potential U.S. policy responses. The diverse views of Yemen's citizens may also affect the outcome of U.S. policy. Recent history suggests no clear answers to the question of how best to achieve U.S.

Manifestations of State Failure in Yemen

Terrorism and Al Qaeda

U.S.-Yemeni Counterterrorism Cooperation: 2009 to the Present[8]

Throughout 2009 and particularly since the attempted attack against Northwest Airlines Flight 253 on Christmas Day 2009, U.S.-Yemeni intelligence cooperation has expanded.[9] The nature and extent of cooperation is a delicate issue. In order to arrest AQAP members and strike AQAP targets inside Yemen's vast remote governorates, the United States requires access to Yemeni security agencies and officials and their cooperation in taking the lead on military operations in order to minimize any U.S. military footprint. In recent times and in previous periods of heightened U.S.-Yemeni cooperation, President Saleh's government has shown some willingness to share intelligence and even attack AQAP targets with reported U.S. assistance, provided that the United States contributes some equipment, training, and financial assistance to Yemen's military and economy respectively.[10]

Whether U.S.-Yemeni security cooperation can be sustained over the long term is the key question for U.S. lawmakers and policymakers. Inevitably, at some point, disagreements arise over Yemen's tendency to release alleged terrorists from prison in order to placate tribal leaders and domestic Islamist politicians who oppose U.S. "interference" in Yemen and U.S. policy in the region in general. One report suggests that in the fall of 2009, U.S. officials met with President Saleh and showed him "irrefutable evidence that Al Qaeda was aiming at him and his relatives," and "that seems to have abruptly changed Saleh's attitude."[11] At times, the United States government itself shares the blame for limiting its bilateral cooperation with Yemen. In the past, high-level U.S. policymakers have shifted focus to what have appeared to be more pressing counterterrorism fronts or areas of the Middle East. Yemeni leaders have grown adept at sensing U.S. interest and have adjusted their level of cooperation accordingly. According to Abdel-Karim al Iryani, a former prime minister, "The trust between the U.S. and Yemen comes and goes.... Everyone has his own calculations on what they want from this relationship."[12]

The Role of the U.S. Military inside Yemen

In 2010, U.S.-Yemeni counterterrorism cooperation appeared to reach its apex. According to one account of U.S. Special Operations forces worldwide, "the Special Operations capabilities requested by the White House go beyond unilateral strikes and include the training of local counterterrorism forces and joint operations with them. In Yemen, for example, 'we are doing all three.'"[13] According to various reports, the United States has provided satellite and surveillance imagery and intercepted communications to help Yemeni security forces carry out air raids against AQAP.[14] Other unclassified sources report that several dozen troops from Joint Special Operations Command (JSOC) are assisting Yemen's security forces in planning missions and developing tactics, in addition to providing weapons.[15] According to one *Reuters* article, U.S. intelligence is being shared with Yemeni security forces to facilitate their strikes against AQAP; as one unnamed intelligence official noted, "there is a tremendous amount of focus on that country."[16] President Saleh has stressed that any U.S. military presence in Yemen is minimal. In one interview, he stated that:

> Those reports are unfounded and there is no U.S. presence on the land of Yemen and there is no treaty or agreement allowing the U.S. presence on our territory, but there is Yemeni-U.S. security cooperation in the field of counterterrorism within the framework of international partnership in this regard.... There are no more than 50 experts contributing to the training of the Yemeni anti-terrorism forces.[17]

The challenges of confronting an Al Qaeda-affiliated local terrorist group are no different in Yemen than they are in other underdeveloped countries with weak central governments and age- old tribal systems of governance in rural areas outside of direct state control. Yemeni public opposition to the presence or activities of foreign military forces is well established and further complicates matters for President Saleh and the United States government. U.S. counterterrorism policy in Yemen, as in Afghanistan, Pakistan, and elsewhere, poses a number of difficult challenges for policymakers; namely, how does the U.S. government combat Al Qaeda-inspired affiliates who live among the local population without creating more radicals? This question is particularly relevant because Al Qaeda seeks to exploit for propaganda purposes any collateral damage inflicted upon civilians.

Collateral Damage and Civilian Casualties

As the United States seeks to weaken the AQAP organization, policymakers have been careful not to alienate local civilian populations. However, inevitably, counterterrorism operations have resulted in some civilian casualties. On December 17, 2009, Yemeni security forces carried out several raids and air strikes in Abyan governorate against AQAP terrorists and training camps, and though an estimated 14 AQAP members were killed in those air strikes, an estimated 35-42 civilians (mostly women and children) also were killed, many of whom were the relatives of AQAP members staying at the training camps. On December 19, the *New York Times* reported that the United States provided firepower, possibly missile strikes, intelligence, and other support to the government of Yemen as it carried out these strikes against AQAP.[18] On June 7, 2010, Amnesty International published a report that included photographs of a U.S.-made cruise missile and an unexploded cluster bomblet it claimed were used in the December 17 strikes.[19] According to one Yemeni researcher:

> Many consider the strike that happened in Abyan to have been American, and that the Yemeni government faces much pressure, and even threats, to accept this American pressure.... The most important issue is that there is a general view of semi- hostility toward the United States, especially among religious groups and tribes, and even some national forces. Any direct interference by the US will cause some of these powers to have sympathy with Al Qaeda.[20]

The United States and Yemeni governments again suffered "blowback" from the mistaken May 24 killing of Jabir Ali al Shabwani, a deputy governor from Marib governorate who allegedly had been killed along with four bodyguards in an air strike. Shabwani reportedly was serving as an intermediary between the government and AQAP and may have been en route to meet with AQAP operatives over their possible surrender.[21] Some Yemenis have charged that he was killed by a missile fired from a U.S. drone. However, the Yemeni government has taken full responsibility and, in order to ease the anger of Shabwani's tribe, President Saleh apologized and formed a committee to investigate the incident. According to Foreign Minister Abubakr al Qirbi, "If there was a drone, and we don't know, then we have to find out if this was used by the Yemeni security forces or by others, but we don't know how the incident happened. We will have to wait for the results of the investigation."[22] Nevertheless, for several days following the attack, Shabwani's larger tribe, the Ubaydah/Abidah, attacked local oil pipelines, set up roadblocks, attacked government buildings, and clashed with the Yemeni army.

Success in Weakening AQAP

Although it is nearly impossible to qualitatively assess whether the United States and Yemen have significantly weakened AQAP, many analysts believe that the 2009-2010 campaign has, at the minimum, put the organization on the defensive. During the past six months, Yemeni units have arrested or killed several mid-level AQAP operatives.[23] Nevertheless, AQAP remains intact and relevant. On April 26, 2010, the group carried out an unsuccessful assassination attempt against British Ambassador to Yemen Timothy Torlot,[24] an operation that many experts believe was designed to demonstrate the group's resilience in the face of pressure. In June 2010, AQAP gunmen attacked a Political Security Organization (P SO) administration building in Aden, killing seven military personnel, three women and a seven-year-old boy. Yemeni authorities also accused AQAP of carrying out several other deadly attacks against government soldiers and policemen in Shabwa and Abyan provinces in July 2010.

According to one report, the Yemeni government claims that an estimated 30 AQAP leaders have been killed since January 2010, though these claims are often unsubstantiated. In several instances, AQAP leaders have resurfaced after having been pronounced dead by the government.[25] In June 2010, the governor of the vast Marib province claimed to a Saudi newspaper that the top leadership of AQAP "have been monitored in the governorate."[26] Though the top leadership of AQAP remains intact, many of its sub-commanders have been killed, captured, or have surrendered to authorities. The following are some recent examples:

- In June 2010, Yemeni authorities claimed that Hamza Saleh al Dayan, one of the 23 Al Qaeda operatives who escaped from a Yemeni jail in 2006, surrendered to provincial authorities in Marib governorate. A week earlier, another operative, Ghalib al Zayedi, surrendered to authorities in Marib governorate.[27]
- In May 2010, AQAP released a video tape confirming earlier deaths of several of its senior operatives, including Abdallah al Mihdar, age 47, killed January 2010, who led the organization in the Shabwa governorate; Muhammad Umayr al Awlaqi, who was killed in an air raid on his hideout in Abyan in late December 2009; and Muhammad Salih al Kazimi, a 38-year-old former Afghanistan fighter, killed during the air strike in Abyan in mid December 2009.[28]
- In May 2010, AQAP leaders announced in an audio tape that a March 2010 airstrike had killed Jamil Nasser Abdullah al Anbari (alt. sp. Ambari), a local leader of AQAP in Abyan governorate. They also verified that another senior leader, Nayyif bin Muhammad al Qahtani, who ran the media arm of AQAP, also had been killed in a

separate incident. On May 11, the Secretary of State designated another two other AQAP leaders as terrorists under Executive Order 13224.[29]

Profiles of AQAP Leaders and Other Radical Yemeni Islamists

Nasir al Wuhayshi

According to a number of sources, the leader of AQAP is a former secretary of Osama bin Laden named Nasir al Wuhayshi (alt. sp. Wahayshi). Like other well-known operatives, Al Wuhayshi was in the 23-person contingent who escaped from a Yemeni prison in 2006. Al Wuhayshi's personal connection to Bin Laden has reportedly enhanced his legitimacy among his followers. After the fall of the Taliban in Afghanistan in 2001, he escaped through Iran, but was arrested there and held for two years until deported to Yemen in 2003. He led Al Qaeda in Yemen until it assumed the mantle of its Saudi counterpart and predecessor organization in January 2009 when he became the overall leader of AQAP, though he is not considered as charismatic as his Saudi counterparts.

Sa'id al Shihri

Al Shihri (alt. sp. Shahri), who is the deputy commander of AQAP, is a Saudi national and former Guantanamo detainee (#372). After his release in 2007, he participated in Saudi Arabia's deradicalization rehabilitation program. After leaving the kingdom and forming AQAP in Yemen, it was believed that his presence in Yemen would boost Al Qaeda's financing and operational capabilities. Al Shihri's family also has been active in AQAP. His wife reportedly was married to an AQAP militant killed by Saudi security forces in 2005. As mentioned earlier, his brother-in- law died in a shootout with Saudi police in Jizan in October 2009. In June 2010, he called for abductions of Saudi ministers and royals.

Qasim al Rimi

Qasim al Rimi is AQAP 's senior military commander and spokesman. Al Rimi is a Yemeni national who is known for his recruitment of new operatives. In AQAP video and audio tapes, he has praised attacks against the United States and threatened more. On May 11, 2010, Secretary of State Clinton designated Rimi a terrorist under E.O. 13224.

Ibrahim Suleiman al Rubaysh

Ibrahim Suleiman al Rubaysh (alt. sp. Rubaish) is a Saudi citizen who is described as AQAP 's theological guide. Rubaysh is a former detainee at Guantanamo Naval Station, Cuba. He was incarcerated there until December 13, 2006, when he was transferred to Saudi Arabia and placed in the Saudi rehabilitation program for jihadists. At some point afterward, he fled to Yemen.

Uthman Ahmad al Ghamidi

Uthman Ahmad al Ghamidi (alt. sp. Othman Ahmed al Ghamdi) is one of the new Saudi leaders of AQAP. He also is a former detainee at Guantanamo who participated in Saudi Arabia's rehabilitation program. He was a soldier in the Saudi military before he went to Afghanistan to train with Al Qaeda and fight the Northern Alliance.

Anwar al Awlaki

Yemeni-American Awlaki (alt. sp. Aulaqi) is infamous for his role in radicalizing Major Nidal M. Hasan in the months prior to the mass shooting at Fort Hood Army Base in Texas. After the failed Christmas Day airline bombing, information suggested that Awlaki also may have played a role in radicalizing Umar Farouk Abdulmutallab. Awlaki was born in New Mexico in 1971, and he hails from a prominent tribal family in the southern governorate of Shabwa. Awlaki lived in Britain and in the United States, where he worked as an imam and lecturer at several mosques, including in Falls Church, VA. He traveled to Yemen in 2004, where he became a lecturer at Al Iman University. He was arrested by Yemeni authorities in 2006 and interrogated by the FBI in September 2007 for his possible contacts with some of the 9/11 hijackers. According to various reports, he began openly supporting the use of violence against the United States after his release from prison. On July 16, the U.S. Treasury Department designated Awlaki, pursuant to Executive Order 13224, for supporting acts of terrorism and for acting for or on behalf of AQAP.

Shaykh Abd al Majid al Zindani

One source of strain in U.S.-Yemeni relations is the status of Shaykh Abd al Majid al Zindani, an alleged Al Qaeda financier and recruiter whom the U.S. Treasury Department designated in February 2004 as a U.S. Specially Designated Global Terrorist. Al Zindani is the leader of Al Iman University located in the capital of Sana'a. U.S. officials have accused Al Zindani of using the university as a recruiting ground for Al Qaeda, as some student groups openly advocate for a violent jihad against the West. According to one report, the university has "a small contingent of students that veer away from the quietist trend of their colleagues. They tend to be foreign students that are drawn to Al Iman by Al Zindani's radical reputation." Yemen has refused to turn Al Zindani over to U.S. authorities, as many observers believe that President Saleh is protecting him for political purposes.

Tribal Support for AQAP?

For many U.S. observers, of greatest concern is the ability of AQAP to transform itself from what is believed to be a group of between 100 to 400 hard-core militants into a mass movement embedded into Yemen's age-old tribal structure. Some policymakers fear that if AQAP were to form permanent alliances with rural tribes, then U.S. objectives in Yemen may have to shift from providing limited support for the Yemeni government's counterterrorism efforts to helping President Saleh combat a much broader and more dangerous nation-wide insurgency. Determining the triangular relationship between the government, AQAP, and tribes may be key to assessing the relative strength of AQAP inside Yemeni society over the long term.

One school of thought rejects the idea that Yemen is becoming more like Pakistan, where the central government faces several revolts from Pakistani Taliban groups which have drawn their inspiration for fighting from Al Qaeda central in Afghanistan, but who are not subordinate to the commands of Osama Bin Laden and other top Al Qaeda leaders. According to Sarah Phillips, an expert on Yemen from the Centre for International Security Studies at Sydney University:

The more they [AQAP] require control of territory, the more likely they are to be in competition with the tribes; this is why al-Qaeda groups are unlikely to pose a systemic challenge to the states in which they exist. That changes, however, if the cells are prepared to accept client status of the tribe, as they have partially done in Pakistan. Even if al-Qaeda attempts to discursively and operationally align itself with the Yemeni tribes against the state, one of the group's broader objectives—establishing political control—consigns tribes to a subordinate status. This exclusion would likely put AQAP in confrontation with the tribes.[30]

Others assert that while a permanent AQAP-tribal alliance is doubtful, there are many factors that could serve as the foundation for closer AQAP-tribal ties in the short to medium terms. Although central governing power in Yemen has always remained weak, many observers in recent years have suggested that President Saleh's ability to secure tribal support in outlying provinces (such as Al Jawf, Marib, Abyan, Shabwa, and Hadramawt) has diminished considerably. This is true particularly in areas where oil is extracted, as local tribes often claim that they rarely receive revenues generated from oil produced on their lands. According to one Yemeni expert, "There is, as in Pakistan, some intertwining of politics, society and the security forces with Al Qaeda.... It can happen.... The enemy of my enemy is my friend, and you can turn it into the Kandahar of Yemen."[31] In addition to economic grievances, some analysts believe that AQAP has toned down its ideological extremism and adapted itself to local tribal customs and culture. According to Gregory Johnsen, a Yemen expert at Princeton University, "They've [AQAP] worked hard to put deep, and what they hope are lasting, roots that will make it very difficult for them to be rooted out of Yemen.... They've done a good job of looking at the mistakes that other versions of al Qaeda have made elsewhere."[32]

Some analysts reject outright the hypothesis that AQAP will develop mass tribal support in Yemen that will enable it to control territory and strike beyond the country's borders. Although many AQAP members are Yemenis, a significant portion are Saudi citizens and foreign fighters,[33] who may be treated as temporary guests by a host tribe, but who would have to marry into the tribe to be considered full-fledged members. Although such marriages do occur, there is no public evidence that they are dramatically increasing, particularly between foreign nationals and Yemeni women.[34] Furthermore, there is no indication that large numbers of Yemeni tribesmen are open to Al Qaeda's ideological appeal. According to former U.S. Ambassador to Yemen Edmund Hull:

In 2002, Abu Ali al Harithi, then Al Qaeda's leader in Yemen, was killed by an American drone in a strike that was coordinated with the Yemeni government. By tribal custom, any perceived illegitimate killing would have been grounds for a claim by the tribe against the government. No such claim was made. In fact, when receiving the body for burial, one of his kinsmen noted that "he had chosen his path, and it had led to his death." This was not an anomaly. In my experience, there is no deep-seeded affinity between Yemeni tribes and the Al Qaeda movement. Tribes tend to be opportunistic, not ideological, so the risk is that Al Qaeda will successfully exploit opportunities created by government neglect. There are also family affinities—cousins, linked to uncles, linked to brothers. These do matter. But what matters most is the 'mujahedeen fraternity'—Yemenis with jihadist experience in Afghanistan, Iraq, Saudi Arabia or elsewhere. Finally, what would matter—and significantly—would be innocent casualties resulting from counterterrorism operations, which could well set off a tribal response.[35]

To a certain extent, a connection between some of Yemen's tribes and AQAP already exists. Yemeni AQAP members tend to operate in their home provinces where they receive a certain level of protection from their host tribe. Protection is granted out of custom and not necessarily due to ideological affinity. Furthermore, this protection is not guaranteed and can become problematic if the tribe's security and well being are put at risk by government reprisals or attacks against AQAP suspects harbored locally, particularly if those suspects are foreign fighters.

Overall, it appears that at present, tribal leaders are using AQAP as a temporary lever to pressure the government for benefits, settle scores with rival, neighboring tribes, or to strike back against the government to avenge some perceived historical injustice. According to one observer, "All view AQAP as a means to pressure the regime, like kidnapping and blocking roads. They hope the damage the government suffers will persuade it to adopt policies more amenable to the tribe. The tribes also exploit the group to keep the regime weak. By putting the government on the defensive, al Qaeda attacks help the tribes preserve their coveted autonomy in regional affairs."[36]

Al Qaeda in Afghanistan/Pakistan and AQAP seem to be acutely aware of the need for tribal support. Their media propaganda continually attempts to persuade certain tribes to back them against the central government. In February 2009, Ayman al Zawahiri, Al Qaeda's second-incommand, released an audio tape in which he said, "I call on the noble and defiant tribes of the Yemen and tell them: Don't be less than your brothers in the defiant Pashtun and Baluch tribes." After the May 24 killing of a local official in Marib governorate set off a series of reprisal attacks from a prominent tribe, postings on jihadist websites began imploring tribes in Marib to fight central government authorities. One posting read, "O People of the Proud Marib [Province]: For God's sake, who is it that destroys your mosques and kills your women and children? Is it the mujahidin, or Ali Abdallah Salih? Who is it that violates the sanctity of your houses and bombs your farms and homes? Is it the mujahidin, or Ali Salih?"[37]

AQAP's Threat to the Homeland and Attempts to Radicalize Foreign Nationals and American Citizens

Though AQAP continues to threaten American and other Western targets inside and around Yemen,[38] it is the ability of Yemeni and Saudi Islamist radicals to recruit foreigners to conduct attacks abroad that may ultimately be of greater concern to U.S. policymakers. In assessing the AQAP threat to the American homeland, a May 2010 Senate Intelligence Committee report concluded that U.S. intelligence agencies previously saw AQAP (before the December 25, 2009, attempted airline bombing) as a threat to American targets in Yemen, not to the United States itself.[39] In February 2010, then-Director of National Intelligence Admiral Dennis C. Blair testified in his annual threat assessment that "We are still exploring the genesis of this plot and what other Homeland plots AQAP and associated Yemeni extremists may have planned. We are concerned that they will continue to try to do so, but we do not know to what extent they are willing to direct core cadre to that effort given the group's prior focus on regional operations."[40]

Thiry-nine-year-old Yemeni-American preacher Anwar al Awlaki has been either directly or indirectly linked to radicalizing Major Nidal M. Hasan (committed the November 2009 mass shooting at Fort Hood Army Base in Texas), Umar Farouk Abdulmutallab (the

Nigerian suspect accused of trying to ignite explosive chemicals to destroy Northwest/Delta Airlines Flight 253 from Amsterdam to Detroit on Christmas Day 2009), and Faisal Shahzad (alleged Times Square failed car bomb), who allegedly told U.S. investigators that Awlaki's online lectures urging jihad helped inspire him to act.[41] According to several reports, the Obama Administration has added Awlaki, an American citizen, to the CIA's list of suspected terrorists who may be captured or killed.[42] To date, Yemen has refused to extradite Awlaki (Article 44 of the Yemeni constitution states that a Yemeni national may not be extradited to a foreign authority), and his tribe has vowed to protect him.[43] Another Muslim-American who claims to have been in contact with Awlaki, 26-year-old New Jersey resident Sharif Mobley, was arrested by Yemeni authorities in March 2010. After his arrest, Mobley shot two security guards in a hospital while attempting to escape. There is some concern that Mobley, who worked as a low-level maintenance worker for six years at several nuclear power plants in New Jersey, could have passed on basic details about American nuclear-plant security to Al Qaeda.[44] In May 2010, the FBI arrested a Texas man who had exchanged emails with Awlaki and was accused of attempting to obtain and deliver global positioning system devices, telephone calling cards, and a military compass for AQAP. He was arrested after boarding a ship bound for the Middle East with the equipment.[45]

In June 2010, multiple reports surfaced suggesting that the Yemeni government has detained dozens for foreign nationals suspected of ties to AQAP, including several Americans, some of whom are believed to be students studying Arabic at Yemeni universities and language schools. On June 7, 2010, U.S. State Department spokesman, Philip J. Crowley said that "If the question is, are we aware that there are Americans in custody in Yemen, we are.... We're trying to find out more information."[46]

The Al Houthi Revolt in Northern Sa'da Province

Although combating Al Qaeda in Yemen may be a top priority for the United States, the Yemeni government faces two other domestic insurgencies that pose a more immediate risk to regime survival. One revolt, which has been raging for nearly six years in the northernmost governorate of Sa'da, is known as the Al Houthi conflict. Its name is derived from the revolt's leaders, the Al Houthi family, a prominent Zaydi religious clan who claim descent from the prophet Muhammad. The late head of the family, Shaykh Hussein Badr ad din al Houthi, believed that Zaydi Shiism and the Zaydi community were becoming marginalized in Yemeni society for a variety of reasons, including government neglect of Sa'da governorate and Saudi Arabian "Wahhabi" or "Salafi" proselytizing in Sa'da. Perhaps in order to seize the attention of central government authorities more forcefully, Shaykh Hussein formed a radical organization called the Organization for Youthful Believers as a revivalist Zaydi group for Al Houthi followers who dispute the legitimacy of the Yemeni government and are firmly opposed to the rule of President Saleh.[47] President Saleh is a Zaydi himself, though with no formal religious training or title.

Shaykh Hussein Badr ad din al Houthi was killed by Yemeni troops in 2004. His son, Abdul Malik al Houthi, is now the leader of the group. The Yemeni government claims that Al Houthi rebels seek to establish a Zaydi theocratic state in Sa'da with Iranian assistance, though some analysts dispute Iranian involvement in northern Yemen, asserting that the

Yemeni authorities are using the specter of Iranian interference to justify large-scale military operations against the insurgents and calls for assistance from neighboring Gulf states.[48]

On February 12, 2010, three weeks after a major international donor conference on Yemen was held in London, the Yemeni government and Al Houthi rebels in the northern province of Sa'da signed yet another cease-fire, the sixth agreement since fighting began in 2004. This last round of fighting, dubbed "Operation Scorched Earth" by the government, resulted in, according to observers on the ground, far more damage to civilian infrastructure than previous episodes. Some international human rights groups, such as Human Rights Watch and Amnesty International, have called for investigations into atrocities committed by both sides during the war, and many experts believe that the government may have used a disproportionate amount of force in order to deter the rebels from launching future attacks. As a result of Operation Scorched Earth, which, for the first time, was accompanied by a major Saudi military intervention[49] on the side of the Yemeni government, an estimated 250,000 people were internally displaced, with up to 30,000 living in temporary camps run by the United Nations High Commissioner for Refugees (UNHCR). USAID has provided emergency food aid to assist refugees in the north.[50]

Since the cease-fire started, there have been several violent incidents, but both sides have shown restraint, signaling possible exhaustion on the part of the rebels and acknowledgement by the government that its armed forces are overstretched. The two sides have exchanged prisoners, and the Al Houthis have removed road blocks and ceded captured areas to local authorities. However, thousands of landmines remain undetected, making the former war zone a difficult challenge for reconstruction activities.

In July 2010, clashes between government-aligned tribes and Al Houthi fighters killed dozens, though President Saleh had pledged earlier that month that "There are no indicators for a seventh war.. ..That would be totally unacceptable." Overall, the fundamental grievances that started the conflict in the first place have not been resolved. Sa'da remains one of the poorest areas of Yemen and, without the government's political will to develop it, Al Houthi leaders may continue to protest against their cultural, religious, economic, and political marginalization in Yemeni society.

Looking ahead, many observers suggest that it is merely a matter of time before the conflict in the north resumes. Should this assumption hold true, possible key questions for policymakers include:

- In the absence of central government political will to resolve the conflict diplomatically, do the Yemeni armed forces have the capability to wage a counter-insurgency campaign indefinitely in an economic climate of diminishing state resources?
- How would a resumption of hostilities in Sa'da affect the government's ability to combat AQAP?
- How would a resumption of hostilities in Sa'da affect Yemen's domestic politics, particularly in light of a possible presidential succession in the near future?[51]
- If the conflict festers and President Saleh and his immediate relatives are delegitimized as a result, could a more radical leader take his place who would be less amenable to cooperate with the United States?
- What about the role of Saudi Arabia and the U.S.-supported Saudi military?

According to a recent RAND study:

> Additionally, the regime itself has cultivated Salafi-leaning elements, either as ideological defenders of the GoY approach or as volunteer fighters. This is not a positive development for the United States. It increases the influence of those who, unlike the Huthis, go beyond rhetoric in their anti-U.S. vehemence. Likewise, at a practical level, it may decrease U.S. influence in San'a as well as the quality of U.S.-Yemeni collaboration on a variety issues, from domestic security to regional cooperation.[52]

Unrest in the South

For years, southern Yemenis have been disaffected because of their perceived second-class status in a unified state from which many of their leaders tried to secede during the civil war in 1994. After the 1990 unification, power sharing arrangements were established, but in practice, north and south were never fully integrated, and the civil war effectively left President Saleh and his allies in no mood for further compromise. As a result, southern Yemen's political and economic marginalization gradually worsened. Although the former People's Democratic Republic of Yemen (PDRY) government had already ruined South Yemen's economy with its socialist policies and was essentially bankrupt due to the loss of its Soviet patron at the time of reunification, historians note that the PDRY, like the British rule of parts of South Yemen before it, had advanced educational development, women's rights, and stamped out tribalism. According to one Yemeni academic, "They [the North] want to push us into backwardness so we are like them.... Aden was tolerant: there were Jews, Christians, Muslims all living together here. The North is not."[53]

Civil unrest in Yemen's southern governorates reemerged in 2007, when civil servants and military officers from the former People's Democratic Republic of Yemen (PDRY) began protesting low salaries and lack of promised-pensions. Since then, what started as a series of demonstrations against low or non-existent government wages has turned into a broader "movement" channeling popular southern anger against President Saleh and his inner circle.

The key demands of south Yemenis include equality, decentralization, and a greater share of state welfare. Many southerners have felt cut off from services and jobs and see persistent infiltration of central government influence in their local area. Southerners have accused Saleh's government of selling off valuable southern land to northerners with links to the regime and have alleged that revenues from oil extraction, which is mostly located in the south, disproportionately benefit northern provinces.[54] In addition, the once prosperous and liberal port city of Aden has deteriorated, as most business must now be conducted in the capital of Sana'a. Furthermore, southerners complain of corruption, as each major southern province is ruled by a military governor with close ties to the president. According to a December 2009 Human Rights Watch report:

> The security forces, and Central Security in particular, have carried out widespread abuses in the south—unlawful killings, arbitrary detentions, beatings, crackdowns on freedom of assembly and speech, arrests of journalists, and others. These abuses have created a climate of fear, but have also increased bitterness and alienation among southerners, who say the north

economically exploits and politically marginalizes them. The security forces have enjoyed impunity for unlawful attacks against southerners, increasing pro-secessionist sentiments in the south and plunging the country into an escalating spiral of repression, protests, and more repression. While the government publicly claims to be willing to listen to southern grievances, its security forces have responded to protests by using lethal force against largely peaceful protestors without cause or warning, in violation of international standards on the use of lethal force. Protestors occasionally behaved violently, burning cars or throwing rocks, usually in response to police violence.[55]

After more than three years, calls for southern autonomy and secession have grown louder, though observers have described southern demands as more of a cacophony, and competition among southern elites has forestalled the creation of a unified agenda to redress grievances with the central, northern-Yemen dominated government in Sana'a.

The Southern Mobility Movement (SMM or, in Arabic, *Al Harakat al Janubi*) is the official title of a decentralized movement set on achieving either greater local autonomy or outright secession. The SMM is organized into local committees, and there is a rudimentary central body to coordinate protest activities. In 2009, 71-year-old former southern secessionist leader Ali Salim al Bidh (alt. sp. Bid or Beidh)[56] announced in a televised speech from Germany that he was resuming his political activities after nearly two decades in exile in Oman. He then declared himself leader of the southern separatist movement and called for the resurrection of the PDRY. He has many supporters, but there are enough rivals to his claimed mantle of leadership to keep the SMM divided and, therefore, less effective in its stance against the government.

Some analysts assert that the April 2009 defection of a former Saleh ally, 42-year-old Shaykh Tariq al Fadhli (alt. sp. Tareq al Fadhli),[57] from the regime to the cause of the southern movement, was a major development that could portend trouble for the central government should other prominent elites follow suit. Shaykh al Fadhli has openly called for separation of the south during rallies in his southern home province of Abyan. Since his defection to the southern cause, his loyalists clashed with government troops until both sides agreed to halt the violence. Then, in June 2010, Al Fadhli declared "I will resume the Southern Movement's activities in the city Zanjabar, but with different means and forms.... We are looking for new mechanisms and potentials that render the Southern Movement's activities successful."[58]

Unrest in the south has grown with each passing year. To date, several hundred have been killed in protest-related violence and many more have been arrested.[59] Nevertheless, with the international community primarily focused on AQAP, President Saleh may have calculated that he has more freedom to suppress dissent in the south. He may exploit the SMM's divisions to his advantage while continuing to use physical repression to stifle further rumblings. It is unclear whether this strategy will work in the long term. Overall, the viability of southern Yemen as an independent entity also is uncertain, leading some experts to believe that some sort of compromise solution is inevitable.

In May 2010, President Saleh's motorcade came under fire in the Radfan district of southern Lahij governorate. Two officers were killed, but the president was not in the car and had already returned to the capital. An assassination attempt against a deputy prime minister had occurred just days earlier. A few weeks after the attack, President Saleh pledged to

The Major Challenges: Subsidies, Water Depletion, Declining Oil Revenues, and Qat

Fuel Subsidies

Although terrorism, provincial revolts, and unrest in the south are all serious concerns related to Yemeni stability, they pale in comparison to the long-term structural resource and economic challenges facing a country with a rapidly growing population. To an outsider, these problems seem almost intractable, as bad government policies and crippling poverty exacerbate existing shortages, creating a feedback loop. For example, the central government subsidizes diesel fuel at a cost to the treasury of several billion dollars annually (nearly 11% of GDP). The diesel subsidy not only drains government revenue but distorts commodity prices, and makes water pumping and trucking costs artificially low, thereby giving farmers no incentive to conserve water. Furthermore, the subsidy encourages smuggling (via the sale of reduced cost fuel at inflated rates to international buyers), which may be officially sanctioned at the highest levels. According to one report, "Diesel smuggling is a facet of elite corruption that has led one international economist working in Yemen to complain that more and more people are being pushed into destitution while a handful of people are living as if there is no tomorrow."[60] However, when the government attempted to lift the diesel subsidy in 2001 and 2005, riots ensued, and the policy was swiftly reversed. In the winter and spring of 2010, the government reduced subsidies on diesel, kerosene, and other oil derivatives by 8%-16% without incident. Nevertheless, according to the World Bank, local energy prices are 60% less than international averages.[61]

Water Scarcity

Water scarcity is perhaps the greatest long-term concern. According to Yemeni government statistics, domestic consumption exceeds renewable fresh water resources by nearly 1 billion cubic meters annually. That deficit stands to double by 2025, when it is estimated the population will have almost doubled to 44 million people. Current inefficient usage is unsustainable, as many of the country's poor in cities such as Ta'izz must obtain water from private truck deliveries, spending a large percentage of their income on fresh water.[62] Public systems only provide water a few days a week in the capital and perhaps as little as a few days a month in other cities. Well drilling has become prohibitively expensive. As farmers drill deeper wells to access freshwater, the water table drops and drinking water becomes contaminated with minerals. Yemenis may now be using fossil water to irrigate crops.

Most analysts believe that if Yemen's major aquifers are depleted, the only realistic solution to the country's water crisis would be a strategy based on increased water-use efficiency and the construction of several large-scale, expensive desalination plants. How such a massive investment in the infrastructure would be financed remains unknown. Although predictions vary as to when underground aquifers will run dry, solutions portend problems for the country's majority of small farmers. For example, if Yemen were to construct desalination plants and pump water from the Red Sea over highlands to the capital, the cost would be affordable enough for household use but too costly to support irrigation for agriculture. According to one Yemen water expert, "Increasing awareness of the country's water scarcity has resulted in a race to the bottom—every man for himself."[63]

Qat Production/Consumption

The cultivation of qat, a stimulant whose leaves are widely chewed throughout the Horn of Africa, also drains Yemen's scarce underground water resources. Qat is a cash crop,[64] and its harvests surpass local coffee and wheat production, which has led to increased demand for food imports. Qat also may use as much as 40% of water resources consumed by local agriculture.

Though it is an age-old tradition and ingrained in Yemeni culture, qat chewing also cripples attempts at promoting sustainable development. Not only does it deplete the country's water resources and reduce food security, low-income chewers spend significant portions of their time and salaries (between 10% and 30%) on qat. According to social critics, "No development can be chieved in Yemen as long as this plant called qat takes up 90 percent of the spare time of the Yemeni people.... Some may argue that this is an old tradition of Yemen just like the arms and *jambiyas* (traditional daggers). But even if that were so, harmful traditions must be thrown away."[65] According to the World Bank, the culture of spending extended afternoon hours chewing qat is inimical to the development of a productive work force, with as much as one-quarter of usable working hours allocated to qat chewing. Chewing qat also suppresses the appetite, and its widespread consumption has been linked to growing child malnutrition rates. Qat chewing also reinforces social and political practices that exclude women, as prominent male politicians and business elites often conduct their business during an afternoon qat chew.

Oil Production/LNG

The loss of oil revenue is another major challenge facing Yemen. Revenue from oil production accounts for nearly all of Yemen's exports and up to 65% of government revenue, yet most economists predict that, barring any new major discoveries,[66] Yemen will deplete its modest oil reserves at some point between 2017 and 2021. Production has dropped precipitously since reaching its peak nearly a decade ago, dropping from 440,000 barrels per day (bpd) in 2001 to an estimated 260,000 bpd in 2010. As consumption has increased, exports have subsequently dropped and, according to the Central Bank of Yemen, state oil receipts fell from $4.4 billion in 2008 to $1.96 billion in 2009. In June 2010, President Saleh announced that the combined impact of falling oil production and rising domestic consumption had made Yemen a net importer of oil.

The Balhaf $4.5 billion liquefied natural gas plant (operated by the Yemeni government in partnership with Total, Hunt Oil, and three South Korean firms: SK Corporation, Korea Gas, and Hyundai), is now online, though experts believe that revenue generated from the project will only slightly stem the hemorrhaging of government funds. It is expected to generate approximately $30 billion to $50 billion in revenue for Yemen's treasury over the next 25 years. However, in the short term, government revenue from LNG sales is expected to reach $370 million in 2010 and will not reach its full level until 2017.[67]

In terms of diversifying its economy, though the government has developed alternative strategies, in reality, Yemen may become even more dependent on international assistance and worker remittances in the future. Its tourism industry suffers from chronic instability and frequent tribal kidnappings of foreigners as well as underdeveloped infrastructure. Growth in non-hydrocarbon sectors of the economy has been stagnant in recent years and is projected to reach a mere 4.4% in 2010.

National Budget

In 2010, the government's fiscal position has weakened, as the national currency, the riyal, has rapidly depreciated, forcing the central bank to spend nearly as much as it did in all of 2009 ($1 billion est.) to stabilize the currency. As previously mentioned, fuel subsidies cost the treasury nearly $1.6 billion annually (about 20% of all budgetary expenditures), though to its credit, the government has modestly reduced some fuel subsidies.[68] Public sector salaries also serve as another drain on the national budget, accounting for another 35% of domestic spending, with perhaps hundreds of thousands of payroll positions unaccounted for. Government jobs are a key source of patronage for President Saleh's government, and positions are routinely dispensed to key elites, though they exist in name only.

In order to buttress its finances, the Yemeni government is seeking assistance from the World Bank and International Monetary Fund and debt relief from its creditors. With food imports rising, its currency devalued, and oil revenue down, many economists are concerned that the Yemeni government is taking on too much debt in order to stem its fiscal hemorrhaging. Many experts believe that the government must pursue alternative means of revenue generation and expand its domestic tax base.

Poor Governance and Uncertainty over Presidential Succession

Although governance issues are far less tangible than the current military conflicts and resource shortages engulfing the Yemeni state, they are at the heart of all of Yemen's major problems. Although President Saleh's government does not resemble those of all-controlling, totalitarian regimes in places like North Korea and Myanmar, critics charge that despite Yemen's decentralized political culture, political and economic power has become far more concentrated in the president's inner circle, a trend that has exacerbated tensions in the north and south, and with tribal leaders whose support is critical in combating Al Qaeda.

President Saleh has been in power for over 30 years and, like many long-serving leaders, has filled the top ranks of his military and intelligence services with extended family members in order to consolidate power. Barring any new constitutional amendments, his term expires in 2013. As mentioned earlier, Saleh's son Ahmed is commander of the Republican Guards and a possible presidential successor. Ali Mohsen al Ahmar, the president's fellow tribesman, is a brigadier general whose forces have fought in Sa'da and who is charged with protecting the capital. He also is considered a potential successor to Saleh and may be in competition with Ahmed Saleh. According to one report, "Mr. Mohsen has signaled that he does not favor a direct succession of Ahmed Saleh to the presidency, diplomats and analysts said. Mr. Mohsen believes, they said, that the younger Mr. Saleh lacks the personal strength and charisma of his father and cannot hold the country together."[69] Another report suggests that Mohsen has close ties to religious extremists and, while such reports have arisen in the past, media speculation over Mohsen's alleged radical ties helps to boost President Saleh's image of moderation and mercurial cooperation with the West.[70] With succession looming as a major uncertainty, juxtaposing Mohsen against more moderate Yemeni leaders may reinforce Western desires to see the status quo maintained in Yemeni domestic politics.

President Saleh's three nephews also hold senior positions in the military and intelligence services. His nephew Colonel Amar Saleh is deputy chief of the National Security Bureau (NSB), an intelligence agency formed in 2002 designed to work in closer cooperation with foreign governments.[71] Another nephew, Yahya Mohammed Abdullah Saleh, is chief of staff of the Central Security Organization (CSO), a division of the Ministry of the Interior which maintains an elite U.S.-trained Counter-Terrorism Unit (CTU).[72] Tariq Saleh is head of the Presidential Guard, the Yemeni equivalent of the U.S. Secret Service. Finally, the president's half-brother, Ali Saleh al Ahmar, is commander of the Air Force.[73]

Yemen's parliamentary elections have been postponed from April 2009 until 2011 in the hope that disagreements over electoral reform and possible amendments to the constitution can be resolved. The Obama Administration noted the decision "with deep concern and disappointment," and argued that the United States finds it "difficult to see how a delay of this duration serves the interests of the Yemeni people or the cause of Yemeni democracy."[74] In December 2009 by- elections to fill several vacant seats in parliament, the ruling General People's Congress (GPC) captured 10 seats, while independent candidates won two seats. The opposition coalition, named the Joint Meeting Parties (JMP), which includes both Islamist and more secular-oriented parties, boycotted the elections. Among many issues, the JMP has protested against the composition of the Supreme Election Committee for Elections and Referendums (SCER), a quasi-governmental body responsible for overseeing elections. The tasks of this independent body include drawing constituency boundaries, engaging in voter education and registration measures, and ensuring that elections proceed according to the law. The SCER is composed of seven members appointed by the president from a list of 15 candidates nominated by the House of Representatives. Candidates must receive nominations from at least two-thirds of parliamentarians. Opposition members accuse the GPC of nominating Saleh loyalists to the committee's board.

One powerful opposition figure in Yemen is Hamid al Ahmar, a son of the late Shaykh Abdullah al Ahmar, who during his lifetime headed Hashid tribal federation (the most powerful tribal coalition in Yemen), was president of the quasi-opposition party known as *Islah* (Reform), and served as speaker of the parliament. Hamid was a major supporter of the primary opposition candidate in the 2006 presidential election. In the summer of 2009, Hamid appeared on *Al Jazeera* television and called on President Saleh to step down from his office. With the death of his father, Hamid along with his brothers became the primary shareholders in the Al Ahmar Group, a Yemeni conglomerate with interests in the banking, telecommunications, oil, and tourism sectors.

On July 17, 2010, the GPC and JMP agreed to engage in a "national dialogue," a process designed to bring about political reconciliation between the ruling and opposition coalitions. Some analysts have speculated that, if successful, the process could lead to the formation of a limited coalition government in 2011. Others cynically assert that the process is designed to satisfy foreign donors which are calling for political reform and successful elections next year.

Foreign Relations

Somalia: Piracy, Terrorism, and Refugees

Somalia is a source of hundreds of thousands of refugees who flee to Yemen each year over treacherous waters, and now a haven for pirates threatening vital international shipping lanes in the Bab al Mandab strait, which oil tankers transit carrying an estimated 3 million barrels per day. Yemen's ability to combat piracy beyond its immediate shoreline and major ports is extremely small. Although the United States helped build Yemen's coast guard after the 2000 *USS Cole attack*, the country's shoreline is vast, and the number of patrol and deep water vessels in its fleet is limited.

Each year, tens of thousands of Somalis cross the Gulf of Aden and the Red Sea in smugglers' boats to reach the shores of Yemen. Many observers believe that smuggler boats unload destitute Somali refugees in Yemen, and then return to Somalia with weapons, fuel, and other cargo purchased inside Yemen. Many refugees die at sea in storms or when forced overboard by accidents or smugglers seeking to avoid security forces.

In 1992, United Nations Security Council Resolution 733 established an arms embargo against Somalia and, according to the U.N. Monitoring Group on Somalia, Yemen remains a primary source of arms flowing into the war-torn country. In its March 2010 report to the Security Council, the Monitoring Group reports that: "Puntland remains the primary gateway for arms and ammunition into Somalia, owing to its Gulf of Aden coastline, historical arms trading relationship with dealers in Yemen, and largely unpoliced territory. The Monitoring Group has learned that arms markets still exist in most major towns, although—as elsewhere in Somalia—they are generally fragmented, informal and run by businessmen with connections to Yemen."[75]

Al Shabaab

Some Western analysts have begun to examine potential linkages between terrorist threats emanating from Somalia and Yemen. To date, the only indication that *Al Shabaab* (translated as, "The Youth"), a radical Somali Islamist group which is a U.S. State Department-designated Foreign Terrorist Organization (FTO), maintains close ties to AQAP is rhetorical. On January 1, 2010, an *Al Shabaab* official, Shaykh Mukhtar Robow Abuu Mansuur, said the group was ready to send reinforcements to AQAP should the United States attack its bases in Yemen. Leaders on both sides have pledged mutual support, and Yemeni and Somalian officials claim that they are providing each other with arms and manpower. [76] Another report suggests that Yemenis "make up a sizeable part of a foreign contingent that fights with Al Shabaab's Somali rank and file and supplies bomb-making and communications expertise."[77] Other observers see less of a direct connection. According to one report, "Shabaab has only recently turned to Al Qaeda, and then it was only from the East Africa cell of Al Qaeda, not from Yemen.... Shabaab has its own major conflict looming with Somalia's Transitional Federal Government."[78]

Relations with the Gulf Cooperation Council (GCC)

Yemen desires to join the 29-year-old Gulf Cooperation Council (GCC), a sub-regional organization which groups Saudi Arabia, Kuwait, Bahrain, Qatar, the United Arab Emirates, and Oman in an economic and security alliance. GCC members have traditionally opposed accession of additional states. Currently, Yemen has partial observer status on some GCC committees, and observers believe that full membership is unlikely. Others assert that it is in the GCC's interest to assist Yemen and prevent it from becoming a failed state, lest its instability spread to neighboring Gulf countries.[79] The impediments to full GCC membership are steep. Reportedly, Kuwait, still bitter over Yemen's support for Saddam Hussein during the first Gulf War, has blocked further discussion of membership. Meanwhile, Yemen needs to export thousands of its workers each year to the Gulf in order to alleviate economic burdens at home. [80] Foreign remittances are, aside from oil exports, Yemen's primary source of hard currency. According to one report, "Unless Yemen is the focus of coherent and sustained GCC action, then Yemen's membership of the GCC will remain a rhetorical ambition rather than a potentially powerful tool to effect change."[81]

Saudi Arabia

By far, Yemen's most important bilateral relationship is with the Kingdom of Saudi Arabia, its wealthier, more powerful, and concerned northern neighbor which in recent years has taken a more active role in attempting to stabilize Yemen. Over decades, Saudi Arabia's perception of Yemen and its interventions there domestically have dramatically shifted from a policy aimed at deliberately weakening the central government to propping up President Saleh's rule in the midst of multiple crises.

Although Saudi Arabia's role in Yemeni domestic affairs is opaque to most Western observers,[82] Saudi goals appear to be geared toward containing threats emanating from Yemen both physically and ideologically. AQAP is a direct threat to the Saudi royal family, as was vividly illustrated by a failed assassination attempt in August 2009 against Assistant Interior Minister Prince Mohammed bin Nayef bin Abdelaziz Al Saud, the director of the kingdom's counterterrorism campaign.

According to one report, two of Saudi Arabia's most powerful intelligence agencies, the Saudi General Intelligence Presidency (GIP), headed since October 2005 by Prince Muqrin bin Abdulaziz, and the General Security Services (GSS), which is attached to the Saudi Interior Ministry, have been working with Yemen's military and special forces units.[83] Though the Al Houthi conflict also physically threatened Saudi Arabia after Houthi rebels crossed the Saudi border[84] and seized territory in November 2009 sparking a major Saudi military intervention there, Saudi leaders fear that the Sunni-Shiite sectarian tinge of the Al Houthi conflict could also spark tensions at home and throughout the Gulf region.

U.S. Relations and Foreign Aid

Historically, close U.S.-Yemeni relations have been hindered by a lack of strong military-tomilitary ties and commercial relations, general Yemeni distrust of U.S. policy in the Middle East, and U.S. distrust of Yemen's commitment to fighting terrorism. Since Yemen's unification, the United States government has been primarily concerned with combating Al Qaeda-affiliated terrorist groups inside Yemen. Al Qaeda's attack against the *USS Cole* in 2000[85] coupled with the attacks of September 11, 2001, a year later officially made Yemen a front in the so-called war on terror. Though Al Qaeda-affiliated terrorist groups operated in Yemen nearly a decade before the 2000 *Cole* bombing, the United States had a minimal presence there during most of the 1990s. After President Saleh lent his support to Iraq during the first Gulf War, the United States drastically reduced its bilateral aid to Yemen. USAID virtually ceased all operations inside Yemen between 1996 and 2003 with the exception of small amounts of food aid (P.L. 480) and democracy assistance to support parliamentary elections.[86] In the late 1990s, though differing views over policy toward the late Saddam Hussein's Iraq continued to divide Yemen and the United States, U.S.-Yemeni military cooperation was revived as policymakers grew more concerned with Al Qaeda.[87]

During the early years of the George W. Bush Administration, relations improved under the rubric of the war on terror, though Yemen's lax policy toward wanted terrorists and U.S. concerns about corruption and governance stalled additional U.S. support. Yemen harbored then and continues to harbor now a number of Al Qaeda operatives and has refused to extradite several known militants on the FBI's list of most wanted terrorists. In 2007, after reports surfaced that one of the *USS Cole* bombers had been released from prison, the Millennium Challenge Corporation canceled a ceremony to inaugurate a $20.6 million threshold grant, which was canceled a few years later.

In 2009, the Obama Administration initiated a major review of U.S. policy toward Yemen. That review, coupled with the attempted airline bombing over Detroit on Christmas Day 2009, led to a new U.S. strategy toward Yemen referred to as the National Security Council's Yemen Strategic Plan. This strategy is essentially three-fold, focusing on combating AQAP in the short term, increasing development assistance to meet long-term challenges, and marshalling international support in order to maximize global efforts to stabilize Yemen.

However, the United States remains concerned over Yemen's deteriorating human rights record, particularly as President Saleh's government combats terrorism and domestic insurgencies. There is concern that should violations continue, Yemen's reliability as a U.S. partner could come into question. According to the U.S. State Department's 2009 report on human rights in Yemen:

> Serious human rights problems increased significantly during the year. Severe limitations on citizens' ability to change their government included corruption, fraudulent voter registration, administrative weakness, and close political-military relationships at high levels. The ruling and opposition parties denied opportunities for change when they agreed to postpone for two years April's parliamentary elections after the two sides failed to reach an agreement on electoral reform. There were reports of arbitrary and unlawful killings by government forces, politically motivated disappearances, and torture in prisons. Prison conditions were poor. Arbitrary arrest, prolonged detention, and other abuses increased, particularly with the ongoing protest movement in the southern governorates, where authorities reportedly

temporarily jailed thousands of southerners during the year. The judiciary was weak, corrupt, and lacked independence. The government significantly increased restrictions on freedom of speech, press, and assembly, and there were reports of government use of excessive force against demonstrators. Journalists and opposition members were harassed and intimidated. Academic freedom was restricted, and official corruption was a problem. International humanitarian groups estimated that more than 175,400 persons were internally displaced as a result of the Saada conflict. Pervasive and significant discrimination against women continued, as did early marriage, child labor, and child trafficking. The right of workers to associate was also restricted.[88]

U.S. Foreign Assistance to Yemen

Over the past two years, U.S. military and economic assistance to Yemen has dramatically increased. For FY2011, the Administration is seeking $106.6 million in foreign assistance for Yemen, a request well above previous amounts ($42 million in FY2009 and $67 million in FY2010). U.S. 1206 Department of Defense (DOD) assistance to Yemen also has increased in recent years. In FY2010, DOD is providing an estimated $150 million in assistance to Yemen, well above the FY2009 level ($66.8 million). Though the Obama Administration has increased aid substantially, it is worth noting that when compared to other regional recipients such as Israel ($2.8 billion in FY2010), Egypt ($1.55 billion in FY20 10), Jordan ($842 million in FY2 10), and even the Palestinians ($500.4 million in FY2010), U.S. aid to Yemen lags far behind.

Military Aid
U.S. military assistance to Yemen is divided between State Department-administered FMF funds and Department of Defense-administered 1206 funds. Overall FMF aid to Yemen is modest by regional standards and helps to maintain U.S. equipment provided to Yemen over several decades. In 2008, both countries signed a first-ever bilateral End Use Monitoring Agreement. The agreement is designed to allow for the verification of articles and services provided to Yemen under U.S.-sponsored military and security assistance, thus preventing the misuse or illicit transfer of these items and services. In November 2009, just days before a series of strikes against AQAP targets inside Yemen, the official news agency of Yemen reported that the United States and Yemen signed a new cooperation agreement to combat terrorism, smuggling, and piracy.[89] The Obama Administration has not divulged the details of any such cooperation agreement to date.

For several years, the United States has provided training to Yemen's elite Counter-Terrorism Unit (CTU) using funds from the State Department-controlled Foreign Military Financing (FMF) and International Narcotics Control and Law Enforcement (INCLE) accounts.[90] Provisions in the FY20 11 defense authorization bills seek to expand funding for the CTU (see below), and the House and Senate versions differ over which agency, State or DOD, should manage the CTU training program. To some extent, this same debate occurred in 2009 over proposed new counterinsurgency funding for Pakistan; ultimately, the State Department was given the responsibility for its management.

Table 1. U.S. Foreign Aid to Yemen (current year $ in millions)

Aid Account Operations) (Foreign	FY2006	FY2007	FY2008	FY2009	FY2010	FY2011 Request
Economic Support Fund (ESF)	7.920	12.000	1.500	19.767a	5.000	34.0
Foreign Military Financing (FMF)	8.415	8.500	3.952	2.800	12.500	35.0
Development Assistance (DA)	—	—	4.913	11.233	35.000	—
Non-Proliferation, Anti-Terrorism, De-mining, and Related Programs (NADR)	1.441	3.751	4.034	2.525	—	4.5
Global Health Child Survival	—	—	2.833	3.000	4.800	21.0
International Military Education and Training (IMET)	.924	1.085	.945	1.000	1.100	1.1
International Narcotics Control and Law Enforcement (INCLE)	—	—	—	—	—	11.0
Totals	18.700	25.336	18.177	30.325	58.400	106.600

a. Congress appropriated an additional $10 million in ESF for Yemen in P.L. 111-32, the Supplemental Appropriations Act, FY2009

Table 2. 1206 Department of Defense Funding for Yemen FY2006-FY2010 ($ in millions)

1206Program	FY2006	FY2007	FY2008	FY2009	FY2010
Cross Border Security and CT Aid	4.3	—	—	—	—
Yemeni Special Operations Capacity Development to Enhance Border Security	—	26.0	—	—	—
Air Force Aerial Surveillance Initiative	—	—	—	5.9	—
Coast Guard Maritime Security Initiative	—	—	—	29.9	—

Table 2. (Continued)

Increased Border Security CT Initiative	—	—	—	25.4	—
Explosive Ordnance Disposal Initiative	—	—	—	5.8	—
Special Operations Forces CT Enhancement Package	—	—	—	—	34.5
Fixed-Wing Aircraft and Support for Yemeni Air Force to Support CT Units	—	—	—	—	38.0
Rotary-Wing Aircraft (4 Huey II) and Support for Yemeni Air Force to Support CT Units	—	—	—	—	52.8
Upgrades and Parts for approx. 10 existing Yemeni Air Force Helicopters	—	—	—	—	30.0
Total	4.3	26.0	0	67.0	155.3

Source: CRS Report RS22855, *Security Assistance Reform: "Section 1206" Background and Issues for Congress*, by Nina M. Serafino.

1206 Defense Department Assistance

In recent years, the Defense Department's 1206 train and equip fund has become the major source of overt U.S. military aid to Yemen. Section 1206 Authority is a Department of Defense account designed to provide equipment, supplies, or training to foreign national military forces engaged in counter-terrorist operations. Between FY2006 and FY2007, Yemen received approximately $30.3 million in 1206 funding. In the last two fiscal years, it has received $221.8 million. As of midFY2010, Yemen is the largest global 1206 recipient, receiving $252.6 million. Pakistan is the second-largest recipient with $203.4 million.

In general, 1206 aid aims to boost the capacities of Yemen's air force, its special operations units, its border control monitoring, and coast guard forces. Approximately $38 million of the FY20 10 1206 assistance will be used to provide Yemen's Air Force with one CASA CN-235 medium- range twin-turbo-prop aircraft to transport its special operations units. The United States also has used 1206 funds to provide special operations units with training, helicopters with night-vision cameras, sniper rifles, secure personal radios, and bullet-proof jackets. Yemen's Coast Guard has received through 1206 funding patrol boats and radios and border security personnel have received armored pickup trucks.

Some observers and lawmakers have concerns regarding increased U.S. military aid to Yemen. Some fear that, despite required U.S. human rights training and vetting of Yemeni units, abuses committed by security forces may still occur or even increase. Others, particularly lawmakers, are concerned that U.S. equipment could be diverted by the Yemeni government away from combating terrorism and toward fighting domestic insurgencies. One January 2010 Senate Foreign Relations Committee report concluded that it was "likely that U.S. counter-terrorism assistance had been diverted for use in the government's war against the Houthis in the north and that this temptation will persist." The report stated that

> This potential misuse of security assistance underscores the importance of enhancing the current end-use monitoring regime for U.S.-provided equipment. Indeed, the existing end- use monitoring protocols in place have revealed discrepancies between U.S. records of security assistance and those that are in the possession of Yemeni defense forces. The Defense Security Cooperation Agency (DSCA), the Department of State, and Embassy's Office of Military Cooperation (OMC) should work to reconcile these differences. In addition, they should conduct a thorough review of physical security and accountability procedures at the Yemeni Special Operations Forces (YSOF) compound.[91]

Economic Aid

Yemen receives U.S. economic aid from three primary sources, the Economic Support Fund (ESF), the Development Assistance (DA) account, and the Global Health Child Survival account (GHCS). In September 2009, the United States and Yemen signed a new bilateral assistance agreement to fund essential development projects in the fields of health, education, democracy and governance, agriculture and economic development. The agreement, subject to congressional appropriations, provides a total of $121 million from FY2009 through FY2011.

USAID 's new country stabilization strategy for Yemen for 2010-2012 features, among other activities, two main programs, the Community Livelihoods Project (CLP) and the Responsive Governance Project (RGP). The CLP seeks to work with NGOs in local communities in Yemen's rural governorates in order to expand access to freshwater, healthcare, and education. Its estimated budget is $80 million for three years, plus up to $45 million for each of two additional option years, for a total of $125 million over five years. The RGP seeks to work with, according to USAID, "key Yemeni ministries, including Health, Education, Agriculture, Planning, Industry & Trade, among others, to address related but broader government policy, institutional, and capacity issues that will help the Government of Yemen be more responsive to the needs of its citizens."[92] Its estimated budget is $27 million for three years, plus up to $16 million for both additional option years, for a total of up to $43 million over five years. The governance program was awarded to Counterpart International.

In FY20 10, USAID obligated an additional $12.8 million to support a containment and stabilization program for northern Yemen. According to USAID, funds will "provide immediate community-based assistance in the governorates surrounding Sa'ada (Hajjah, Amran, northern districts of Al Jawf) in order to contain the Sa'ada conflict from spilling into these areas, support the current ceasefire, mitigate the possibility for a renewed outbreak of violence, and position USAID to enter Sa'ada to deliver similar assistance as the basis for future reconstruction should access open up."[93]

Democracy Assistance/Tribal Outreach

U.S. economic aid to Yemen also supports democracy and governance programming. For several years, U.S. democracy promotion organizations have run programs in Yemen's outlying provinces to support conflict resolution strategies designed to end revenge killings among tribes. Some NGOs receive U.S. funding to facilitate discussions between tribal leaders in Mareb province and government officials, donors, and the private sector. U.S. assistance also works to monitor voter registration issues in anticipation of parliamentary elections scheduled for April 2011, enhance the electoral competitiveness of Yemen's main political opposition parties, train members of parliament, and provide technical assistance to parliamentary oversight and budget committees. The State Department's Middle East Partnership Initiative (MEPI) also provides small grants to a number of local Yemeni NGOs.[94]

Yemeni Detainees at Guantanamo Bay

A large portion (between 60 and 90) of the estimated 181 detainees who remain incarcerated in the U.S. detention facility at Guantanamo Naval Base, Cuba, are Yemenis. The Obama Administration suspended repatriations to Yemen after the December 25 failed airline bomb attack. In April 2010, Spain accepted one Yemeni detainee. The United States is seeking other third party countries to accept the remaining prisoners, as there is a widespread belief, particularly among U.S. lawmakers, that many of them would return to militancy if under Yemeni government custody.

In recent months, federal judges in separate cases ordered that two Yemeni detainees be freed. In May 2010, one judge ordered that Mohamed Mohamed Hassan Odaini be repatriated. In June 2010, another court ordered the Administration to release Hussain Salem Mohammed Almerfedi, who had been incarcerated for eight years without trial. In May, the Administration reaffirmed its commitment to its moratorium on transfers to Yemen, stating that "We are not lifting the overall suspension on detainee transfers to Yemen, and this should not be viewed as a reflection of a broader policy for other Yemeni detainees."[95] Prior to the moratorium, an Administration interagency task force on Guantanamo had cleared 29 Yemenis to return home and conditionally cleared another 30 if Yemen's security conditions improve.

Recent Legislation

FY2011 Defense Authorization Bills

Both House and Senate FY20 11 defense authorization bills feature significant policy directives on Yemen. Section 1203 of S. 3454, the National Defense Authorization Act for Fiscal Year 2011, would authorize the Secretary of Defense to use up to $75 million (from FY20 11 DOD operations and maintenance funds) to enhance the ability of the Yemen Ministry of Interior counterterrorism forces to conduct counterterrorism operations against AQAP.[96] According to the Senate Report accompanying the bill:

> The committee recognizes the importance of the ongoing efforts by the Department of Defense (DOD) to use `section 1206' train and equip assistance to build the capacity of various elements of the Yemeni military. However, the committee is concerned that too little assistance is being provided to the more capable and responsive Counter Terrorism Unit (CTU) of the Government of Yemen's Ministry of Interior. The Department has indicated that the ongoing `section 1206' train and equip efforts are critical, but the committee is concerned that the results of this effort will not be demonstrated in the near term. With this in mind, the committee believes it is critical to provide DOD with the authority to expand its train and equip efforts to include CTU. This assistance will help to ensure that DOD has a reliable partner to rely on for counterterrorism operations in this very sensitive area of the world and provide the Department with additional flexibility and agility in dealing with the threats emanating from Yemen. The committee notes explicitly in the provision that these funds shall be used to enhance the ability of CTU to conduct operations against `al Qaeda in the Arabian Peninsula and its affiliates.' The committee notes that there have been public reports suggesting that the Government of Yemen may have used equipment provided by the United States to conduct operations against government opposition elements in both the North and South. The committee believes this would be a misuse of this assistance and any other security assistance provided to the Government of Yemen.[97]

In addition to supporting Yemen's CTU, S. 3454 also calls for a comprehensive audit and report on U.S. assistance to Yemen. The bill would direct the Comptroller General to report on the following issues:

> (1) the amount and types of assistance the United States has provided to the Government of Yemen to include support from the U.S. Department of State, Department of Defense, U.S. Agency for International Development, and other U.S. Government departments and agencies; (2) an assessment of the effectiveness of U.S. assistance to the Government of Yemen; (3) an assessment of the extent to which the Government of Yemen has been able to utilize U.S. assistance to counter the AQAP threat; (4) a discussion of the capability and reliability of security forces units within the Government of Yemen; (5) an assessment of how effectively the United States coordinated its assistance among the various federal agencies and other major donors and regional allies; and (6) other issues deemed appropriate by the Comptroller General. The Comptroller General shall provide this chapter to the appropriate congressional committees no later than January 31, 2011.[98]

Other Recent Legislation

- H.Res. 1288. Urges that a certificate of loss of nationality should be issued by the appropriate diplomatic or consular officer for approval by the Secretary of State and forwarded to U.S. Citizen and Immigration Services finding that Anwar al Awlaki voluntarily relinquished his status as a United States citizen by, among other things, voluntarily participating in and collaborating with Armed Forces seeking to carry out hostilities against the United States. Bill Status: Referred to the Subcommittee on Immigration, Citizenship, Refugees, Border Security, and International Law, House Committee on the Judiciary, 6/15/2010.
- S.Res. 400. Among other things, requests that the Secretary of State, the Secretary of Defense, and the Director of National Intelligence submit a joint, comprehensive strategy for Yemen, in classified and unclassified form, to the Senate, including (a) counterterrorism cooperation; (b) development, humanitarian, and security assistance; (c) regional and international diplomatic coordination; and (s) democracy, human rights, and governance promotion. Bill Status: Placed on Senate Legislative Calendar.
- H.R. 4464. States that no individual who is detained at Naval Station, Guantanamo Bay, Cuba, as of the date of the enactment of this Act, may be transferred or repatriated, for the purposes of release or detention, into a nation or region that is recognized by the Department of State or the Department of Defense as a haven of any manner, kind, or fashion for terrorist activity or that has been classified as a state sponsor of terrorism. Bill Status: Referred to House Committee on Armed Services, 1/19/20 10.
- S.Res. 341. Among other things, calls on the President to give sufficient weight to the situation in Yemen in efforts to prevent terrorist attacks on the United States, United States allies, and Yemeni civilians and calls on the President to promote economic and political reforms necessary to advance economic development and good governance in Yemen. Bill Status: Passed in the Senate, 12/4/2009.

INTERNATIONAL AID AND CALLS FOR REFORM IN YEMEN

Despite increased economic and military aid, the Administration recognizes that the United States cannot be solely responsible for Yemen's development and security. In order to increase donor coordination and widen the scope of support, the United States and Great Britain helped form the Friends of Yemen Group, a multilateral forum of 24 concerned countries that was launched at a January 2010 conference in London.[99] Since then, a meeting between Yemen and Arab donors was held in Riyadh, Saudi Arabia, in order to accelerate the delivery of pledges made at an earlier 2006 conference in London. In March, the Friends of Yemen group convened in Abu Dhabi, where Yemeni officials stated that the country requires $44 billion in aid and investment over the next five years to support development. The Friends of Yemen are scheduled to meet again in New York in September.

Yemen: Background and U.S. Relations

Table 3. International Pledges to Yemen: London Donors Conference 2006 Funds in U.S. millions ($)

Donor	Pledge (in U.S. $)
GCC Bilateral Countries	
Saudi Arabia	1,181
UAE	650
Qatar	500
Kuwait	200
Oman	100
Total	**2,631**
Multilateral Regional Agencies	
Arab Fund for Social Development	785
Word Bank (IDA)	400
Arab Monetary Fund	220
Islamic Development Bank	200
U.N. System	90
European Commission	100
IFDA	70
OPEC Fund for International Development	20
Global Fund	32
Total	**1,917**
Traditional Bilateral Countries	
United Kingdom	230
Germany	190
France	130
Netherlands	91
South Korea	40
Spain	26
United States	21
Japan	15
Italy	12
Denmark	9
Total	764
Grand Total	5,312

Source: http://www.yemencg.org/library/2008/goverment_report08_en.pdf

Note: Media reports indicate that donors pledged a total of $5.7 billion, and therefore this table does not include the sources for an additional $400 million in pledged aid.

In general, Yemen is not a large recipient of official development assistance. According to the World Bank, in 2008 the country received $305.4 million from donors worldwide, though most experts agree that figure does not include unofficial cash transfers from Yemen's wealthy Gulf Arab neighbors. Countries attending the 2006 London Donors Conference pledged $5.7 billion for Yemen, and since the 2009 Christmas Day attempted airline bombing, the Administration and others have recognized that the fulfillment of these pledges would be critical not only for development purposes, but for demonstrating to Yemeni leaders that there is international political will to stabilize the country. As of early 2010, a mere 10% of the 2006 pledges had been actually disbursed.

In essence, Yemen requires external aid, both political and financial, to improve its capacity to provide security, governance, and economic development, but donors are hesitant to commit to Yemen, fearing that its government's lack of capacity to absorb aid will inevitably lead to their funds being squandered. Furthermore, though the United States has taken a leading role in marshalling international support for Yemen in recent years, Western countries are constantly pushing for Yemen's Arab neighbors to take a more active and positive role in the country's development. However, many Gulf countries themselves lack the human expertise or desire to implement aid projects on the ground in Yemen, preferring to donate cash to Yemen's coffers or outsource development work to Western aid agencies. According to one report,

> The GCC states do not discuss common developmental approaches. In part this reflects a lack of national capacity, highlighted by a leading GCC official's suggestion at the February 2010 Riyadh meeting of paying "outside experts" (Western aid agencies) to meet Yemen's developmental needs. No individual GCC state has an aid office in Sana'a, nor is there a collective GCC one, despite Yemeni encouragement of on-the-ground Arab support. At present this is limited to a few Saudi and Egyptian experts advising on economic management in Aden.[100]

Overall, though it is not nearly at the level desired by the Yemeni government, foreign countries have increased their aid to Yemen out of growing fear of state failure. In December 2009, the Abu Dhabi Fund for Development (ADFD) made a $650 million commitment to fund over a dozen projects inside Yemen. The World Bank has disbursed several hundred million dollars for dozens of projects inside the country for its five-year program. Yemen's Social Fund for Development is a primary recipient of foreign aid and is well regarded by the international community for its transparency and wide reach outside the capital. It spent $218 million on projects inside Yemen in 2009.

Reform in Yemen

Many observers believe that the international community is willing to assist Yemen in boosting its internal capacity to take necessary political and economic reforms that would somewhat alleviate the country's woeful state of development; however, it is unclear whether or not the Yemeni government itself is seriously committed to tackling difficult challenges.

At present, Yemen is negotiating with the International Monetary Fund in order to launch an economic reform plan. After Yemen's latest Article IV Consultation with the IMF that concluded in January 2010, the IMF recommended that:

> Given the sizable increase in domestic debt to finance the 2009 budget deficit, including use of central bank financing, Directors encouraged ambitious fiscal consolidation, focusing on aligning expenditures with revenues, reducing structural rigidities in expenditures and boosting non-oil revenue. Key priorities in this regard include full implementation of the General Sales Tax and reducing fuel subsidies. At the same time, Directors stressed the need for larger and better-targeted direct transfers to protect the poor. Continued efforts to reform

the income tax regime, eliminate exemptions and strengthen public financial management are also crucial.[101]

President Saleh himself has initiated his own 10-point reform plan that includes, among other things, fuel subsidy reductions, land reform, civil service reform, and enhanced water-use efficiency. In response, Secretary of State Hillary Rodham Clinton remarked that:

> President Salih has a 10-point economic plan, and we have made clear that we have expectations and we have the right to work with the Government of Yemen as we do provide development [aid] because we want it to go for the benefit of the people of Yemen. We want to see results on the ground. We're seeing results in the counterterrorism efforts and we want to see similar results when it comes to development. But I believe that the foreign minister and other high officials in Yemen understand that. They're committed to this new course and we want to assist them in being successful.[102]

The government of Yemen insists that is committed to making difficult choices. As mentioned earlier, fuel subsides have been modestly reduced in 2010. According to Yemen's Deputy Minister of Planning and International Cooperation Hisham Sharaf, "Our emergency and urgent program includes such reforms. The brother president considers that the reforms will emerge before the world, and that this developing country which is said to have corruption and problems should follow a course of reform that would attract the others as investors, donors, and also as countries to deal with us. These reforms will not be mere ink on paper, or postponed from one year to another."[103]

CONCLUSION AND U.S. POLICY OPTIONS

There are a number of challenges to expanded U.S. military and non-military action in Yemen, including limited local political support, limited local capacity to absorb or effectively administer U.S. assistance, a strong public antipathy to U.S. security cooperation, a local government that does not identify Al Qaeda as its primary domestic problem, limited U.S. government knowledge of Yemen's internal political dynamics, and a precarious security situation on the ground that prohibits direct U.S. support in outlying areas. Given these challenges, many observers have suggested that the range of options before Congress and the Obama Administration for dealing with AQAP and Yemen's long-term viability as a nation-state is limited. The following summaries describe some options that have been proffered; the selection is not exhaustive:

- **Condition U.S. Assistance.** There is some concern that just like after the 2000 *USS Cole* bombing in Aden harbor, the United States might repeat a familiar pattern—an attack occurs, the United States scrambles to react, and then gradually the U.S. government loses focus, as the Yemeni government reduces the capabilities of Al Qaeda-inspired militants to an internationally tolerable level without eliminating them. In this regard, some argue that, in crafting his government's response, President Saleh is likely to seek to avoid exacerbating political opposition at home while meeting the demands of the United States or other potential donors. This time, some suggest that the United States condition additional U.S. aid, either overtly or behind closed doors, on political and economic reform in order to improve Yemen's long-term prospects and stabilize existing political crises. Based on other cases, it is likely that the Administration would seek waiver authority for any congressionally mandated conditions or certification requirements on U.S. assistance.

- **Internationalize Assistance.** For years, the United States has advocated for more development assistance for Yemen at the World Bank and International Monetary Fund. However, some analysts suggest that due to the political sensitivities of greater U.S. involvement in Yemen, the United States should work multilaterally with Saudi Arabia, the EU, and other countries in both expanding military and economic cooperation there. The potentially competing short-term priorities of regional, international, and multilateral parties may make it less likely that external assistance would affect Yemen's long-term prognosis in a decisive way.

- **The Minimalist Approach.** Despite the flurry of recent media attention since the Flight 253 incident, some observers anticipate that the AQAP threat to the U.S. homeland is not nearly as dire as advertised and that the United States risks exacerbating the problem by becoming too involved in Yemen. While doing nothing may not be an option, these same observers suggest that a quiet, sustained, and deliberate approach focused on minimizing short-term threats and addressing long-term systemic challenges may be best.

END NOTES

[1] Media reports indicate that Saudi Arabia's intelligence chief, Mohammed bin Nayef, himself a target of an AQAP bombing, called John Brennan, the Deputy National Security Advisor for Homeland Security and Counterterrorism, and Assistant to the President late Thursday evening. Reportedly, Bin Nayef may have received critical information on the plot from Jaber al Faifi, a former detainee at the U.S. detention facility in Guantanamo Bay, Cuba, who went through a rehabilitation program in Saudi Arabia before rejoining AQAP. Al Faifi had surrendered to Saudi authorities just two weeks ago.

[2] The bomb discovered in Dubai left Yemen on October 28. It was flown to Doha, Qatar, and then on to Dubai. The device discovered in Britain traveled through Cologne, Germany, before making its way to Nottingham, England.

[3] On October 31, the *Washington Times* reported that Western officials were now reevaluating whether a UPS 747 cargo plane that crashed in Dubai on Sept. 3, killing two crew members, was downed by an explosive package in its cargo bay and not by an onboard fire, as initially suspected. See, "Package bombers not 'quite there yet'," *Washington Times*, October 31, 2010. However, UAE investigators claim that there is no evidence that the UPS cargo plane that crashed in Dubai in September was brought down by an explosion.

[4] On October 31, Brennan said that "We're looking at the potential that they would have been detonated en route to those synagogues aboard the aircraft as well as at the destinations.... But at this point, I think, we would agree with the British that they were designed to be detonated in flight."

[5] "Yemen Covert Role Pushed ," *Wall Street Journal*, November 1, 2010.

[6] "More U.S. Funds Sought for Yemen's Forces," *Wall Street Journal*, September 3, 2010.

[7] The population of Yemen is almost entirely Muslim, divided between Zaydis, found in much of the north (and a majority in the northwest), and Shafi'is, found mainly in the south and east. Zaydis belong to a branch of Shi'a Islam, while Shafi'is follow one of several Sunni Muslim legal schools. Yemen's Zaydis take their name from their fifth Imam, Zayd ibn Ali. They are doctrinally distinct from the Twelvers, the dominant branch of Shi'a Islam in Iran and Lebanon. Twelver Shiites believe that the 12th Imam, Muhammad al Mahdi, has been hidden by *Allah* and will reappear on Earth as the savior of mankind. For more information, see CRS Report RS2 1745, *Islam: Sunnis and Shiites*, by Christopher M. Blanchard.

[8] For more background on AQAP see, CRS Report R41070, *Al Qaeda and Affiliates: Historical Perspective, Global Presence, and Implications for U.S. Policy*, coordinated by John Rollins

[9] In May 2010, the *New York Times* reported that former CENTCOM commander General David H. Petraeus signed a classified directive, known as the Joint Unconventional Warfare Task Force Execute Order, on September 30, 2009 authorizing an expansion of clandestine military activity throughout some parts of the Middle East, including Yemen. See, "U.S. Is Said to Expand Secret Military Acts in Mideast Region," *New York Times*, May 24, 2010.

[10] According to one article, after the attacks of September 11, 2001, former CIA Director George Tenet "won Saleh's approval to fly Predator drones armed with Hellfire missiles over the country." See, "U.S. Playing a Key Role in Yemen Attacks; Providing data, weapons Six top leaders of al-Qaeda affiliate killed," *Washington Post*, January 27, 2010.

[11] "I s Yemen the Next Afghanistan?," *New York Times*, July 6, 2010.

[12] "Yemen Walks Fine Line in Aiding U.S," *Washington Post*, January 5, 2010.

[13] "U.S. 'secret war' Expands Globally," *Washington Post*, June 4, 2010.

[14] "US to Expand Yemen's Air Forces to Counter Al Qaeda," *Reuters*, February 25, 2010.

[15] Op.cit., "U.S. Playing a Key Role in Yemen Attacks; Providing data, weapons Six top leaders of al-Qaeda affiliate killed," *Washington Post*, January 27, 2010. The Yemeni government allowed U.S. personnel to launch a missile strike from an unmanned aircraft against an automobile in eastern Yemen in November 2002, killing six alleged terrorists, including Qaid Salim Sinan al Harithi, the leader of Al Qaeda in Yemen and a key planner of the attack on the USS Cole.

[16] "U.S. Expands Intelligence Operations in Yemen," *Reuters*, May 25, 2010.

[17] Open Source Center, "No US Military Presence In Yemen: Saleh," *SABA Online in English*, GMP201003 19950047, March 19, 2010.

[18] "U.S. Aids Yemeni Raids on Al Qaeda, Officials Say," *New York Times*, December 19, 2009.

[19] Amnesty International, *Yemen: Images of Missile and Cluster Munitions Point to US role in Fatal Attack* , June 7, 2010, http://www.amnesty.org/en/news-and-updates/yemen-images-

[20] "US Cluster Bombs in Yemen: The Right Weapon in Al Qaeda Fight?," *Christian Science Monitor*, June 7, 2010.

[21] "Yemen Tribe in new Pipeline Blast over Airstrike," *Reuters*, May 27, 2010.

[22] "INTERVIEW-Yemen may Review Methods in Al Qaeda Fight -formin," *Reuters*, May 31, 2010.

[23] According to Ambassador Daniel Benjamin, State Department Coordinator For Counterterrorism, "This intensified engagement has paid off. In the last month, Yemen has conducted multiple air and ground operations designed to disrupt AQAP's operational planning and deprive its leadership of safe haven within Yemen's national territory. Yemen has significantly increased the pressure on Al Qaida, and the United States commends the Yemeni government on these successful operations." See, U.S. Congress, House Armed Services Subcommittee on Terrorism, Unconventional Threats and Capabilities, Threats Posed by Al Qaeda, 111th Cong., 2nd sess., January 20, 2010.

[24] A suicide bomber detonated his explosive belt moments after the ambassador passed by in an armored convoy just outside the British Embassy in Sana'a.

[25] "Al Qaeda's hive stings Yemen," *Washington Times*, April 2, 2010.

[26] Open Source Center, "Yemeni Sources Report AQAP Leaders, Wanted Saudi Fugitives in Ma'rib Governorate," *Jedda Ukaz Online in Arabic*, June 14, 2010, GMP20100614614002.

[27] "Yemen 'al-Qaeda man' surrenders," *BBC News Middle East*, June 7, 2010.

[28] BBC Monitoring Middle East, "Al-Qa'idah video identifies new Saudi leader in Yemen," *Al Arabiya TV*, May 27, 2010.

[29] On January 19, 2010, Secretary of State Clinton designated AQAP as a Foreign Terrorist Organization (FTO) under Section 219 of the Immigration and Nationality Act, as amended (INA). In addition, the Secretary also designated AQAP and its two top leaders Nasir al Wahishi and Said al Shihri under E.O. 13224, which would, among other things, block "all property and interests in property" of these designated terrorists and individuals and entities materially supporting them. On May 11, the Secretary designated another two other AQAP leaders under E.O. 13224, Qasim al Rimi (Raymi) and Nayif al Qahtani (now deceased).

[30] Sarah Phillips, *What Comes Next in Yemen? Al Qaeda, the Tribes, and State-Building*, Carnegie Endowment for International Peace, March 2010.

[31] "Yemen's Chaos Aids the Evolution of a Qaeda Cell," *New York Times*, January 2, 2010.

[32] "Al Qaeda's Deep Tribal Ties Make Yemen a Terror Hub," *Wall Street Journal*, January 22, 2010.

[33] According to one analyst, based on a rudimentary analysis of known members of the organization, Yemenis make up 56% of the AQAP's total membership, Saudis 37%, and foreigners 7%. See, Murad Batal al Shishani, *Terrorism Monitor*, Jamestown Foundation, vol. 8, issue 9, March 5, 2010. Yemen's national security agency director, Gen. Mohammed al Anisi, says that AQAP is approximately 90% Yemeni, with only 10% foreign fighters rounding out the ranks. See, op.cit., *Wall Street Journal*, January 22, 2010.

[34] Experts note that one factor that led Sunni tribes in Iraq to break away from Al Qaeda in Iraq (AQI) and cooperate with U.S. forces was AQI's attempts to replace tribal customs with its own extreme version of Islamic law (*Sharia*) and arrange forced marriages between its members and local Iraqi women. According to one expert, "Al Qa'ida in Iraq pushed too hard against the Sunni tribes that they relied on for support when they insisted on extracting oaths from the sheikhs to reject tribal legal traditions – a blatant infringement of

tribal autonomy. Al Qa'ida leaders also alienated themselves by attempting to impose themselves in marriage to prominent tribal families, despite cultural norms against women marrying beyond the clan." See, Sarah Phillips, "Yemen's Postcards from the Edge: al Qa'ida, Tribes, and Nervous Neighbours," Centre for International Security Studies, Sydney University.

[35] "Al Qaeda's Shadowland," *New York Times*, January 12, 2010.

[36] Barak Barfi, *Yemen on the Brink? The Resurgence of Al Qaeda in Yemen*, New America Foundation, January 2010.

[37] Open Source Center, "AQAP Statement Condemns Airstrikes in Yemen, 'Silence' From Tribes," *Al-Fallujah Islamic Forums* in Arabic, June 17, 2010, GMP20100618836001.

[38] In March 2010, the U.S. Department of Transportation's Maritime Administration issued a warning stating that "Information suggests that Al Qaeda remains interested in maritime attacks in the Bab Al Mandab strait, Red Sea, and the Gulf of Aden along the coast of Yemen."

[39] U.S. Congress, Senate Select Committee on Intelligence, *ATTEMPTED TERRORIST ATTACK ON NORTHWEST AIRLINES FLIGHT 253*, 111th Cong., 2nd sess., May 24, 2010, 111-199 (Washington: GPO, 2010).

[40] U.S. Congress, House Permanent Select Committee on Intelligence, *ANNUAL THREATS ASSESSMENT – DENNIS C. BLAIR*, 111th Cong., 2nd sess., February 3, 2010.

[41] "Imam's Journey from Messenger of Peace to Voice of Jihad," *International Herald Tribune*, May 10, 2010.

[42] "U.S. Approves Targeted Killing of American Cleric," *New York Times*, April 6, 2010.

[43] Awlaki's tribe publicly stated that "the Al Awlak tribes are renown for their bravery and for the protection of all their sons. Therefore, we are warning anyone of the consequences of his collaboration with the Americans by giving information about him." See, Open Source Center, "Yemeni Tribe Extends Protection to Al-Awlaki, Rejects US Accusations," *Al Quds Al Arabi* (London, in Arabic), April 12, 2010, GMP20100412825007. Yemeni Foreign Minister Abu Bakr al Qirbi said that "Anwar al Awlaki has always been looked at as a preacher rather than a terrorist and shouldn't be considered as a terrorist unless the Americans have evidence that he has been involved in terrorism." See, "Yemen Balks at Possible US strike on Cleric Anwar al-Awlaki," *Christian Science Monitor*, April 12, 2010.

[44] "Al Qaeda's Nuclear Plant," *New York Times*, May 6, 2010.

[45] "Texas: Man Accused of Aiding Al Qaeda," *New York Times*, June 4, 2010.

[46] "12 Americans Arrested in Yemen," *New York Times*, June 8, 2010.

[47] According to Yemen expert Philip McCrum, historical Zaydi doctrine believes that rebelling against an unjust ruler is a religious duty. This belief originated from the actions of the sect's founder, Zayd bin Ali, who led an unsuccessful uprising against Umayyad Caliph Hisham in 740 because of the Caliph's despotic rule. See, Juan Cole's blog Informed Comment, "The Houthi Rebellion in Yemen," available online at http://www.j uancole.com/2009/09/huthi-rebellion-inyemen.html

[48] In a February interview with the Arabic language pan-Arab daily *Al Hayat* newspaper, Assistant Secretary of State for Near Eastern Affairs Jeffrey Feltman stated that "We do not see the degree of Iranian interference that some have suggested. Yet we are still open (to listening to the evidence) but quite simply we do not have at present the evidence that the Iranian interference with the Huthists is as deep as the one with (the Lebanese) Hezbollah." See, BBC Monitoring Middle East, "USA's Feltman denies presence of US forces inside Yemen fighting Al-Qa'idah," Text of report by London-based newspaper *Al-Hayat* website on 31 January, published February 1, 2010.

[49] Saudi Arabia launched a three month air and ground campaign along the border of its southernmost province of Jizan and Sa'da in an attempt to repel reported Houthi infiltration of Saudi territory. It is estimated that Saudi Arabia lost 133 soldiers in its war against the Al Houthis. Saudi Arabia agreed to a ceasefire with the Houthis in late February 2010 after an exchange of prisoners and remains.

[50] USAID's Bureau For Democracy, Conflict, and Humanitarian Assistance (DCHA) and Office Of U.S. Foreign Disaster Assistance (OFDA) have provided $15.8 million in FY2010 disaster aid for displaced Yemenis in the north.

[51] Some analysts see the conflict tied to the behind-the-scenes-struggle for presidential succession in Yemen between two of the front-runners, the President's son Ahmed and head of the Republican Guards and Ali Mohsen al Ahmar, the commander of the army's northern forces. According to one *New York Times* article, "The tension between the two old comrades [President Saleh and Ali Mohsen] is visible in the criticism of the way the war in the north is being handled, with government officials sometimes complaining that Mr. Mohsen set off renewed fighting there by occupying or destroying the mosques and holy places of the Houthis and building Sunni mosques and schools in the area. Mr. Mohsen's supporters have countered that the war has not been fully supported by the central government." See, "In Yemen, U.S. Faces Leader Who Puts Family First," *New York Times*, January 5, 2010.

[52] Barak A. Salmoni, Bryce Loidolt, and Madeleine Wells, *Regime and Periphery in Northern Yemen: The Houthi Phenomenom*, RAND, 2010.

[53] "In Yemen's South, Protests Could Cause More Instability," *New York Times*, February 27, 2010.

[54] "Yemen: Southern Secession Threat Adds to Instability," *Oxford Analytica*, May 27, 2009.

[55] Human Rights Watch, *In the Name of Unity: The Yemeni Government's Brutal Response to Southern Movement Protests*, December 14, 2009.

[56] Al Bidh also was the former leader of the Yemeni Socialist Party (YSP) and led the unsuccessful southern revolt against the north in the 1994 civil war in which an estimated 3,000 people were killed.

[57] After the British withdrawal from Yemen in 1967 and the formation of the socialist PDRY in southern Yemen, Al Fadhli's prominent family (his father was a Sultan) in Abyan lost its vast estates, and he moved to Saudi Arabia where he was raised. At age 19, Al Fadhli left to fight in Afghanistan alongside Osama Bin Laden against the Soviet army largely to exact retribution on a Communist country. When he returned to Yemen, he regained much of his family's holdings and helped recruit jihadists to fight for the north in the civil war of 1994. His sister is married to Ali Mohsen, one of the country's top military commanders. For a full profile, see, "Ex-Jihadist Defies Yemen's Leader, and Easy Labels," *New York Times*, Feb 26, 2010.

[58] Open Source Center, "Yemen: Southern Movement Figure Declares End of Truce With Govt," *London Quds Press (in Arabic)* , June 18, 2010, GMP20100618615001.

[59] In an official Interior Ministry report to parliament, the government itself claims that 18 people had been killed and 120 injured in violence in the south of Yemen during the first quarter of the 2010. See, *Economist Intelligence Unit*, Country Report - Main report: May 1, 2010.

[60] Ginny Hill, *Yemen: Fear of Failure*, Chatham House, Middle East Programme, November 2008.

[61] Open Source Center, "Yemeni Govt Raises Fuel Prices for 2nd Time in 3 Months; Riots Expected ," *Yemen Times*, May 13, 2010, GMP20100514054001.

[62] "Alarm as Water Taps Run Dry," *The National (UAE)*, September 24, 2009.

[63] Gerhard Lichtenthaeler, "Water Conflict and Cooperation in Yemen," *Middle East Report*, Spring 2010.

[64] The World Bank estimates that qat cultivation employs one out of every seven Yemeni workers.

[65] Lenard Milich and Mohammed Al-Sabbry, "The "Rational Peasant" vs Sustainable Livelihoods: The Case of Qat in Yemen," *Development - Society for International Development*, 1995.

[66] With the exception of the French firm Total, most major international oil companies have avoided investing in Yemen due to the lack of government transparency and the security situation in its remote governorates.

[67] "2010 could be the Year for an Upturn in Yemen's Economy," *Yemen Times*, May 13, 2010.

[68] At current prices, fuel subsidies could reach as high as $2.2 billion in 2010. See, "Yemen raises Diesel Prices by 13 percent," *Reuters*, June 7, 2010.

[69] *New York Times*, January 5, 2010, op.cit.

[70] One senior Yemeni official who spoke on the condition of anonymity remarked that Mohsen/Muhsin is "building up his ambitions. If he becomes president, it will be a bad sign.... Muhsin sides more with the religious extremists, not necessarily al-Qaeda, but with extremists like Sheik Abdul Majid al Zindani." See, "Yemen's Alliance with Radical Sunnis in Internal War Poses Complication for U.S.," *Washington Post*, February 11, 2010.

[71] According to one recent report, the NSB was established to "provide Western intelligence agencies with a more palatable local partner than the Political Security Organization (PSO). The NSB is now responsible for dispensing $3.4 million of U.S.-provided tribal engagement funds to support the campaign against AQAP. See, Michael Knights, "Strengthening Yemeni Counterterrorism Forces: Challenges and Political Considerations," *Policywatch* #16 16, The Washington Institute for Near East Policy, January 6, 2010. In general, due to previous allegations of PSO sympathy and direct support of Al Qaeda, the United States government deeply distrusts that security agency and does not work with its units which are responsible for day-to-day security inside the country. See, "Yemen Security Agency Prone to Inside Threats, Officials Say," *Washington Post*, February 10, 2010.

[72] Andrew McGregor, Yemen and the U.S.: Different Approaches to the War on Terrorism, The Jamestown Foundation, *Terrorism Monitor*, May 10, 2007.

[73] *New York Times*, January 5, 2010, op.cit.

[74] U.S. Acting Deputy State Department Spokesman Gordon Duguid, "Statement on Yemen Parliamentary Elections Postponement," Washington, DC, March 3, 2009.

[75] United Nations Security Council, Letter dated 10 March 2010 from the Chairman of the Security Council Committee pursuant to resolutions 751 (1992) and 1907 (2009) concerning Somalia and Eritrea addressed to the President of the Security Council, S/2010/91, March 10, 2010.

[76] "Somalis fleeing to Yemen prompt new worries in fight against al-Qaeda," *Washington Post*, January 12, 2010.

[77] "Q+A-Somali-Yemeni Militant Ties in the Spotlight," *Reuters*, January 6, 2010.

[78] "Is Al Qaeda in Yemen connected to Al Qaeda in Somalia?," *Christian Science Monitor*, January 7, 2010.

[79] Bernard Haykel, "Act locally: why the GCC needs to help save Yemen," *The National* (UAE), January 7, 2010.

[80] Yemeni expatriates are to a large extent located in Saudi Arabia. There are smaller communities in Bahrain and the UAE.

[81] Oxford Analytica, *GULF STATES: GCC lacks policy coordination for Yemen*, March 24, 2010.

[82] According to experts, Crown Prince and Defense Minister Sultan bin Abdel Aziz al Saud, his son Prince Khalid bin Sultan, Interior Minister Prince Nayef Abdel Aziz al Saud, and his son Prince Mohammed bin Nayef are the four primary Saudi leaders charged with managing the Yemen portfolio.

[83] Ed Blanche, "Saudis lead the Charge against Al Qaeda," *The Middle East*, February 1, 2010.

[84] The boundary between Yemen and Saudi Arabia was partially defined by the 1934 Treaty of Taif. The permanent (and current) definition of the border took place as a result of a June 2000 treaty between the two countries.

[85] In 1999, the Clinton Administration reached a naval refueling agreement with Yemen at Aden harbor. After the Cole bombing a year later, some critics charged that this refueling agreement had placed U.S. vessels at risk in order to improve U.S.-Yemeni relations. In testimony before the Senate Armed Services Committee, former CENTCOM commander and retired Marine Corps General Anthony Zinni said that "The refueling of that ship in Aden was my decision.... I pass that buck on to nobody.... I don't want anyone to think we ever in any instance, anywhere, in any evolution or event that took place in CENTCOM ever took a risk for the purpose of a better relationship with a country and put soldier, sailor, airman, marine at risk for that reason. Absolutely not.... At no time was this a gratuitous offer to be made just to improve relations with the Yemenis." See, "Retired Commander takes Responsibility for Decision to Refuel Ships in Aden," *Agence France Presse*, October 19, 2000.

[86] Edward Prados, *The US and Yemen: A Half-Century of Engagement*, Center for Contemporary Arab Studies, Georgetown University, 2005.

[87] "For Yemen, an Evolving U.S. Relationship; As Both Seek to Improve Ties, Sanctions Against Iraq Remain a Point of Division," *Washington Post*, October 24, 2000.

[88] See, http://www.state

[89] "Yemen signs military deal with US," *The National Newspaper (UAE)*, November 11, 2009.

[90] In testimony before the House Foreign Affairs Committee, Assistant Secretary of State for Near Eastern Affairs Jeffrey Feltman remarked that "On the security front, the Departments of State and Defense provide training and assistance to Yemen's key counterterrorism units. Through Diplomatic Security Antiterrorism Assistance (DS/ATA) programs we provide training to security forces in the Ministry of Interior, including the Yemeni Coast Guard and the Central Security Force's Counterterrorism Unit (CTU)." See, *Yemen on the Brink: Implications for U.S. Policy*, Jeffrey D. Feltman Assistant Secretary, Bureau of Near Eastern Affairs Ambassador, House Foreign Affairs Committee, February 4, 2010.

[91] U.S. Congress, Senate Committee on Foreign Relations, Following the Money in Yemen and Lebanon: Maximizing the Effectiveness of US Security Assistance and International Financial Institution Lending, committee print, 111th Cong., 1st sess., January 5, 2010 (Washington: GPO, 2010).

[92] USAID, Fact Sheet: USAID New Strategy for Yemen, February 5, 2010.

[93] USAID, *United States Agency For International Development*, Advice of Program Change, CN#58, June 10, 2010.

[94] For a list of ongoing MEPI grants in Yemen, see http://www.abudhabi.mepi.state

[95] "Rulings Raise Doubts on Policy On Transfer Of Yemenis," *New York Times*, July 9, 2010.

[96] Section 1203 of H.R. 5136, the House-passed National Defense Authorization Act for FY20 11, also authorizes $75 million in 1206 funding for U.S. assistance to Yemeni Ministry of Interior forces with the stipulation that the funds be transferred to the Department of State, which would assume responsibility for the program. The SASC version of the bill, S. 3454, would provide a new, separate, and discrete authority for DOD to train and equip the Yemini Ministry of Interior forces.

[97] S. 3454

[98] S. 3454

[99] Traditional foreign donors to Yemen include the United States, GCC states, United Kingdom, Germany, France, Netherlands, Italy, Japan, South Korea, the World Bank, European Commission, various United Nations agencies (UNDP, HCR, WFP, UNFPA, UNICEF, FAO, WHO, UNHCR), and Arab multilateral development funds (Arab Fund for Economic and Social Development, the Islamic Development Bank, the OPEC Fund, the Arab Monetary Fund).

[100] "GULF STATES: GCC lacks policy coordination for Yemen," *Oxford Analytica*, March 24, 2010.

[101] IMF Executive Board Concludes 2009 Article IV Consultation with Yemen, Public Information Notice (PIN) No. 10/15, January 27, 2010.

[102] U. S. Department of State, *Remarks by Clinton with Yemeni Foreign Minister Abubakr al-Qirbi*, January 21, 2010.

[103] Open Source Center, "Yemeni Deputy Planning Minister Hisham Sharaf on New Yemeni Economic Plan," *London Al-Sharq al-A wsat Online in Arabic* , February 28, 2010, GMP20100228001007 .

CHAPTER SOURCES

The following chapters have been previously published:

Chapter 1 – This is an edited, excerpted and augmented edition of a United States Congressional Research Service publication, Report Order Code RL30588, dated November 19, 2010.

Chapter 2 – This is an edited, excerpted and augmented edition of a United States Congressional Research Service publication, Report Order Code RS21922, dated November 12, 2010.

Chapter 3 – This is an edited, excerpted and augmented edition of a United States Congressional Research Service publication, Report Order Code RL32686, dated July 15, 2010.

Chapter 4 – This is an edited, excerpted and augmented edition of a United States Congressional Research Service publication, Report Order Code RL34170, dated November 1, 2010.

INDEX

A

abuse, 113, 116
access, 5, 39, 54, 62, 67, 122, 166, 177, 187, 188
accessibility, 119
accountability, 13, 187
accounting, 22, 59, 124, 179
activism, 13, 61
administrators, 18
advancement, 115
Afghan insurgency, vii, 1, 23
Afghan Interim Government, 4
Afghan political establishment, vii, 1
Afghan Provincial Protection Program (APPP), 36
Africa, 23, 45, 115, 178, 181
age, 5, 96, 167, 168, 170, 178, 197
agencies, 15, 35, 43, 44, 65, 69, 98, 104, 108, 110,
    112, 149, 166, 172, 182, 189, 192, 197, 198
agility, 189
agricultural sector, 144
agriculture, 6, 68, 70, 144, 153, 178, 187
Air Force, 47, 51, 180, 185, 187, 195
Al Qaeda, 8, 9, 10, 11, 21, 22, 23, 24, 25, 34, 35, 36,
    45, 50, 52, 54, 55, 59, 61, 62, 63, 81, 82, 83, 84,
    86, 88, 121, 131, 147, 156, 160, 161, 162, 165,
    166, 167, 168, 169, 170, 171, 172, 173, 179, 181,
    183, 193, 194, 195, 196, 197
Al Qaeda cells, 23
Al Qaeda in the Arabian Peninsula (AQAP), 162,
    165
Albania, 80
Alexander the Great, 2
alienation, 175
Amin, Hafizullah , 3, 132
ammonium, 22
Amrollah Saleh, 10, 15, 92
Andijon, 51, 61
apex, 166
appetite, 178
appointees, 96, 117, 126
appointments, 13, 96, 105, 110, 112

appropriations, 49, 64, 65, 66, 86, 103, 117, 144,
    152, 156, 187
Appropriations Act, 155, 156, 159, 185
Arab world, 161, 163
Arabian Peninsula, 162, 163, 165, 189
arbokai, 3, 37
armed conflict, 146, 150, 159
armed forces, 99, 100, 150, 174
armed groups, 21, 38, 57, 129
Armenia, 80, 157
arms sales, 86
arrest, 23, 27, 35, 54, 58, 99, 107, 157, 166, 173, 183
arrests, 113, 149, 175
Asia, 27, 40, 57, 59, 60, 61, 62, 66, 67, 68, 71, 103,
    115, 158
Asian Development Bank (ADB), 66
assassination, 14, 27, 54, 111, 168, 176, 182
assault, 94, 115
assertiveness, 13
assessment, 21, 27, 28, 31, 50, 98, 104, 134, 152,
    172, 189
assets, 57, 84, 86, 87, 105, 106, 150, 152, 154, 157
atrocities, 174
audit, 106, 108, 189
audits, 65, 135
Austria, 80
authorities, 12, 38, 39, 91, 103, 108, 110, 115, 138,
    139, 145, 146, 147, 148, 149, 152, 154, 155, 158,
    159, 162, 163, 168, 170, 172, 173, 174, 184, 194
authority, 7, 9, 16, 18, 24, 29, 65, 68, 84, 90, 91, 101,
    106, 108, 110, 129, 146, 147, 148, 151, 156, 158,
    160, 173, 189, 194, 198
automobiles, 70
autonomy, 17, 95, 172, 176, 195
aversion, 93
awareness, 79, 109, 139, 178
Ayman al Zawahiri, 172
Azerbaijan, 80, 157

B

backlash, viii, 26, 30, 89, 130, 162

backwardness, 175
Bagram airfield, 3
Bahrain, 43, 51, 158, 182, 197
Bamiyan,, 8, 31, 82
ban, 20, 86, 141
bank financing, 192
banking, 48, 180
banks, 5, 108
base, vii, 1, 6, 7, 21, 47, 51, 56, 61, 63, 67, 81, 82, 94, 95, 100, 155, 159, 179, 188
Belgium, 42, 80
benchmarks, 31, 54, 65
beneficial effect, 110
beneficiaries, 158
benefits, 99, 102, 103, 110, 172
beverages, 114
bilateral aid, 86, 183
bilateral relationship, 182
blame, 22, 130, 166
blasphemy, 114
bomb attack, 162, 165, 188
bonds, viii, 89
bonuses, 103
border control, 186
border crossing, 54, 55, 69, 157
border security, 187
Bosnia-Herzegovina, 80
bribes, 2, 48, 104, 105, 107, 108
Britain, 3, 20, 25, 26, 34, 39, 40, 41, 42, 43, 47, 56, 57, 68, 81, 101, 106, 107, 108, 162, 170, 190, 194
brothers, 14, 132, 171, 172, 180
Buddhism, 2
budget deficit, 192
Bulgaria, 40, 80
bureaucracy, 49
burn, 114
businesses, 33, 38, 68, 151
buyers, 68, 83, 151, 177

C

Cabinet, 125, 135
cabinet members, 20
caliber, 152
campaign strategies, 91
campaigns, 91, 123, 139, 154, 163
canals, 18, 32
cancer, 143
candidates, 42, 58, 91, 93, 94, 117, 120, 122, 123, 128, 129, 130, 131, 134, 180
capital goods, 6
cash, 33, 58, 79, 93, 108, 154, 178, 191, 192
cash crops, 154
casting, 86, 124

category a, 79, 118
ceasefire, 188, 196
Central Asia, 59, 60, 61, 62, 66, 67, 68, 71, 115, 157
central bank, 179, 192
certificate, 190
certification, 20, 76, 77, 109, 111, 124, 134, 156, 194
challenges, vii, viii, 53, 140, 141, 145, 146, 148, 156, 161, 162, 164, 167, 177, 183, 192, 193, 194
checks and balances, 126
chemical, 23, 86
chemicals, 22, 151, 173
Chief Justice, 113, 132
Chief of Staff, 132
child labor, 184
children, 64, 67, 167, 172
China, 11, 40, 41, 59, 62, 70, 88, 107, 115, 157, 165
Christianity, 115
Christians, 5, 114, 175
CIA, 4, 6, 10, 14, 23, 35, 45, 83, 88, 101, 104, 162, 173, 195
cities, 41, 177
citizens, 48, 63, 109, 165, 171
citizenship, 104
civil servants, 102, 103, 105, 175
civil service, 103, 193
civil service reform, 193
civil society, 113, 118
civil war, 7, 46, 139, 163, 175, 196, 197
cleaning, 18
climate, 140, 162, 174, 175
Clinton Administration, 8, 9, 71, 197
cluster bomb, 167
C-N, 77
CNN, 23, 88, 134
coal, 70
Coast Guard, 185, 187, 198
coffee, 178
cold war, 163
Cold War, 3
collaboration, 175, 196
collateral, 167
collateral damage, 167
commerce, 32, 52, 127
commercial, 42, 83, 183
commodity, 177
Communist Party, 3
communities, 34, 36, 48, 67, 90, 92, 93, 151, 187, 197
community, 11, 12, 16, 17, 20, 24, 29, 33, 34, 35, 65, 70, 91, 93, 98, 109, 114, 115, 128, 143, 161, 173, 176, 188, 192
compensation, 109, 151
competition, 58, 90, 118, 121, 170, 176, 179

competitiveness, 188
complexity, 131
compliance, 38, 108
composition, 93, 180
computer, 97
conference, 12, 16, 31, 34, 39, 40, 49, 63, 65, 66, 88, 90, 97, 103, 104, 105, 106, 107, 108, 109, 113, 117, 125, 128, 159, 174, 190
conflict, 4, 7, 16, 18, 50, 52, 54, 58, 59, 60, 82, 90, 104, 107, 116, 139, 140, 146, 147, 148, 150, 159, 165, 173, 174, 181, 182, 184, 188, 196
conflict resolution, 16, 188
confrontation, 146, 171
consensus, 35, 47, 53, 103, 118, 125
Consolidated Appropriations Act, 156
consolidation, 143, 192
constituents, 101
Constitution, 12, 119, 131
constitutional amendment, 164, 179
construction, 17, 34, 43, 49, 51, 59, 62, 67, 68, 70, 79, 108, 177
consumption, 177, 178
containers, 82, 87
controversial, 116, 128, 159
cooperation, 4, 10, 16, 20, 21, 30, 33, 53, 54, 56, 58, 61, 76, 77, 104, 111, 138, 161, 162, 166, 167, 175, 180, 183, 184, 190, 193, 194
coordination, 16, 38, 51, 55, 157, 190, 197, 198
corruption, vii, viii, 2, 5, 15, 17, 18, 26, 45, 48, 49, 50, 51, 53, 70, 79, 89, 90, 96, 97, 98, 102, 103, 104, 105, 106, 107, 108, 109, 110, 111, 121, 123, 125, 126, 137, 138, 139, 140, 143, 144, 145, 146, 148, 152, 161, 175, 177, 183, 193
cost, 2, 41, 50, 51, 59, 71, 83, 120, 150, 154, 177, 178, 179
Counternarcotics Infantry Kandak (CNIK), 154
counterterrorism, 138, 147, 148, 149, 155, 161, 162, 165, 166, 167, 170, 171, 182, 189, 190, 193, 198
covering, 22, 64, 117, 153
creditors, 6, 179
criticism, 6, 15, 48, 54, 96, 97, 98, 99, 106, 107, 114, 122, 159, 196
Croatia, 47, 80
crop, 19, 66, 68, 70, 139, 140, 144, 146, 153, 157, 159, 178
crops, 68, 79, 110, 141, 149, 151, 154, 177
cruise missiles, 8
Cuba, 22, 169, 188, 190, 194
cultivation, viii, 16, 19, 20, 66, 68, 70, 101, 102, 110, 137, 138, 139, 140, 141, 142, 143, 145, 146, 148, 149, 151, 153, 154, 155, 156, 157, 160, 178, 197
cultural norms, 195
culture, 171, 178, 179

currency, 108, 179, 182
current prices, 197
cycles, 140, 146
Czech Republic, 47, 80, 81

D

Daoud, Mohammad, 3
Dai Kundi, 8, 25, 82, 114, 143
database, 43
death penalty, 114, 115
deaths, 22, 38, 45, 57, 168
debts, 151
decentralization, 2, 175
deficiencies, 65
deficiency, 18
deficit, 18, 177, 192
degenerate, 11
degradation, 150
delegates, 12, 39, 91, 95, 117
Delta, 88, 173
democracy, 10, 11, 19, 89, 91, 118, 180, 183, 187, 188, 190
Democratic Party, 3
demonstrations, 125, 130, 175
denial, 86, 115
Denmark, 39, 57, 80, 81, 191
Department of Agriculture, 68, 112, 144, 153
Department of Defense, 20, 27, 46, 87, 135, 145, 149, 151, 158, 159, 184, 185, 186, 189, 190
Department of Justice, 102
Department of Transportation, 196
depth, 40, 53, 59, 110
derivatives, 177
destruction, 73, 157
detainees, 113, 188
detection, 152, 159, 162
detention, 183, 188, 190, 194
development assistance, 16, 138, 139, 140, 144, 146, 153, 165, 183, 191, 194
development policy, 138
diesel fuel, 177
direct action, 140
directives, 149, 189
disappointment, 100, 180
disaster, 196
discrimination, 8, 114, 184
discussion groups, 12
dissidents, 163
distribution, 85, 92, 133, 153
Doha, 194
domestic laws, 149
domestic policy, 50
dominance, 95

donations, 20, 34, 49, 63

donors, viii, 5, 16, 18, 30, 34, 38, 40, 49, 57, 63, 65, 66, 71, 89, 103, 104, 112, 117, 120, 128, 161, 180, 188, 189, 190, 191, 192, 193, 198

Dostam, General Abdul Rashid, 8

draft, 39, 87, 98, 109

drawing, 131, 180

drinking water, 177

drought, 69, 137, 141

drug trafficking, viii, 46, 56, 101, 137, 138, 145, 146, 155, 156, 160

drugs, 48, 137, 149, 158

durability, 139

duty free, 72

duty-free treatment, 72

E

earnings, 109

economic activity, viii, 89, 140, 146

economic assistance, 17, 20, 144, 156, 184

economic cooperation, 194

economic cycle, 151

economic development, 1, 21, 26, 29, 43, 56, 64, 67, 110, 187, 190, 192

economic growth, 68, 110

economic integration, 68, 141

economic power, 179

economic reform, 192, 193

economic reforms, 192

education, 11, 44, 59, 66, 114, 127, 180, 187

Egypt, 67, 163, 184

elders, 26, 32, 34, 54, 55

election, 13, 14, 15, 16, 27, 28, 34, 40, 82, 89, 90, 91, 94, 95, 96, 97, 99, 100, 101, 103, 111, 117, 118, 119, 120, 121, 122, 123, 124, 125, 127, 128, 129, 130, 131, 134, 135, 138, 154, 159, 164, 180

election fraud, 14, 123, 130

Electoral Complaints Commission (ECC), 16, 89

electricity, 58, 59, 61, 66, 67, 68, 70, 79

e-mail, 134

embargo, 181

embassy, 5, 8, 17, 23, 54

emergency, 12, 51, 62, 86, 131, 174, 193

employees, 105, 112

employment, 115

employment opportunities, 115

empowerment, 117, 158

encouragement, 192

endowments, 127

energy, 62, 67, 71, 81, 100, 126, 165, 177

energy prices, 177

enforcement, 138, 141, 144, 146, 148, 149, 150, 159

England, 194

environment, 163

equality, 175

equipment, 42, 46, 47, 48, 49, 51, 60, 61, 62, 66, 68, 97, 101, 105, 152, 159, 161, 166, 173, 184, 186, 187, 189

equity, 98

Eritrea, 197

Estonia, 40, 80, 81

ethnic groups, 91

ethnic minority, 58

ethnicity, 48, 91, 92, 102, 122

EU, 194

Europe, 88, 100, 120, 123, 139, 154, 158

European Commission, 57, 191, 198

European Union, 16, 46, 120

evidence, 36, 82, 99, 120, 123, 150, 166, 171, 194, 196

evolution, 26, 44, 198

exclusion, 171

executive branch, 138, 156, 157

Executive Order, 24, 57, 84, 86, 149, 158, 169, 170

exercise, 91

exile, 11, 22, 63, 82, 99, 101, 111, 176

expenditures, 179, 192

expertise, 126, 181, 192

exploitation, 115

explosives, 57, 162

exporter, 68

exports, 6, 68, 69, 84, 86, 178, 182

extremists, 55, 172, 179, 197

F

facilitators, 23, 158

factories, 68, 70

fairness, 123

faith, 104, 114, 128

families, 28, 32, 46, 59, 106, 154, 195

family members, 179

farmers, 20, 67, 70, 110, 117, 137, 138, 139, 140, 141, 147, 151, 153, 154, 177

farms, 172

FBI, 107, 170, 173, 183

fear, 3, 33, 36, 38, 52, 58, 61, 90, 93, 99, 111, 146, 162, 170, 175, 182, 187, 192

fears, 53, 56, 61, 62, 127

Federal Government, 181

Federal Register, 159

fights, 181

financial, viii, 9, 17, 24, 30, 33, 43, 70, 90, 93, 101, 118, 128, 137, 140, 150, 155, 161, 163, 166, 192

financial institutions, viii, 161

financial support, 140, 163

flexibility, 42, 151, 189

food, 6, 69, 116, 174, 178, 179, 183
force, 2, 3, 10, 12, 16, 20, 21, 23, 27, 28, 34, 37, 38, 40, 41, 45, 46, 47, 48, 53, 63, 80, 99, 101, 108, 117, 149, 150, 152, 174, 176, 178, 184, 186, 188
foreign aid, 46, 78, 103, 161, 192
foreign assistance, 138, 145, 184
foreign nationals, 119, 157, 171, 173
foreign policy, 161
Foreign Terrorist Organization (FTO), 25, 181, 195
formation, 11, 95, 116, 127, 180, 196
Fort Hood, 170, 172
France, 39, 40, 41, 43, 46, 47, 51, 80, 191, 198
fraud, 14, 15, 16, 89, 95, 119, 120, 123, 124, 125, 129, 130, 134
free trade, 72
freedom, 114, 115, 175, 176, 184
Freedom Support Act, 53, 65, 66, 117
funding, 4, 6, 17, 19, 20, 31, 33, 34, 37, 49, 59, 63, 64, 65, 66, 70, 71, 72, 87, 104, 105, 109, 117, 118, 119, 128, 138, 144, 146, 154, 155, 156, 159, 184, 186, 187, 188, 198
fundraising, 123
funds, 5, 14, 18, 19, 20, 32, 33, 34, 37, 38, 46, 49, 53, 54, 57, 58, 64, 65, 67, 68, 71, 73, 74, 75, 76, 77, 78, 79, 83, 84, 102, 105, 108, 109, 117, 118, 120, 128, 144, 145, 150, 151, 155, 156, 160, 178, 184, 187, 188, 189, 192, 197, 198

G

GDP, viii, 5, 140, 161, 177
Gen. Petraeus, 2, 24, 28, 29, 31, 32, 33, 34, 36, 37, 43, 45, 46, 50, 56, 57, 70
General Security Services (GSS), 182
Generalized System of Preferences, 84
Georgia, 41, 51, 60, 80
Germany, 6, 11, 12, 30, 40, 41, 42, 47, 49, 57, 61, 80, 81, 91, 99, 111, 176, 191, 194, 198
Ghazni provinces, 8
governance, vii, 1, 11, 15, 16, 17, 18, 19, 21, 26, 29, 31, 32, 33, 40, 48, 49, 59, 65, 78, 79, 89, 90, 91, 94, 95, 98, 101, 103, 110, 111, 116, 118, 126, 161, 166, 167, 179, 183, 187, 188, 190, 192
government funds, 108, 178
government intervention, 143
government policy, 187
governments, 33, 40, 51, 53, 111, 116, 125, 167, 180
governor, 7, 14, 19, 23, 32, 36, 51, 96, 99, 100, 101, 102, 110, 117, 121, 127, 132, 139, 148, 153, 154, 167, 168, 175
GPC, 180
graduate students, 54
grants, 71, 106, 118, 188, 198
grass, 143

Great Britain, 190
Greece, 40, 49, 80
greed, 4, 40, 41
grouping, 62, 81, 95, 120
growth, vii, viii, 68, 110, 139, 161
Guantanamo, 22, 169, 188, 190, 194
guidance, 48, 104, 149, 150, 159
gynecologist, 14

H

hard currency, 182
Hazara tribes, 8, 82, 114
healing, 51
health, 5, 7, 14, 44, 66, 67, 69, 117, 144, 155, 187
health care, 7, 44, 67
health care sector, 67
herbicide, 155, 159
heroin, 139, 140, 151, 157
Hezbollah, 196
higher education, 59, 127
history, 2, 62, 91, 165
homeland security, 162, 165
host, 39, 149, 171, 172
hostile acts, 159
hostilities, 18, 150, 159, 174, 190
House, vii, 1, 10, 18, 29, 32, 52, 53, 66, 72, 78, 87, 94, 95, 96, 97, 107, 109, 115, 131, 134, 149, 152, 157, 158, 159, 160, 166, 180, 184, 189, 190, 195, 196, 197, 198
House of Representatives, 134, 180
housing, 63
hub, 51, 55, 100
human, 6, 18, 19, 20, 33, 46, 48, 56, 65, 77, 99, 109, 113, 115, 116, 118, 128, 134, 150, 166, 174, 183, 187, 190, 192
Human Development Index, viii, 161
human right, 6, 18, 19, 20, 33, 46, 48, 56, 65, 77, 99, 109, 113, 115, 116, 118, 128, 134, 166, 174, 183, 187, 190
human rights, 6, 18, 19, 20, 33, 46, 48, 56, 65, 77, 99, 109, 113, 115, 116, 118, 128, 134, 166, 174, 183, 187, 190
humanitarian aid, 58, 61
Hungary, 80, 81
hydrocarbons, 67
hypothesis, 171
Hyundai, 88, 178

I

identity, 95, 99, 129, 162
ideology, 82
illiteracy, vii, viii, 48, 161

image, 44, 180
imagery, 166
images, 80, 195
IMF, 54, 66, 192, 198
Immigration and Nationality Act, 195
immunity, 6
imports, 6, 72, 178, 179
improvements, 140
inauguration, 55, 95
income, 140, 153, 177, 178, 192
income tax, 192
independence, 3, 16, 61, 108, 113, 184
Independent Directorate for Local Governance (IDLG), 110
India, vii, 1, 2, 3, 6, 13, 25, 40, 51, 52, 53, 54, 56, 57, 59, 63, 69, 71, 83, 86, 93, 103, 112, 114, 126, 157
individuals, 131, 139, 146, 150, 151, 195
industries, 70, 141
industry, 67, 68, 70, 140, 144, 179
information technology, 106, 114
infrastructure, 3, 11, 21, 29, 34, 61, 62, 68, 79, 149, 163, 174, 177, 179
insecurity, viii, 137, 138, 140, 145, 146
inspectors, 108
institution building, 103
institutions, viii, 11, 17, 30, 44, 45, 66, 89, 91, 93, 97, 103, 113, 115, 122, 128, 146
insurgency, vii, 1, 18, 19, 21, 22, 23, 26, 28, 29, 32, 42, 47, 52, 53, 54, 57, 92, 101, 104, 111, 121, 139, 144, 149, 150, 152, 158, 165, 170, 174
integration, 30, 48, 68, 141
intelligence, 4, 9, 10, 15, 20, 23, 35, 55, 63, 83, 92, 95, 137, 149, 152, 158, 162, 166, 167, 172, 179, 180, 182, 194, 197
Intelligence Reform and Terrorism Prevention Act, 157, 160
interest groups, 101
interference, 52, 107, 166, 167, 174, 196
internally displaced, 174, 184
international financial institutions, viii, 161
international meetings, 11, 15
International Monetary Fund, 179, 192, 194
International Narcotics Control, 20, 118, 143, 144, 145, 160, 184, 185
international standards, 19, 91, 176
international terrorism, 57
Inter-Service Intelligence directorate (ISI), 4
intervention, 91, 143, 182
intimidation, 101, 113, 123
investment, 62, 70, 72, 140, 177, 190
investments, 62, 105
investors, 193

Iran, 2, 7, 11, 12, 23, 30, 51, 52, 56, 57, 58, 62, 63, 69, 71, 82, 83, 88, 93, 114, 115, 165, 169, 194
Iraq, 2, 16, 27, 34, 36, 51, 53, 64, 65, 82, 125, 158, 163, 165, 171, 183, 195, 198
Ireland, 80
iron, 62, 70
irrigation, 18, 178
Islam, 2, 7, 61, 63, 82, 94, 114, 115, 120, 131, 194
Islamic law, 35, 96, 113, 195
Islamic Movement of Uzbekistan (IMU), 23, 61
Islamic movements, 3, 61
isolation, 163
Israel, 72, 184
issues, 9, 11, 17, 42, 53, 56, 61, 82, 95, 108, 109, 113, 116, 117, 128, 130, 138, 146, 157, 165, 175, 179, 180, 187, 188, 189
Italy, 3, 11, 40, 41, 42, 43, 45, 46, 47, 57, 80, 81, 191, 198

J

Jamestown, 195, 197
Japan, 34, 37, 38, 40, 41, 43, 49, 57, 88, 103, 191, 198
Jews, 5, 175
jihad, 170, 173
jihadist, 171, 172
Jirga, 34, 35, 37, 94, 95, 96, 111, 115, 129, 130, 131, 134
job creation, 144
Jordan, 67, 72, 80, 184
journalists, 9, 113, 117, 175
judiciary, 184
jurisdiction, 39, 107
justification, 96, 156

K

Kabul Bank,, viii, 14, 89, 99, 105
Kazakhstan, 51, 61, 62, 67, 157
Kenya, 8, 83
kerosene, 177
kidnapping, 107, 172
kill, 150, 155
King Mohammad Zahir Shah, 3
kinship, 102
Korea, 40, 80, 81, 83, 88, 178, 179, 191, 198
Kuwait, 23, 82, 158, 182, 191
Kyrgyzstan, 51, 61, 62, 145, 157

L

Latvia, 51, 80
law enforcement, 138, 141, 144, 146, 149, 159
laws, 66, 100, 107, 108, 149

lead, vii, 1, 2, 13, 25, 26, 31, 38, 41, 42, 44, 45, 46, 50, 81, 92, 93, 129, 131, 146, 150, 152, 165, 166, 180, 192, 197
leadership, vii, viii, 1, 8, 12, 16, 21, 23, 24, 26, 27, 28, 29, 30, 31, 35, 39, 40, 42, 50, 52, 58, 62, 66, 71, 89, 91, 102, 104, 134, 168, 176, 195
Leahy, 79
learning, 117
Lebanon, 194, 198
legislation, 18, 52, 78, 109, 156
legislative authority, 68
legislative proposals, 152
lending, 66, 99
lifetime, 180
light, 101, 140, 162, 165, 166, 174
Lion, 26
liquefied natural gas, 178
loans, viii, 86, 89, 99, 105
local authorities, 154, 174
local government, 17, 18, 91, 163, 193

M

Macedonia, 80
majority, 15, 25, 43, 63, 115, 128, 177, 194
Malaysia, 41, 80
malnutrition, 178
man, 83, 115, 158, 173, 178, 195
management, 17, 54, 70, 112, 118, 144, 184, 192
marginalization, 93, 174, 175
marriage, 2, 70, 94, 184, 195
mass, 82, 87, 95, 134, 170, 171, 172
media, 69, 87, 96, 113, 122, 123, 168, 172, 179, 194
mentoring, 44, 109
Mexico, 170
Middle East, 1, 2, iii, 166, 173, 183, 188, 194, 195, 196, 197
militancy, 61, 188
military aid, 4, 66, 186, 187, 190
military-to-military, 161
militia, 6, 8, 9, 10, 23, 24, 37, 38, 91, 94, 99, 101, 147
militias, 3, 17, 36, 37, 38, 73, 79
Ministry of Education, 105
Ministry of Rural Rehabilitation and Development (MRRD), 106
minorities, 2, 3, 33, 38, 58, 93, 95, 98
mission, 16, 18, 19, 20, 25, 28, 30, 40, 41, 42, 43, 44, 45, 50, 64, 102, 104, 107, 149, 150, 152
missions, 20, 39, 40, 42, 51, 120, 148, 149, 166
misuse, 108, 184, 187, 189
models, 18
modernization, 3, 91
momentum, 2, 21, 28, 32, 36

moratorium, 114, 188
morphine, 151
mortality, 5, 67
Moscow, 4, 62, 87, 88
mujahedin, 3, 4, 6, 7, 9, 12, 24, 46, 55, 82, 83, 86, 91, 92, 93, 94, 95, 96, 99, 100, 121, 122, 126, 131, 132, 134

N

naming, 47
narcotics, 12, 14, 19, 20, 45, 53, 56, 63, 64, 65, 66, 74, 76, 77, 79, 99, 101, 104, 109, 110, 118, 137, 138, 139, 141, 144, 145, 146, 147, 148, 149, 150, 151, 152, 158, 159
National Defense Authorization Act, 34, 37, 39, 52, 53, 71, 157, 158, 159, 189, 198
national emergency, 86
national identity, 129
national interests, 58
National Islamic Movement of Afghanistan, 8
National Public Radio, 158
national security, 28, 74, 93, 126, 135, 143, 145, 149, 156, 160, 165, 195
National Security Council, 14, 35, 88, 92, 104, 126, 144, 183
nationalism, 163
nationality, 190
nation-building, 11, 21
NATO, vii, 1, 16, 20, 21, 23, 25, 26, 27, 28, 29, 30, 31, 32, 34, 35, 38, 39, 40, 41, 42, 43, 44, 45, 51, 55, 56, 57, 60, 61, 68, 80, 81, 87, 98, 104, 112, 120, 121, 123, 129, 149, 158, 159
natural gas, 62, 71, 178
natural resources, vii, viii, 161
neglect, 171, 173
negotiating, 30, 192
Netherlands, 25, 40, 41, 43, 44, 47, 57, 80, 81, 191, 198
neutral, 24
New Zealand, 80, 81
NGOs, 69, 71, 115, 117, 187, 188
Niyazov, 71
nodes, 55
nominee, 100
Noorzai clan, 10
North Korea, 83, 179
Northern Alliance, 8, 9, 10, 12, 13, 14, 36, 38, 47, 52, 58, 59, 61, 67, 95, 96, 99, 131, 141, 142, 169
Northwest Airlines, 162, 165, 166
Norway, 47, 57, 80, 81
nuclear program, 56
nutrition, 117

O

Obama Administration, vii, 1, 11, 15, 16, 17, 18, 19, 21, 27, 28, 29, 30, 31, 34, 35, 39, 40, 44, 46, 50, 52, 54, 55, 56, 64, 97, 98, 99, 103, 104, 105, 106, 112, 113, 118, 119, 125, 134, 138, 139, 144, 146, 153, 154, 155, 161, 162, 165, 173, 180, 183, 184, 188, 193

obstacles, 138, 165

oil, 6, 43, 51, 70, 71, 163, 165, 168, 171, 175, 177, 178, 179, 180, 181, 182, 192, 197

oil production, 6, 178

Omnibus Appropriations Act,, 155, 156

online lectures, 173

Operation Anaconda, 10

Operation Enduring Freedom, 9, 10, 14, 25, 39, 40, 41, 43

operations, 2, 10, 17, 20, 21, 23, 25, 26, 27, 28, 29, 32, 33, 38, 39, 41, 42, 43, 46, 47, 50, 51, 53, 55, 59, 63, 64, 65, 76, 79, 82, 101, 115, 120, 121, 137, 138, 139, 144, 146, 147, 148, 149, 151, 152, 153, 154, 155, 157, 158, 159, 162, 165, 166, 167, 171, 172, 174, 183, 186, 189, 195

ophthalmologist, 121

opiates, 151

opportunities, 8, 34, 115, 146, 148, 171, 183

opposition parties, 183, 188

Organization of Islamic Conference (OIC), 11

organize, 14, 16, 40

organs, 36, 92

Osama Bin Laden, 170, 197

OSCE, 120

outreach, 34, 95

oversight, 59, 65, 94, 97, 113, 118, 157, 188

P

Pakistan, vii, 1, 4, 6, 7, 9, 11, 13, 15, 18, 20, 22, 23, 24, 25, 26, 29, 30, 31, 33, 35, 36, 45, 46, 47, 50, 51, 52, 53, 54, 55, 56, 58, 59, 61, 63, 64, 66, 68, 69, 71, 72, 82, 84, 87, 88, 93, 95, 98, 101, 115, 121, 132, 135, 144, 145, 157, 158, 167, 170, 171, 172, 184, 186

parallel, 166

Pashtun, 4, 5, 7, 8, 9, 10, 13, 14, 15, 18, 33, 37, 47, 56, 57, 81, 82, 92, 93, 94, 95, 98, 101, 102, 121, 122, 130, 131, 132, 134, 172

payroll, 179

peace, 10, 12, 16, 24, 34, 35, 36, 38, 41, 51, 53, 55, 90, 91, 95, 113, 117

peace plan, 36

peacekeeping, 12, 16, 41, 51, 53

peacekeeping forces, 12

peer review, 65

penalties, 30

Pentagon, 126, 150, 158

Persian Gulf, viii, 14, 20, 43, 51, 63, 158, 161

persuasion, 38

pessimism, 32

petroleum, 6

pharmaceutical, 86

Philippines, 45

phosphates, 84

photographs, 167

physicians, 67

piracy, 181, 184

plants, 155, 173, 177

platform, 51, 96

playing, 20, 66, 103

Poland, 39, 40, 42, 47, 80, 81

police, 2, 5, 20, 24, 37, 41, 44, 45, 46, 47, 48, 49, 84, 99, 101, 105, 107, 108, 114, 117, 145, 146, 147, 157, 169, 176

policy responses, 138, 165

policymakers, 165, 166, 167, 170, 172, 174, 183

political force, 164

political instability, 146

political opposition, 95, 188, 193

political participation, 113

political parties, 93, 120, 131, 164

politics, 8, 33, 171, 174, 180

polling, 120, 123, 124, 125, 129

popular support, 7

population, vii, viii, 5, 6, 18, 28, 29, 32, 33, 37, 67, 85, 92, 93, 98, 108, 114, 133, 134, 140, 149, 151, 152, 161, 162, 163, 165, 167, 177, 194

population growth, vii, viii, 161

portfolio, 197

Portugal, 40, 41, 80

positive relationship, 138

poverty, viii, 146, 161, 165, 177

poverty line, viii, 161

presidency, 8, 29, 92, 119, 131, 179

president, 3, 6, 9, 12, 13, 36, 91, 94, 95, 96, 98, 99, 111, 117, 120, 121, 122, 164, 175, 176, 179, 180, 193, 197

presidential campaign, 91, 123

presidential campaigns, 123

press conferences, 16

principles, 48, 94

prisoners, 39, 82, 88, 100, 134, 174, 188, 196

prisons, 183

private investment, 70

privatization, 100

producers, 146

professionals, 14, 67

profit, 105, 143
prognosis, 194
programming, 144, 188
project, 6, 43, 59, 62, 65, 66, 67, 70, 71, 79, 88, 107, 158, 178
proliferation, 43, 51
propaganda, 167, 172
prosperity, 100
protection, 14, 21, 34, 51, 72, 74, 76, 149, 172, 196
provincial councils, 91, 95, 96, 111, 120, 131
public awareness, 139
public health, 155
public support, 21, 121
punishment, 114
purchasing power, 5
purchasing power parity, 5

Q

qualifications, 102, 125

R

Rab, 4, 9, 82, 94
radicals, 61, 167, 172
Reagan Administration, 4, 83
recognition, 8, 151
recommendations, iv, 21, 28, 66, 84
reconciliation, 2, 9, 22, 24, 25, 35, 38, 93, 115, 117, 180
reconstruction, 14, 21, 26, 42, 43, 44, 53, 54, 59, 65, 66, 67, 71, 131, 138, 144, 146, 158, 174, 188
recruiting, 111, 170
recurrence, 29
reelection, 159, 164
reform, 65, 97, 98, 102, 103, 128, 134, 139, 146, 157, 180, 183, 192, 193
reform, 17, 128, 134, 157, 158, 160, 180, 186
reforms, 15, 124, 190, 192, 193
refugee camps, 64
refugees, 56, 58, 64, 69, 127, 174, 181
regional cooperation, 175
regulations, 86, 105, 108
regulatory framework, 109
rehabilitation, 76, 169, 194
rehabilitation program, 169, 194
rejection, 127
relatives, viii, 14, 70, 89, 166, 167, 174
relevance, 158, 165
reliability, 165, 183, 189
relief, 44, 46, 60, 64, 66, 69, 115, 179
religion, 2
remittances, 179, 182
repair, 32, 159

repression, 8, 176
reputation, 6, 100, 130, 170
requirements, 30, 53, 90, 128, 139, 152, 159, 194
resentment, 61, 98
reserves, 70, 71, 117, 163, 178
resilience, 168
resistance, 2, 14, 33, 63, 97, 154
resolution, 16, 37, 41, 52, 109, 124, 188
resources, vii, viii, 16, 17, 27, 44, 45, 49, 71, 117, 146, 149, 150, 151, 161, 162, 165, 174, 177, 178
response, 10, 26, 99, 119, 151, 152, 154, 158, 159, 171, 176, 193
restaurants, 114
restrictions, 55, 68, 86, 96, 105, 113, 150, 184
revenue, 64, 137, 177, 178, 179, 192
Revolutionary Guard, 57
rights, iv, 6, 8, 18, 19, 20, 33, 46, 48, 56, 65, 77, 90, 99, 109, 113, 115, 116, 117, 118, 128, 131, 134, 166, 174, 175, 183, 187, 190
risk, vii, viii, 151, 158, 161, 171, 172, 173, 197
risks, 138, 155, 165, 194
Romania, 39, 40, 80
root, vii, 29, 52, 161, 165
roots, 143, 171
routes, 61, 62, 68
rule of law, viii, 16, 17, 18, 19, 49, 78, 89, 109, 110, 118, 146
rules, 29, 42, 149, 150
runoff, 13, 16, 89, 124, 125, 131
rural areas, 5, 26, 67, 68, 90, 167
rural poverty, 146
Russia, 11, 36, 40, 47, 51, 53, 59, 60, 61, 62, 67, 88, 165

S

Saddam Hussein, 43, 82, 182, 183
safe haven, 11, 21, 22, 26, 42, 50, 61, 162, 195
safe havens, 42
safety, 20, 47, 70, 154, 155
sanctions, 8, 24, 36, 84, 86
Saudi Arabia, 7, 22, 30, 36, 41, 55, 57, 63, 82, 83, 88, 158, 162, 163, 165, 169, 171, 173, 174, 182, 190, 191, 194, 196, 197
Saur (April) Revolution, 3
scarcity, 177, 178
school, 5, 7, 32, 58, 67, 79, 86, 116, 170, 173, 194, 196
scope, 16, 29, 31, 103, 146, 190
Secret Service, 180
Secretary of Defense, 10, 27, 28, 97, 145, 152, 157, 158, 189, 190
security assistance, 184, 187, 189, 190

security forces, 26, 28, 29, 37, 39, 40, 43, 49, 50, 59, 73, 74, 93, 108, 113, 123, 126, 129, 143, 147, 148, 149, 161, 166, 167, 168, 169, 171, 175, 181, 187, 189, 198

security guard, 173

seizure, 3

Senate, 8, 10, 28, 29, 52, 66, 87, 107, 112, 150, 158, 159, 160, 172, 184, 187, 189, 190, 196, 197, 198

Senate Foreign Relations Committee, 107, 112, 150, 187

senses, 61

sensing, 62, 166

Shanghai Cooperation Organization, 52, 62

shape, 29, 54, 121

shareholders, viii, 89, 180

Sharia, 113, 195

Sharif, Mazar-e, 10, 17, 47, 67, 82, 100, 112

Shiite Muslims, 8

Shiites, 8, 82, 114, 127, 194

shoreline, 181

showing, 64, 66, 92, 111, 130

signs, 1, 32, 54, 198

Singapore, 80, 103

siphon, 105

skimming, 48

Slovakia, 40, 41, 80

small businesses, 38

smuggling, 43, 51, 53, 150, 177, 184

social fabric, 139

social structure, 163

society, 2, 3, 58, 64, 90, 91, 93, 113, 118, 146, 170, 171, 173, 174

solution, 176, 177

Somalia, 165, 181, 197

South Asia, 27, 52

South Asian Association for Regional Cooperation, 52

South Korea, 40, 80, 81, 88, 178, 191, 198

Soviet helicopters, 4

Soviet Union, 3, 4, 5, 24, 27, 84, 93, 163, 164

Spain, 40, 41, 47, 57, 80, 81, 188, 191

Special Representative for Afghanistan and Pakistan (SRAP), 98

specter, 174

speculation, 179

speech, 16, 21, 28, 39, 63, 87, 112, 117, 121, 125, 175, 176, 184

stability, 7, 12, 32, 50, 54, 59, 62, 68, 100, 135, 138, 140, 141, 146, 149, 150, 154, 157, 158, 165, 177

stabilization, 20, 26, 28, 42, 97, 98, 144, 158, 162, 165, 187, 188

staffing, 65, 111, 144

stakeholders, 30

state, vii, viii, 3, 86, 87, 106, 122, 134, 135, 158, 161, 162, 163, 164, 165, 167, 171, 173, 174, 175, 178, 179, 182, 190, 192, 193, 198

state control, 167

states, 11, 12, 14, 39, 59, 61, 62, 63, 67, 70, 80, 83, 84, 143, 144, 149, 150, 156, 163, 164, 165, 171, 173, 174, 182, 192, 198

statistics, 67, 139, 177

stimulant, 178

Stingers, 4, 79, 83

structure, 16, 25, 26, 32, 90, 94, 163, 170

style, 4, 17, 91, 93

subsidy, 177, 193

substitution, 66, 144, 153, 159

succession, 11, 174, 179, 196

Sudan, 86

suicide, 27, 54, 123, 195

Sun, 18, 49, 90, 110, 135

Sunnis, 194, 197

suppliers, 51, 67, 165

Supreme Court, 96, 107, 113, 114, 115, 119, 124, 132

surrogates, 93

surveillance, 56, 166

sustainable development, 178

Sweden, 41, 47, 80, 81

swelling, 67, 112

sympathy, 167, 197

T

tactics, 21, 22, 57, 148, 166

Tajikistan, 11, 51, 53, 59, 61, 62, 67, 145, 157

takeover, 3, 41

Taraki, Nur Mohammad, 3

target, 14, 24, 25, 37, 38, 39, 45, 46, 57, 105, 116, 150, 152, 157, 194

targeting individuals, 150

tariff, 86

tax base, 179

taxes, 105

teacher training, 79

teachers, 5

teams, 21, 83, 152, 154

technical assistance, 61, 103, 153, 188

technology, 9, 106, 114

telecommunications, 66, 70, 127, 180

tensions, 131, 161, 179, 182

territory, 2, 35, 86, 90, 110, 115, 167, 170, 171, 181, 182, 195, 196

terrorism, 11, 12, 25, 46, 50, 51, 52, 55, 57, 59, 72, 74, 86, 149, 150, 162, 167, 170, 177, 183, 184, 187, 190, 196

terrorist groups, vii, 34, 157, 161, 162, 165, 183

terrorist organization, 88, 163

terrorists, 36, 54, 150, 157, 161, 162, 166, 167, 169, 173, 183, 195

the Central Intelligence Agency (CIA), 4

Third World, 4

threats, 10, 120, 138, 149, 167, 181, 182, 189, 194

time frame, 11, 30, 31, 39, 46

Title I, 60, 69, 72, 74

Title II, 69, 72, 74

Tonga, 80

Tora Bora mountains, 23

torture, 113, 183

tourism, 179, 180

trade, 6, 54, 59, 63, 67, 68, 72, 86, 101, 104, 138, 139, 140, 143, 145, 146, 147, 148, 149, 150, 156, 158, 161, 165

trade agreement, 6, 54, 69, 72

traditional practices, 109

traditions, 7, 17, 113, 115, 178, 195

trafficking, viii, 14, 19, 20, 46, 56, 64, 66, 99, 101, 110, 115, 137, 138, 139, 140, 141, 142, 143, 145, 146, 147, 148, 150, 151, 152, 155, 156, 158, 160, 184

training, 8, 20, 21, 40, 44, 46, 47, 48, 49, 54, 57, 59, 69, 79, 102, 103, 107, 109, 117, 119, 150, 152, 157, 159, 161, 166, 167, 173, 184, 186, 187, 198

translation, 97

transparency, 59, 89, 102, 192, 197

transport, 42, 51, 127, 187

transportation, 14, 49, 68, 86, 127, 159

Treasury, 57, 88, 170

treatment, 3, 72, 86, 99

trial, 114, 115, 188

tribesmen, 171

trust fund, 49

Trust Fund, 5, 49, 64, 71, 75, 76, 78, 79, 105

Turkey, 30, 40, 41, 44, 45, 51, 52, 80, 81, 82, 99, 113

Turkmenistan, 11, 61, 62, 71, 88, 145, 157

turnout, 101, 123, 130

turnover, 31

U

U.N. Assistance Mission Afghanistan (UNAMA), 90

U.N. Security Council, 8, 9, 12, 16, 36, 41, 88

U.S. assistance, 4, 49, 53, 67, 84, 88, 156, 166, 188, 189, 193, 194, 198

U.S. Central Command (CENTCOM), 25, 149

U.S. policy, 17, 18, 21, 24, 30, 33, 53, 54, 68, 88, 90, 97, 110, 113, 121, 140, 144, 161, 165, 166, 172, 183

U.S. Treasury, 88, 170

Ukraine, 80

Umar, Mullah, 8, 10, 14, 22, 26, 35, 36, 62, 63, 82, 132

UNHCR, 64, 69, 174, 198

unification, 175, 183

United Kingdom, 80, 153, 191, 198

United Nations, viii, 8, 10, 11, 12, 16, 30, 31, 40, 56, 83, 90, 91, 139, 140, 141, 157, 158, 161, 174, 181, 197, 198

United Nations High Commissioner for Refugees, 174

universities, 5, 58, 173

urban, 67, 127

urban areas, 67

USDA, 138, 144, 153, 159

USS Cole, 181, 183, 193, 195

Uzbek militia, 8

Uzbekistan, 2, 11, 23, 45, 47, 51, 61, 62, 67, 68

V

variables, 141

vehicles, 42, 48, 105, 111, 120, 152

vessels, 181, 197

veto, 12

violence, 15, 26, 32, 34, 35, 91, 110, 123, 125, 127, 129, 140, 146, 170, 176, 188, 197

vote, 13, 52, 94, 117, 120, 121, 123, 124, 127, 130, 131, 164

voters, 91, 101, 119, 120, 121, 123, 124, 128, 129, 131

voting, 15, 90, 119, 123, 129

W

wages, 175

Wahhabism, 7

waiver, 20, 145, 156, 160, 194

war, 3, 4, 6, 7, 8, 9, 10, 11, 13, 16, 21, 22, 31, 39, 41, 46, 51, 58, 62, 72, 79, 82, 83, 90, 92, 93, 96, 100, 134, 139, 149, 151, 161, 163, 174, 175, 181, 183, 187, 195, 196, 197

War on Terror, 64, 197

warlords, 8, 17, 98, 140, 158

Washington, 4, 8, 29, 55, 83, 87, 88, 95, 97, 104, 134, 135, 154, 157, 158, 159, 194, 195, 196, 197, 198

water, 69, 70, 71, 100, 126, 165, 177, 178, 181, 193

water resources, 177, 178

Waziristan, 133

weakness, 13, 99, 183

weapons, 4, 7, 23, 37, 38, 47, 57, 83, 84, 86, 99, 150, 152, 158, 166, 181, 195

Western aid, 192

Western countries, 16, 192

Western Europe, 139
White House, vii, 1, 29, 32, 53, 87, 97, 166
WHO, 198
withdrawal, 4, 6, 7, 24, 55, 61, 196
WMD, 73, 74, 75, 76
workers, 33, 42, 59, 102, 123, 129, 130, 163, 182, 184, 197
working class, 9
working hours, 178
World Bank, 5, 57, 64, 66, 71, 105, 121, 147, 158, 177, 178, 179, 191, 192, 194, 197, 198
World Trade Organization, 72
worldwide, 104, 156, 166, 191

worry, 15, 22

Y

Yemen, vii, viii, 24, 161, 162, 163, 164, 165, 166, 167, 168, 169, 170, 171, 172, 173, 174, 175, 176, 177, 178, 179, 180, 181, 182, 183, 184, 185, 186, 187, 188, 189, 190, 191, 192, 193, 194, 195, 196, 197, 198
Yemen Arab Republic (YAR), 163
Yemeni instability, vii, 161, 165
yield, 124, 140